AQUAMAN
THE BECOMING

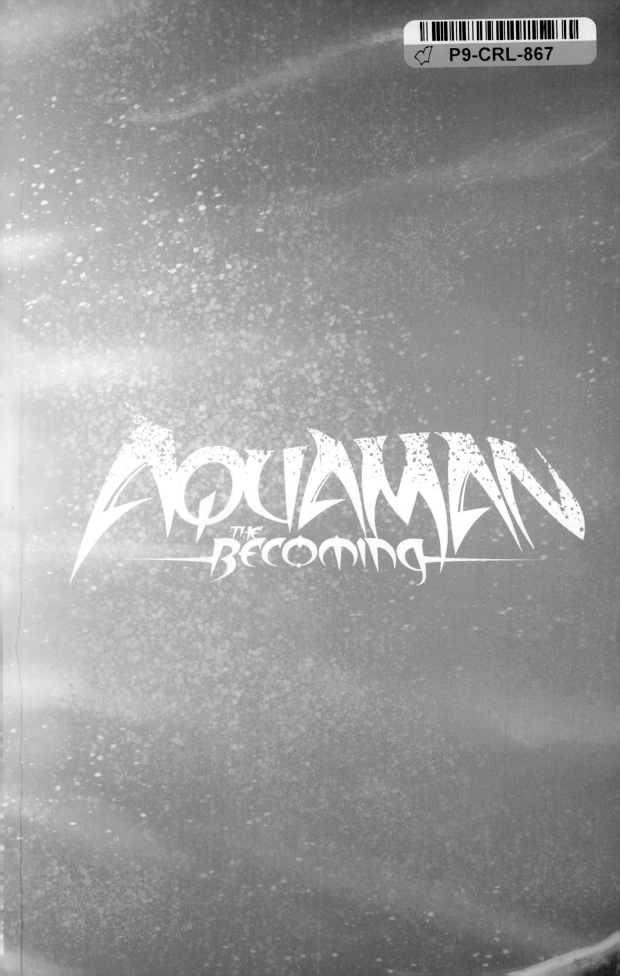

AQUAMAN
THE BECOMING

BRANDON THOMAS writer

DIEGO OLORTEGUI   SCOTT KOBLISH   DANIEL SAMPERE
PAUL PELLETIER   SKYLAR PATRIDGE   SERG ACUÑA pencillers

WADE VON GRAWBADGER   DANIEL SAMPERE   NORM RAPMUND
SKYLAR PATRIDGE   SERG ACUÑA inkers

ADRIANO LUCAS   ALEX GUIMARÃES colorists

ANDWORLD DESIGN letterer   DAVID TALASKI collection cover artist

The "Progress" Pride Flag in the DC logo designed by DANIEL QUASAR

AQUAMAN created by PAUL NORRIS

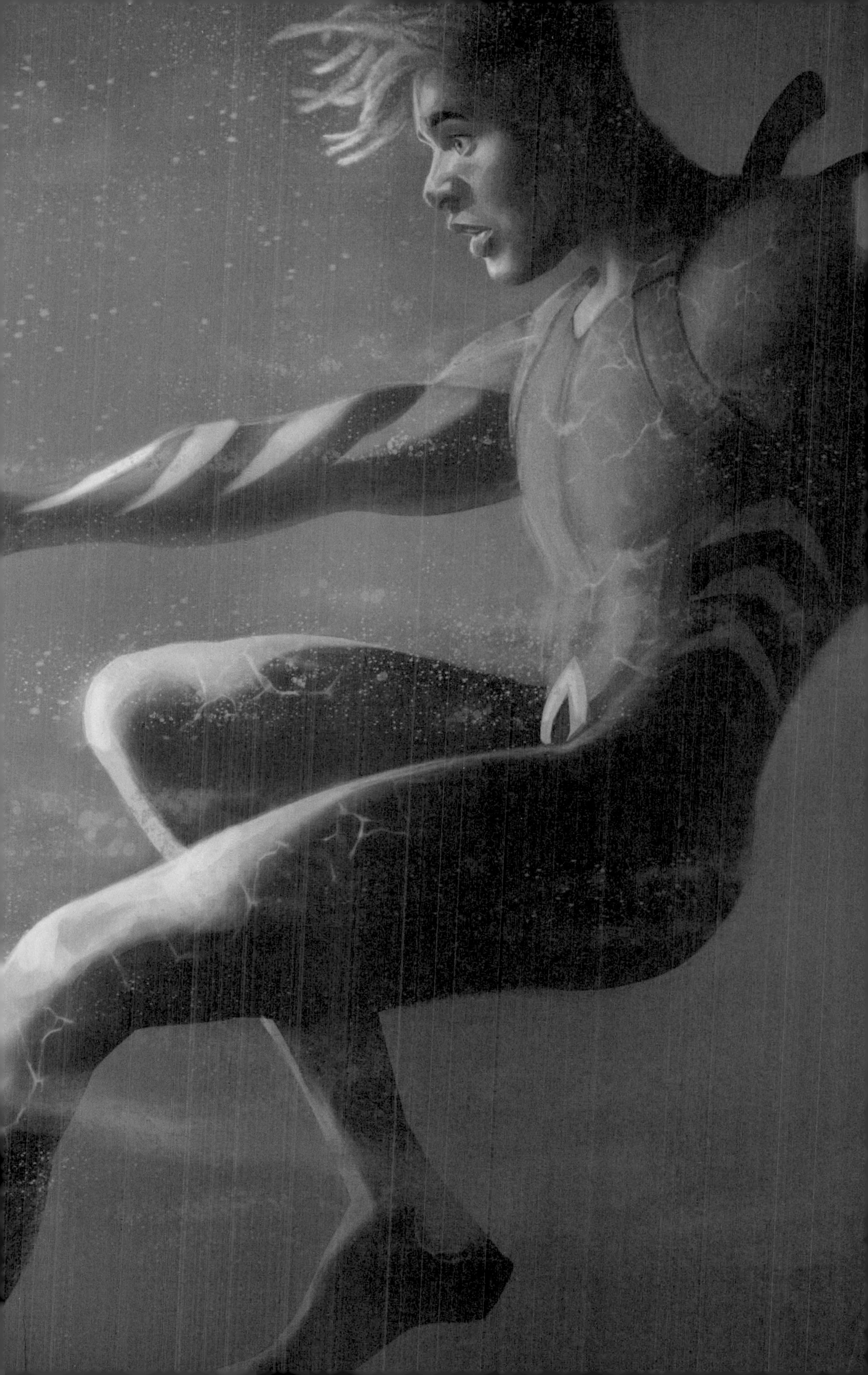

Andrea Shea Editor – Original Series & Collected Edition
Marquis Draper Assistant Editor – Original Series
Steve Cook Design Director – Books
Louis Prandi Publication Design
Christy Sawyer Publication Production

Marie Javins Editor-in-Chief, DC Comics

Anne DePies Senior VP – General Manager
Jim Lee Publisher & Chief Creative Officer
Don Falletti VP – Manufacturing Operations & Workflow Management
Lawrence Ganem VP – Talent Services
Alison Gill Senior VP – Manufacturing & Operations
Jeffrey Kaufman VP – Editorial Strategy & Programming
Nick J. Napolitano VP – Manufacturing Administration & Design
Nancy Spears VP – Revenue

AQUAMAN: THE BECOMING

DC Comics,
2900 West Alameda Ave.,
Burbank, CA 91505
Printed by Solisco Printers,
Scott, QC, Canada. 4/15/22.
First Printing.
ISBN: 978-1-77951-645-9

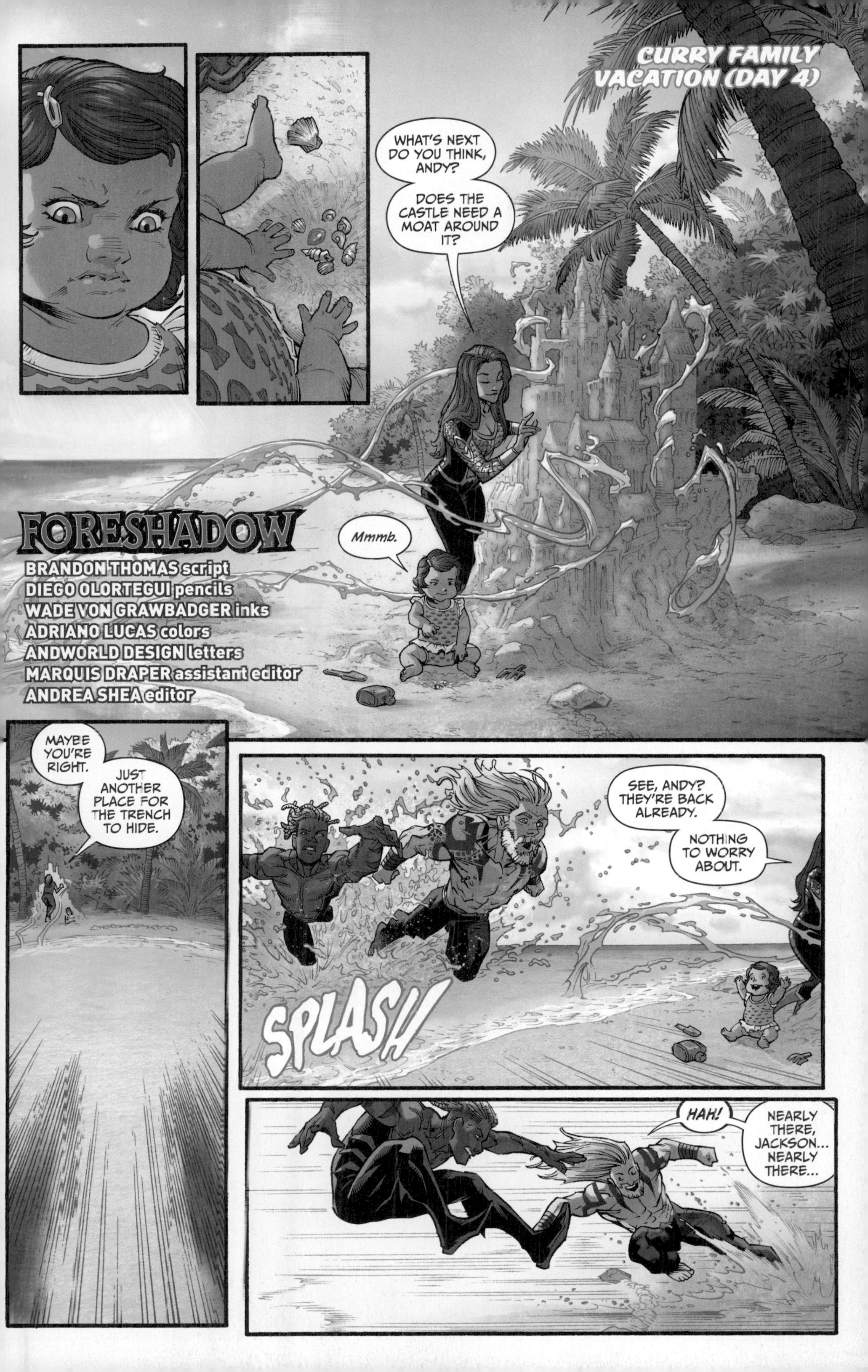
CURRY FAMILY VACATION (DAY 4)
WHAT'S NEXT DO YOU THINK, ANDY?
DOES THE CASTLE NEED A MOAT AROUND IT?
Mmmb.
FORESHADOW
BRANDON THOMAS script
DIEGO OLORTEGUI pencils
WADE VON GRAWBADGER inks
ADRIANO LUCAS colors
ANDWORLD DESIGN letters
MARQUIS DRAPER assistant editor
ANDREA SHEA editor
MAYBE YOU'RE RIGHT.
JUST ANOTHER PLACE FOR THE TRENCH TO HIDE.
SEE, ANDY? THEY'RE BACK ALREADY.
NOTHING TO WORRY ABOUT.
SPLASH
HAH!
NEARLY THERE, JACKSON... NEARLY THERE...

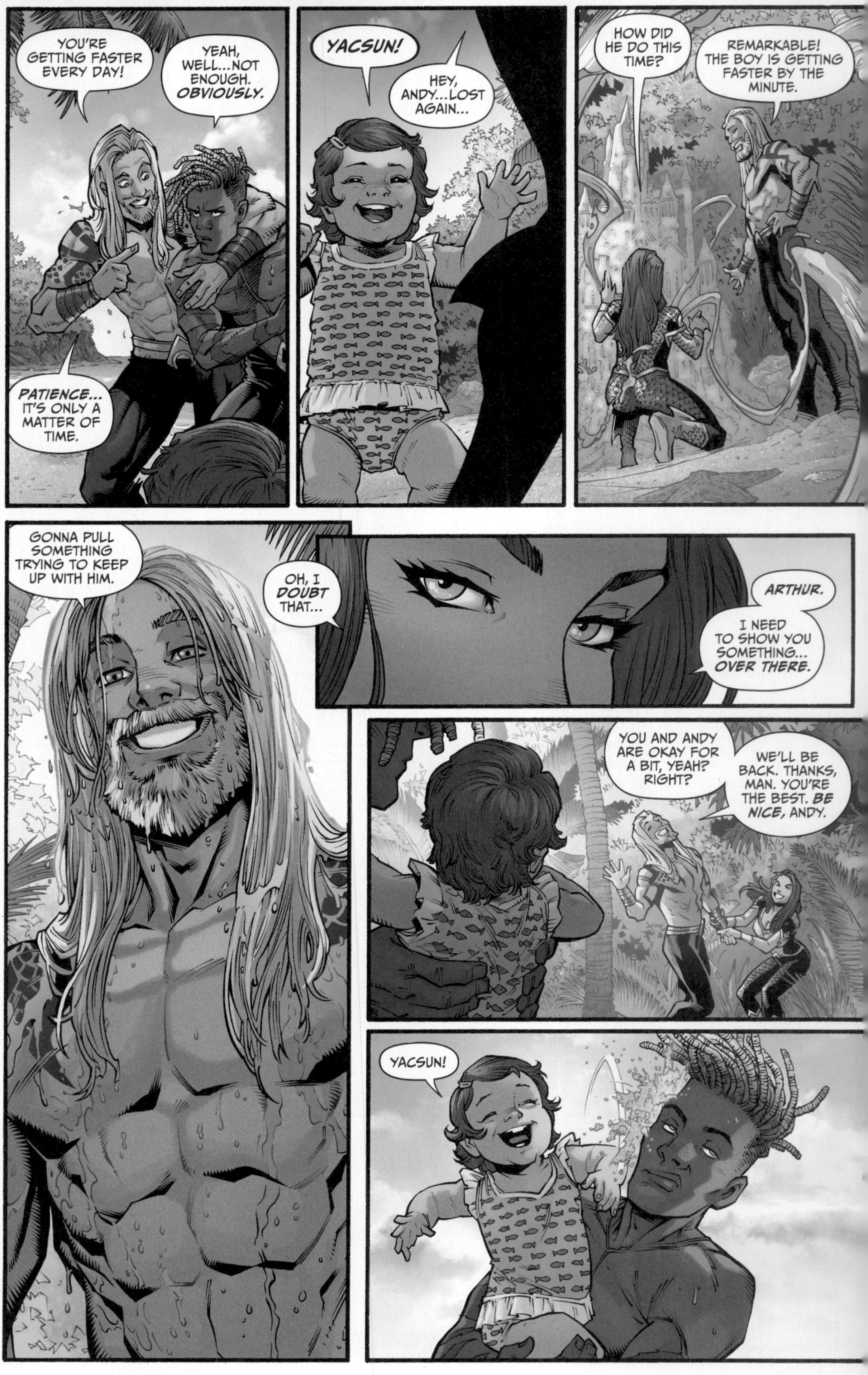
YOU'RE GETTING FASTER EVERY DAY!
YEAH, WELL...NOT ENOUGH. OBVIOUSLY.
PATIENCE... IT'S ONLY A MATTER OF TIME.
YACSUN!
HEY, ANDY...LOST AGAIN...
HOW DID HE DO THIS TIME?
REMARKABLE! THE BOY IS GETTING FASTER BY THE MINUTE.
GONNA PULL SOMETHING TRYING TO KEEP UP WITH HIM.
OH, I DOUBT THAT...
ARTHUR.
I NEED TO SHOW YOU SOMETHING... OVER THERE.
YOU AND ANDY ARE OKAY FOR A BIT, YEAH? RIGHT?
WE'LL BE BACK. THANKS, MAN. YOU'RE THE BEST. BE NICE, ANDY.
YACSUN!

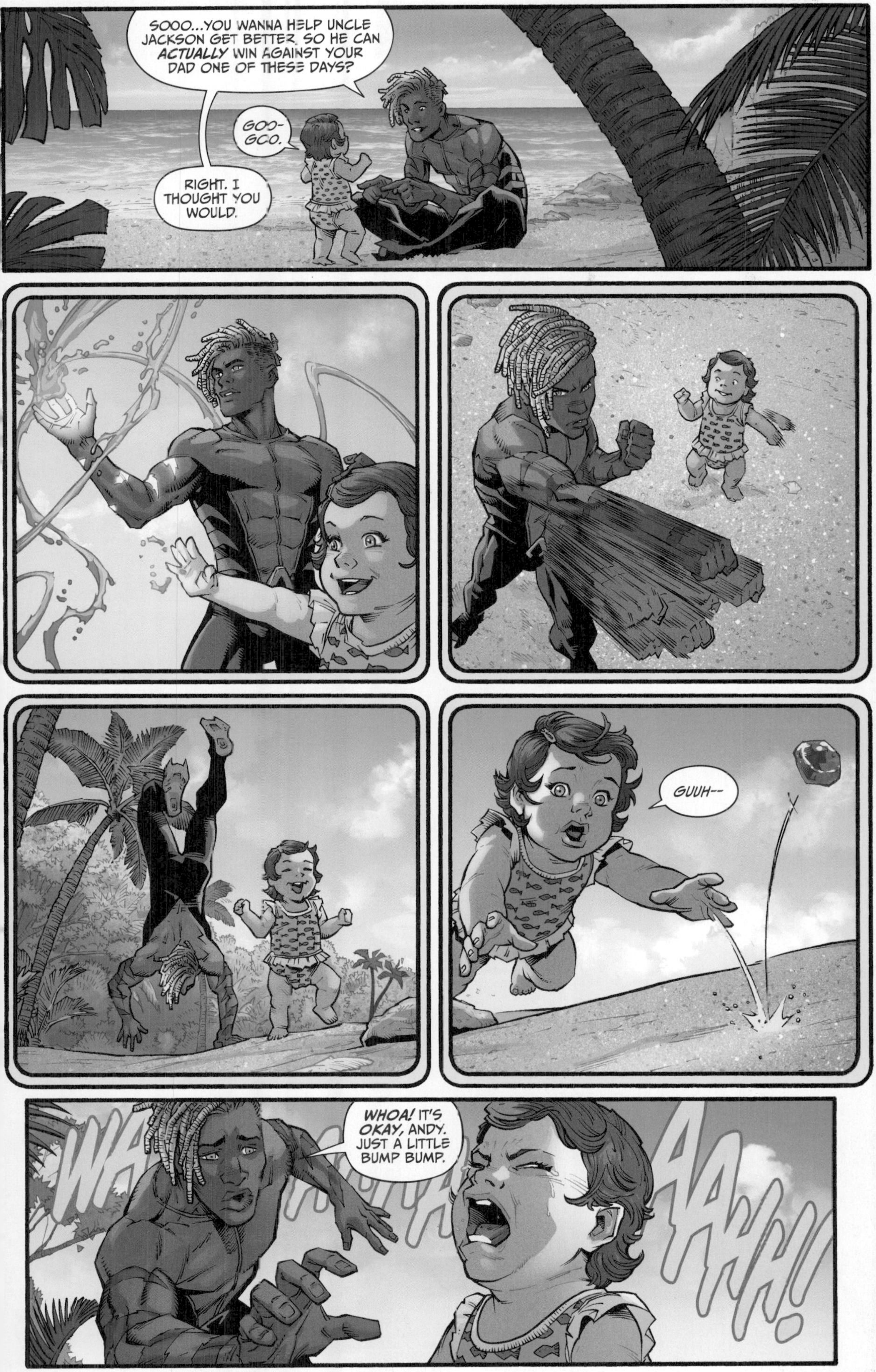
SOOO...YOU WANNA HELP UNCLE JACKSON GET BETTER, SO HE CAN ACTUALLY WIN AGAINST YOUR DAD ONE OF THESE DAYS?
GOO-GOO.
RIGHT. I THOUGHT YOU WOULD.
GUUH--
WHOA! IT'S OKAY, ANDY. JUST A LITTLE BUMP BUMP.
AAH!

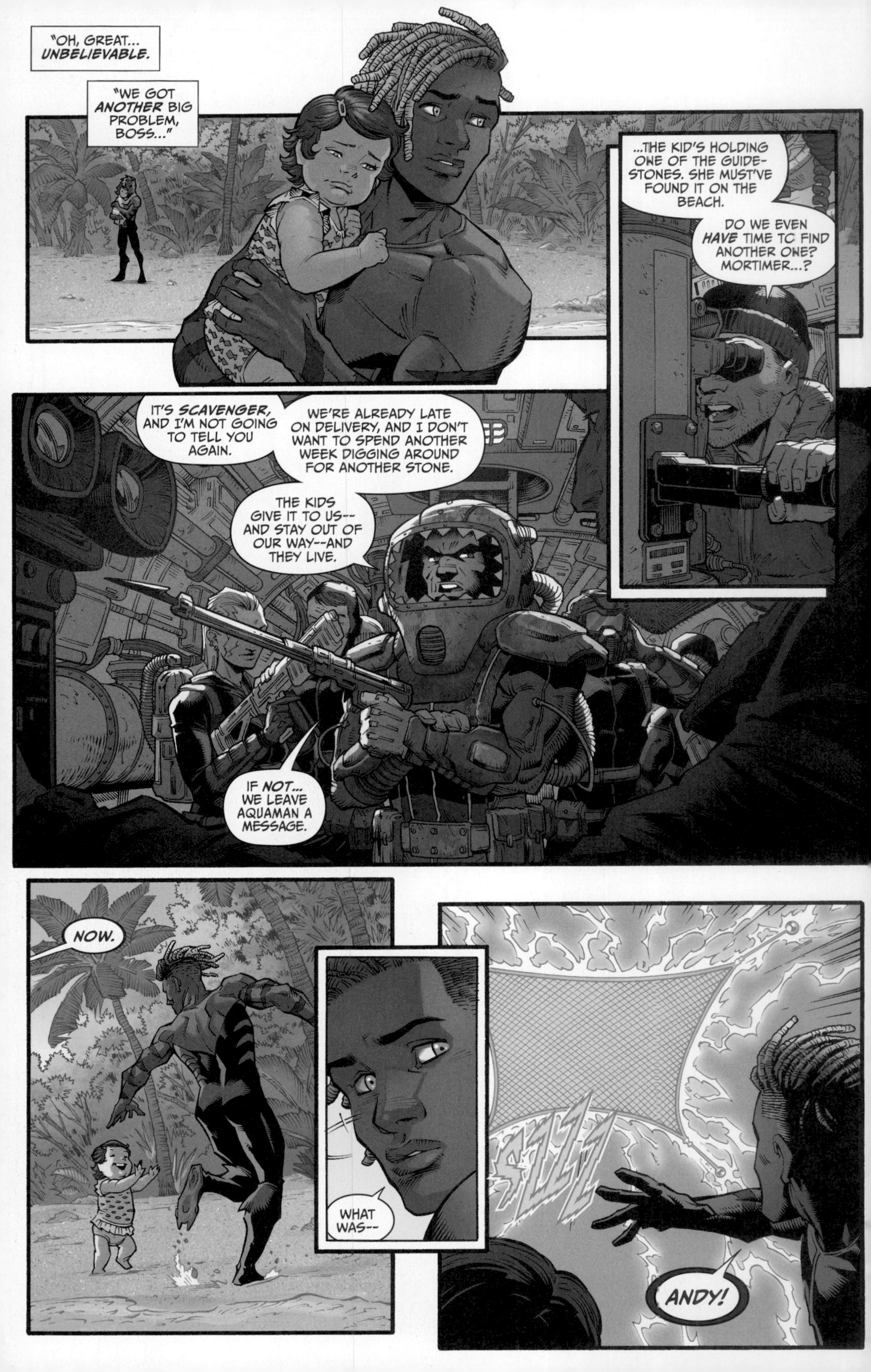
"OH, GREAT... UNBELIEVABLE.
"WE GOT ANOTHER BIG PROBLEM, BOSS..."
...THE KID'S HOLDING ONE OF THE GUIDE-STONES. SHE MUST'VE FOUND IT ON THE BEACH.
DO WE EVEN HAVE TIME TO FIND ANOTHER ONE? MORTIMER...?
IT'S SCAVENGER, AND I'M NOT GOING TO TELL YOU AGAIN.
WE'RE ALREADY LATE ON DELIVERY, AND I DON'T WANT TO SPEND ANOTHER WEEK DIGGING AROUND FOR ANOTHER STONE.
THE KIDS GIVE IT TO US--AND STAY OUT OF OUR WAY--AND THEY LIVE.
IF NOT... WE LEAVE AQUAMAN A MESSAGE.
NOW.
WHAT WAS--
SZZZ
ANDY!

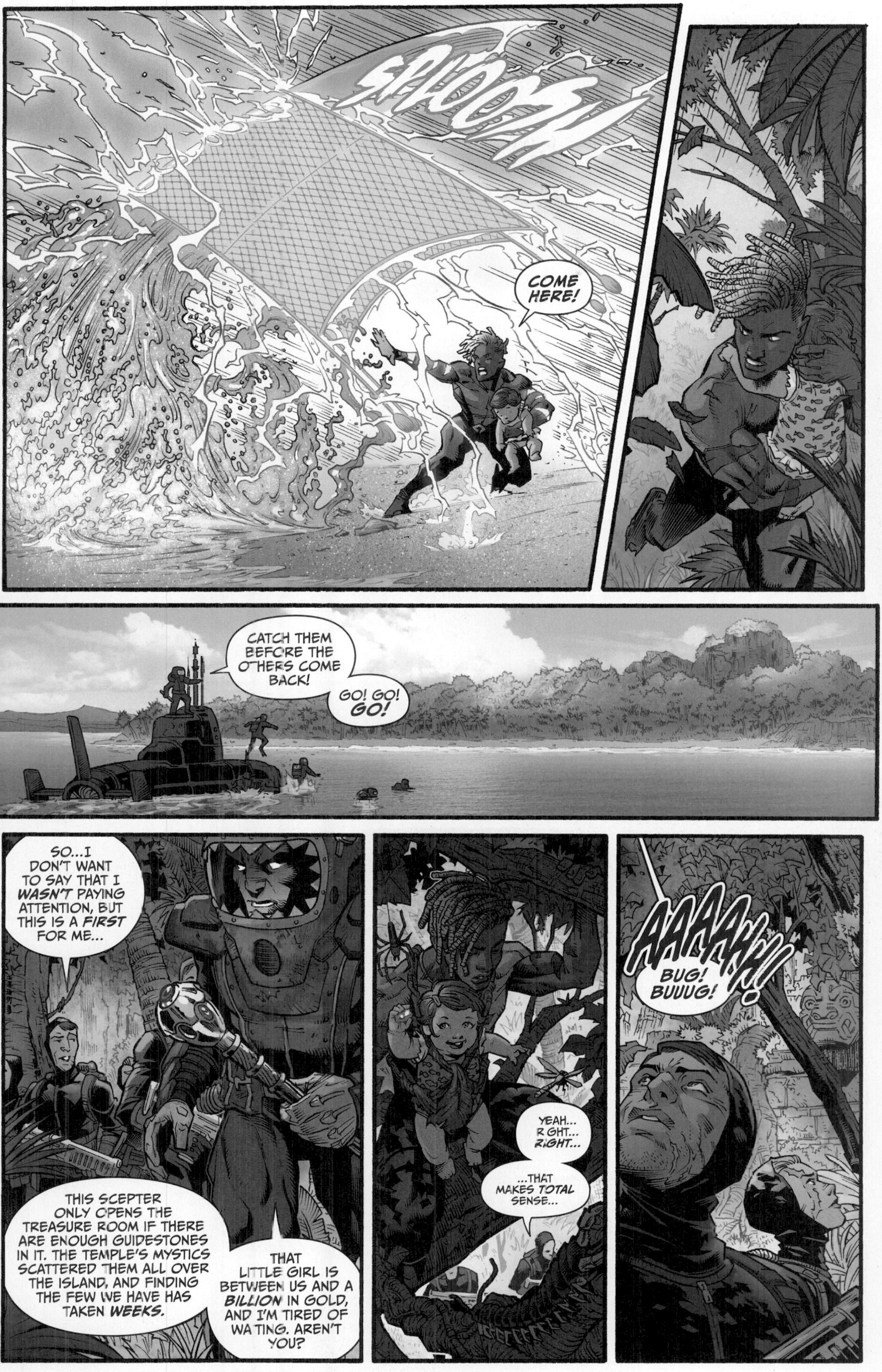
SPLOOSH!
COME HERE!
CATCH THEM BEFORE THE OTHERS COME BACK!
GO! GO! GO!
SO...I DON'T WANT TO SAY THAT I WASN'T PAYING ATTENTION, BUT THIS IS A FIRST FOR ME...
THIS SCEPTER ONLY OPENS THE TREASURE ROOM IF THERE ARE ENOUGH GUIDESTONES IN IT. THE TEMPLE'S MYSTICS SCATTERED THEM ALL OVER THE ISLAND, AND FINDING THE FEW WE HAVE HAS TAKEN WEEKS.
THAT LITTLE GIRL IS BETWEEN US AND A BILLION IN GOLD, AND I'M TIRED OF WAITING. AREN'T YOU?
YEAH... RIGHT... RIGHT...
...THAT MAKES TOTAL SENSE...
AAAAAHH!!
BUG! BUUUG!

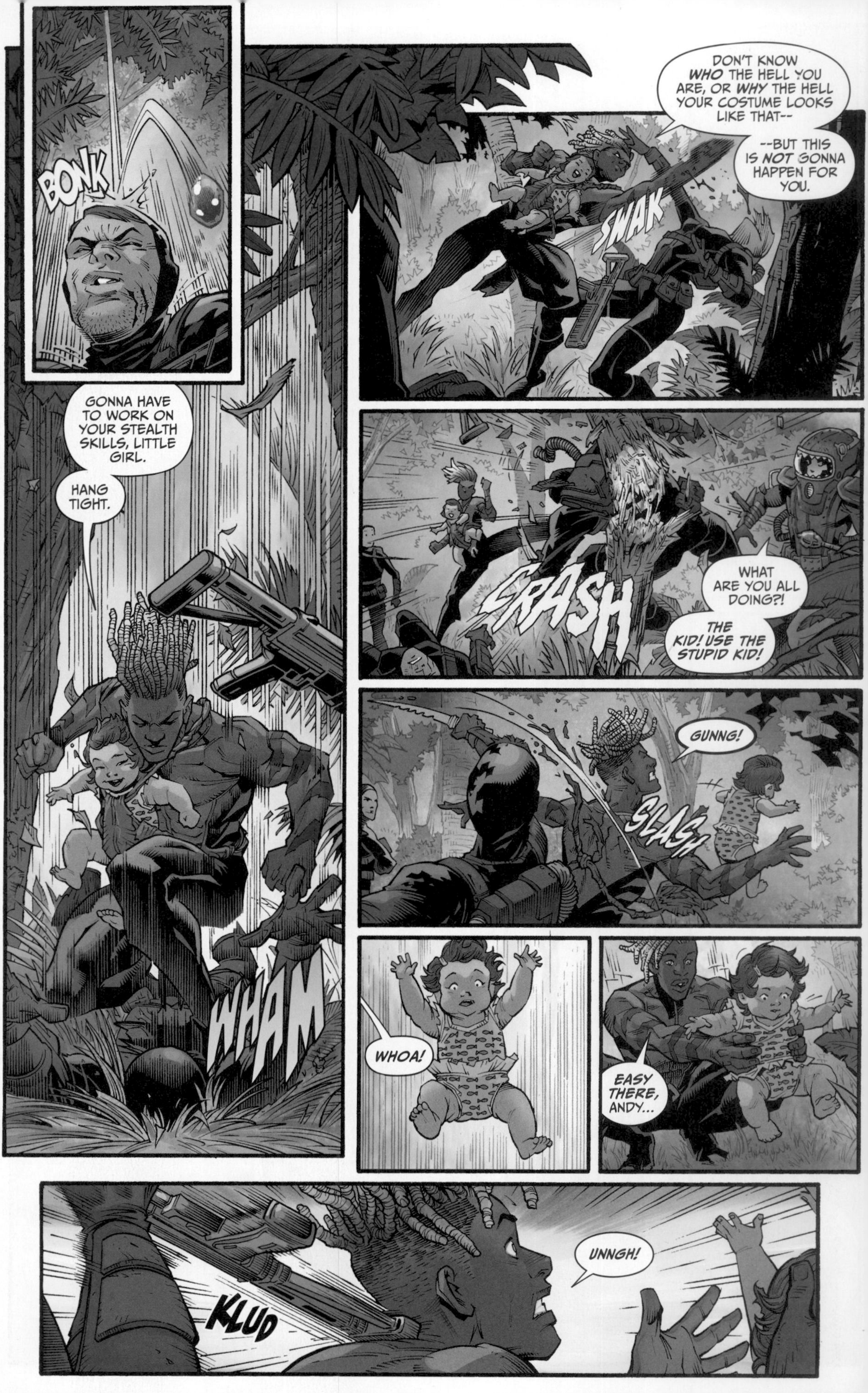
BONK
DON'T KNOW WHO THE HELL YOU ARE, OR WHY THE HELL YOUR COSTUME LOOKS LIKE THAT--
--BUT THIS IS NOT GONNA HAPPEN FOR YOU.
SWAK
GONNA HAVE TO WORK ON YOUR STEALTH SKILLS, LITTLE GIRL.
HANG TIGHT.
WHAM
CRASH
WHAT ARE YOU ALL DOING?!
THE KID! USE THE STUPID KID!
GUNNG!
SLASH
WHOA!
EASY THERE, ANDY...
KLUD
UNNGH!

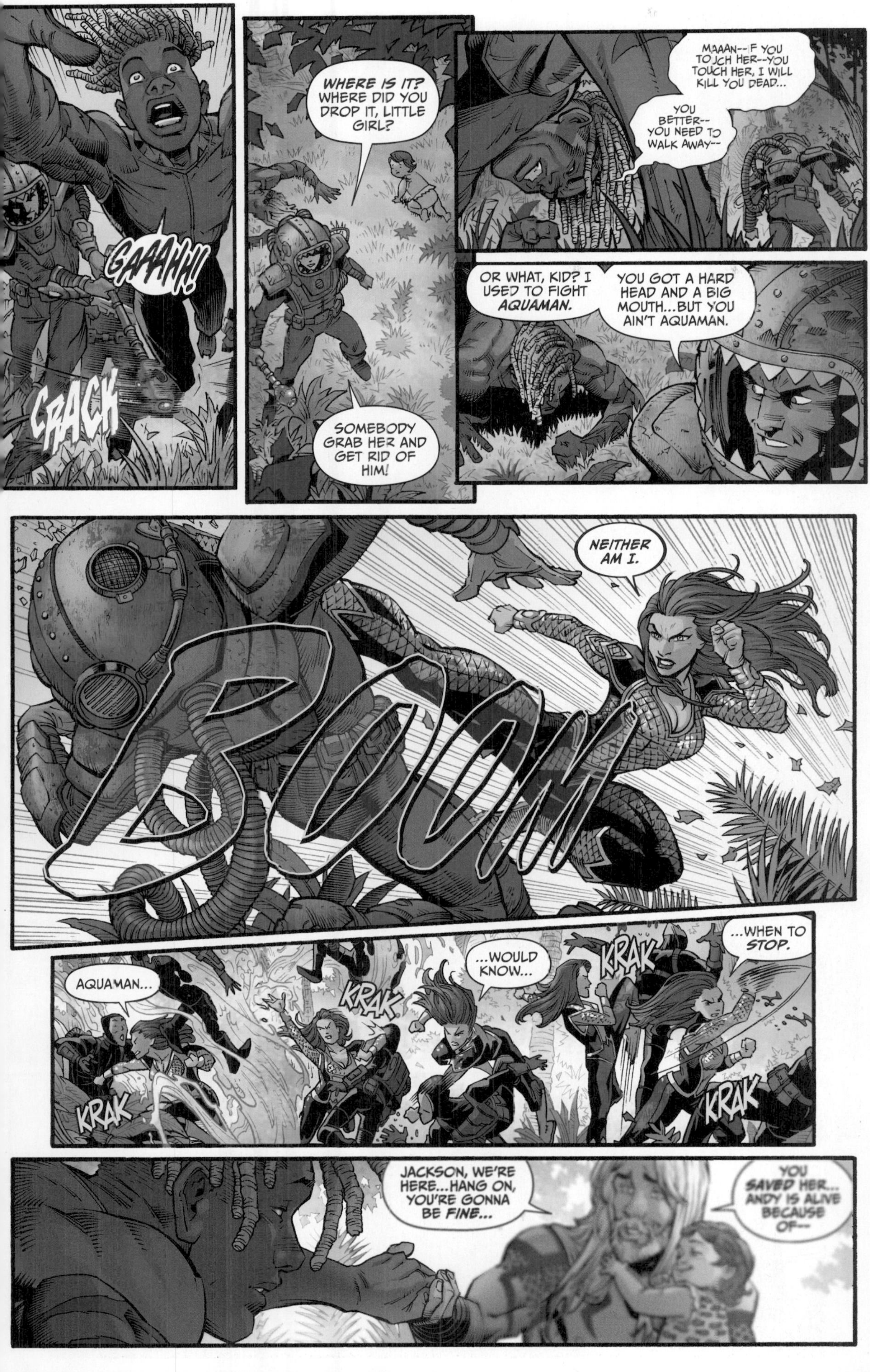
GAAAHH!
CRACK
WHERE IS IT? WHERE DID YOU DROP IT, LITTLE GIRL?
SOMEBODY GRAB HER AND GET RID OF HIM!
MAAAN--IF YOU TOUCH HER--YOU TOUCH HER, I WILL KILL YOU DEAD...
YOU BETTER-- YOU NEED TO WALK AWAY--
OR WHAT, KID? I USED TO FIGHT AQUAMAN.
YOU GOT A HARD HEAD AND A BIG MOUTH...BUT YOU AIN'T AQUAMAN.
NEITHER AM I.
BOOM
AQUAMAN...
KRAK
...WOULD KNOW...
KRAK
...WHEN TO STOP.
KRAK
KRAK
JACKSON, WE'RE HERE...HANG ON, YOU'RE GONNA BE FINE...
YOU SAVED HER... ANDY IS ALIVE BECAUSE OF--

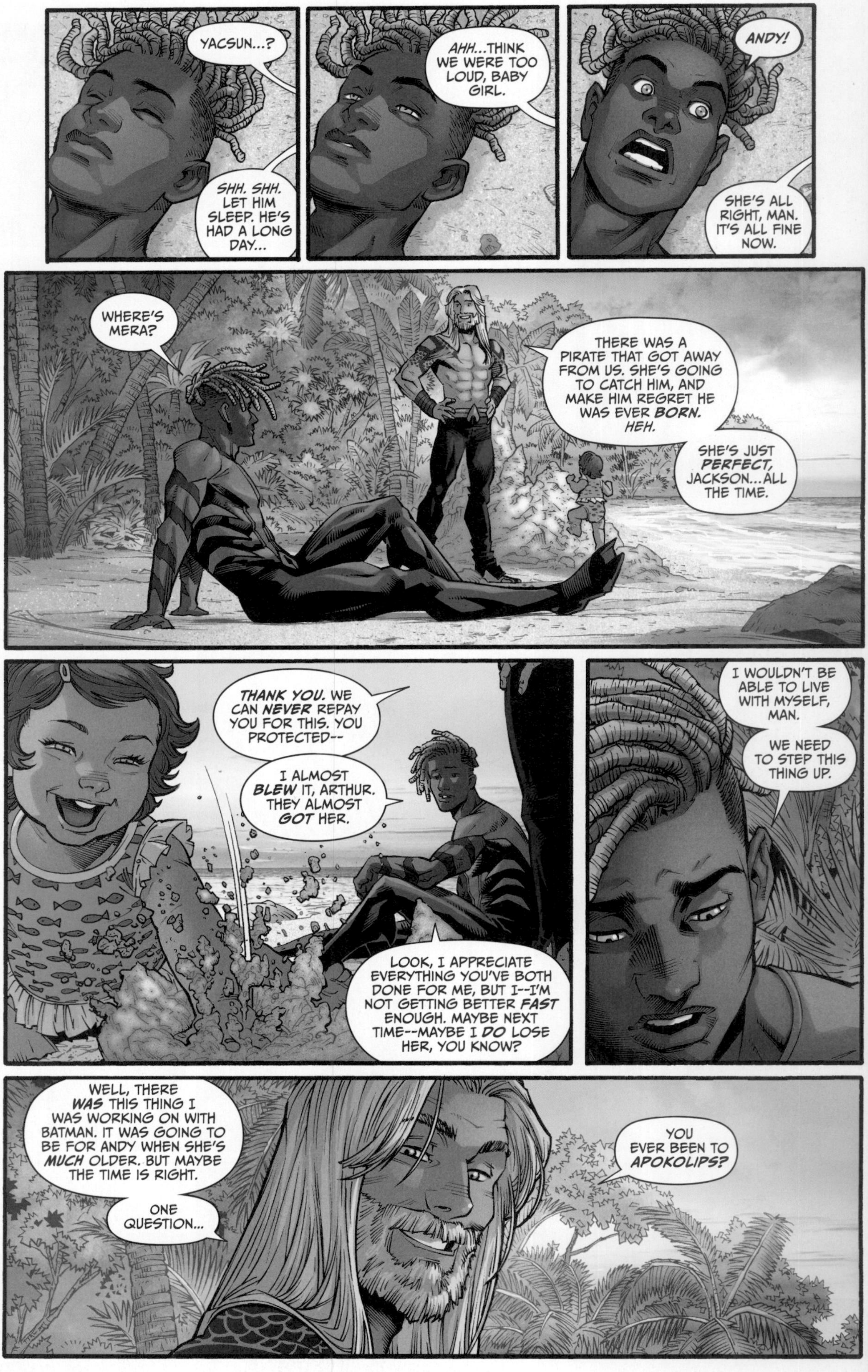

YACSUN...?
SHH. SHH. LET HIM SLEEP. HE'S HAD A LONG DAY...
AHH...THINK WE WERE TOO LOUD, BABY GIRL.
ANDY!
SHE'S ALL RIGHT, MAN. IT'S ALL FINE NOW.
WHERE'S MERA?
THERE WAS A PIRATE THAT GOT AWAY FROM US. SHE'S GOING TO CATCH HIM, AND MAKE HIM REGRET HE WAS EVER BORN. HEH.
SHE'S JUST PERFECT, JACKSON...ALL THE TIME.
THANK YOU. WE CAN NEVER REPAY YOU FOR THIS. YOU PROTECTED--
I ALMOST BLEW IT, ARTHUR. THEY ALMOST GOT HER.
LOOK, I APPRECIATE EVERYTHING YOU'VE BOTH DONE FOR ME, BUT I--I'M NOT GETTING BETTER FAST ENOUGH. MAYBE NEXT TIME--MAYBE I DO LOSE HER, YOU KNOW?
I WOULDN'T BE ABLE TO LIVE WITH MYSELF, MAN.
WE NEED TO STEP THIS THING UP.
WELL, THERE WAS THIS THING I WAS WORKING ON WITH BATMAN. IT WAS GOING TO BE FOR ANDY WHEN SHE'S MUCH OLDER. BUT MAYBE THE TIME IS RIGHT.
ONE QUESTION...
YOU EVER BEEN TO APOKOLIPS?

AQUAMAN: THE BECOMING #1 cover by DAVID TALASKI

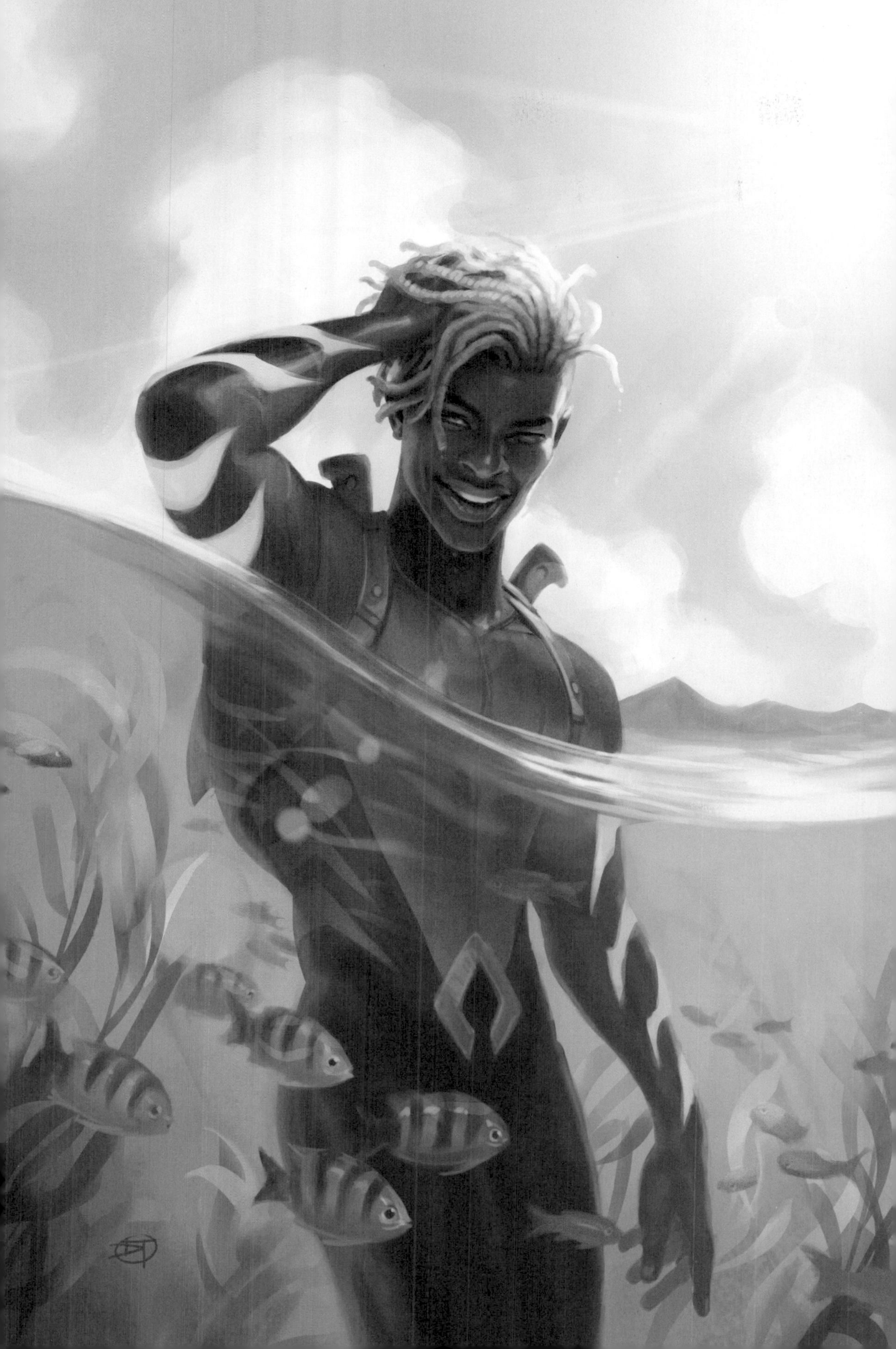

AQUAMAN: THE BECOMING #1 variant cover
by KHARY RANDOLPH and EMILIO LOPEZ

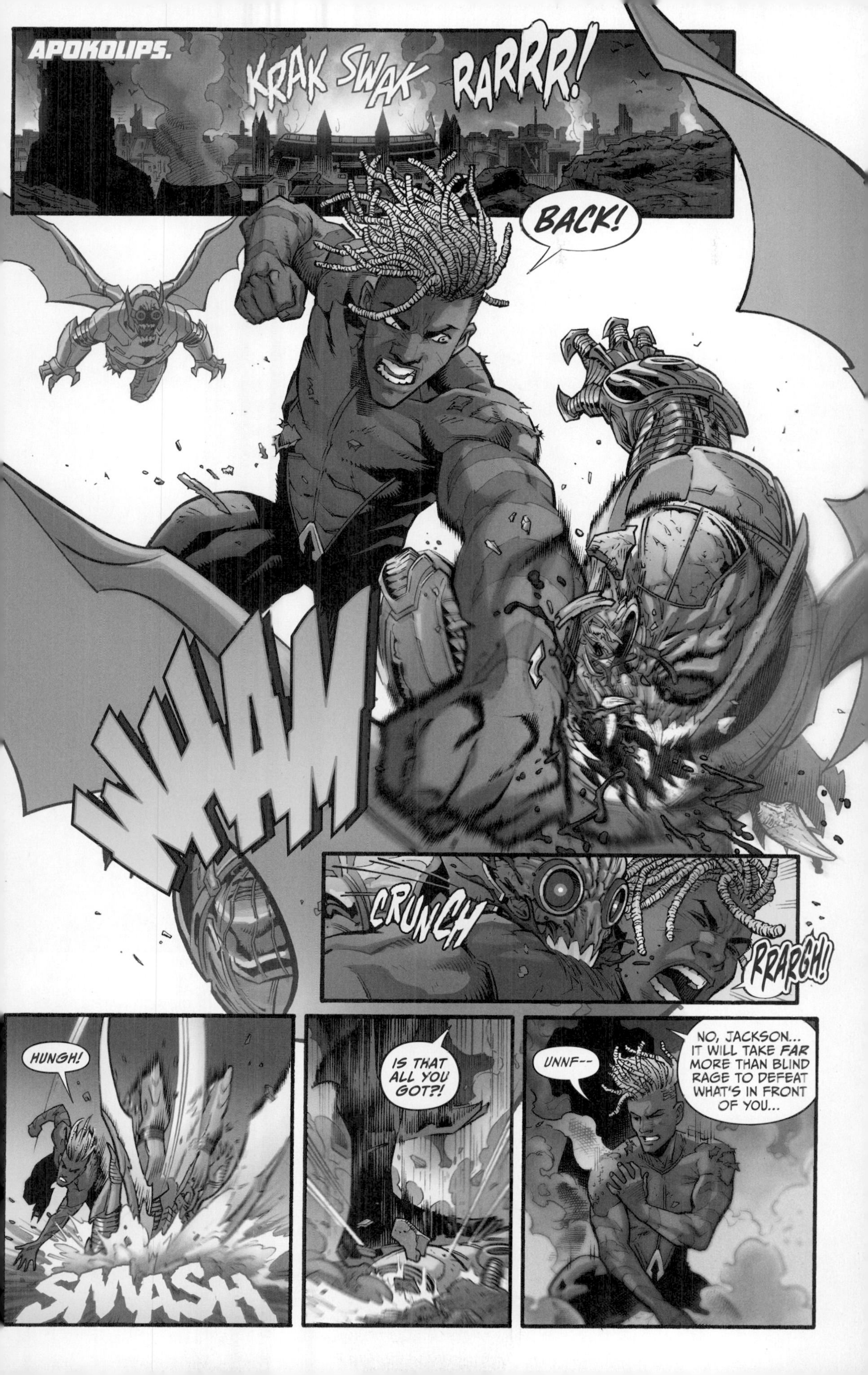

APOKOLIPS.
KRAK SWAK RARRR!
BACK!
WHAM
CRUNCH
RRARGH!
HUNGH!
SMASH
IS THAT ALL YOU GOT?!
UNNF--
NO, JACKSON... IT WILL TAKE FAR MORE THAN BLIND RAGE TO DEFEAT WHAT'S IN FRONT OF YOU...

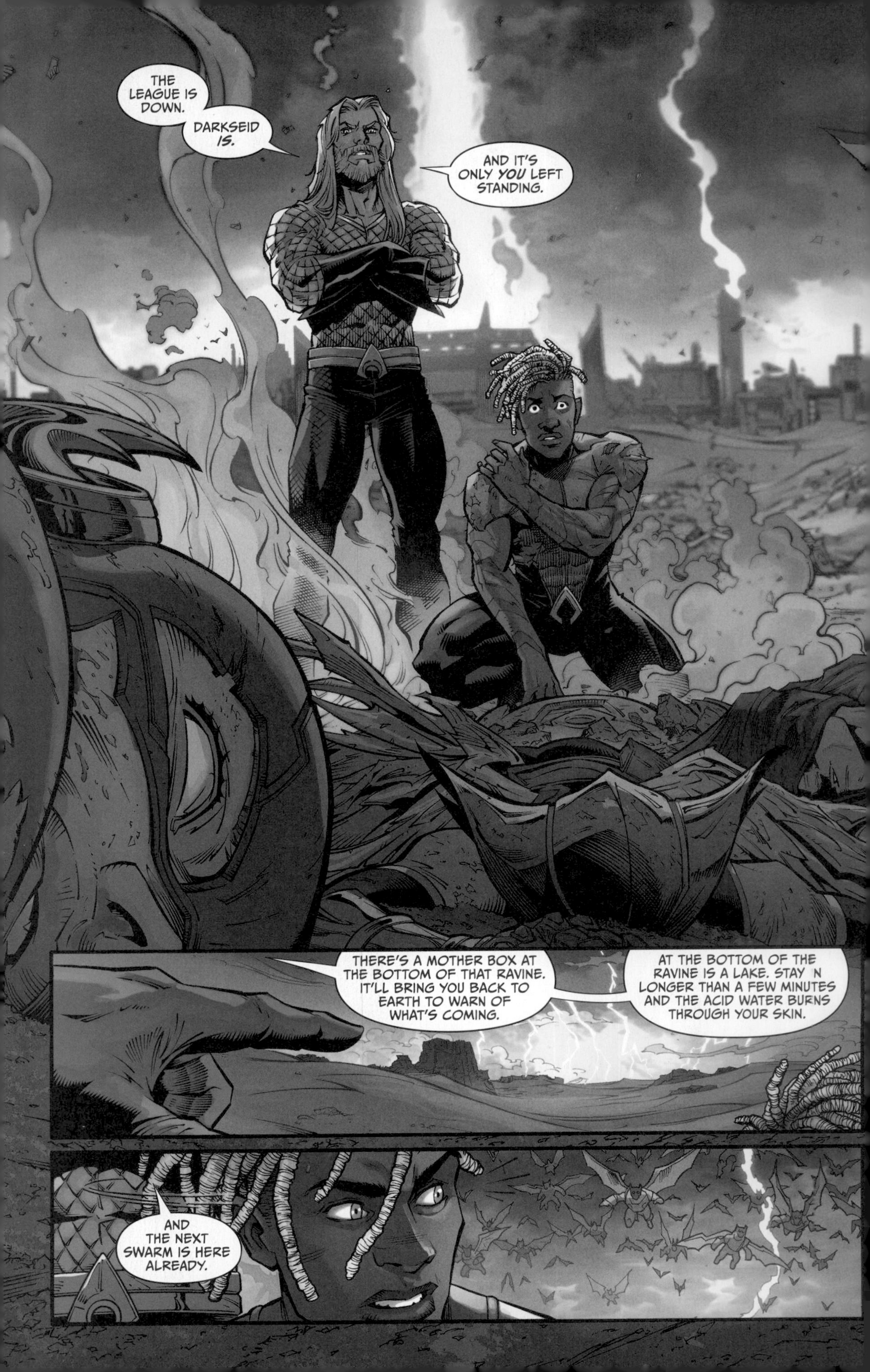
THE LEAGUE IS DOWN.
DARKSEID *IS.*
AND IT'S ONLY *YOU* LEFT STANDING.
THERE'S A MOTHER BOX AT THE BOTTOM OF THAT RAVINE. IT'LL BRING YOU BACK TO EARTH TO WARN OF WHAT'S COMING.
AT THE BOTTOM OF THE RAVINE IS A LAKE. STAY IN LONGER THAN A FEW MINUTES AND THE ACID WATER BURNS THROUGH YOUR SKIN.
AND THE NEXT SWARM IS HERE ALREADY.

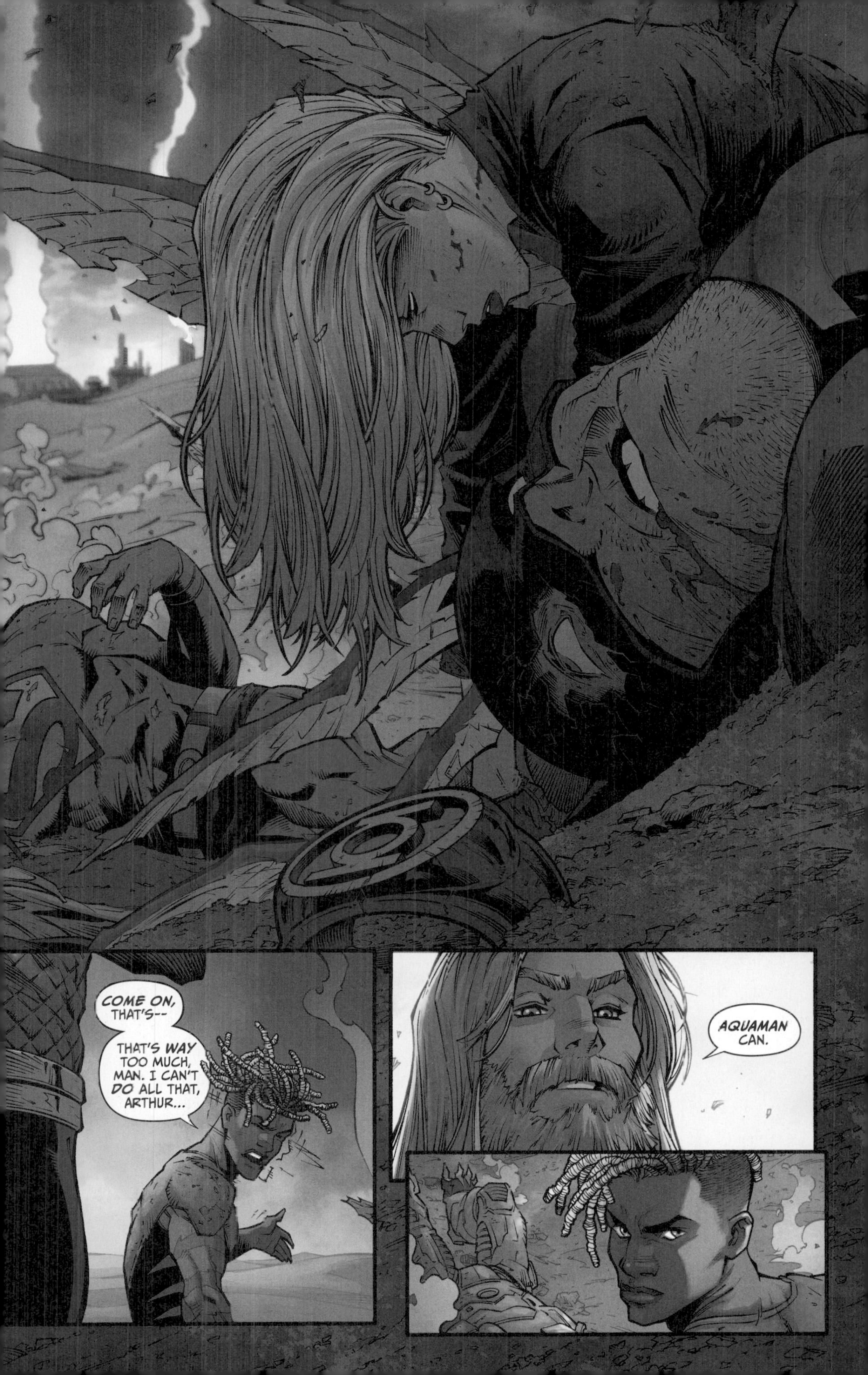
COME ON, THAT'S--
THAT'S WAY TOO MUCH, MAN. I CAN'T DO ALL THAT, ARTHUR...
AQUAMAN CAN.

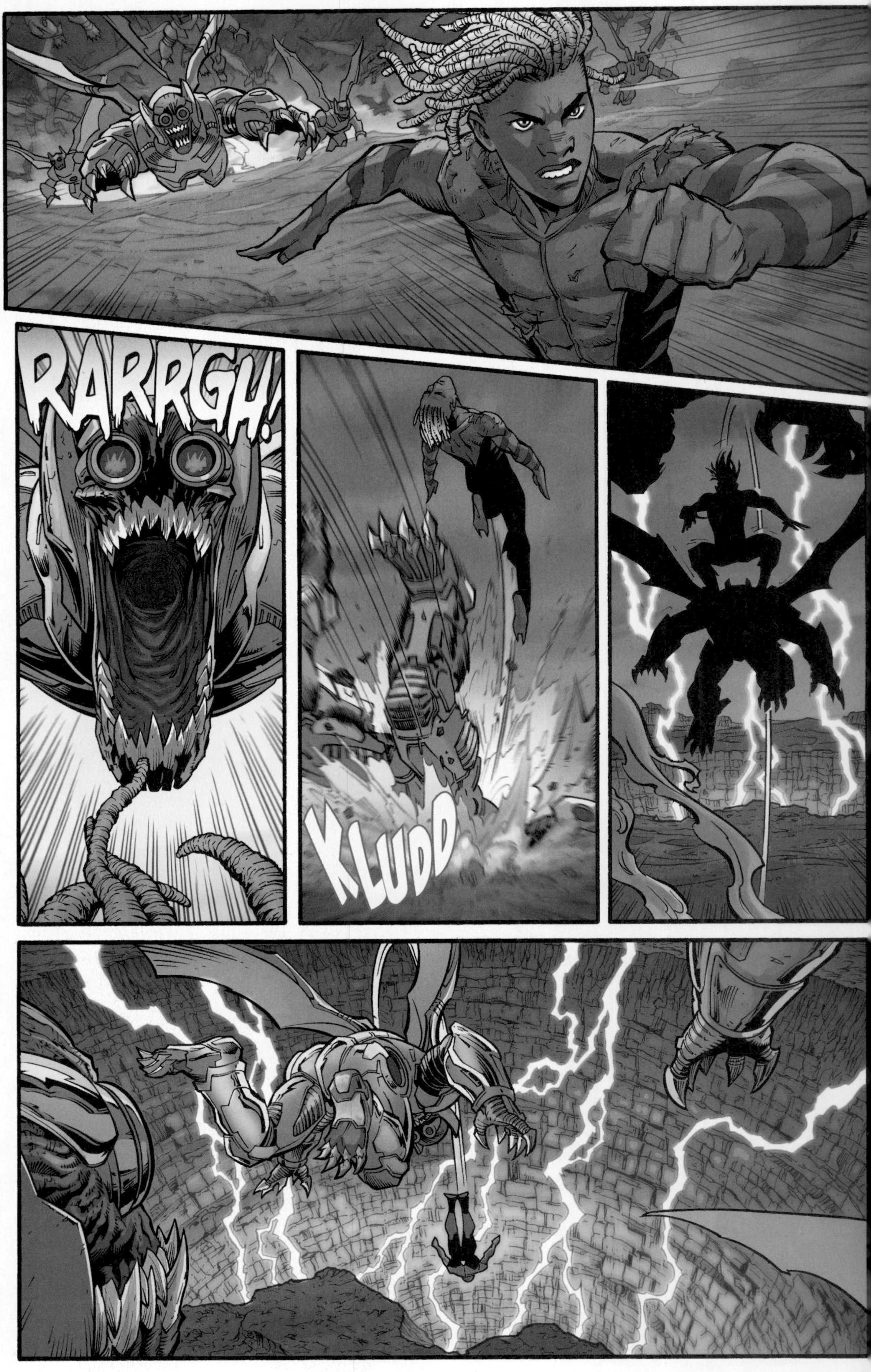
RARRGH!
KLUDD

KA-PLOOSH

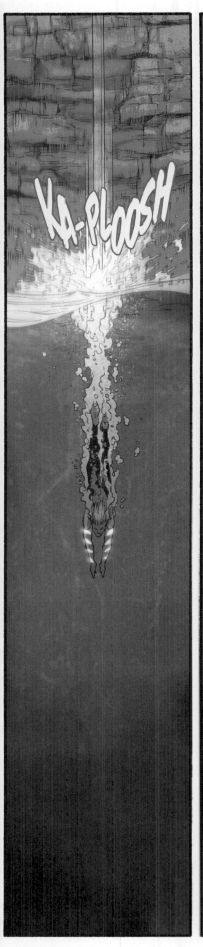

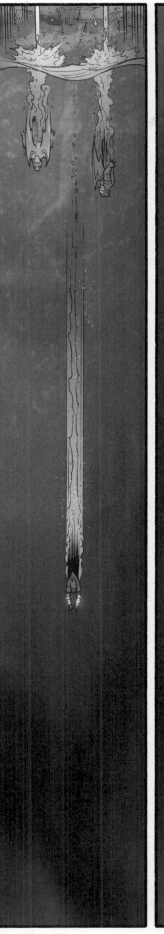

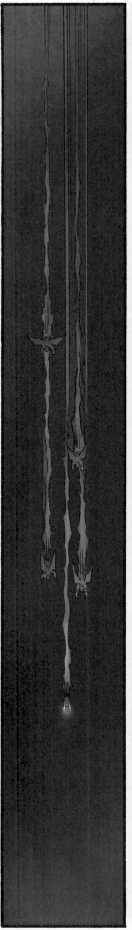

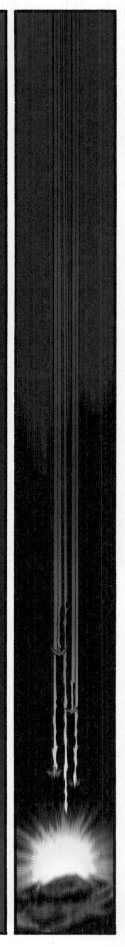

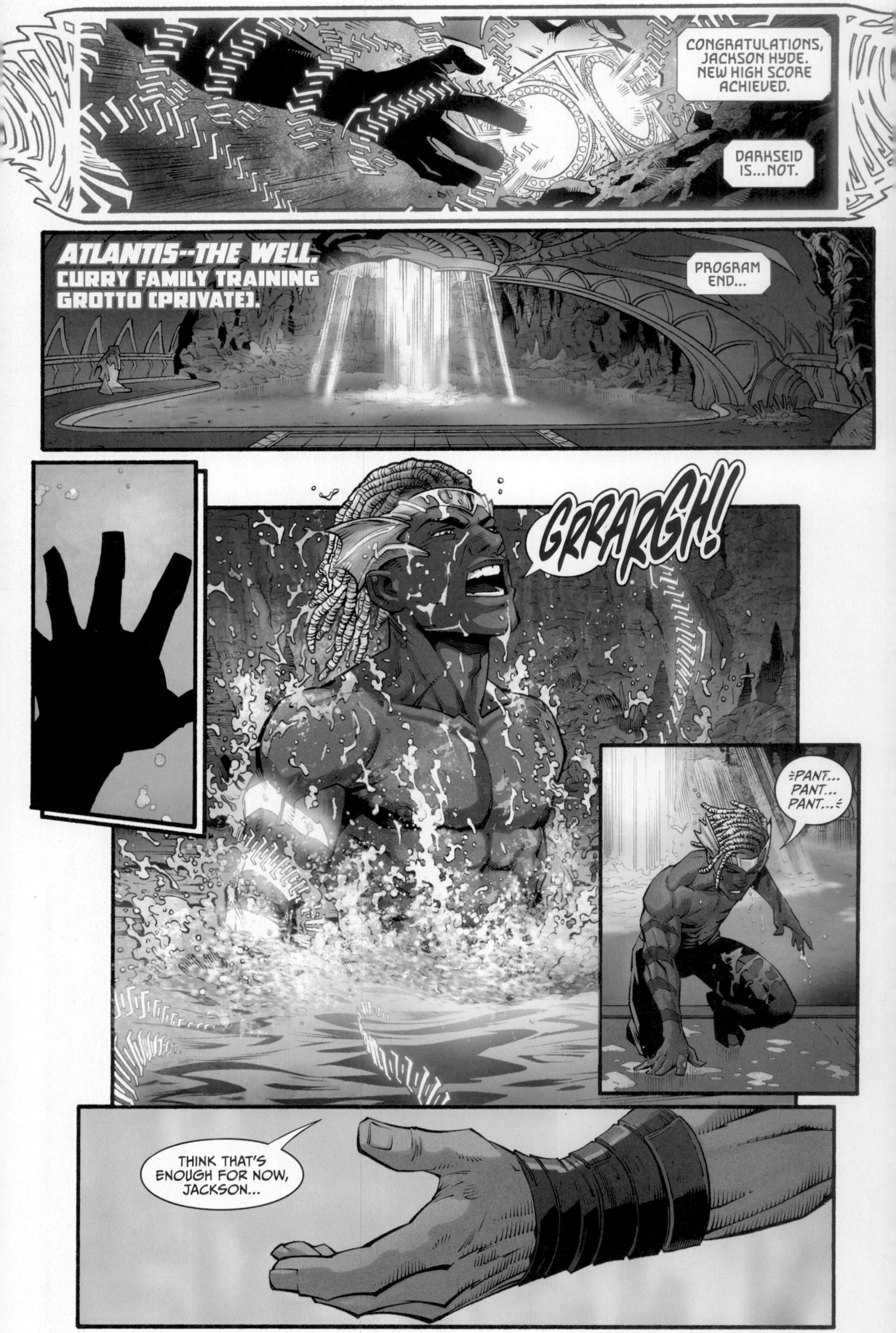
CONGRATULATIONS, JACKSON HYDE. NEW HIGH SCORE ACHIEVED.
DARKSEID IS...NOT.
ATLANTIS--THE WELL. CURRY FAMILY TRAINING GROTTO (PRIVATE).
PROGRAM END...
GRRARGH!
PANT... PANT... PANT...
THINK THAT'S ENOUGH FOR NOW, JACKSON...

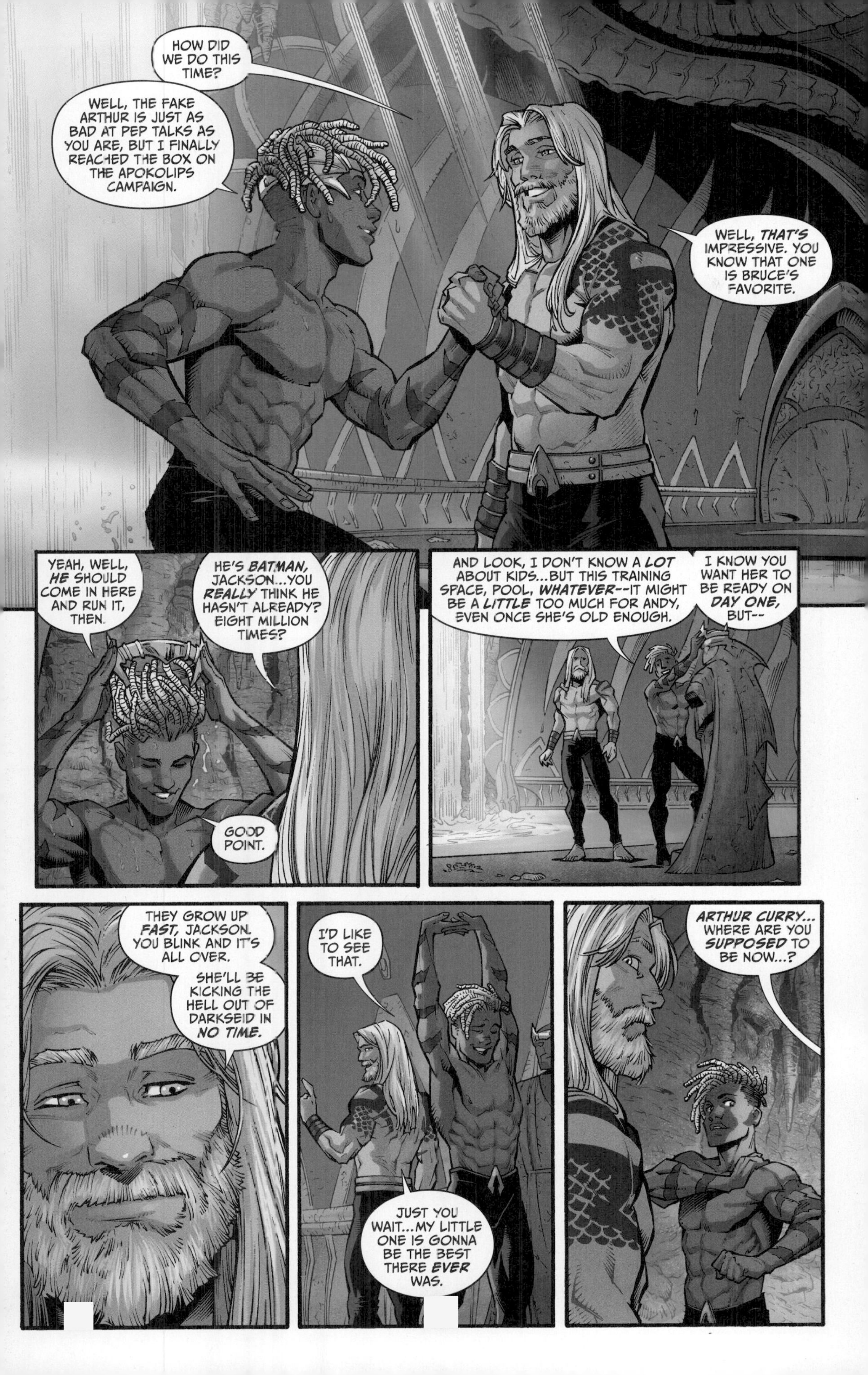
HOW DID WE DO THIS TIME?
WELL, THE FAKE ARTHUR IS JUST AS BAD AT PEP TALKS AS YOU ARE, BUT I FINALLY REACHED THE BOX ON THE APOKOLIPS CAMPAIGN.
WELL, THAT'S IMPRESSIVE. YOU KNOW THAT ONE IS BRUCE'S FAVORITE.
YEAH, WELL, HE SHOULD COME IN HERE AND RUN IT, THEN.
HE'S BATMAN, JACKSON...YOU REALLY THINK HE HASN'T ALREADY? EIGHT MILLION TIMES?
GOOD POINT.
AND LOOK, I DON'T KNOW A LOT ABOUT KIDS...BUT THIS TRAINING SPACE, POOL, WHATEVER--IT MIGHT BE A LITTLE TOO MUCH FOR ANDY, EVEN ONCE SHE'S OLD ENOUGH.
I KNOW YOU WANT HER TO BE READY ON DAY ONE, BUT--
THEY GROW UP FAST, JACKSON. YOU BLINK AND IT'S ALL OVER.
SHE'LL BE KICKING THE HELL OUT OF DARKSEID IN NO TIME.
I'D LIKE TO SEE THAT.
JUST YOU WAIT...MY LITTLE ONE IS GONNA BE THE BEST THERE EVER WAS.
ARTHUR CURRY... WHERE ARE YOU SUPPOSED TO BE NOW...?

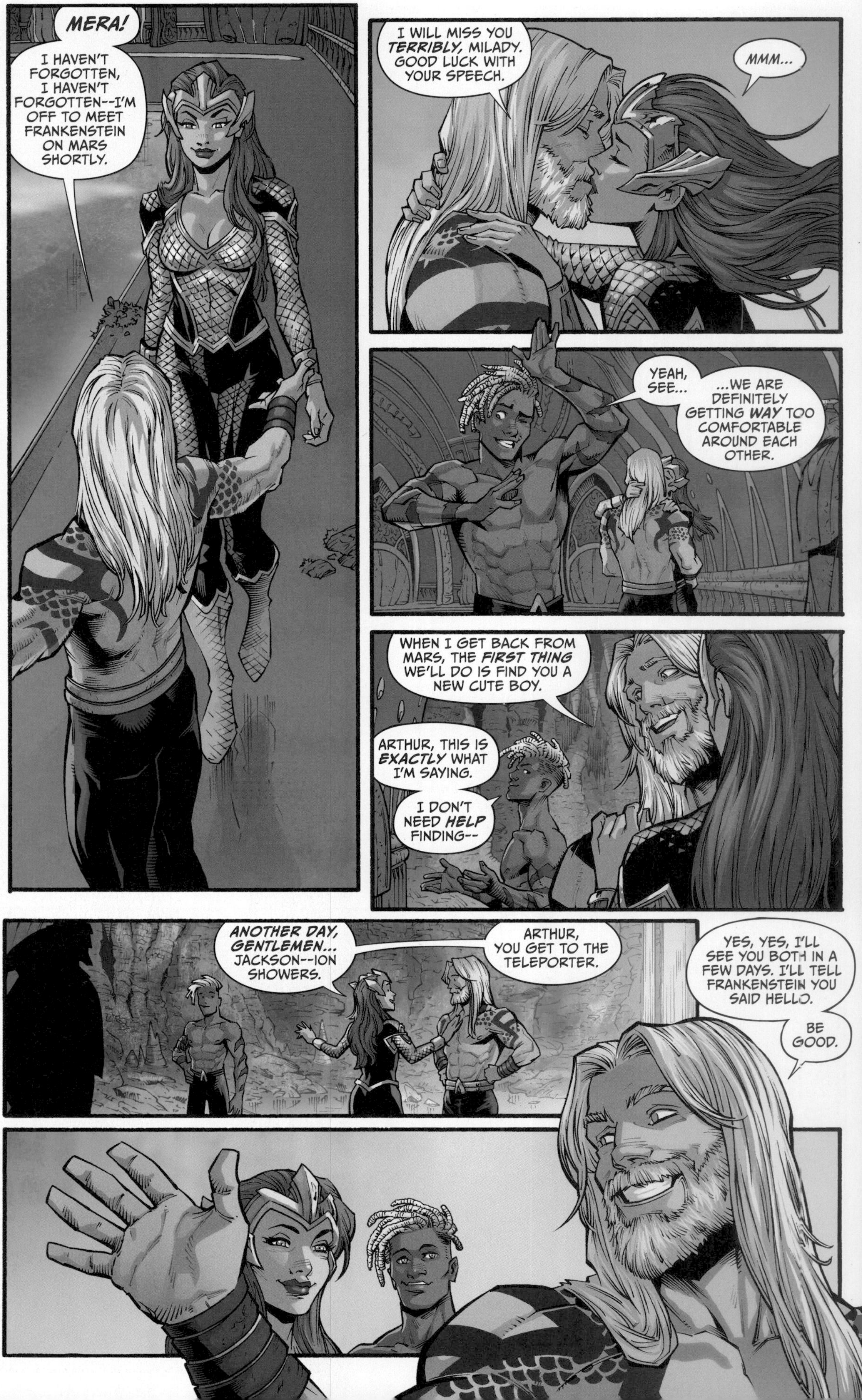

MERA!
I HAVEN'T FORGOTTEN, I HAVEN'T FORGOTTEN--I'M OFF TO MEET FRANKENSTEIN ON MARS SHORTLY.
I WILL MISS YOU TERRIBLY, MILADY. GOOD LUCK WITH YOUR SPEECH.
MMM...
YEAH, SEE...
...WE ARE DEFINITELY GETTING WAY TOO COMFORTABLE AROUND EACH OTHER.
WHEN I GET BACK FROM MARS, THE FIRST THING WE'LL DO IS FIND YOU A NEW CUTE BOY.
ARTHUR, THIS IS EXACTLY WHAT I'M SAYING.
I DON'T NEED HELP FINDING--
ANOTHER DAY, GENTLEMEN... JACKSON--ION SHOWERS.
ARTHUR, YOU GET TO THE TELEPORTER.
YES, YES, I'LL SEE YOU BOTH IN A FEW DAYS. I'LL TELL FRANKENSTEIN YOU SAID HELLO.
BE GOOD.

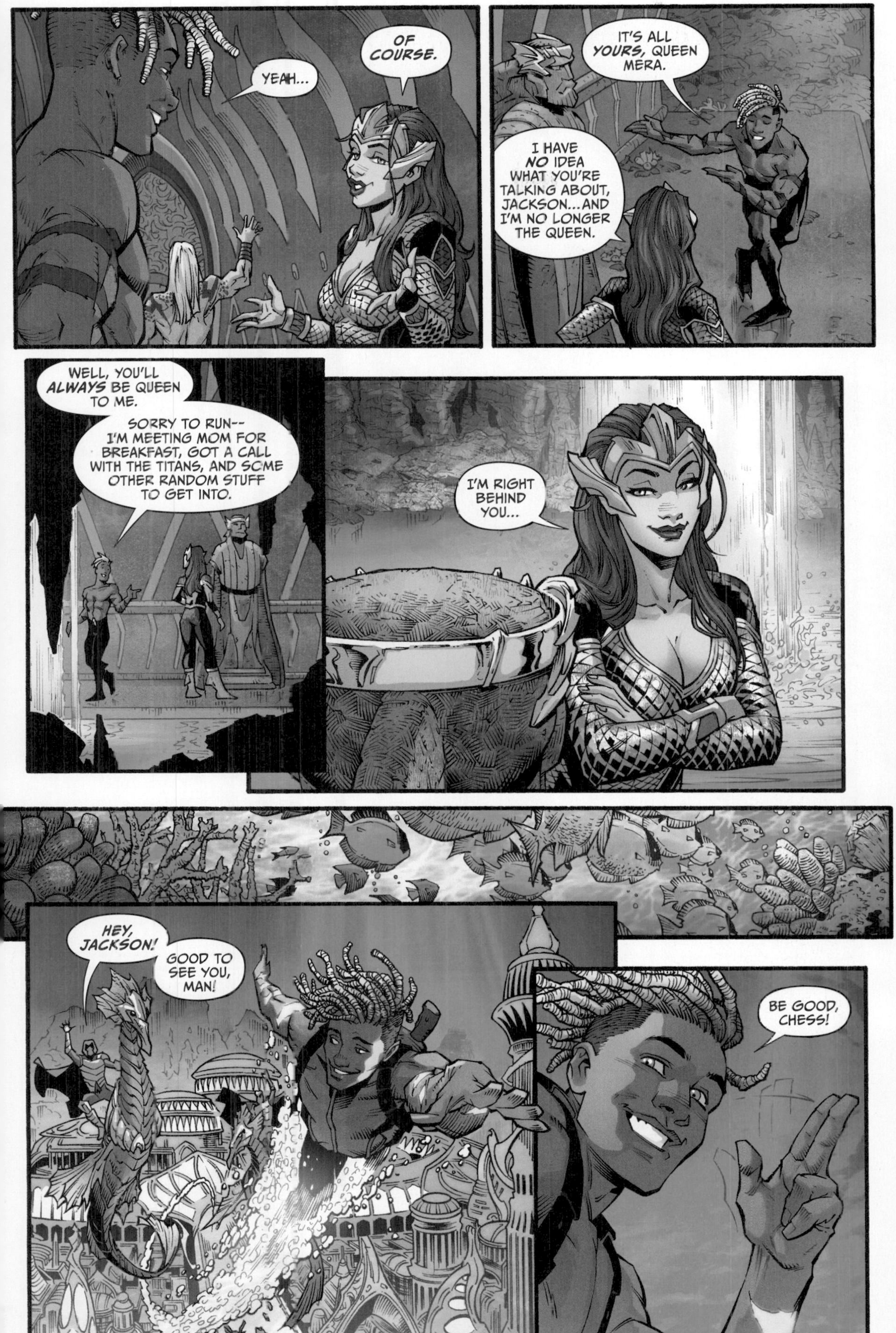
YEAH...
OF COURSE.
IT'S ALL YOURS, QUEEN MERA.
I HAVE NO IDEA WHAT YOU'RE TALKING ABOUT, JACKSON...AND I'M NO LONGER THE QUEEN.
WELL, YOU'LL ALWAYS BE QUEEN TO ME.
SORRY TO RUN-- I'M MEETING MOM FOR BREAKFAST, GOT A CALL WITH THE TITANS, AND SOME OTHER RANDOM STUFF TO GET INTO.
I'M RIGHT BEHIND YOU...
HEY, JACKSON!
GOOD TO SEE YOU, MAN!
BE GOOD, CHESS!

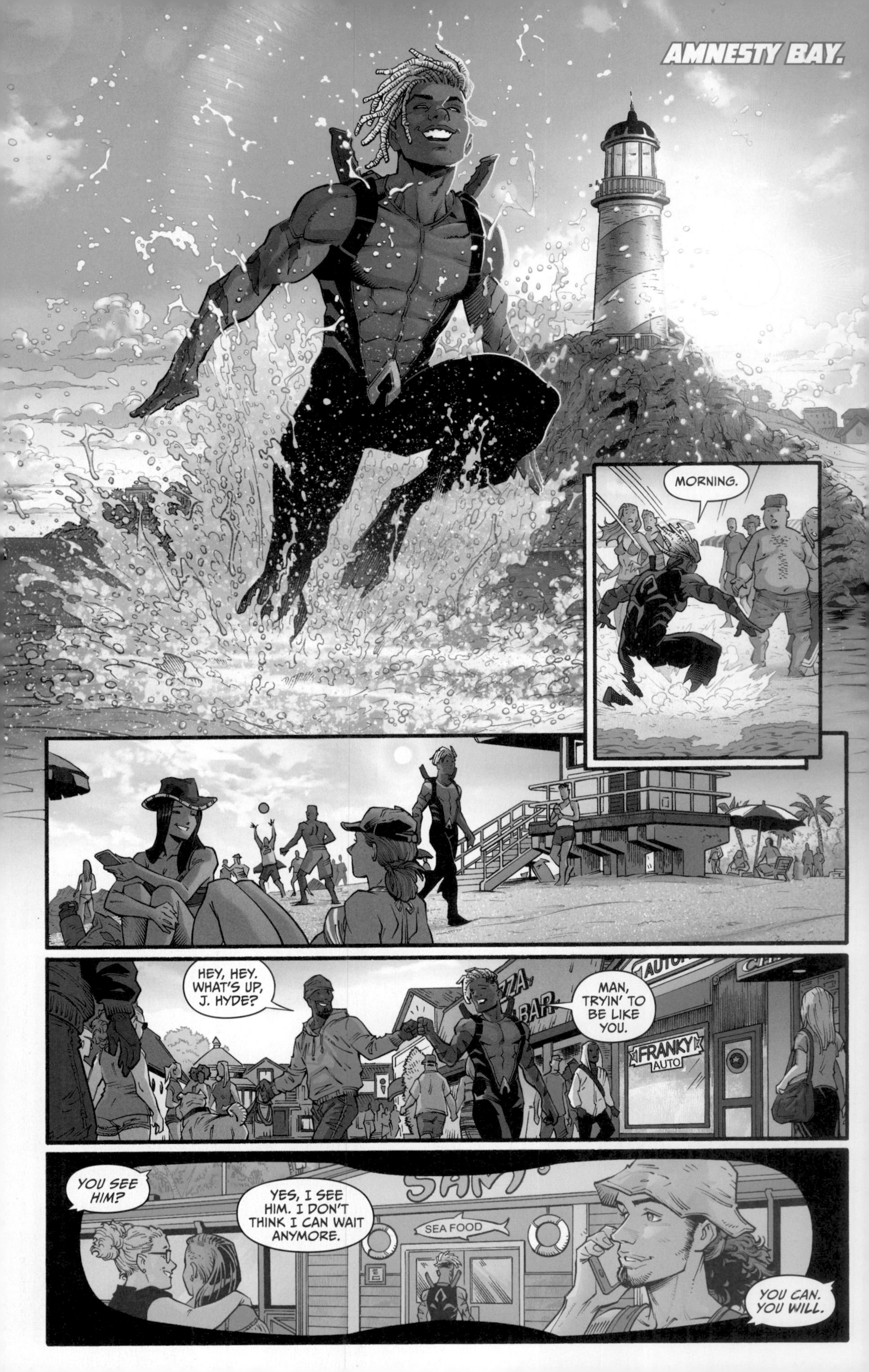
AMNESTY BAY.
MORNING.
HEY, HEY. WHAT'S UP, J. HYDE?
MAN, TRYIN' TO BE LIKE YOU.
FRANKY AUTO
YOU SEE HIM?
YES, I SEE HIM. I DON'T THINK I CAN WAIT ANYMORE.
SEA FOOD
YOU CAN. YOU WILL.

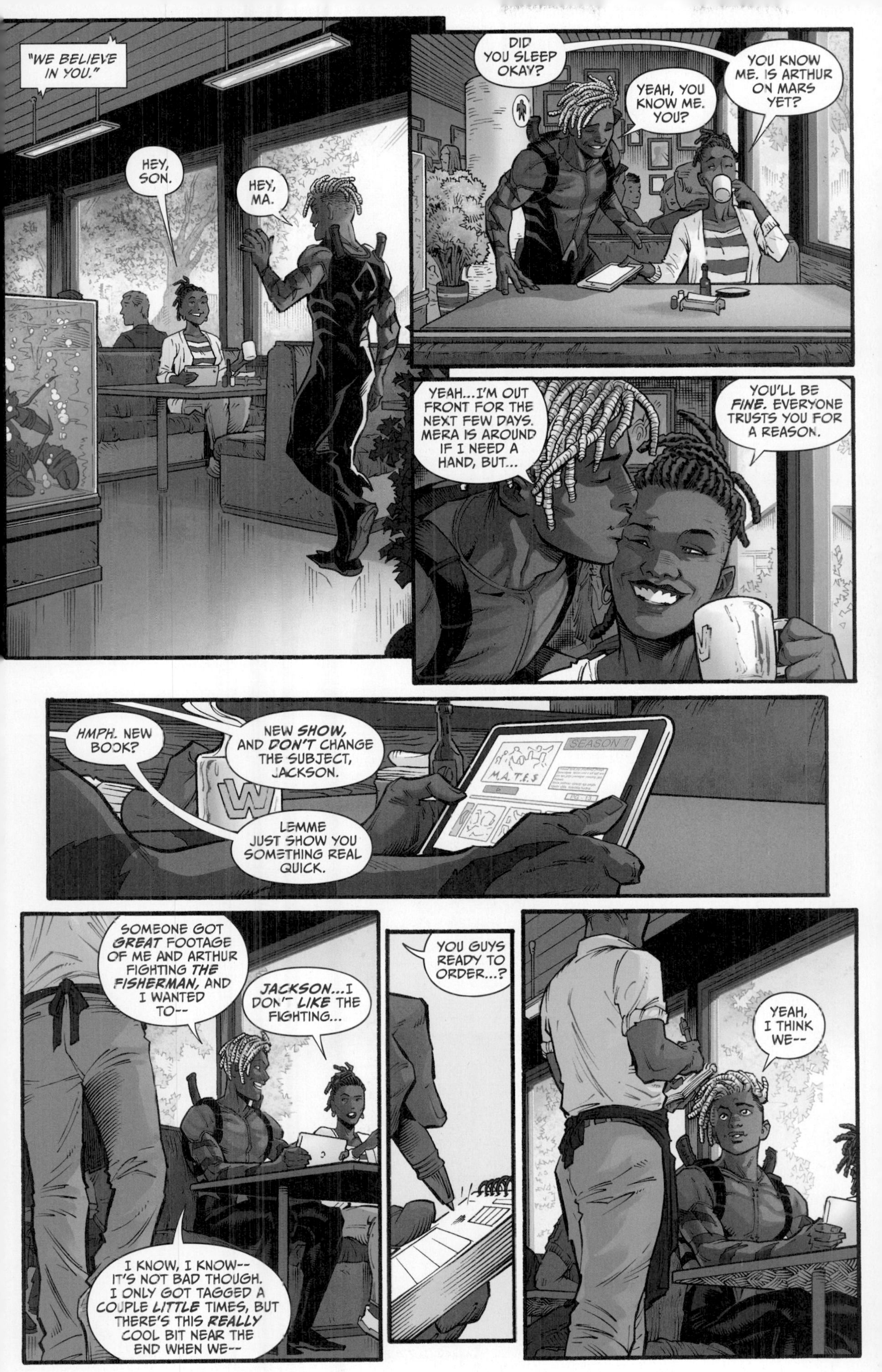
"WE BELIEVE IN YOU."
HEY, SON.
HEY, MA.
DID YOU SLEEP OKAY?
YEAH, YOU KNOW ME. YOU?
YOU KNOW ME. IS ARTHUR ON MARS YET?
YEAH...I'M OUT FRONT FOR THE NEXT FEW DAYS. MERA IS AROUND IF I NEED A HAND, BUT...
YOU'LL BE FINE. EVERYONE TRUSTS YOU FOR A REASON.
HMPH. NEW BOOK?
NEW SHOW, AND DON'T CHANGE THE SUBJECT, JACKSON.
LEMME JUST SHOW YOU SOMETHING REAL QUICK.
SEASON 1
M.A.T.E.S
SOMEONE GOT GREAT FOOTAGE OF ME AND ARTHUR FIGHTING THE FISHERMAN, AND I WANTED TO--
JACKSON...I DON'T LIKE THE FIGHTING...
I KNOW, I KNOW-- IT'S NOT BAD THOUGH. I ONLY GOT TAGGED A COUPLE LITTLE TIMES, BUT THERE'S THIS REALLY COOL BIT NEAR THE END WHEN WE--
YOU GUYS READY TO ORDER...?
YEAH, I THINK WE--

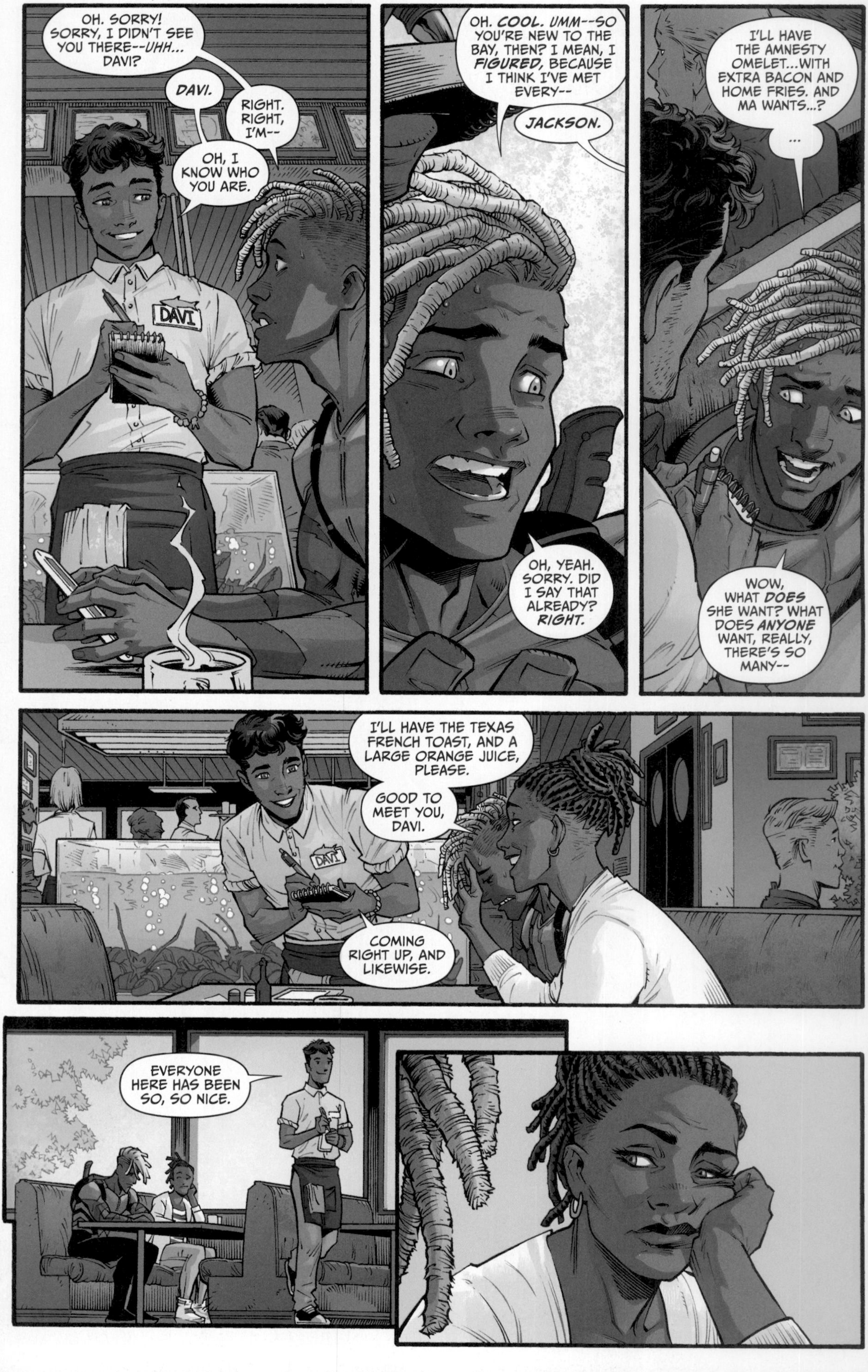
OH. SORRY! SORRY, I DIDN'T SEE YOU THERE--UHH... DAVI?
DAVI.
RIGHT. RIGHT, I'M--
OH, I KNOW WHO YOU ARE.
DAVI
OH. COOL. UMM--SO YOU'RE NEW TO THE BAY, THEN? I MEAN, I FIGURED, BECAUSE I THINK I'VE MET EVERY--
JACKSON.
OH, YEAH. SORRY. DID I SAY THAT ALREADY? RIGHT.
I'LL HAVE THE AMNESTY OMELET...WITH EXTRA BACON AND HOME FRIES. AND MA WANTS...?
...
WOW, WHAT DOES SHE WANT? WHAT DOES ANYONE WANT, REALLY, THERE'S SO MANY--
I'LL HAVE THE TEXAS FRENCH TOAST, AND A LARGE ORANGE JUICE, PLEASE.
GOOD TO MEET YOU, DAVI.
DAVI
COMING RIGHT UP, AND LIKEWISE.
EVERYONE HERE HAS BEEN SO, SO NICE.

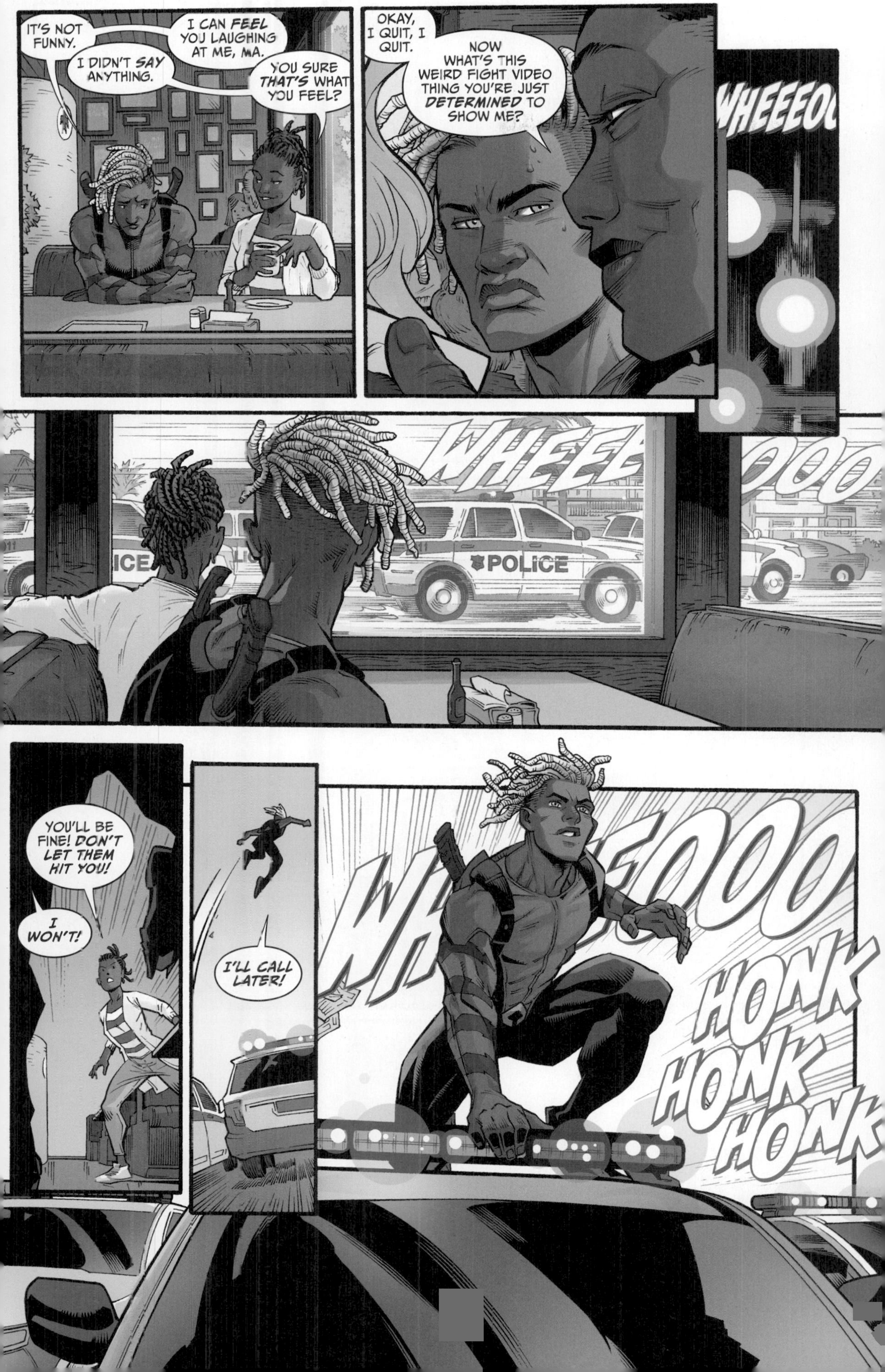
IT'S NOT FUNNY.
I CAN FEEL YOU LAUGHING AT ME, MA.
I DIDN'T SAY ANYTHING.
YOU SURE THAT'S WHAT YOU FEEL?
OKAY, I QUIT, I QUIT.
NOW WHAT'S THIS WEIRD FIGHT VIDEO THING YOU'RE JUST DETERMINED TO SHOW ME?
WHEEEOO
WHEEE
OOOO
POLICE
YOU'LL BE FINE! DON'T LET THEM HIT YOU!
I WON'T!
I'LL CALL LATER!
HONK
HONK
HONK

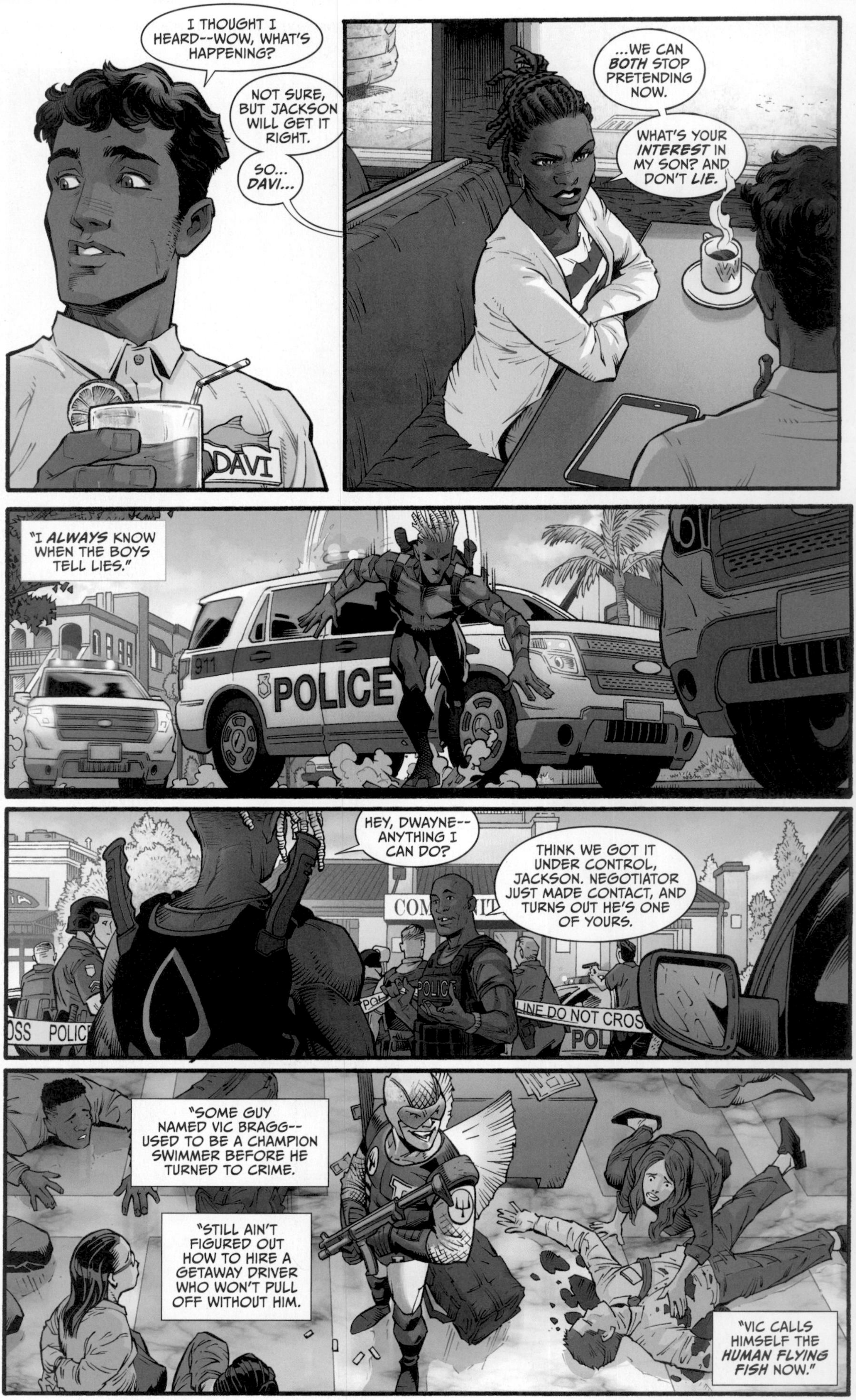
I THOUGHT I HEARD--WOW, WHAT'S HAPPENING?
NOT SURE, BUT JACKSON WILL GET IT RIGHT.
SO... DAVI...
DAVI
...WE CAN BOTH STOP PRETENDING NOW.
WHAT'S YOUR INTEREST IN MY SON? AND DON'T LIE.
"I ALWAYS KNOW WHEN THE BOYS TELL LIES."
911
POLICE
HEY, DWAYNE--ANYTHING I CAN DO?
THINK WE GOT IT UNDER CONTROL, JACKSON. NEGOTIATOR JUST MADE CONTACT, AND TURNS OUT HE'S ONE OF YOURS.
POLICE
LINE DO NOT CROS
"SOME GUY NAMED VIC BRAGG--USED TO BE A CHAMPION SWIMMER BEFORE HE TURNED TO CRIME.
"STILL AIN'T FIGURED OUT HOW TO HIRE A GETAWAY DRIVER WHO WON'T PULL OFF WITHOUT HIM.
"VIC CALLS HIMSELF THE HUMAN FLYING FISH NOW."

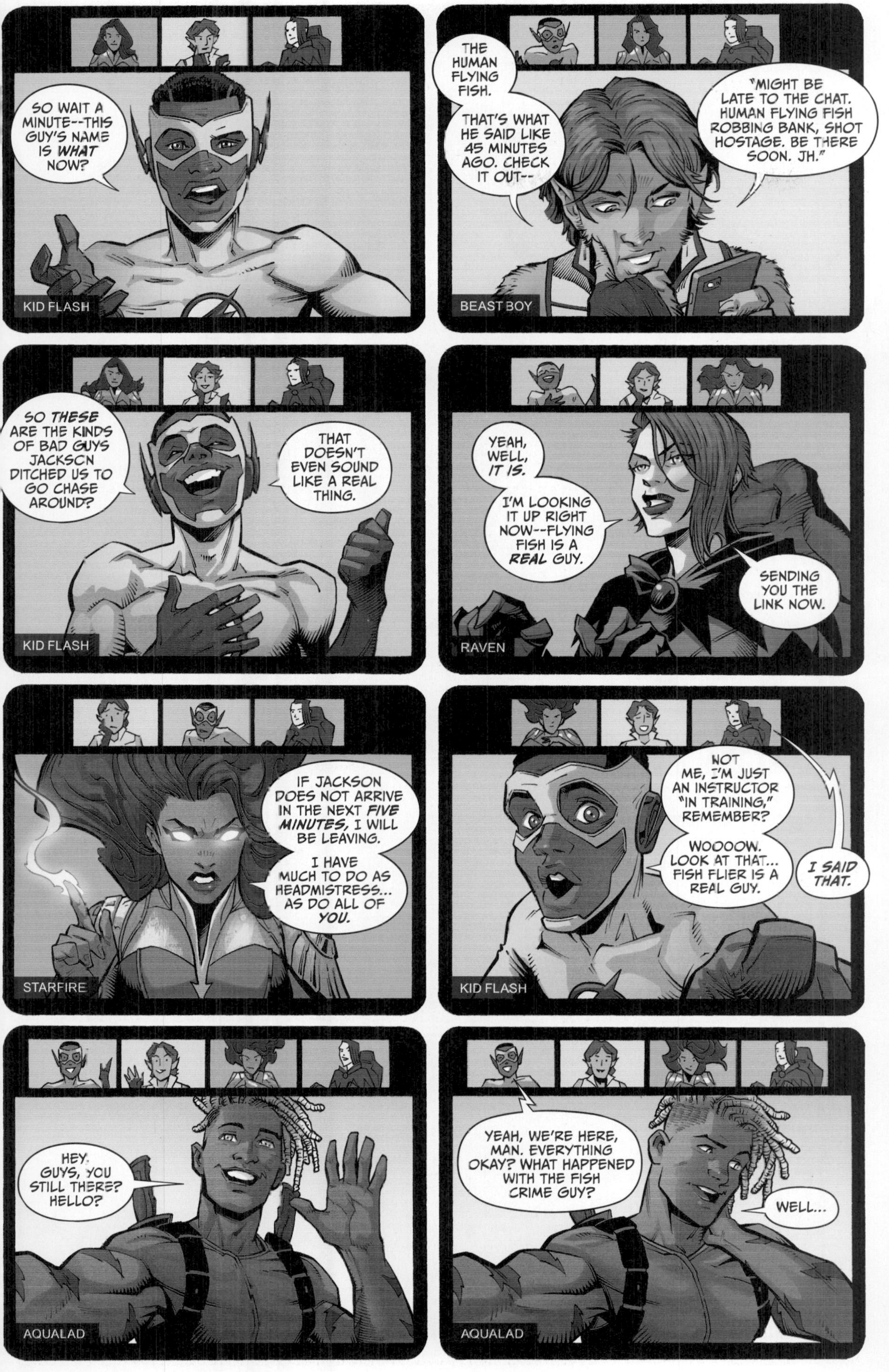
SO WAIT A MINUTE--THIS GUY'S NAME IS WHAT NOW?
KID FLASH
THE HUMAN FLYING FISH.
THAT'S WHAT HE SAID LIKE 45 MINUTES AGO. CHECK IT OUT--
"MIGHT BE LATE TO THE CHAT. HUMAN FLYING FISH ROBBING BANK, SHOT HOSTAGE. BE THERE SOON. JH."
BEAST BOY
SO THESE ARE THE KINDS OF BAD GUYS JACKSON DITCHED US TO GO CHASE AROUND?
THAT DOESN'T EVEN SOUND LIKE A REAL THING.
KID FLASH
YEAH, WELL, IT IS.
I'M LOOKING IT UP RIGHT NOW--FLYING FISH IS A REAL GUY.
SENDING YOU THE LINK NOW.
RAVEN
IF JACKSON DOES NOT ARRIVE IN THE NEXT FIVE MINUTES, I WILL BE LEAVING.
I HAVE MUCH TO DO AS HEADMISTRESS... AS DO ALL OF YOU.
STARFIRE
NOT ME, I'M JUST AN INSTRUCTOR "IN TRAINING," REMEMBER?
WOOOOW. LOOK AT THAT... FISH FLIER IS A REAL GUY.
I SAID THAT.
KID FLASH
HEY. GUYS, YOU STILL THERE? HELLO?
AQUALAD
YEAH, WE'RE HERE, MAN. EVERYTHING OKAY? WHAT HAPPENED WITH THE FISH CRIME GUY?
WELL...
AQUALAD

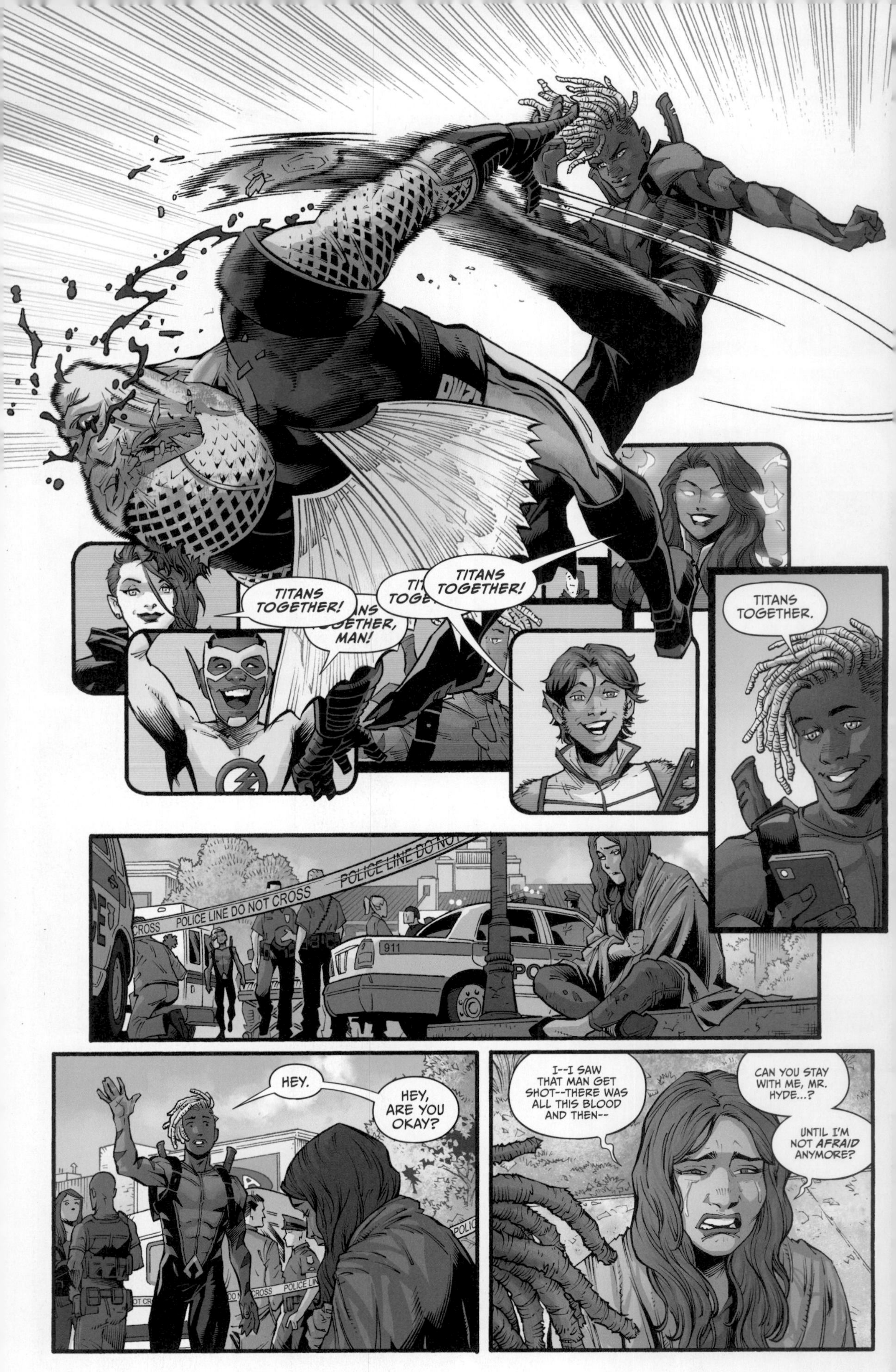
TITANS TOGETHER!
ANS TOGETHER, MAN!
TITANS TOGETHER!
TITANS TOGETHER.
POLICE LINE DO NOT CROSS
HEY.
HEY, ARE YOU OKAY?
I--I SAW THAT MAN GET SHOT--THERE WAS ALL THIS BLOOD AND THEN--
CAN YOU STAY WITH ME, MR. HYDE...?
UNTIL I'M NOT *AFRAID* ANYMORE?

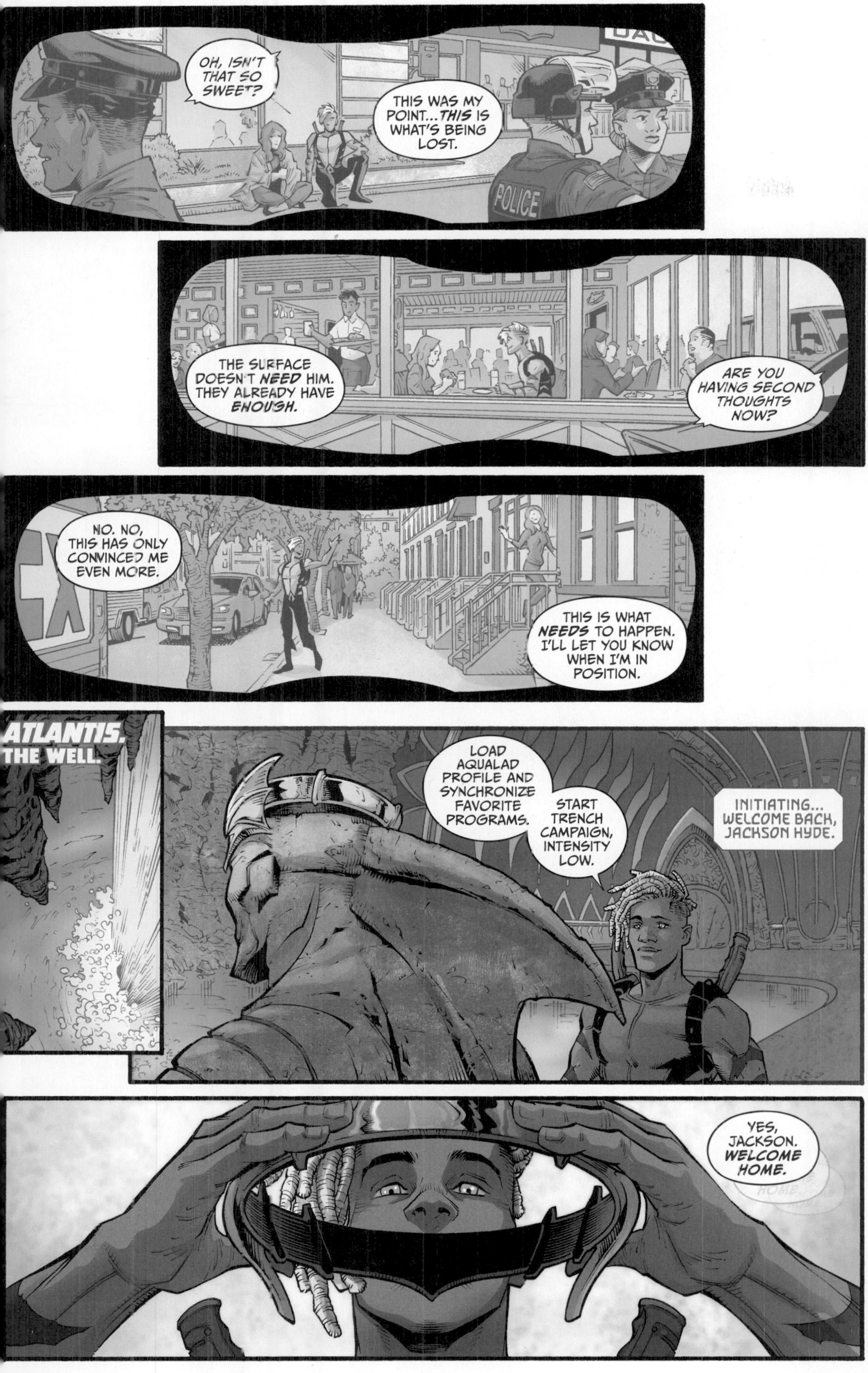
OH, ISN'T THAT SO SWEET?
THIS WAS MY POINT...THIS IS WHAT'S BEING LOST.
POLICE
THE SURFACE DOESN'T NEED HIM. THEY ALREADY HAVE ENOUGH.
ARE YOU HAVING SECOND THOUGHTS NOW?
NO. NO, THIS HAS ONLY CONVINCED ME EVEN MORE.
THIS IS WHAT NEEDS TO HAPPEN. I'LL LET YOU KNOW WHEN I'M IN POSITION.
ATLANTIS. THE WELL.
LOAD AQUALAD PROFILE AND SYNCHRONIZE FAVORITE PROGRAMS.
START TRENCH CAMPAIGN, INTENSITY LOW.
INITIATING... WELCOME BACK, JACKSON HYDE.
YES, JACKSON. WELCOME HOME.

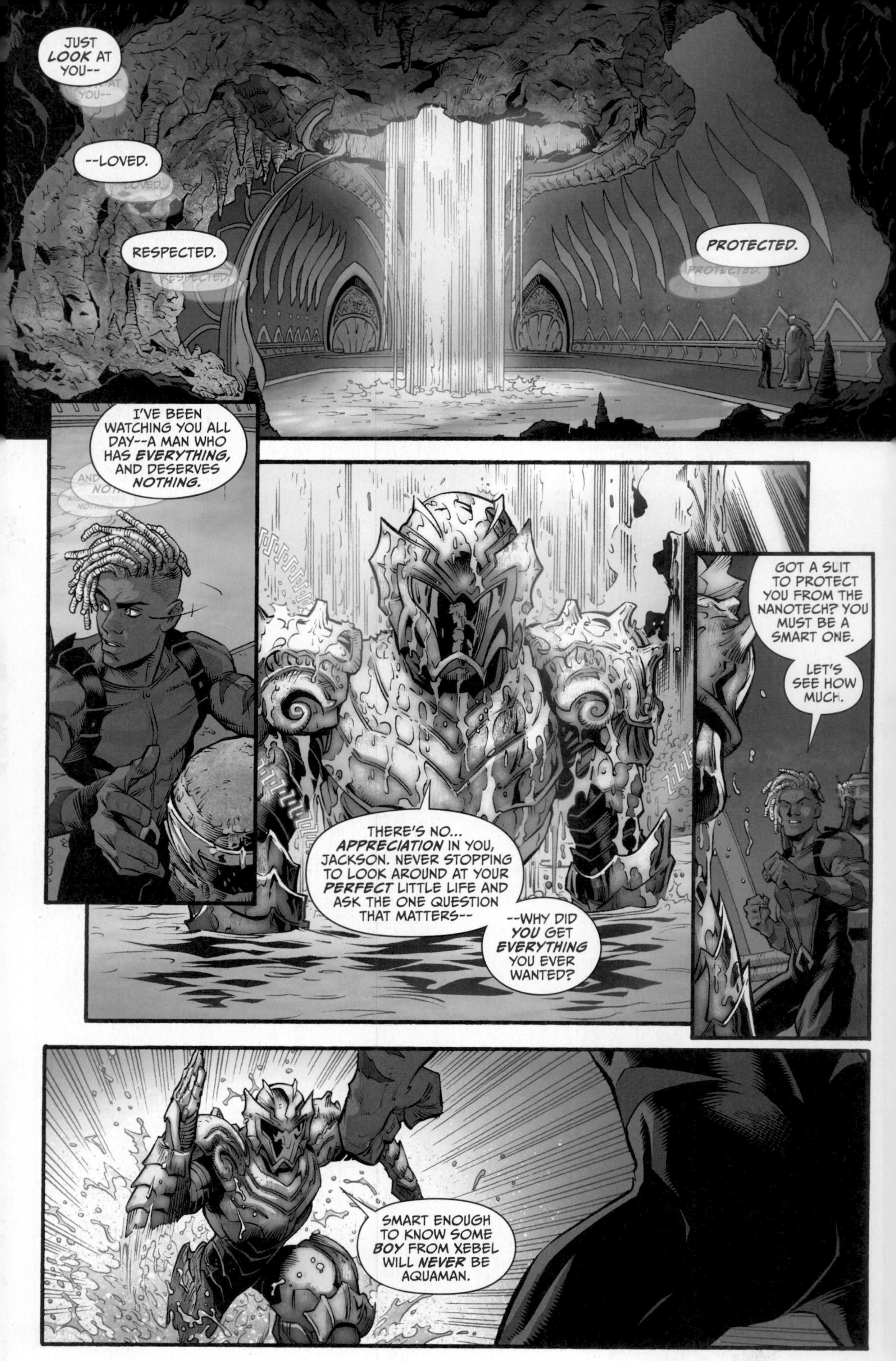
JUST LOOK AT YOU--
--LOVED.
RESPECTED.
PROTECTED.
I'VE BEEN WATCHING YOU ALL DAY--A MAN WHO HAS EVERYTHING, AND DESERVES NOTHING.
THERE'S NO... APPRECIATION IN YOU, JACKSON. NEVER STOPPING TO LOOK AROUND AT YOUR PERFECT LITTLE LIFE AND ASK THE ONE QUESTION THAT MATTERS--
--WHY DID YOU GET EVERYTHING YOU EVER WANTED?
GOT A SUIT TO PROTECT YOU FROM THE NANOTECH? YOU MUST BE A SMART ONE.
LET'S SEE HOW MUCH.
SMART ENOUGH TO KNOW SOME BOY FROM XEBEL WILL NEVER BE AQUAMAN.

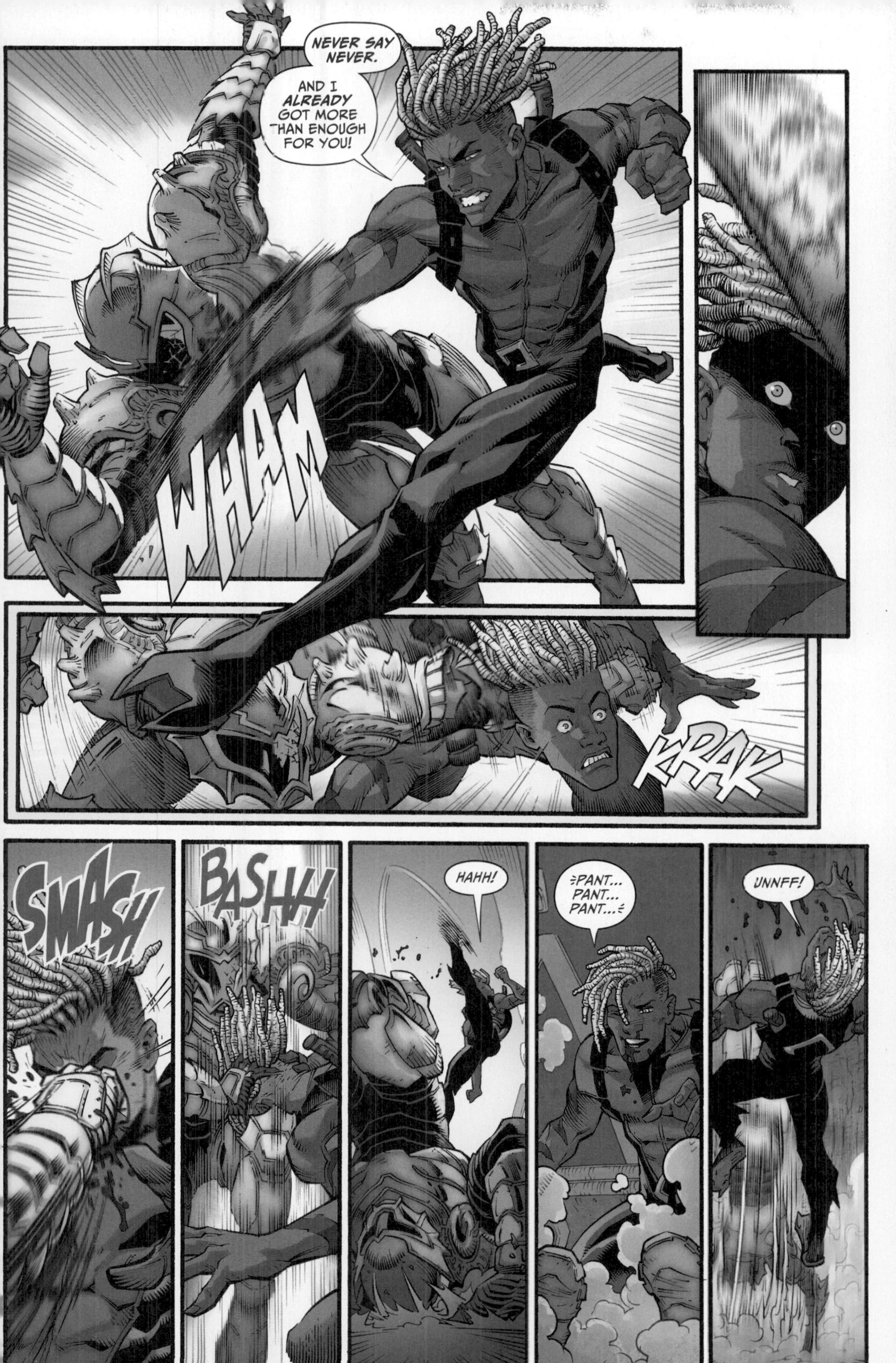
NEVER SAY NEVER.
AND I ALREADY GOT MORE THAN ENOUGH FOR YOU!
WHAM
KRAK
SMASH
BASHH
HAHH!
PANT... PANT... PANT...
UNNFF!

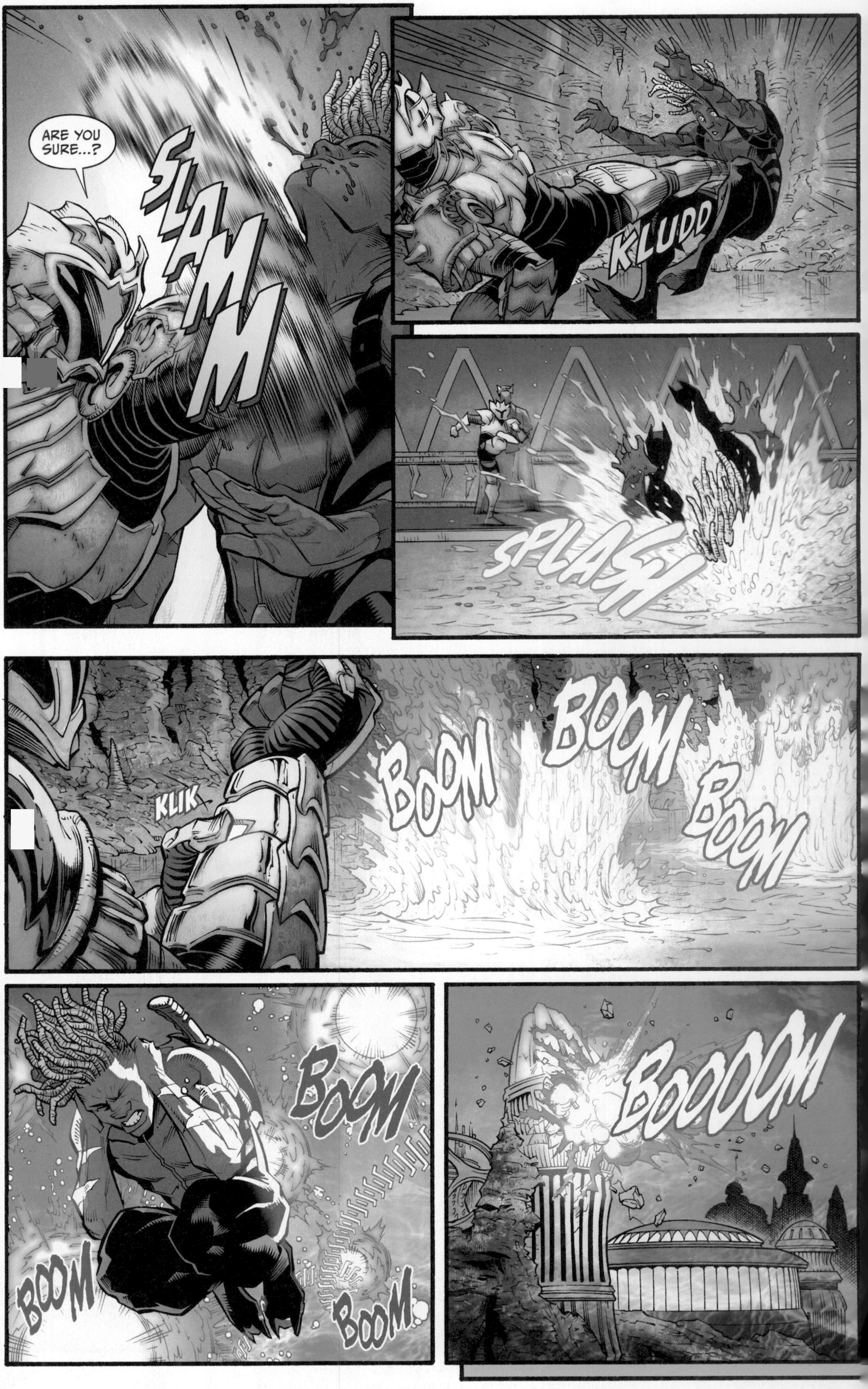
ARE YOU SURE...?
SLAMM
KLUDD
SPLASH
KLIK
BOOM
BOOM
BOOM
BOOM
BOOM
BOOM
BOOOOM

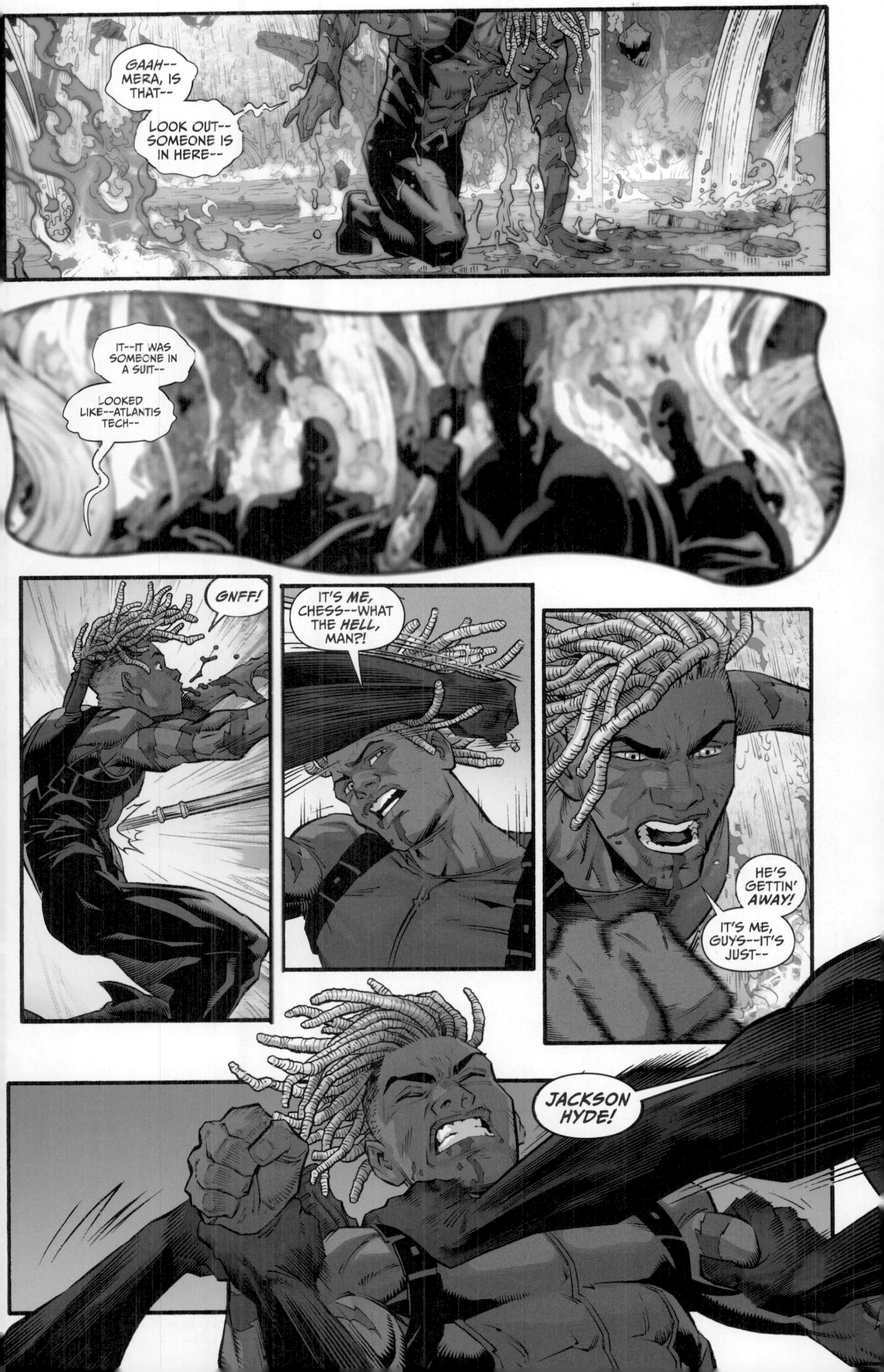
GAAH--
MERA, IS
THAT--
LOOK OUT--
SOMEONE IS
IN HERE--
IT--IT WAS
SOMEONE IN
A SUIT--
LOOKED
LIKE--ATLANTIS
TECH--
GNFF!
IT'S ME,
CHESS--WHAT
THE HELL,
MAN?!
HE'S
GETTIN'
AWAY!
IT'S ME,
GUYS--IT'S
JUST--
JACKSON
HYDE!

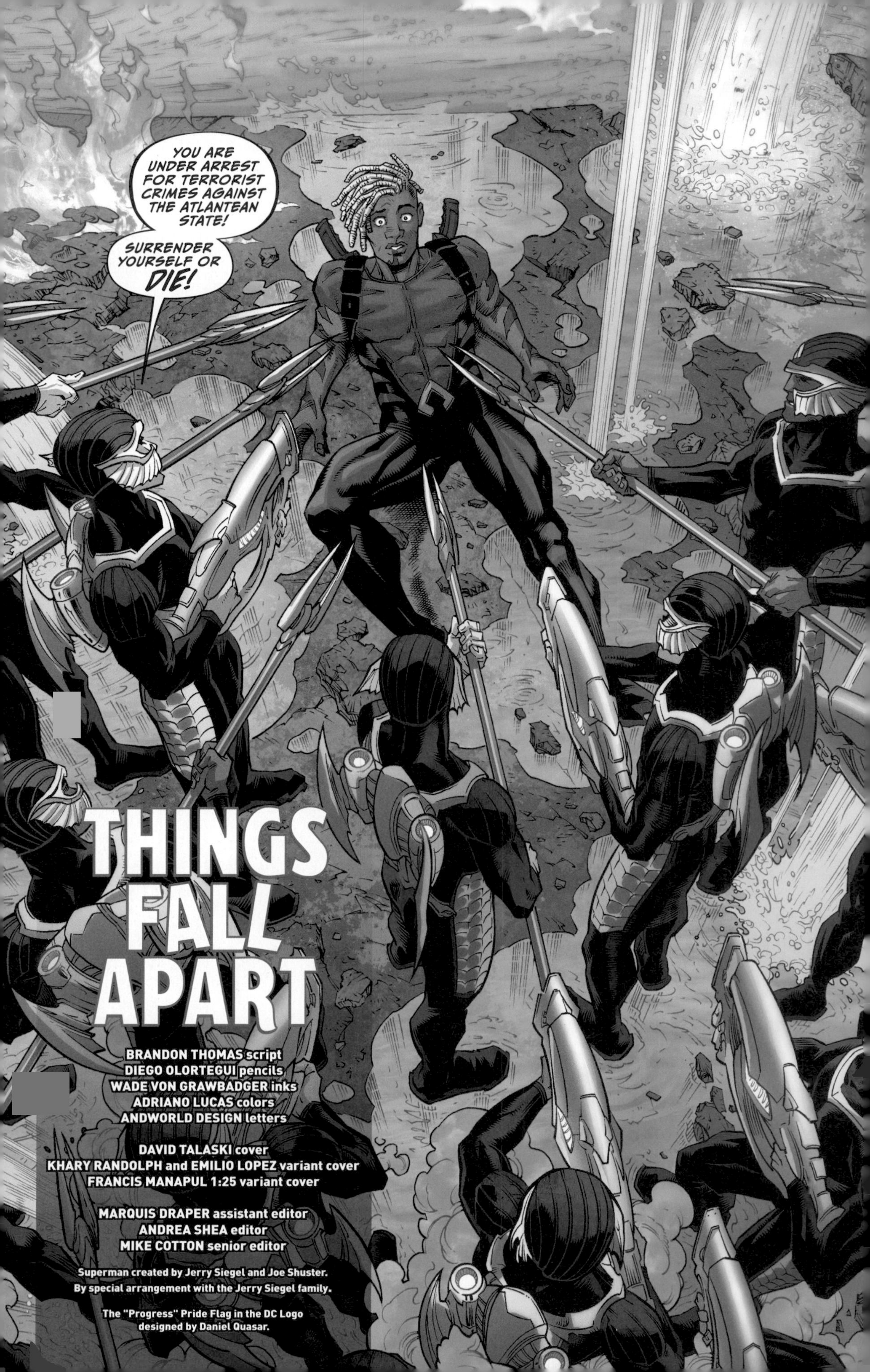
YOU ARE UNDER ARREST FOR TERRORIST CRIMES AGAINST THE ATLANTEAN STATE!
SURRENDER YOURSELF OR DIE!
THINGS FALL APART
BRANDON THOMAS script
DIEGO OLORTEGUI pencils
WADE VON GRAWBADGER inks
ADRIANO LUCAS colors
ANDWORLD DESIGN letters
DAVID TALASKI cover
KHARY RANDOLPH and EMILIO LOPEZ variant cover
FRANCIS MANAPUL 1:25 variant cover
MARQUIS DRAPER assistant editor
ANDREA SHEA editor
MIKE COTTON senior editor
Superman created by Jerry Siegel and Joe Shuster.
By special arrangement with the Jerry Siegel family.
The "Progress" Pride Flag in the DC Logo designed by Daniel Quasar.

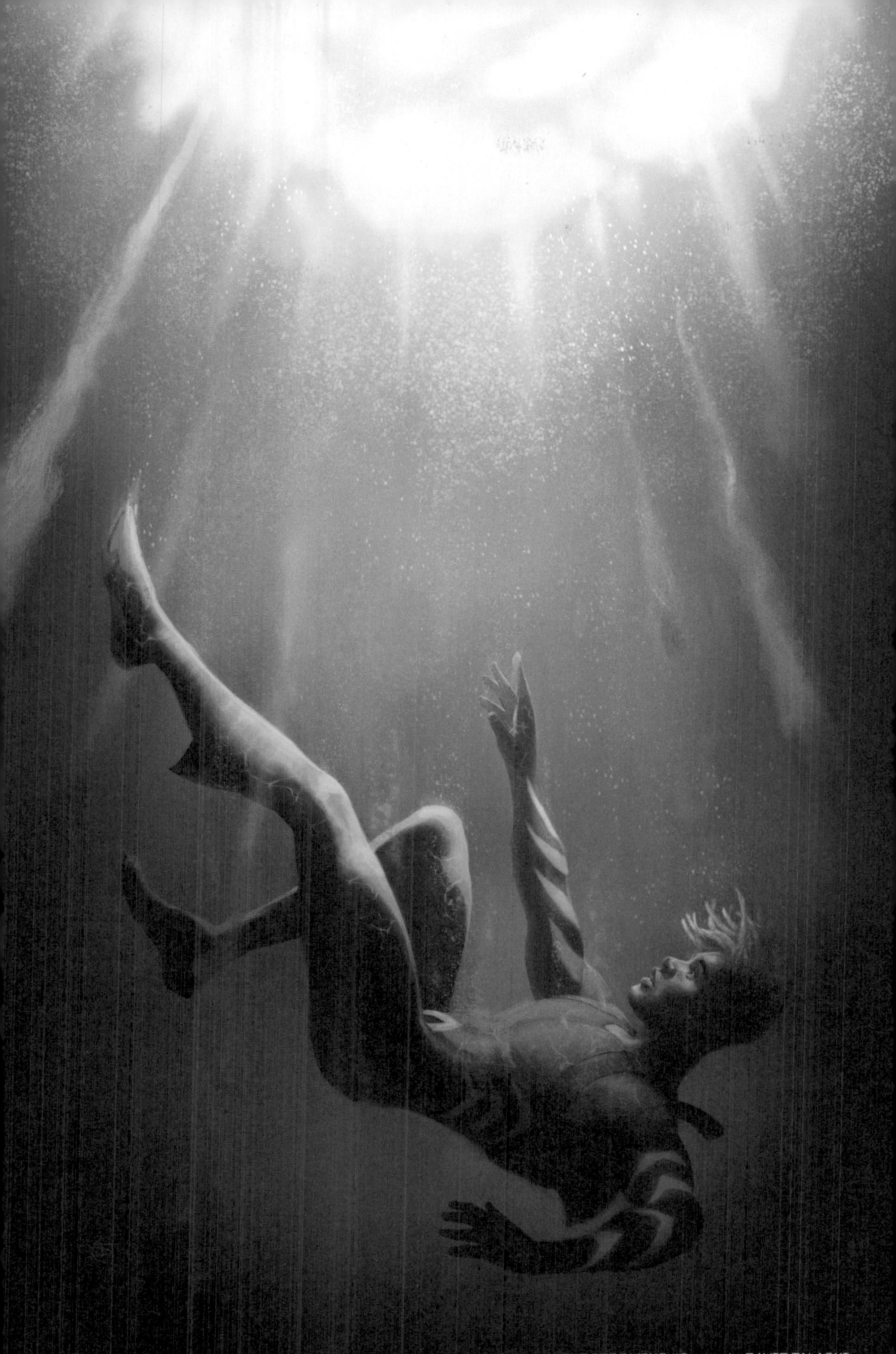

AQUAMAN: THE BECOMING #2 cover by DAVID TALASKI

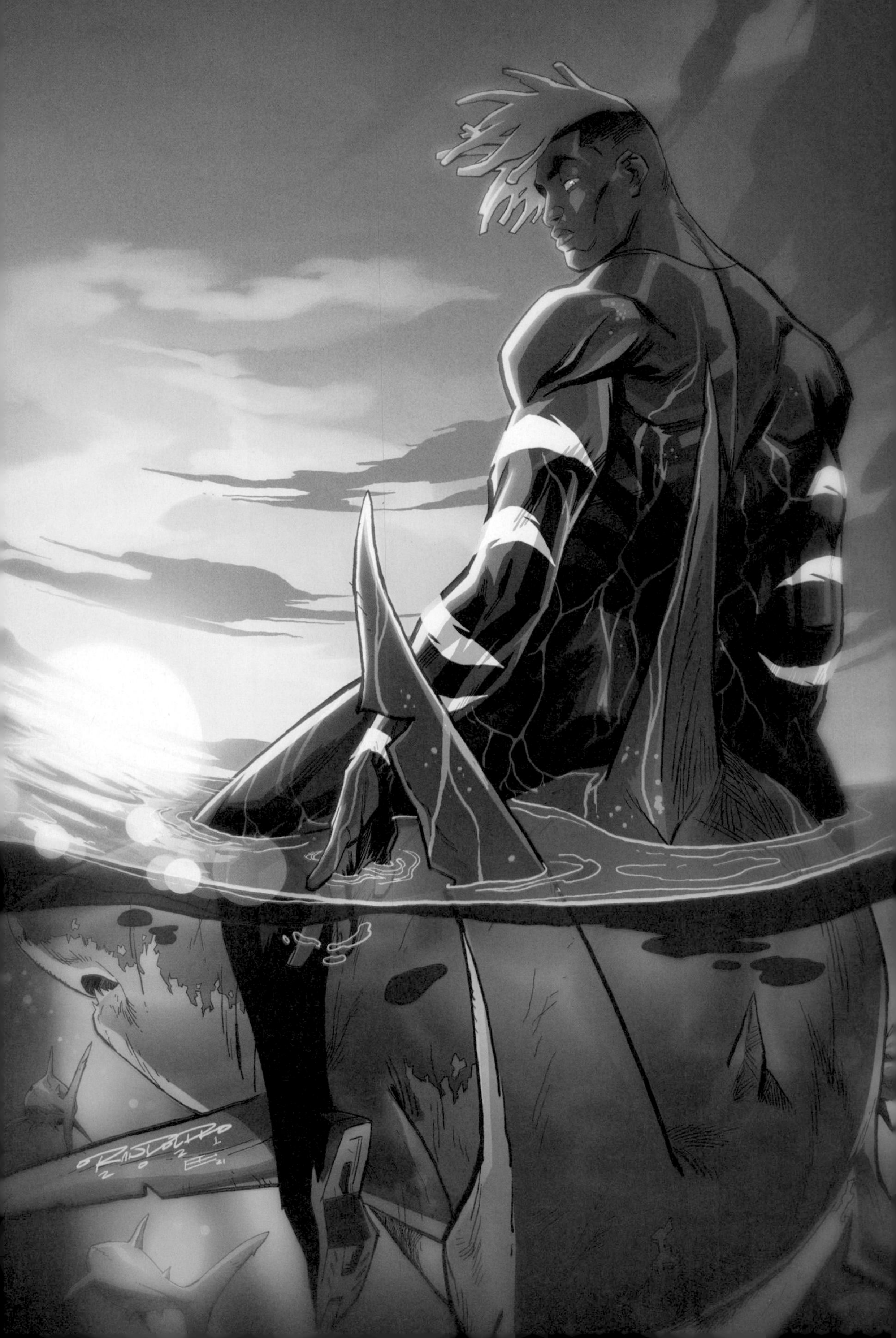

AQUAMAN: THE BECOMING #2 variant cover by
KHARY RANDOLPH and EMILIO LOPEZ

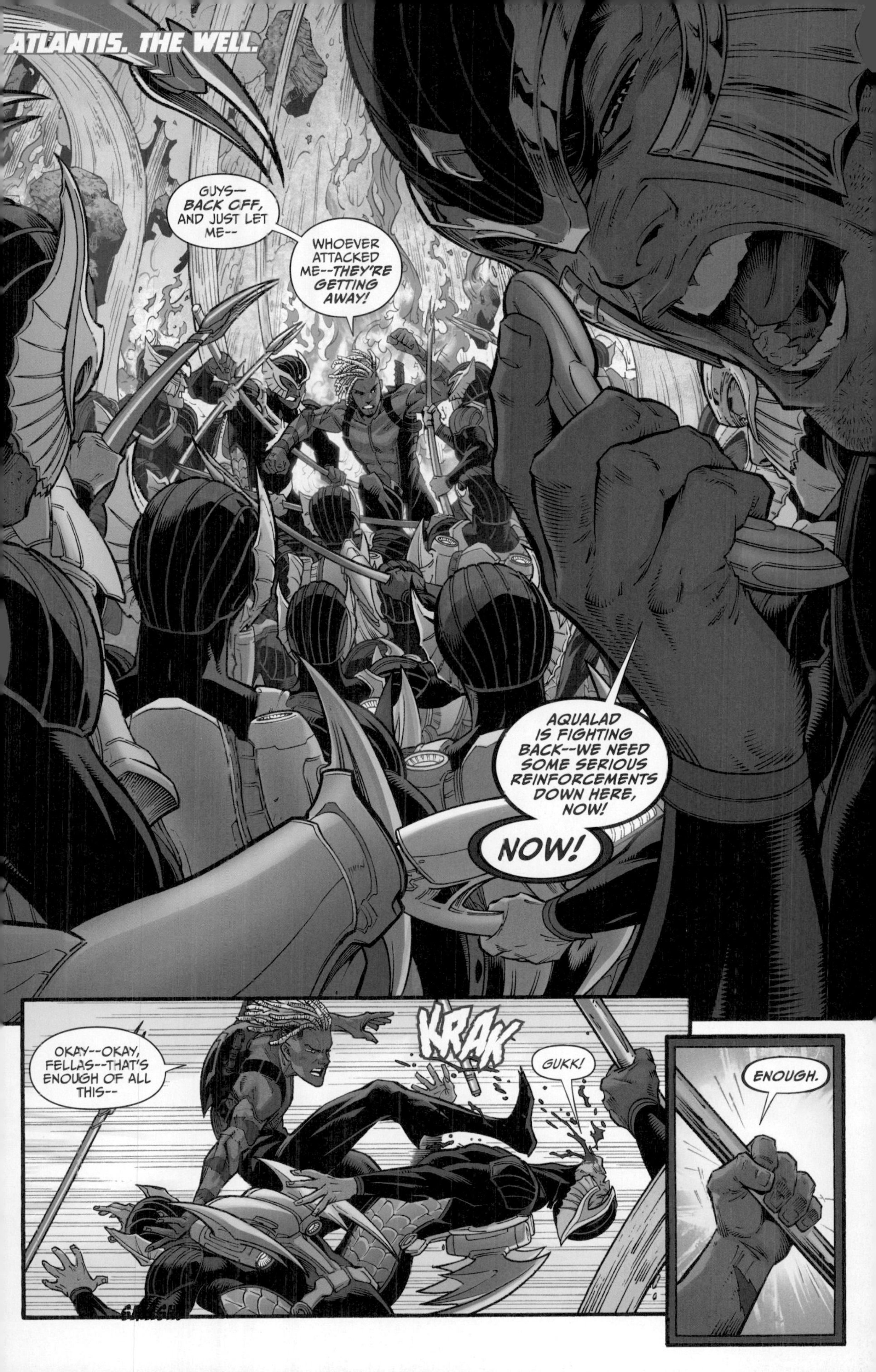
ATLANTIS. THE WELL.
GUYS— BACK OFF, AND JUST LET ME--
WHOEVER ATTACKED ME--THEY'RE GETTING AWAY!
AQUALAD IS FIGHTING BACK--WE NEED SOME SERIOUS REINFORCEMENTS DOWN HERE, NOW!
NOW!
OKAY--OKAY, FELLAS--THAT'S ENOUGH OF ALL THIS--
KRAK
GUKK!
ENOUGH.

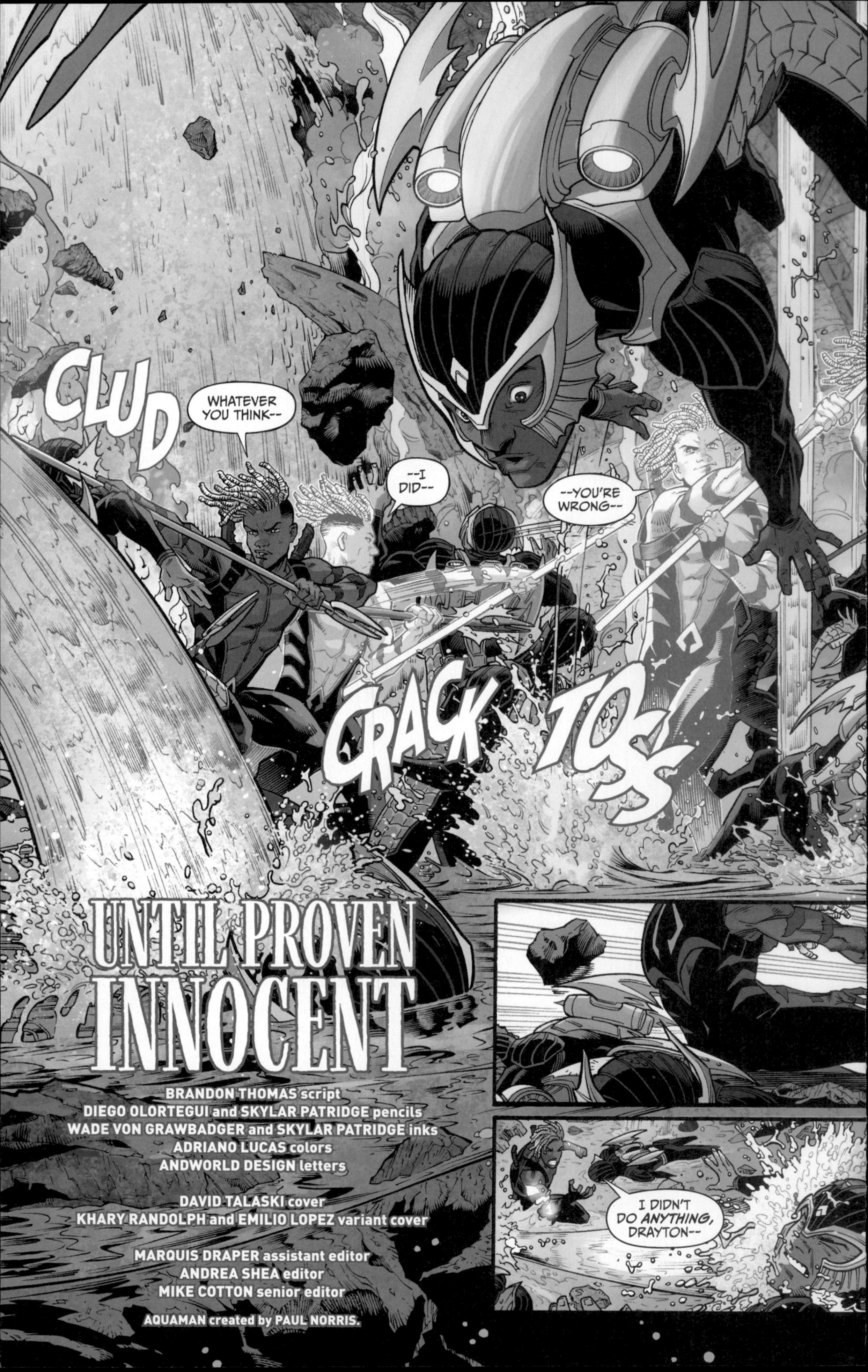
CLUD
WHATEVER YOU THINK--
--I DID--
--YOU'RE WRONG--
CRACK
TOSS
I DIDN'T DO *ANYTHING*, DRAYTON--

UNTIL PROVEN INNOCENT

BRANDON THOMAS script
DIEGO OLORTEGUI and **SKYLAR PATRIDGE** pencils
WADE VON GRAWBADGER and **SKYLAR PATRIDGE** inks
ADRIANO LUCAS colors
ANDWORLD DESIGN letters

DAVID TALASKI cover
KHARY RANDOLPH and **EMILIO LOPEZ** variant cover

MARQUIS DRAPER assistant editor
ANDREA SHEA editor
MIKE COTTON senior editor

AQUAMAN created by **PAUL NORRIS.**

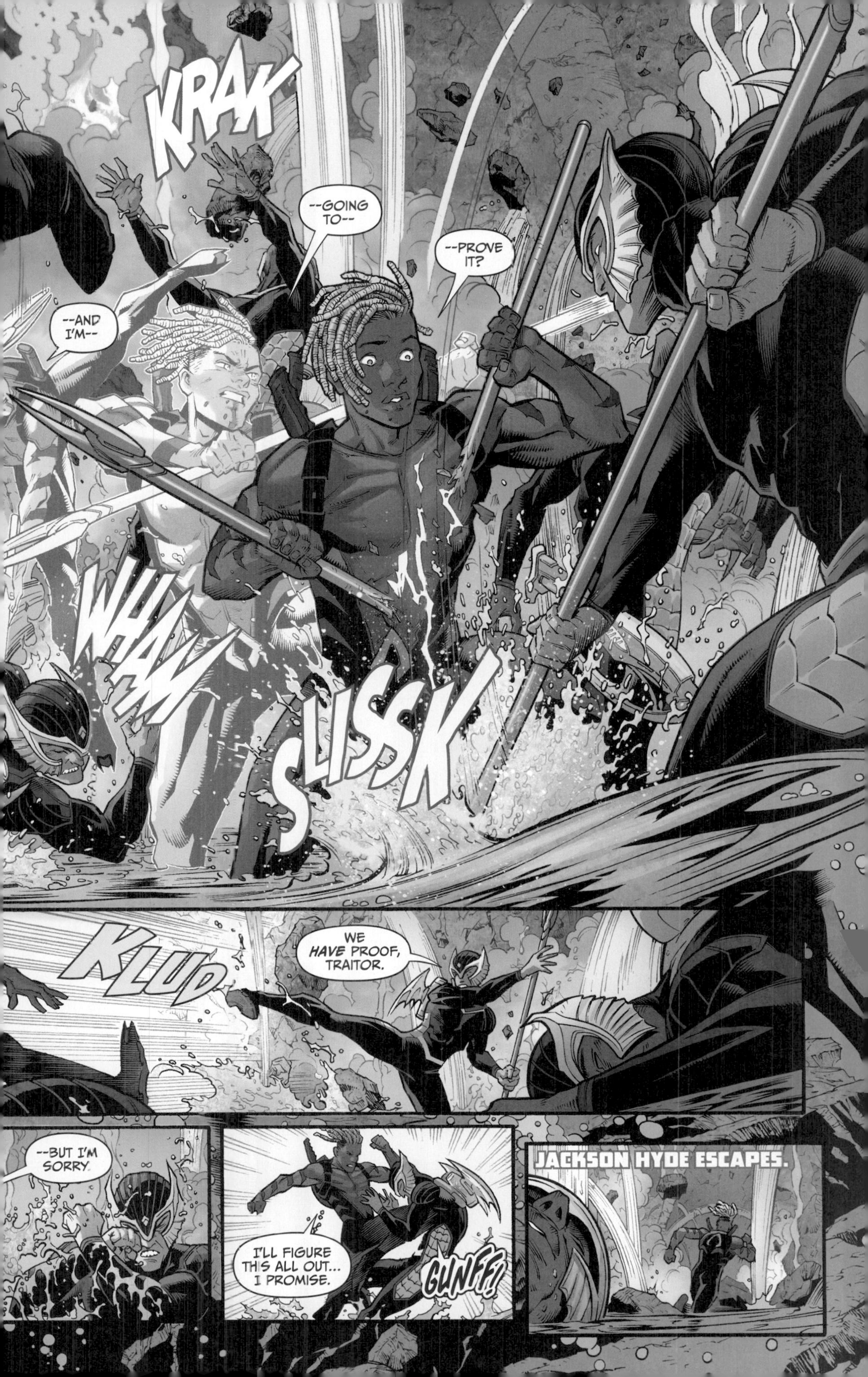
KRAK
--AND I'M--
--GOING TO--
--PROVE IT?
WHAM
SLISSK
KLUD
WE HAVE PROOF, TRAITOR.
--BUT I'M SORRY.
I'LL FIGURE THIS ALL OUT... I PROMISE.
GUNFF!
JACKSON HYDE ESCAPES.

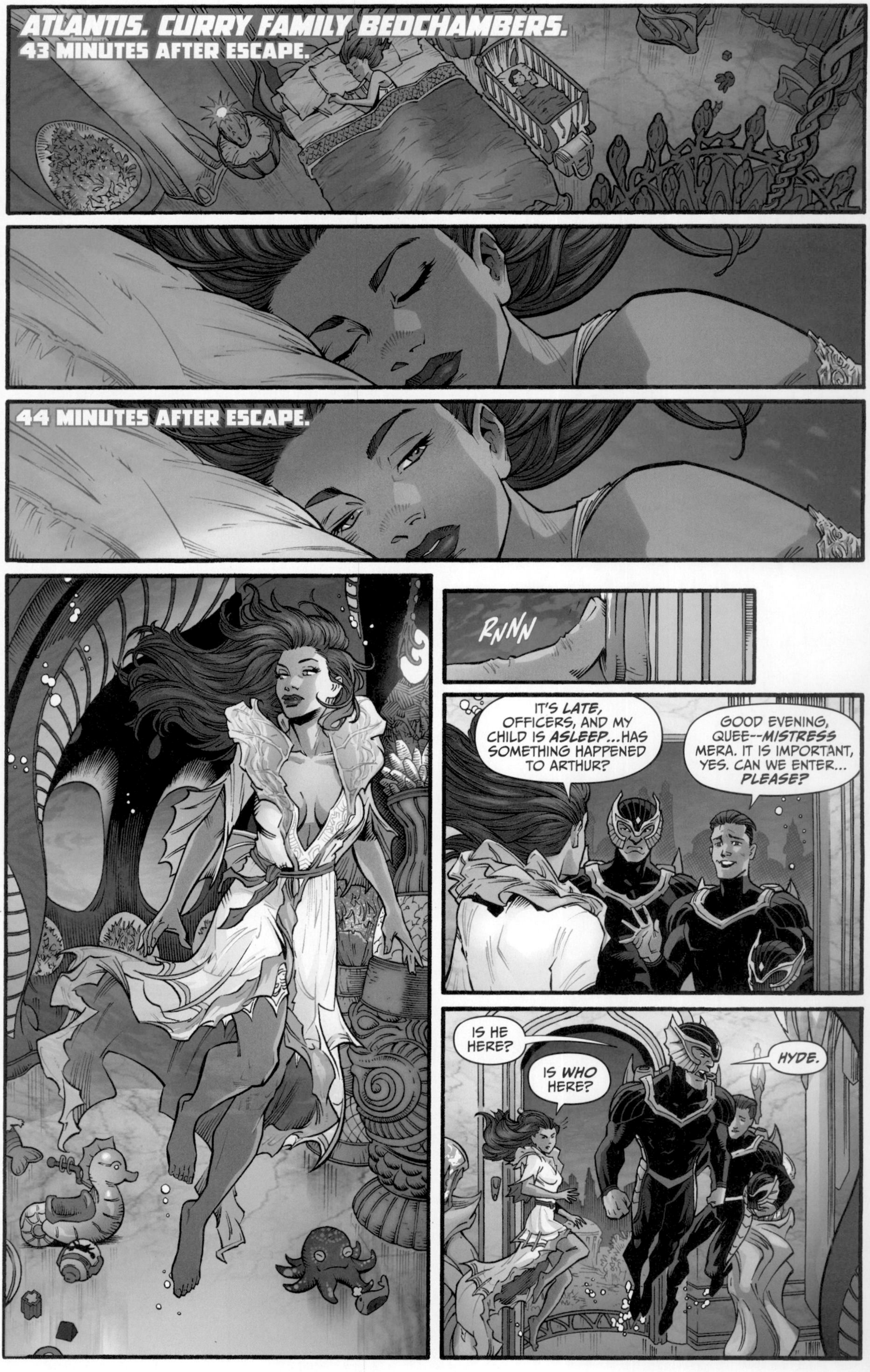
ATLANTIS. CURRY FAMILY BEDCHAMBERS.
43 MINUTES AFTER ESCAPE.
44 MINUTES AFTER ESCAPE.
RNNN
IT'S LATE, OFFICERS, AND MY CHILD IS ASLEEP...HAS SOMETHING HAPPENED TO ARTHUR?
GOOD EVENING, QUEE--MISTRESS MERA. IT IS IMPORTANT, YES. CAN WE ENTER... PLEASE?
IS HE HERE?
IS WHO HERE?
HYDE.

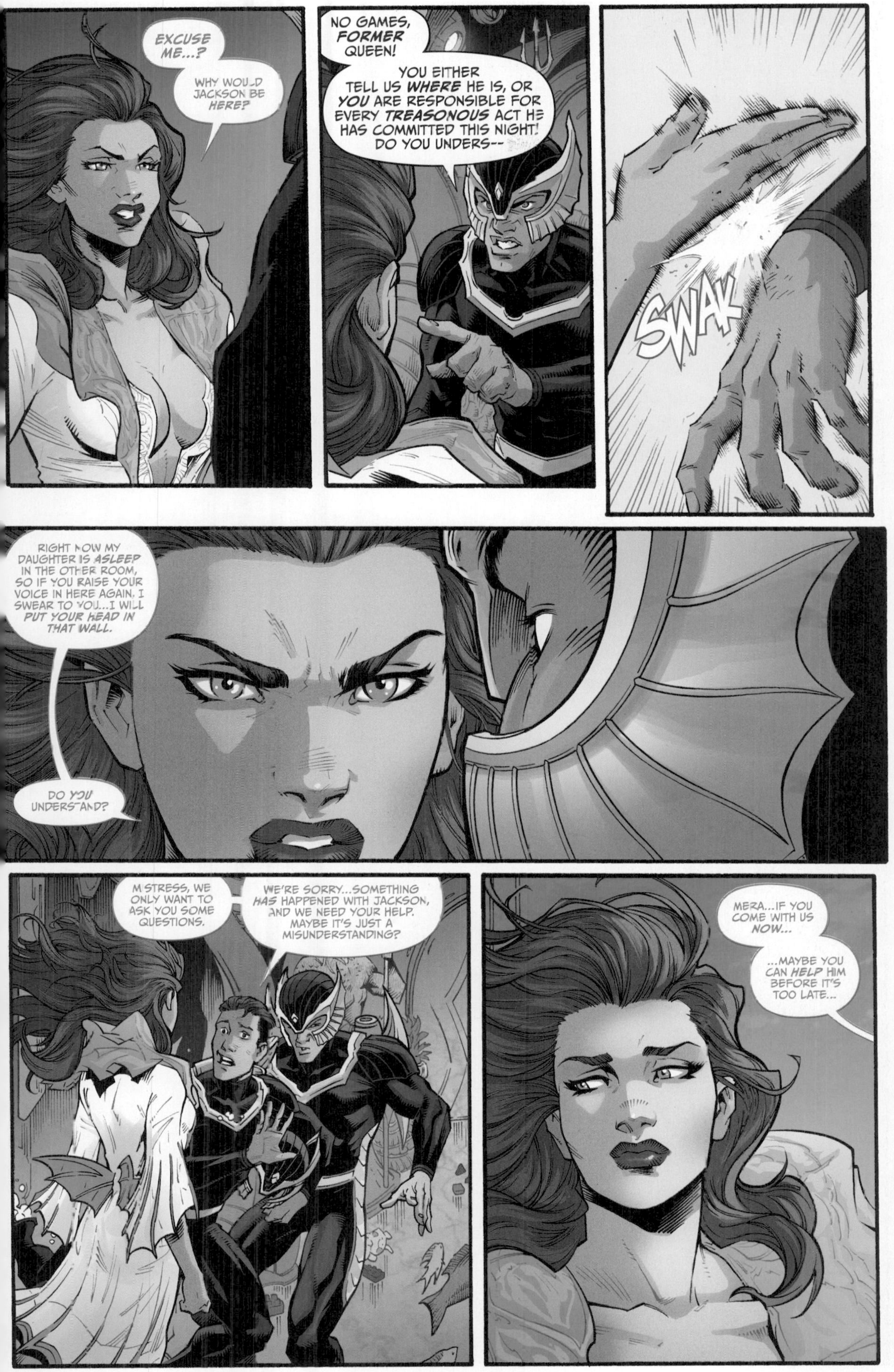
EXCUSE ME...?
WHY WOULD JACKSON BE HERE?
NO GAMES, FORMER QUEEN!
YOU EITHER TELL US WHERE HE IS, OR YOU ARE RESPONSIBLE FOR EVERY TREASONOUS ACT HE HAS COMMITTED THIS NIGHT! DO YOU UNDERS--
SWAK
RIGHT NOW MY DAUGHTER IS ASLEEP IN THE OTHER ROOM, SO IF YOU RAISE YOUR VOICE IN HERE AGAIN, I SWEAR TO YOU...I WILL PUT YOUR HEAD IN THAT WALL.
DO YOU UNDERSTAND?
MISTRESS, WE ONLY WANT TO ASK YOU SOME QUESTIONS.
WE'RE SORRY...SOMETHING HAS HAPPENED WITH JACKSON, AND WE NEED YOUR HELP. MAYBE IT'S JUST A MISUNDERSTANDING?
MERA...IF YOU COME WITH US NOW...
...MAYBE YOU CAN HELP HIM BEFORE IT'S TOO LATE...

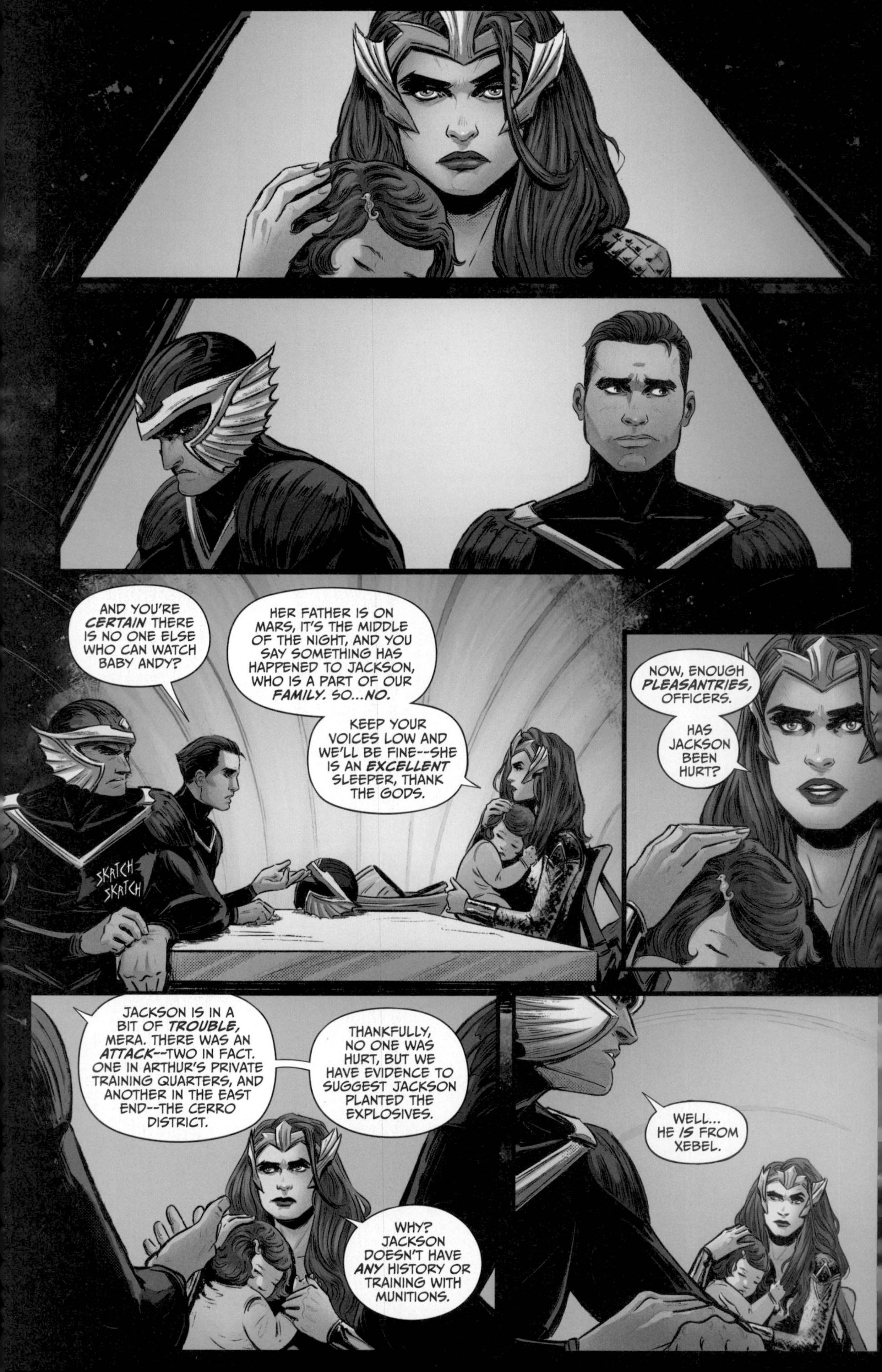
AND YOU'RE CERTAIN THERE IS NO ONE ELSE WHO CAN WATCH BABY ANDY?
HER FATHER IS ON MARS, IT'S THE MIDDLE OF THE NIGHT, AND YOU SAY SOMETHING HAS HAPPENED TO JACKSON, WHO IS A PART OF OUR FAMILY. SO...NO.
KEEP YOUR VOICES LOW AND WE'LL BE FINE--SHE IS AN EXCELLENT SLEEPER, THANK THE GODS.
SKRATCH SKRATCH
NOW, ENOUGH PLEASANTRIES, OFFICERS.
HAS JACKSON BEEN HURT?
JACKSON IS IN A BIT OF TROUBLE, MERA. THERE WAS AN ATTACK--TWO IN FACT. ONE IN ARTHUR'S PRIVATE TRAINING QUARTERS, AND ANOTHER IN THE EAST END--THE CERRO DISTRICT.
THANKFULLY, NO ONE WAS HURT, BUT WE HAVE EVIDENCE TO SUGGEST JACKSON PLANTED THE EXPLOSIVES.
WHY? JACKSON DOESN'T HAVE ANY HISTORY OR TRAINING WITH MUNITIONS.
WELL... HE IS FROM XEBEL.

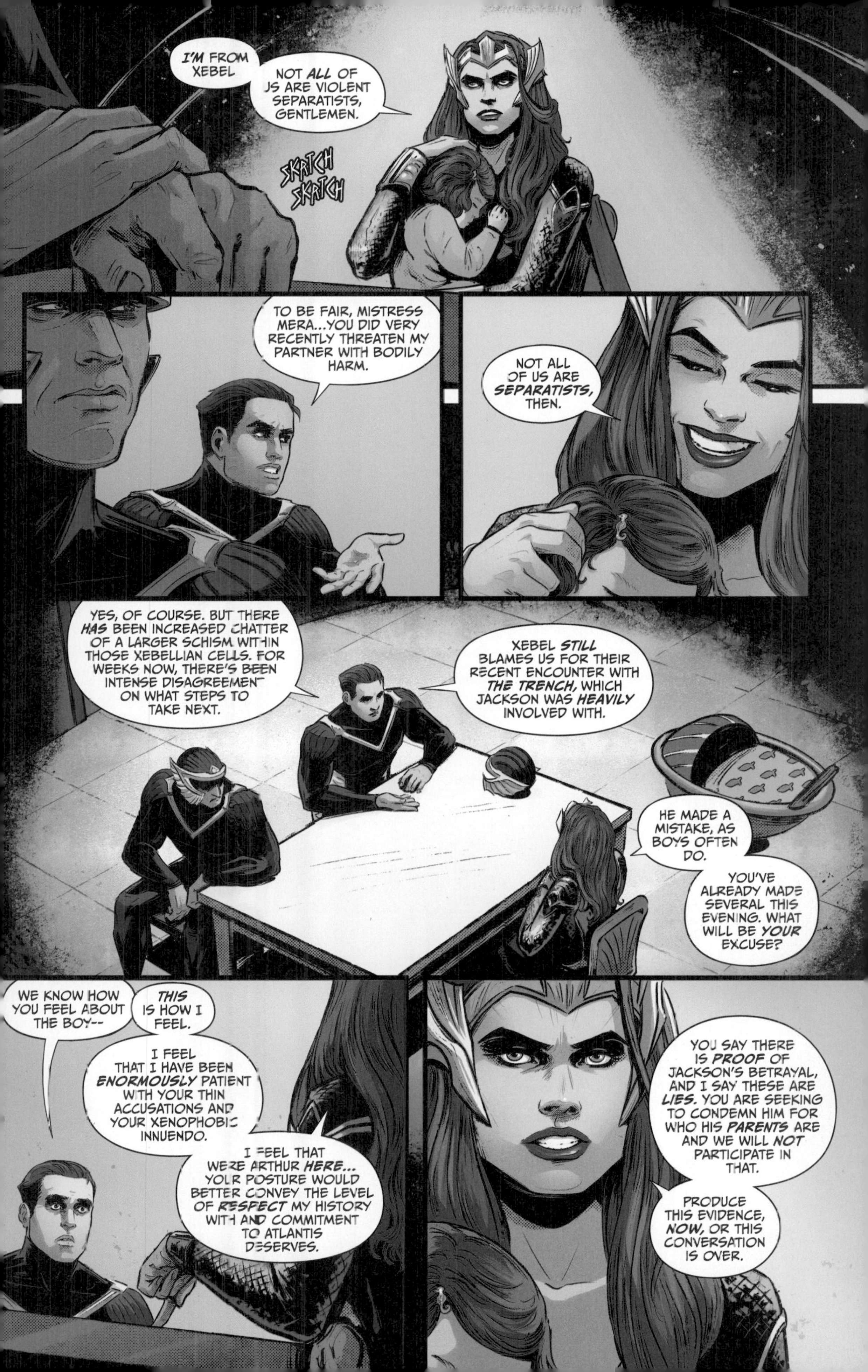
I'M FROM XEBEL
NOT ALL OF US ARE VIOLENT SEPARATISTS, GENTLEMEN.
SKRTCH SKRTCH
TO BE FAIR, MISTRESS MERA...YOU DID VERY RECENTLY THREATEN MY PARTNER WITH BODILY HARM.
NOT ALL OF US ARE SEPARATISTS, THEN.
YES, OF COURSE. BUT THERE HAS BEEN INCREASED CHATTER OF A LARGER SCHISM WITHIN THOSE XEBELLIAN CELLS. FOR WEEKS NOW, THERE'S BEEN INTENSE DISAGREEMENT ON WHAT STEPS TO TAKE NEXT.
XEBEL STILL BLAMES US FOR THEIR RECENT ENCOUNTER WITH THE TRENCH, WHICH JACKSON WAS HEAVILY INVOLVED WITH.
HE MADE A MISTAKE, AS BOYS OFTEN DO.
YOU'VE ALREADY MADE SEVERAL THIS EVENING. WHAT WILL BE YOUR EXCUSE?
WE KNOW HOW YOU FEEL ABOUT THE BOY--
THIS IS HOW I FEEL.
I FEEL THAT I HAVE BEEN ENORMOUSLY PATIENT WITH YOUR THIN ACCUSATIONS AND YOUR XENOPHOBIC INNUENDO.
I FEEL THAT WERE ARTHUR HERE... YOUR POSTURE WOULD BETTER CONVEY THE LEVEL OF RESPECT MY HISTORY WITH AND COMMITMENT TO ATLANTIS DESERVES.
YOU SAY THERE IS PROOF OF JACKSON'S BETRAYAL, AND I SAY THESE ARE LIES. YOU ARE SEEKING TO CONDEMN HIM FOR WHO HIS PARENTS ARE AND WE WILL NOT PARTICIPATE IN THAT.
PRODUCE THIS EVIDENCE, NOW, OR THIS CONVERSATION IS OVER.

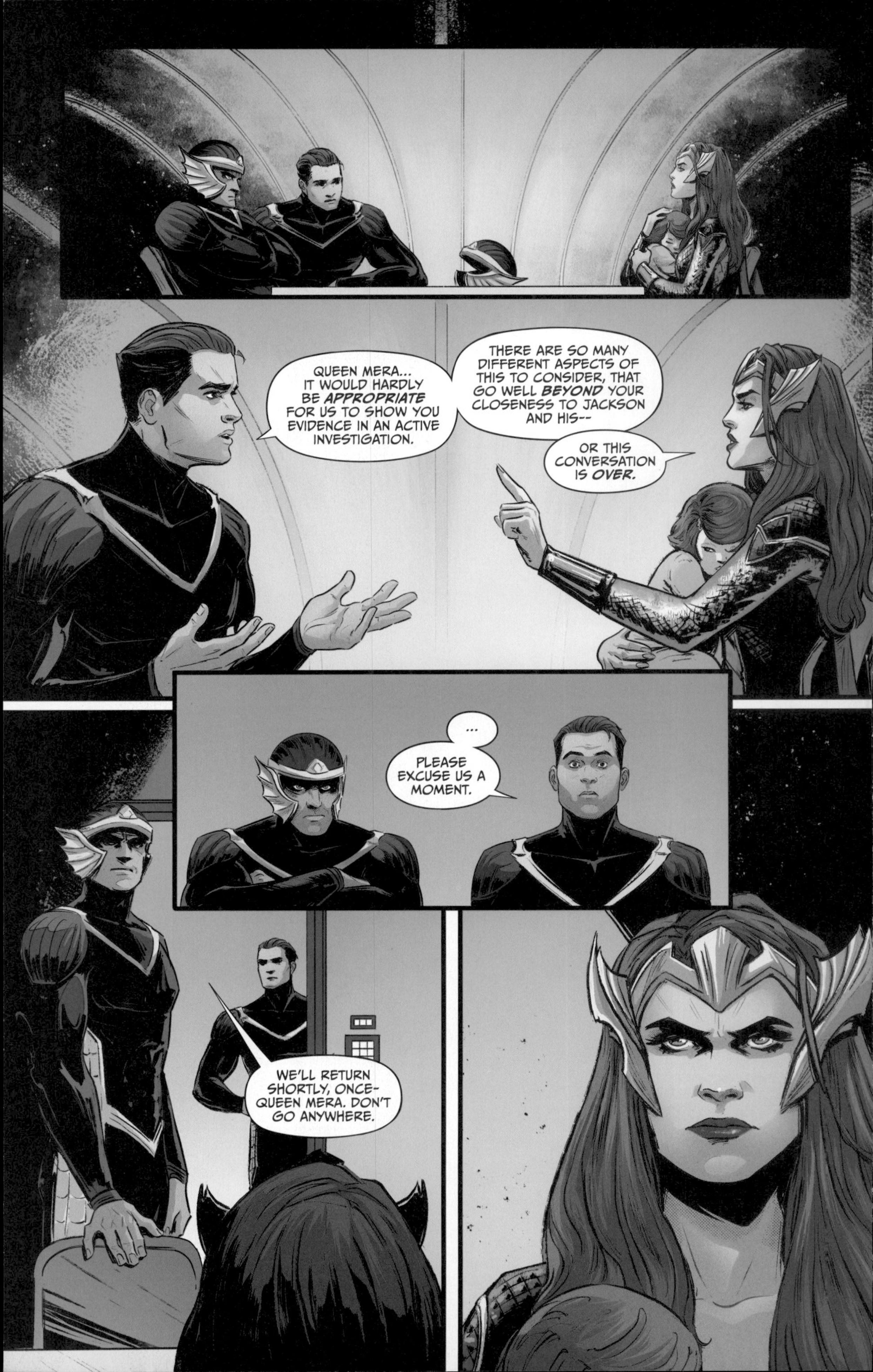
QUEEN MERA... IT WOULD HARDLY BE APPROPRIATE FOR US TO SHOW YOU EVIDENCE IN AN ACTIVE INVESTIGATION.
THERE ARE SO MANY DIFFERENT ASPECTS OF THIS TO CONSIDER, THAT GO WELL BEYOND YOUR CLOSENESS TO JACKSON AND HIS--
OR THIS CONVERSATION IS OVER.
...
PLEASE EXCUSE US A MOMENT.
WE'LL RETURN SHORTLY, ONCE-QUEEN MERA. DON'T GO ANYWHERE.

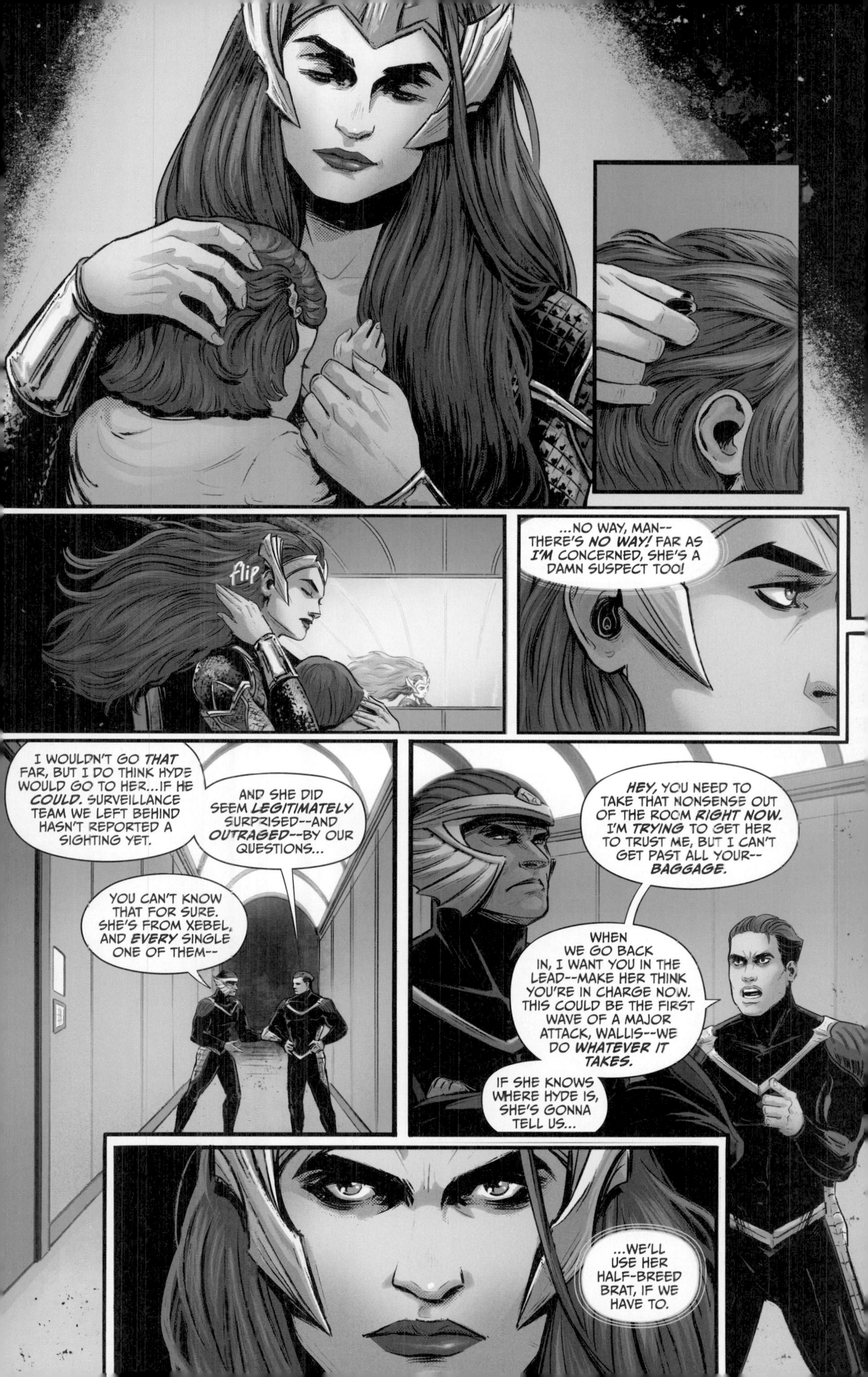

flip
...NO WAY, MAN-- THERE'S NO WAY! FAR AS I'M CONCERNED, SHE'S A DAMN SUSPECT TOO!
I WOULDN'T GO THAT FAR, BUT I DO THINK HYDE WOULD GO TO HER...IF HE COULD. SURVEILLANCE TEAM WE LEFT BEHIND HASN'T REPORTED A SIGHTING YET.
AND SHE DID SEEM LEGITIMATELY SURPRISED--AND OUTRAGED--BY OUR QUESTIONS...
YOU CAN'T KNOW THAT FOR SURE. SHE'S FROM XEBEL, AND EVERY SINGLE ONE OF THEM--
HEY, YOU NEED TO TAKE THAT NONSENSE OUT OF THE ROOM RIGHT NOW. I'M TRYING TO GET HER TO TRUST ME, BUT I CAN'T GET PAST ALL YOUR--BAGGAGE.
WHEN WE GO BACK IN, I WANT YOU IN THE LEAD--MAKE HER THINK YOU'RE IN CHARGE NOW. THIS COULD BE THE FIRST WAVE OF A MAJOR ATTACK, WALLIS--WE DO WHATEVER IT TAKES.
IF SHE KNOWS WHERE HYDE IS, SHE'S GONNA TELL US...
...WE'LL USE HER HALF-BREED BRAT, IF WE HAVE TO.

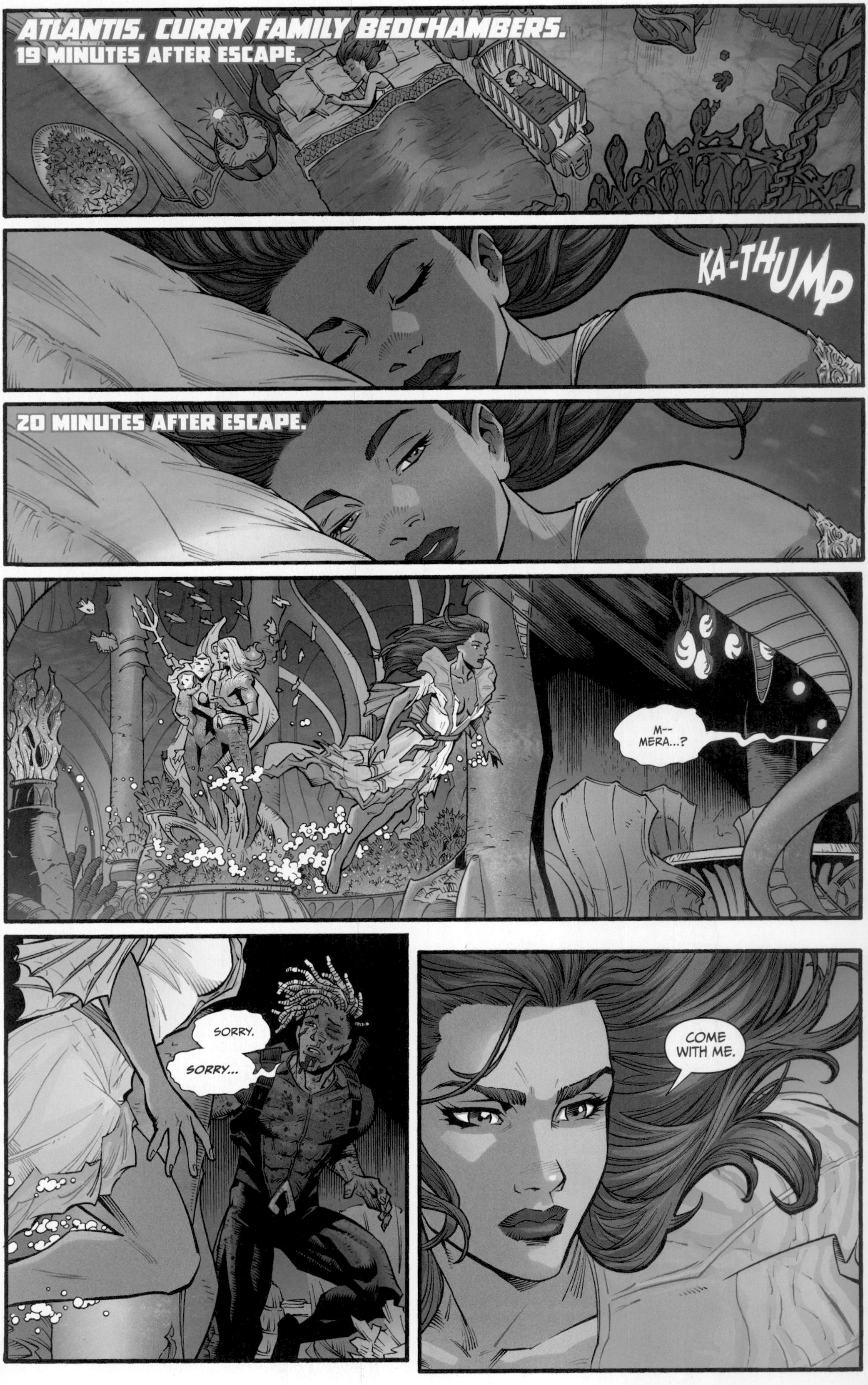
ATLANTIS. CURRY FAMILY BEDCHAMBERS.
19 MINUTES AFTER ESCAPE.
KA-THUMP
20 MINUTES AFTER ESCAPE.
M-- MERA...?
SORRY.
SORRY...
COME WITH ME.

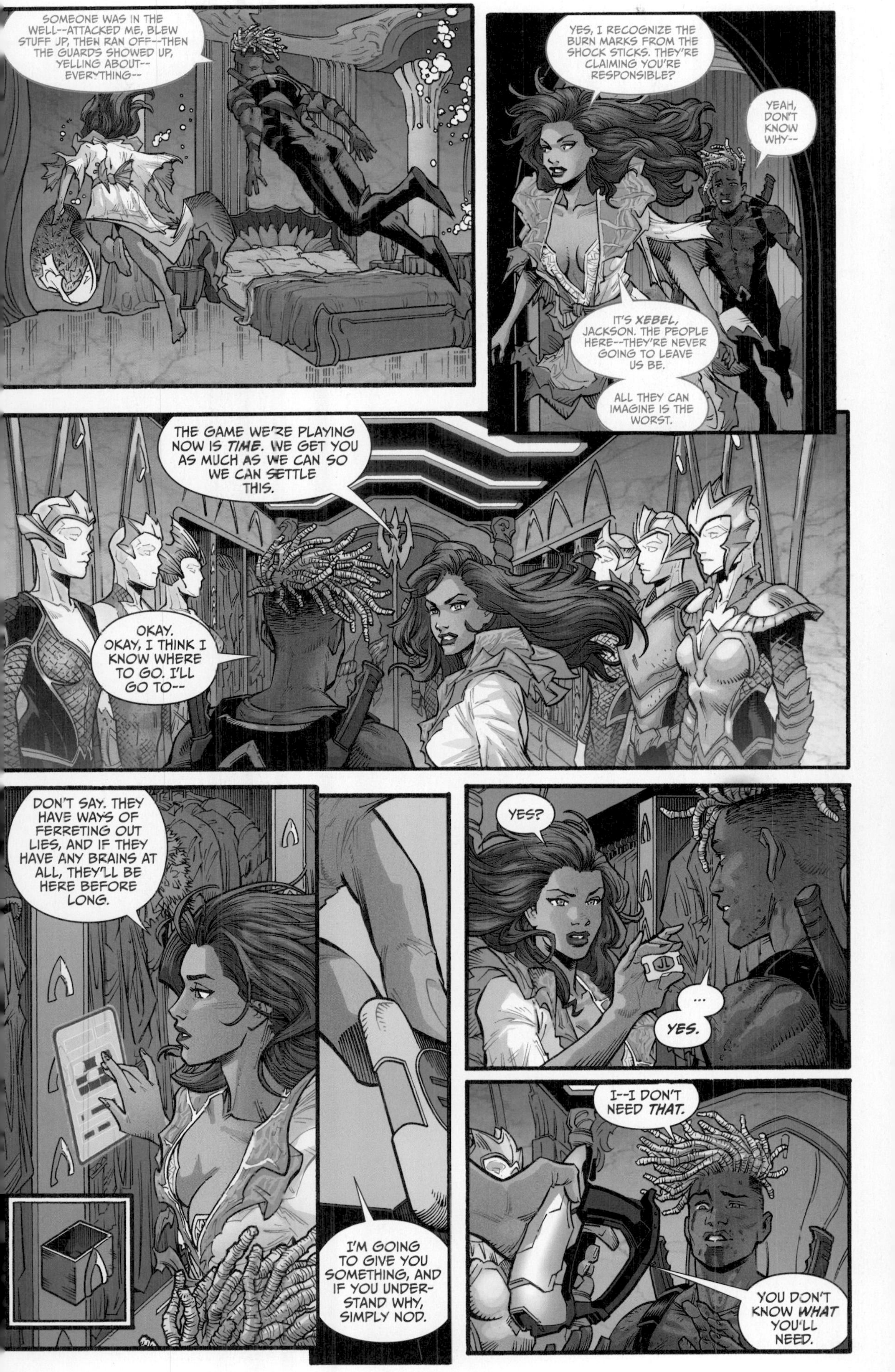
SOMEONE WAS IN THE WELL--ATTACKED ME, BLEW STUFF UP, THEN RAN OFF--THEN THE GUARDS SHOWED UP, YELLING ABOUT-- EVERYTHING--
YES, I RECOGNIZE THE BURN MARKS FROM THE SHOCK STICKS. THEY'RE CLAIMING YOU'RE RESPONSIBLE?
YEAH, DON'T KNOW WHY--
IT'S XEBEL, JACKSON. THE PEOPLE HERE--THEY'RE NEVER GOING TO LEAVE US BE.
ALL THEY CAN IMAGINE IS THE WORST.
THE GAME WE'RE PLAYING NOW IS TIME. WE GET YOU AS MUCH AS WE CAN SO WE CAN SETTLE THIS.
OKAY. OKAY, I THINK I KNOW WHERE TO GO. I'LL GO TO--
DON'T SAY. THEY HAVE WAYS OF FERRETING OUT LIES, AND IF THEY HAVE ANY BRAINS AT ALL, THEY'LL BE HERE BEFORE LONG.
I'M GOING TO GIVE YOU SOMETHING, AND IF YOU UNDERSTAND WHY, SIMPLY NOD.
YES?
... YES.
I--I DON'T NEED THAT.
YOU DON'T KNOW WHAT YOU'LL NEED.

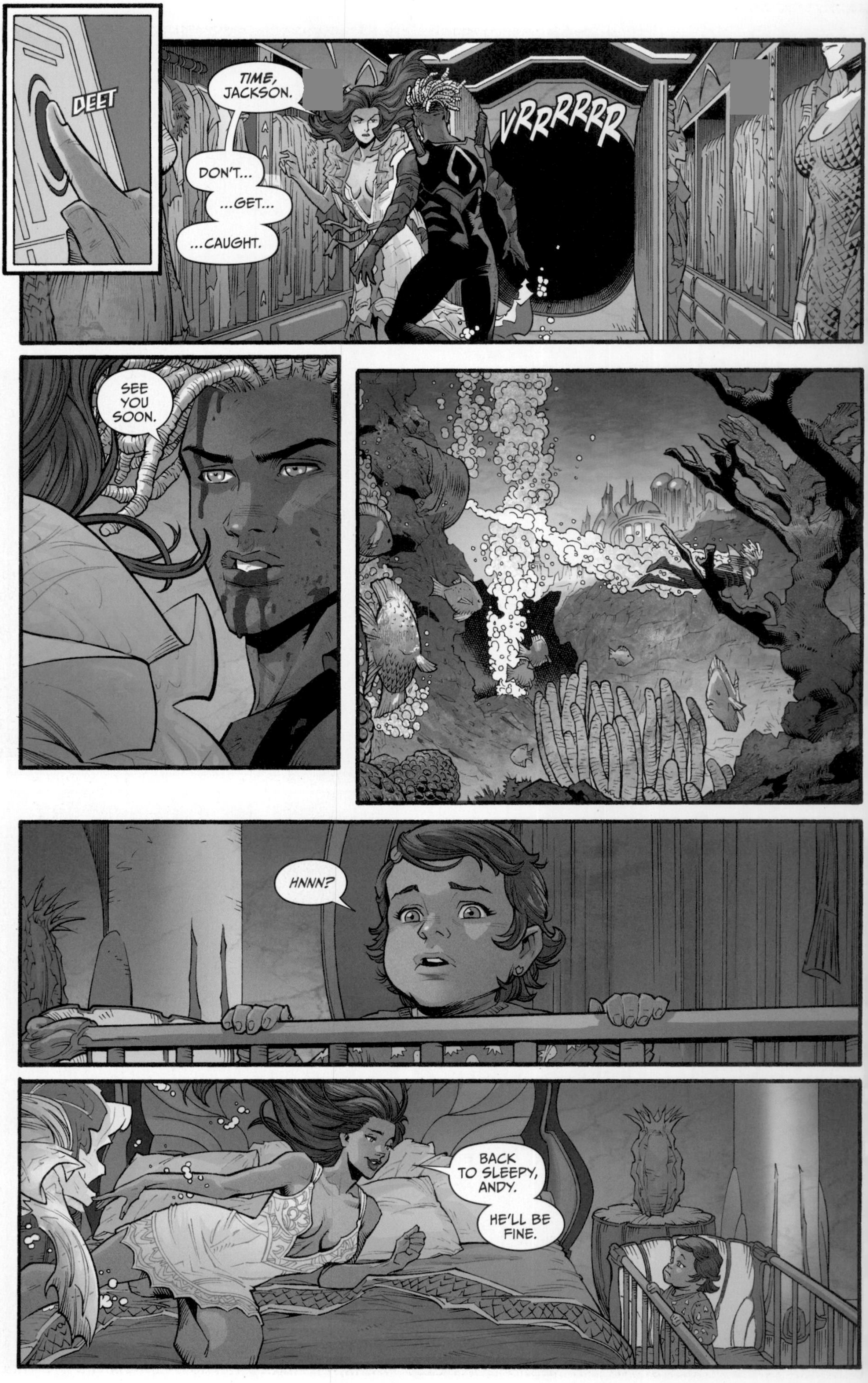
DEET
TIME, JACKSON.
DON'T...
...GET...
...CAUGHT.
VRRRRRR
SEE YOU SOON.
HNNN?
BACK TO SLEEPY, ANDY.
HE'LL BE FINE.

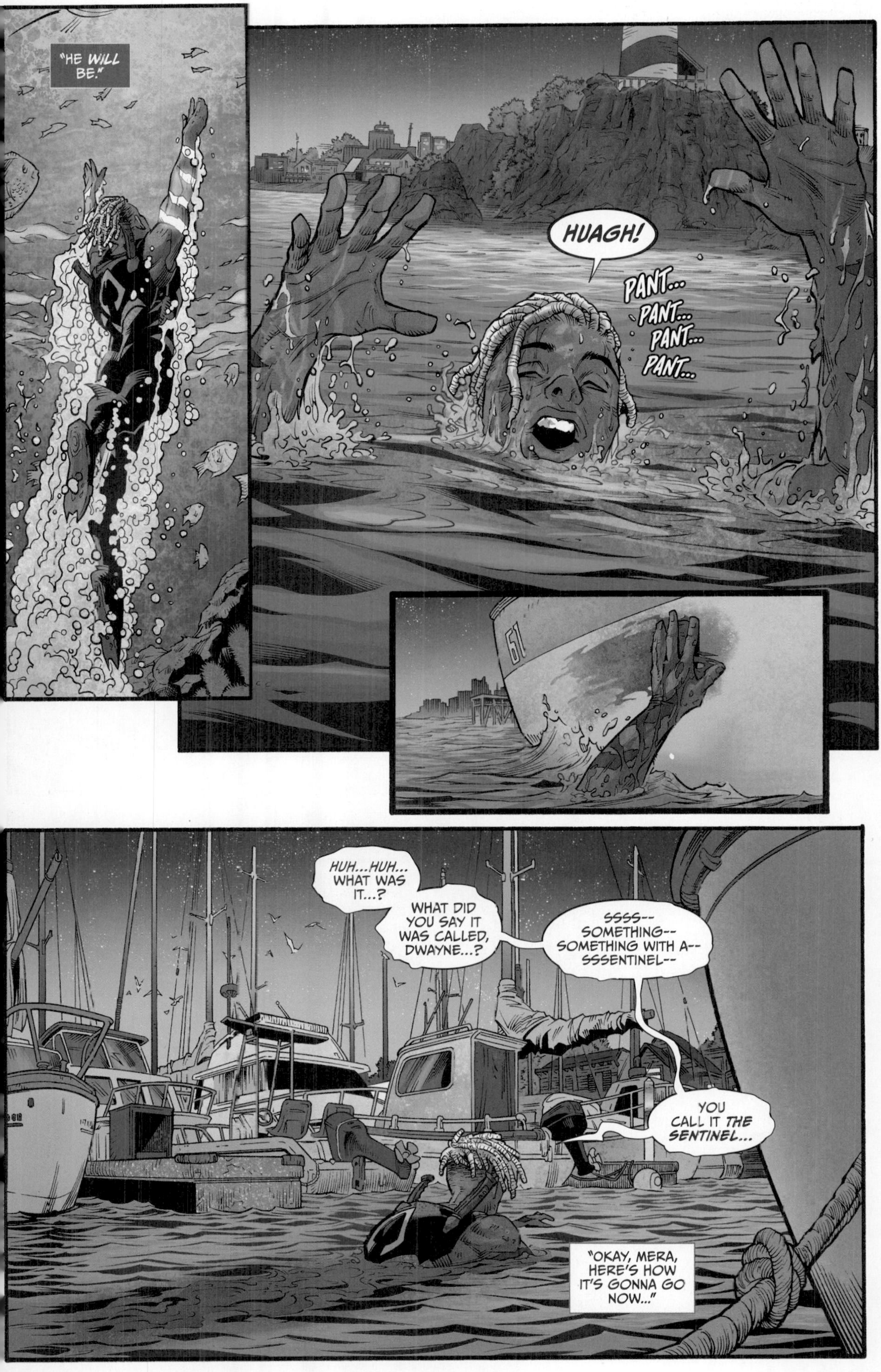
"HE WILL BE."
HUAGH!
PANT... PANT... PANT... PANT...
HUH...HUH... WHAT WAS IT...?
WHAT DID YOU SAY IT WAS CALLED, DWAYNE...?
SSSS-- SOMETHING-- SOMETHING WITH A-- SSSENTINEL--
YOU CALL IT THE SENTINEL...
"OKAY, MERA, HERE'S HOW IT'S GONNA GO NOW..."

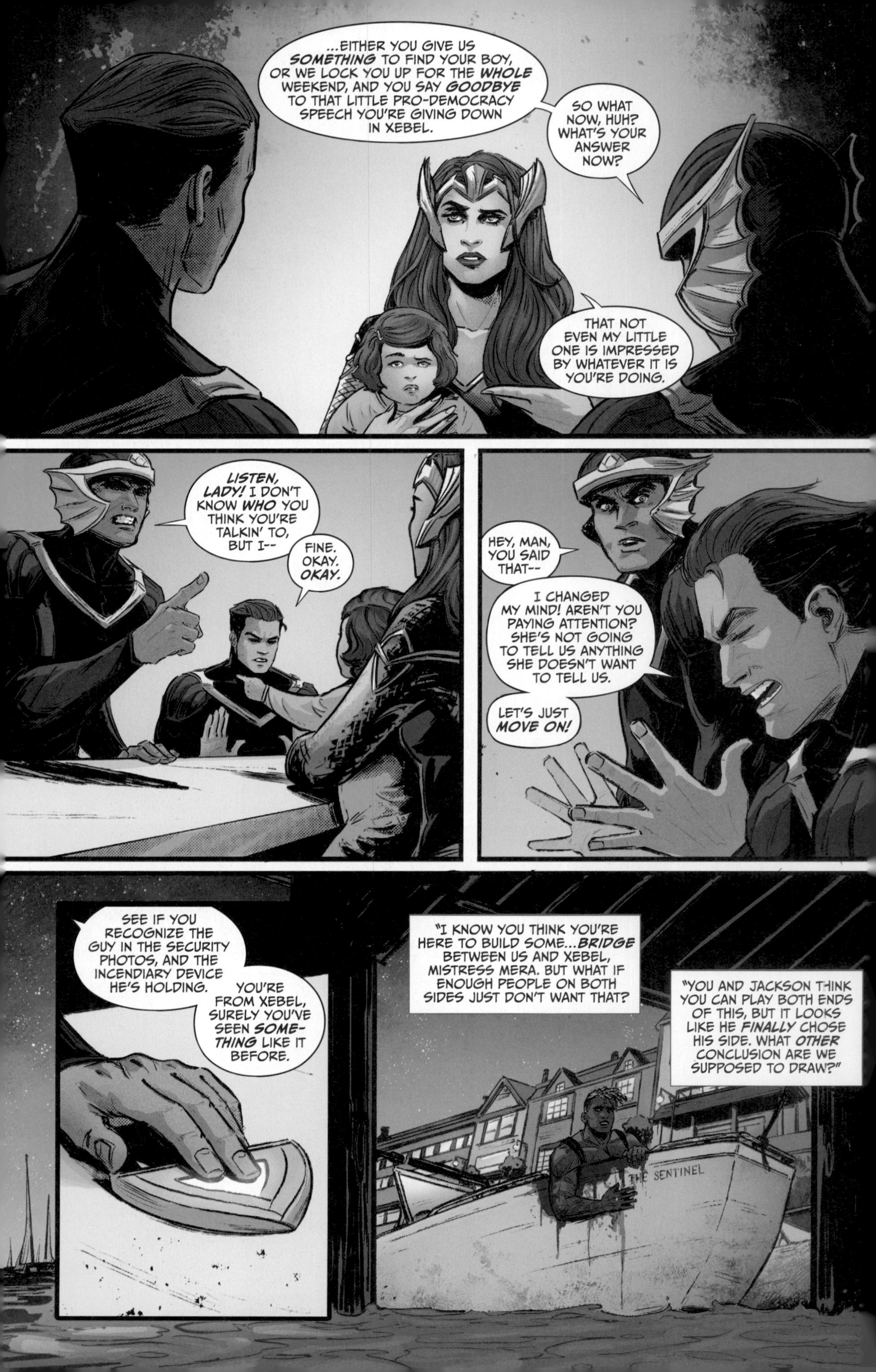
...EITHER YOU GIVE US SOMETHING TO FIND YOUR BOY, OR WE LOCK YOU UP FOR THE WHOLE WEEKEND, AND YOU SAY GOODBYE TO THAT LITTLE PRO-DEMOCRACY SPEECH YOU'RE GIVING DOWN IN XEBEL.
SO WHAT NOW, HUH? WHAT'S YOUR ANSWER NOW?
THAT NOT EVEN MY LITTLE ONE IS IMPRESSED BY WHATEVER IT IS YOU'RE DOING.
LISTEN, LADY! I DON'T KNOW WHO YOU THINK YOU'RE TALKIN' TO, BUT I--
FINE. OKAY. OKAY.
HEY, MAN, YOU SAID THAT--
I CHANGED MY MIND! AREN'T YOU PAYING ATTENTION? SHE'S NOT GOING TO TELL US ANYTHING SHE DOESN'T WANT TO TELL US.
LET'S JUST MOVE ON!
SEE IF YOU RECOGNIZE THE GUY IN THE SECURITY PHOTOS, AND THE INCENDIARY DEVICE HE'S HOLDING.
YOU'RE FROM XEBEL, SURELY YOU'VE SEEN SOMETHING LIKE IT BEFORE.
"I KNOW YOU THINK YOU'RE HERE TO BUILD SOME...BRIDGE BETWEEN US AND XEBEL, MISTRESS MERA. BUT WHAT IF ENOUGH PEOPLE ON BOTH SIDES JUST DON'T WANT THAT?
"YOU AND JACKSON THINK YOU CAN PLAY BOTH ENDS OF THIS, BUT IT LOOKS LIKE HE FINALLY CHOSE HIS SIDE. WHAT OTHER CONCLUSION ARE WE SUPPOSED TO DRAW?"
THE SENTINEL

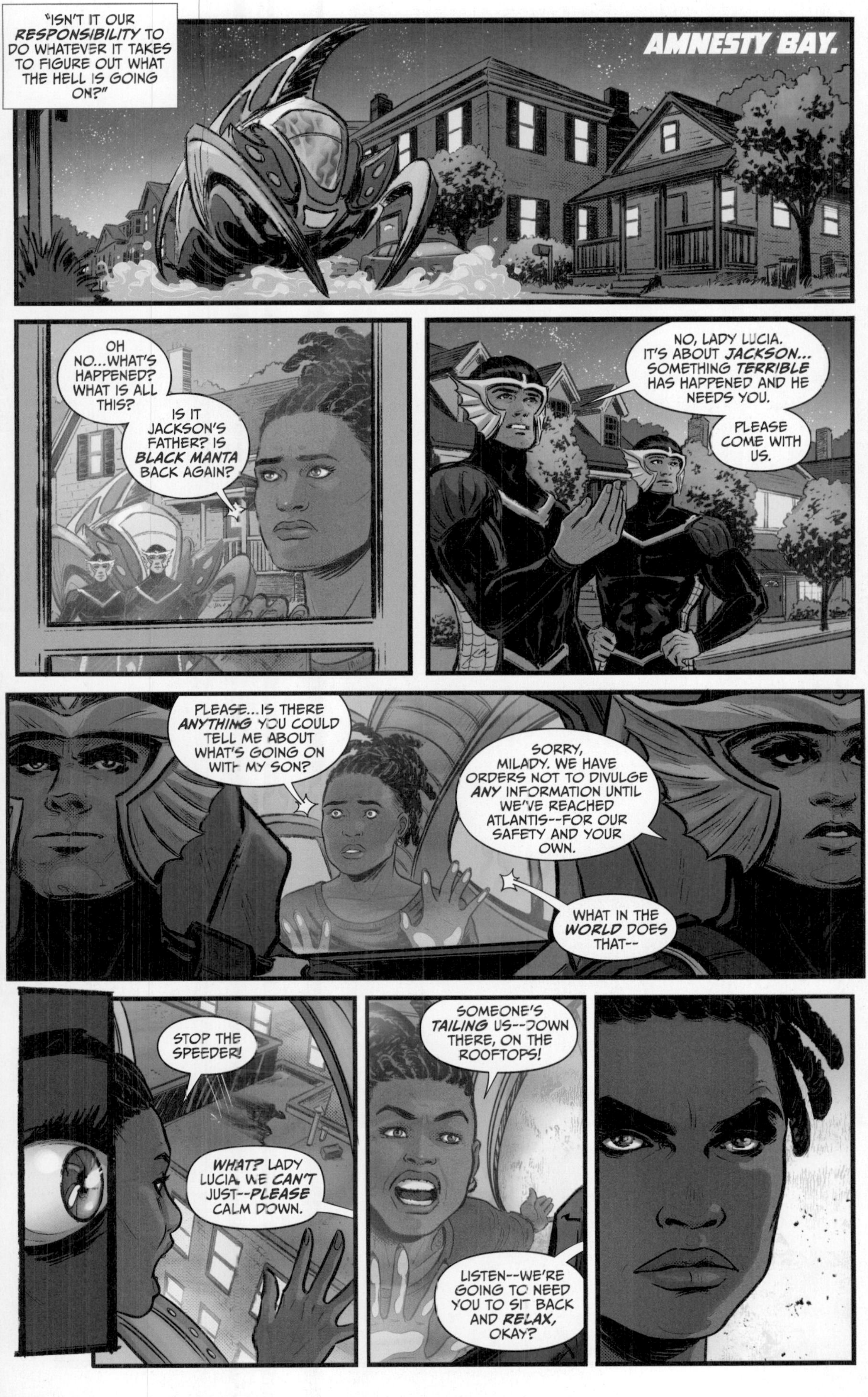
"ISN'T IT OUR RESPONSIBILITY TO DO WHATEVER IT TAKES TO FIGURE OUT WHAT THE HELL IS GOING ON?"
AMNESTY BAY.
OH NO...WHAT'S HAPPENED? WHAT IS ALL THIS?
IS IT JACKSON'S FATHER? IS BLACK MANTA BACK AGAIN?
NO, LADY LUCIA. IT'S ABOUT JACKSON... SOMETHING TERRIBLE HAS HAPPENED AND HE NEEDS YOU.
PLEASE COME WITH US.
PLEASE...IS THERE ANYTHING YOU COULD TELL ME ABOUT WHAT'S GOING ON WITH MY SON?
SORRY, MILADY. WE HAVE ORDERS NOT TO DIVULGE ANY INFORMATION UNTIL WE'VE REACHED ATLANTIS--FOR OUR SAFETY AND YOUR OWN.
WHAT IN THE WORLD DOES THAT--
STOP THE SPEEDER!
WHAT? LADY LUCIA, WE CAN'T JUST--PLEASE CALM DOWN.
SOMEONE'S TAILING US--DOWN THERE, ON THE ROOFTOPS!
LISTEN--WE'RE GOING TO NEED YOU TO SIT BACK AND RELAX, OKAY?

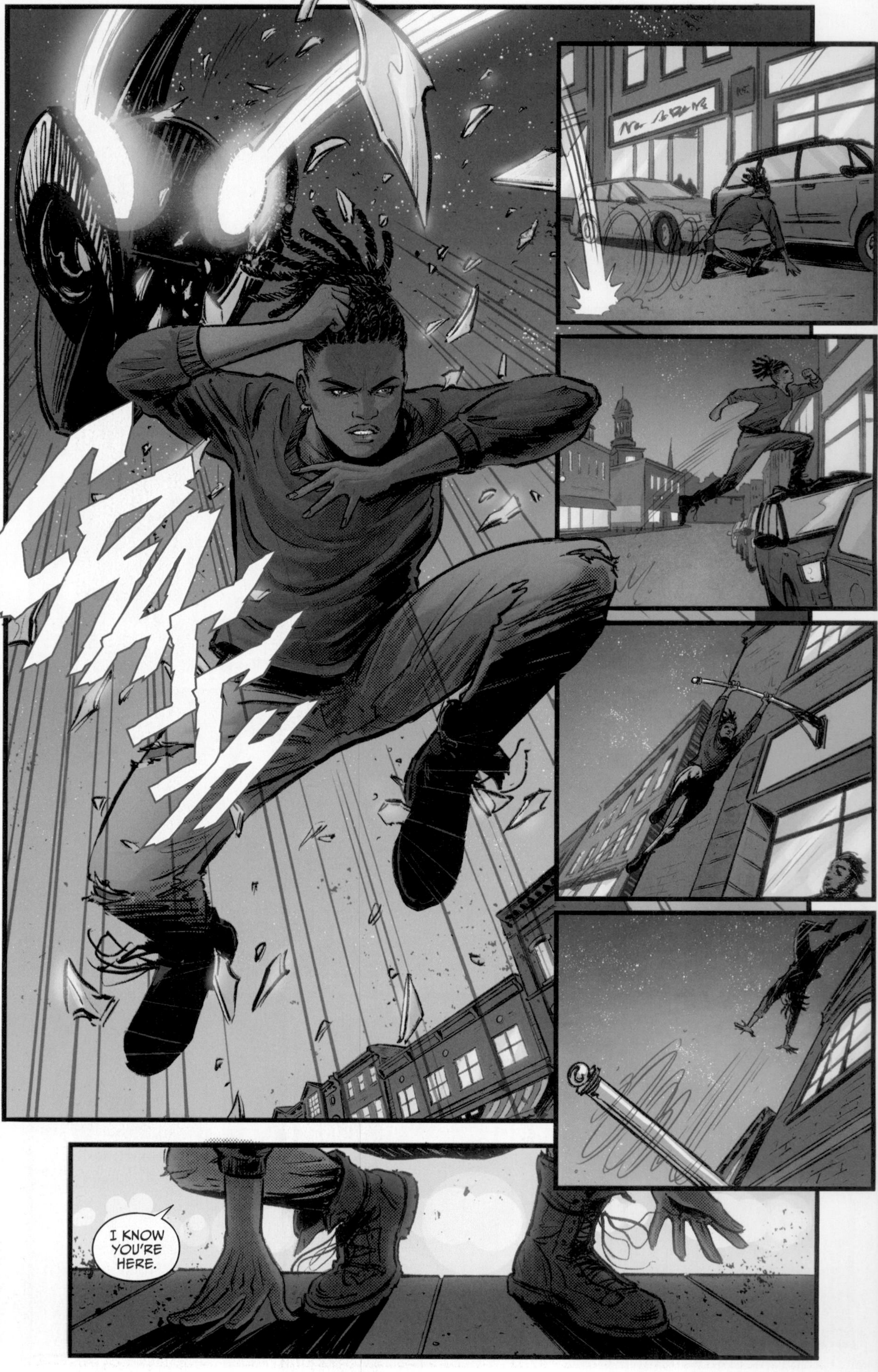
CRASH
I KNOW YOU'RE HERE.

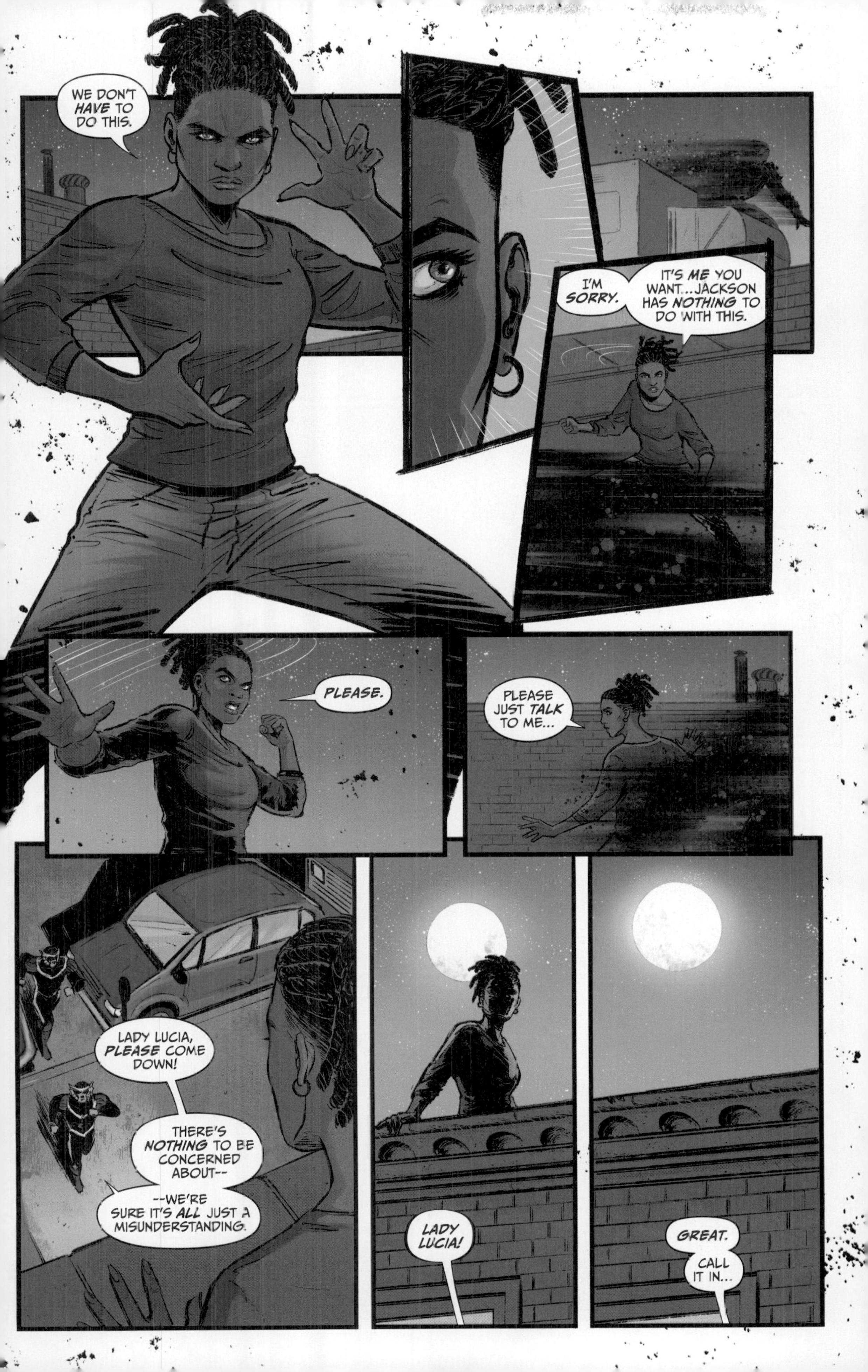
WE DON'T HAVE TO DO THIS.
I'M SORRY.
IT'S ME YOU WANT...JACKSON HAS NOTHING TO DO WITH THIS.
PLEASE.
PLEASE JUST TALK TO ME...
LADY LUCIA, PLEASE COME DOWN!
THERE'S NOTHING TO BE CONCERNED ABOUT--
--WE'RE SURE IT'S ALL JUST A MISUNDERSTANDING.
LADY LUCIA!
GREAT.
CALL IT IN...

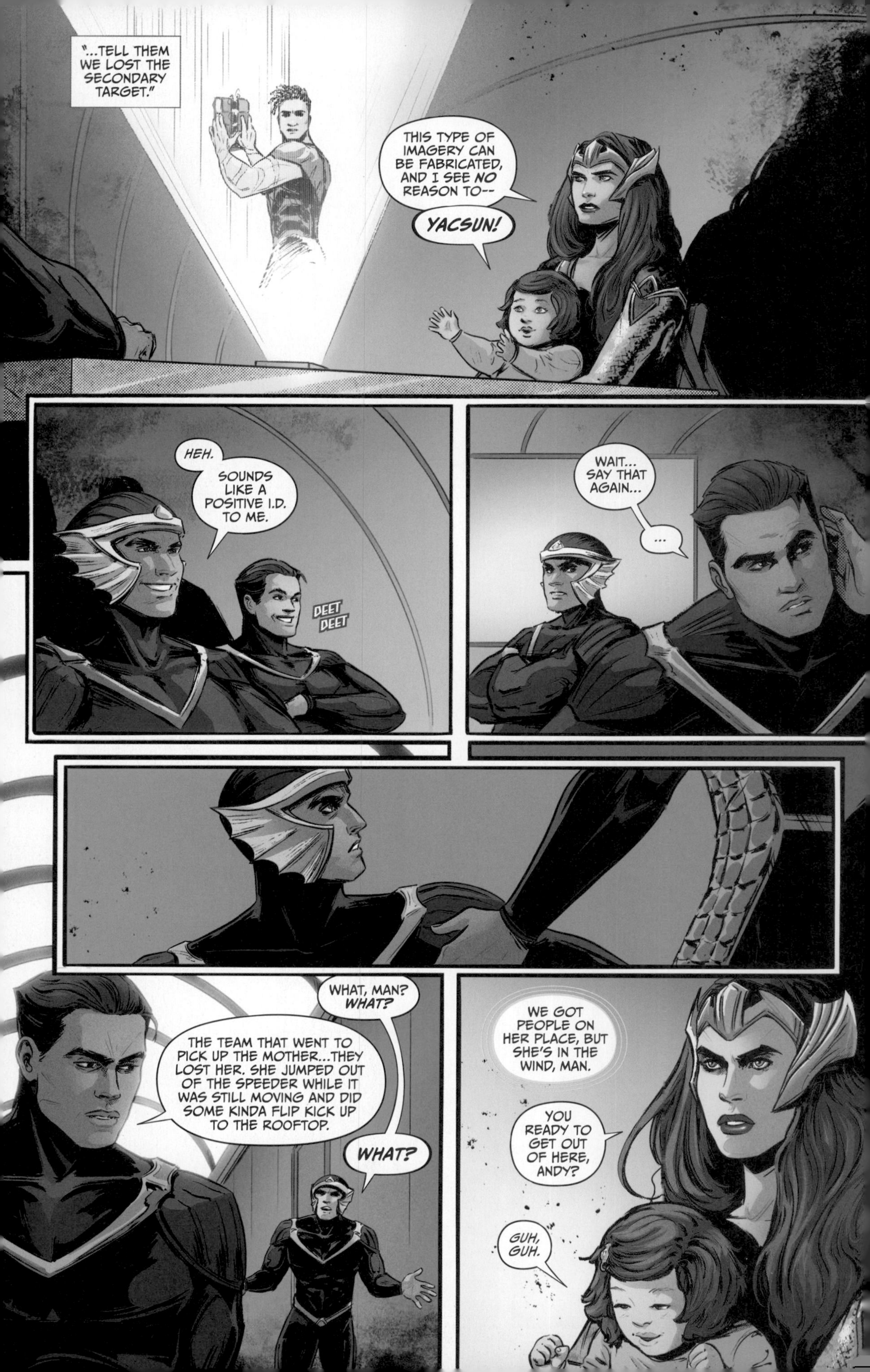

"...TELL THEM WE LOST THE SECONDARY TARGET."
THIS TYPE OF IMAGERY CAN BE FABRICATED, AND I SEE NO REASON TO--
YACSUN!
HEH.
SOUNDS LIKE A POSITIVE I.D. TO ME.
DEET DEET
WAIT... SAY THAT AGAIN...
...
WHAT, MAN? WHAT?
THE TEAM THAT WENT TO PICK UP THE MOTHER...THEY LOST HER. SHE JUMPED OUT OF THE SPEEDER WHILE IT WAS STILL MOVING AND DID SOME KINDA FLIP KICK UP TO THE ROOFTOP.
WHAT?
WE GOT PEOPLE ON HER PLACE, BUT SHE'S IN THE WIND, MAN.
YOU READY TO GET OUT OF HERE, ANDY?
GUH, GUH.

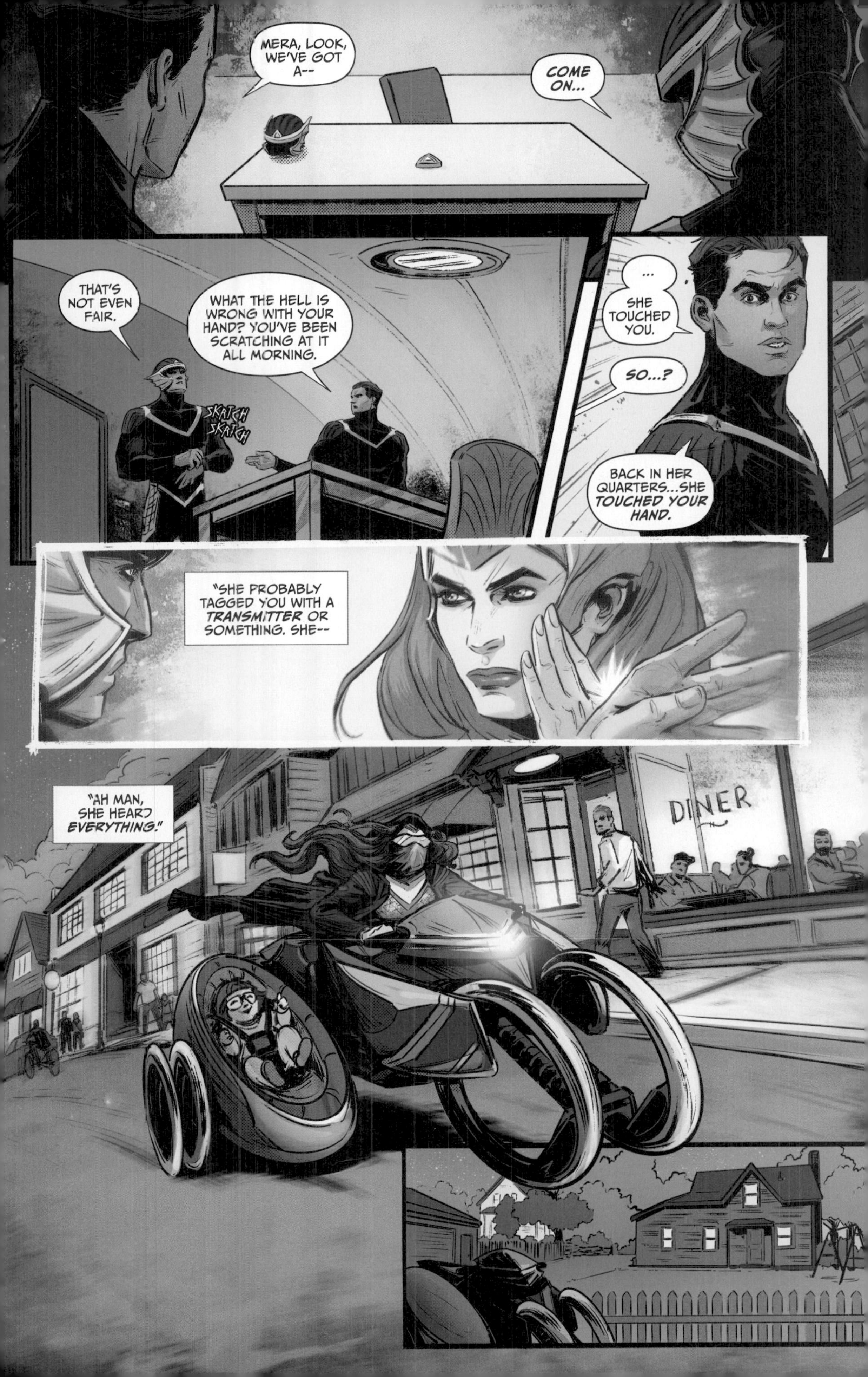
MERA, LOOK, WE'VE GOT A--
COME ON...
THAT'S NOT EVEN FAIR.
WHAT THE HELL IS WRONG WITH YOUR HAND? YOU'VE BEEN SCRATCHING AT IT ALL MORNING.
SKRATCH SKRATCH
...
SHE TOUCHED YOU.
SO...?
BACK IN HER QUARTERS...SHE TOUCHED YOUR HAND.
"SHE PROBABLY TAGGED YOU WITH A TRANSMITTER OR SOMETHING. SHE--
"AH MAN, SHE HEARD EVERYTHING."
DINER

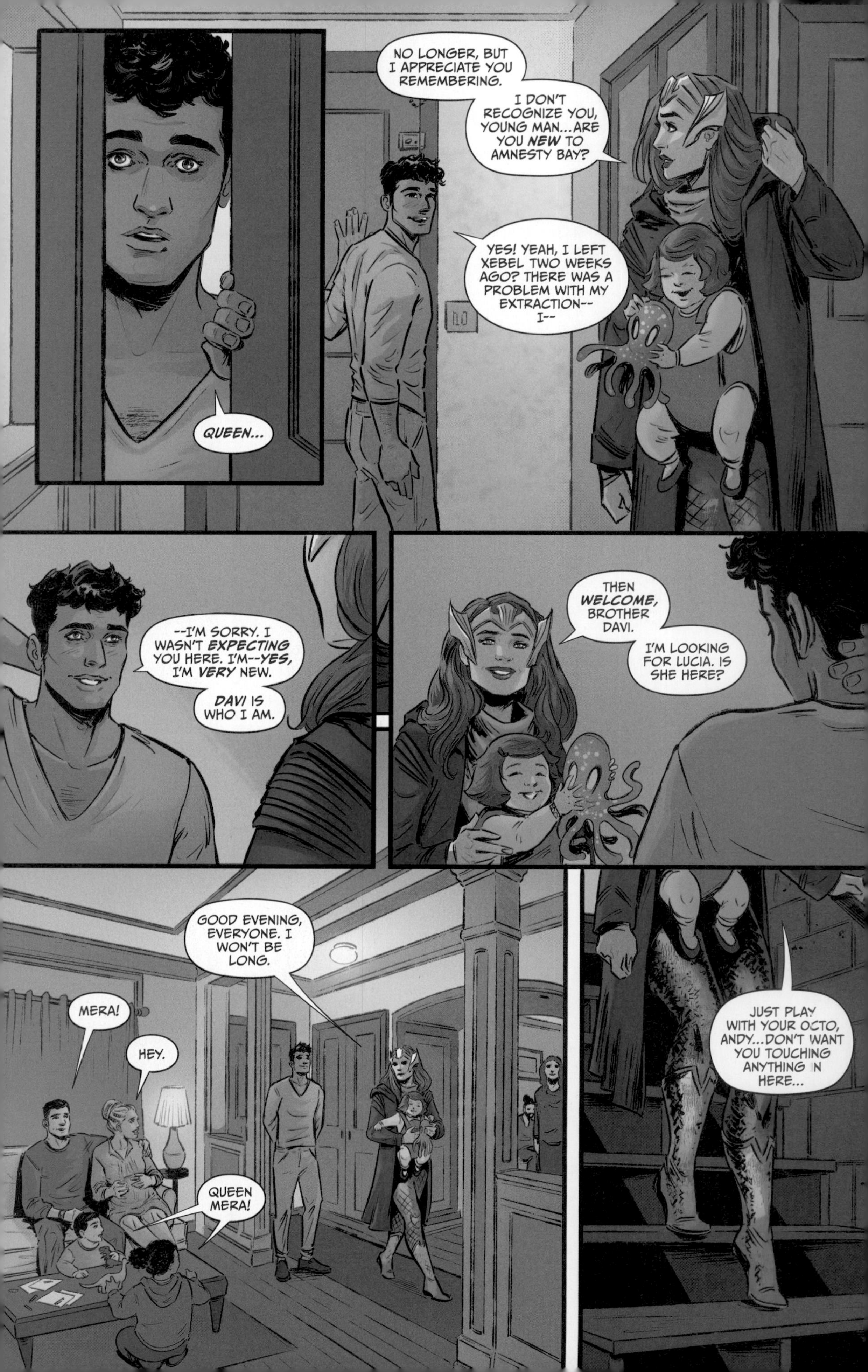
QUEEN...
NO LONGER, BUT I APPRECIATE YOU REMEMBERING.
I DON'T RECOGNIZE YOU, YOUNG MAN...ARE YOU *NEW* TO AMNESTY BAY?
YES! YEAH, I LEFT XEBEL TWO WEEKS AGO? THERE WAS A PROBLEM WITH MY EXTRACTION-- I--
--I'M SORRY. I WASN'T *EXPECTING* YOU HERE. I'M--*YES*, I'M *VERY* NEW.
DAVI IS WHO I AM.
THEN *WELCOME*, BROTHER DAVI.
I'M LOOKING FOR LUCIA. IS SHE HERE?
GOOD EVENING, EVERYONE. I WON'T BE LONG.
MERA!
HEY.
QUEEN MERA!
JUST PLAY WITH YOUR OCTO, ANDY...DON'T WANT YOU TOUCHING ANYTHING IN HERE...

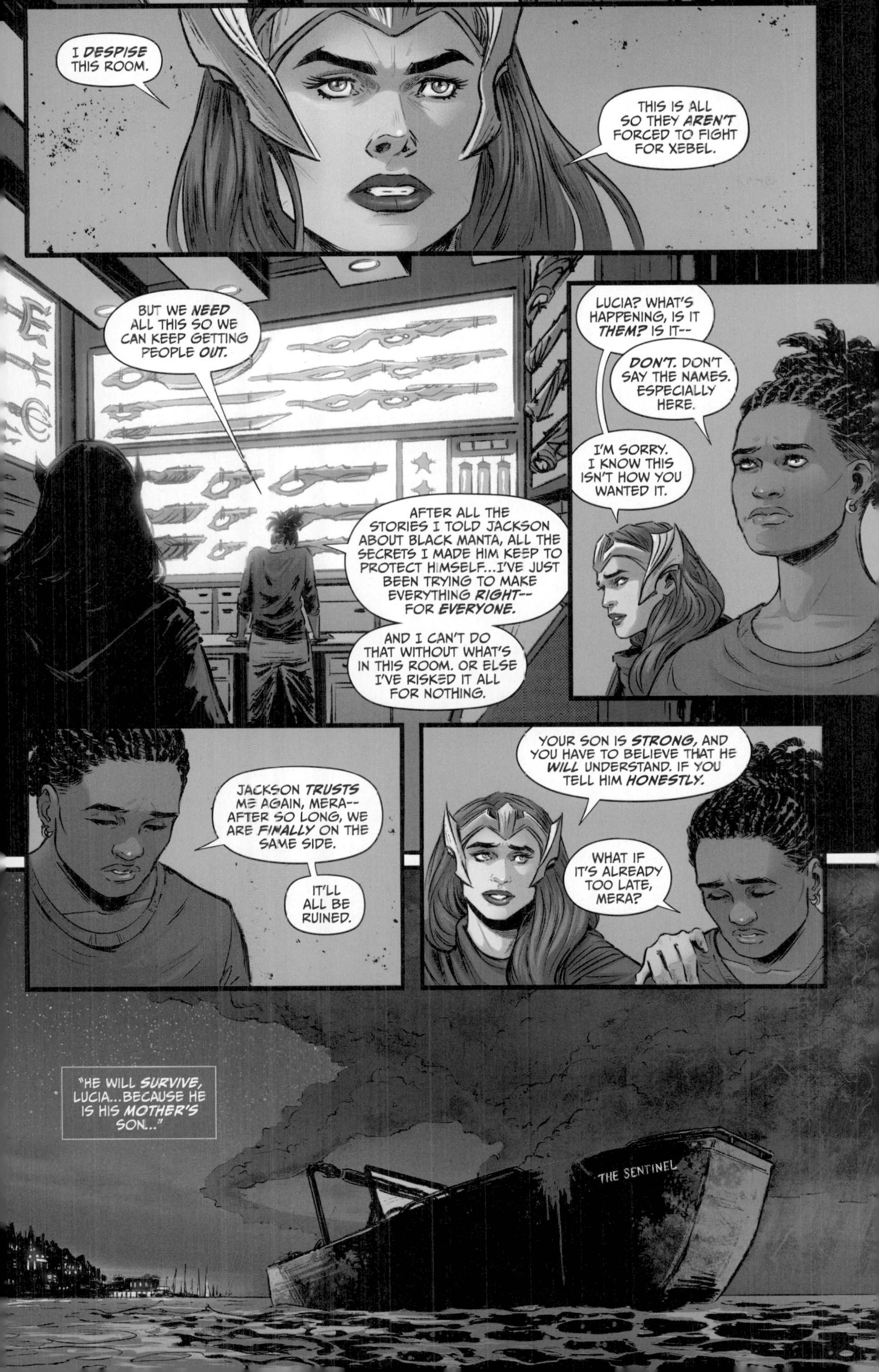
I DESPISE THIS ROOM.
THIS IS ALL SO THEY AREN'T FORCED TO FIGHT FOR XEBEL.
BUT WE NEED ALL THIS SO WE CAN KEEP GETTING PEOPLE OUT.
AFTER ALL THE STORIES I TOLD JACKSON ABOUT BLACK MANTA, ALL THE SECRETS I MADE HIM KEEP TO PROTECT HIMSELF...I'VE JUST BEEN TRYING TO MAKE EVERYTHING RIGHT-- FOR EVERYONE.
AND I CAN'T DO THAT WITHOUT WHAT'S IN THIS ROOM. OR ELSE I'VE RISKED IT ALL FOR NOTHING.
LUCIA? WHAT'S HAPPENING, IS IT THEM? IS IT--
DON'T. DON'T SAY THE NAMES. ESPECIALLY HERE.
I'M SORRY. I KNOW THIS ISN'T HOW YOU WANTED IT.
JACKSON TRUSTS ME AGAIN, MERA-- AFTER SO LONG, WE ARE FINALLY ON THE SAME SIDE.
IT'LL ALL BE RUINED.
YOUR SON IS STRONG, AND YOU HAVE TO BELIEVE THAT HE WILL UNDERSTAND. IF YOU TELL HIM HONESTLY.
WHAT IF IT'S ALREADY TOO LATE, MERA?
"HE WILL SURVIVE, LUCIA...BECAUSE HE IS HIS MOTHER'S SON..."
THE SENTINEL

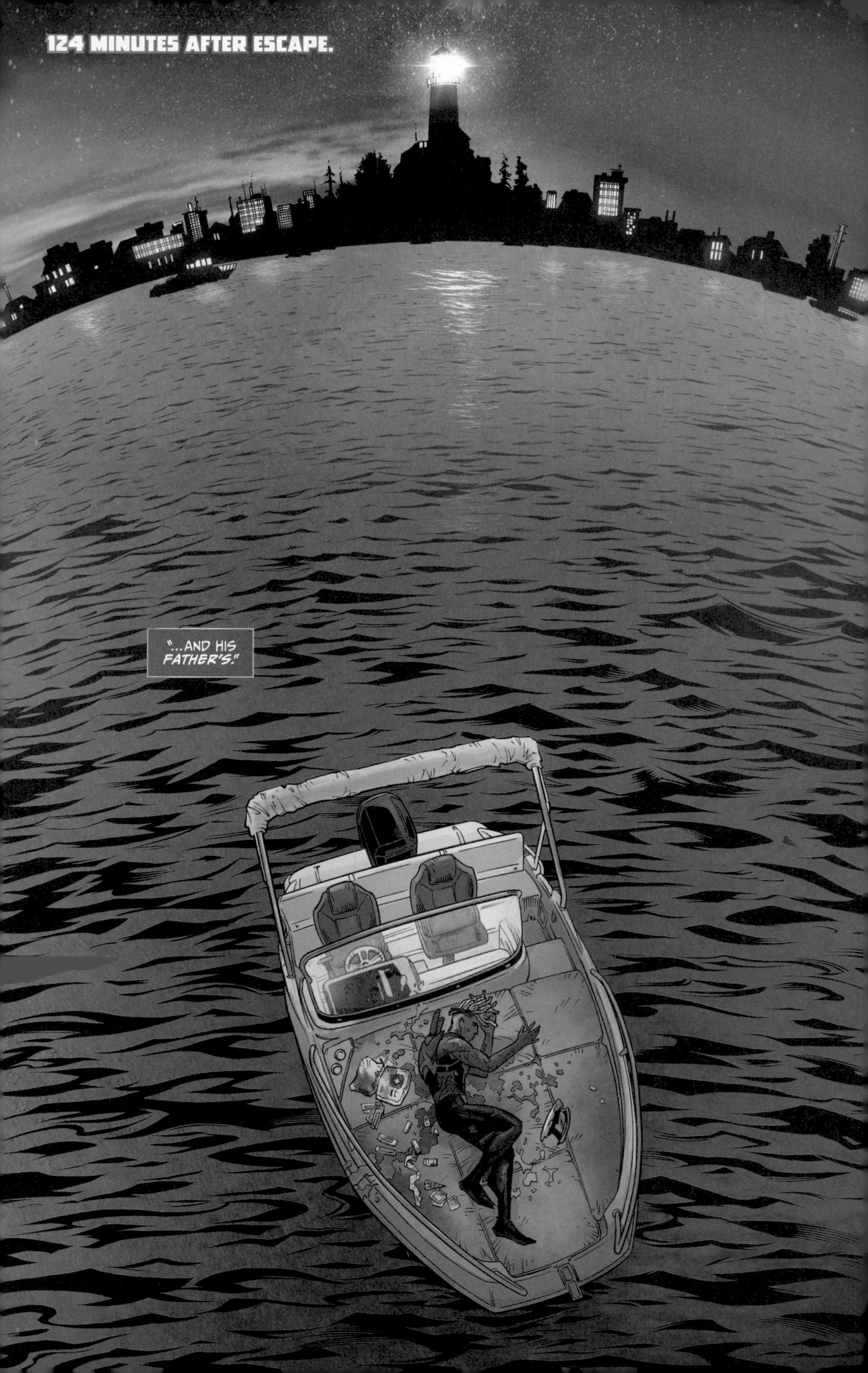
124 MINUTES AFTER ESCAPE.
"...AND HIS FATHER'S."

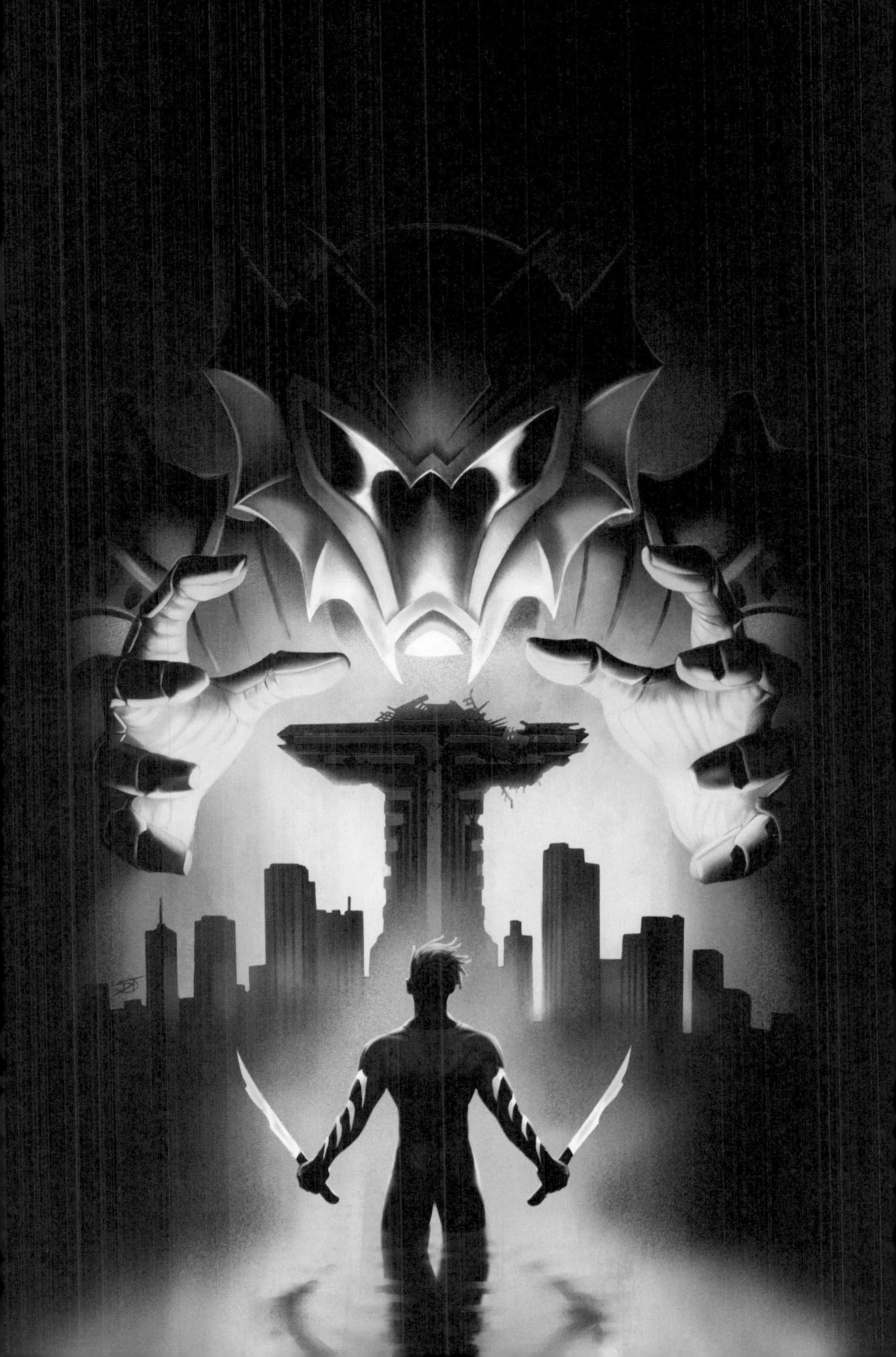

AQUAMAN: THE BECOMING #3 cover by DAVID TALASKI

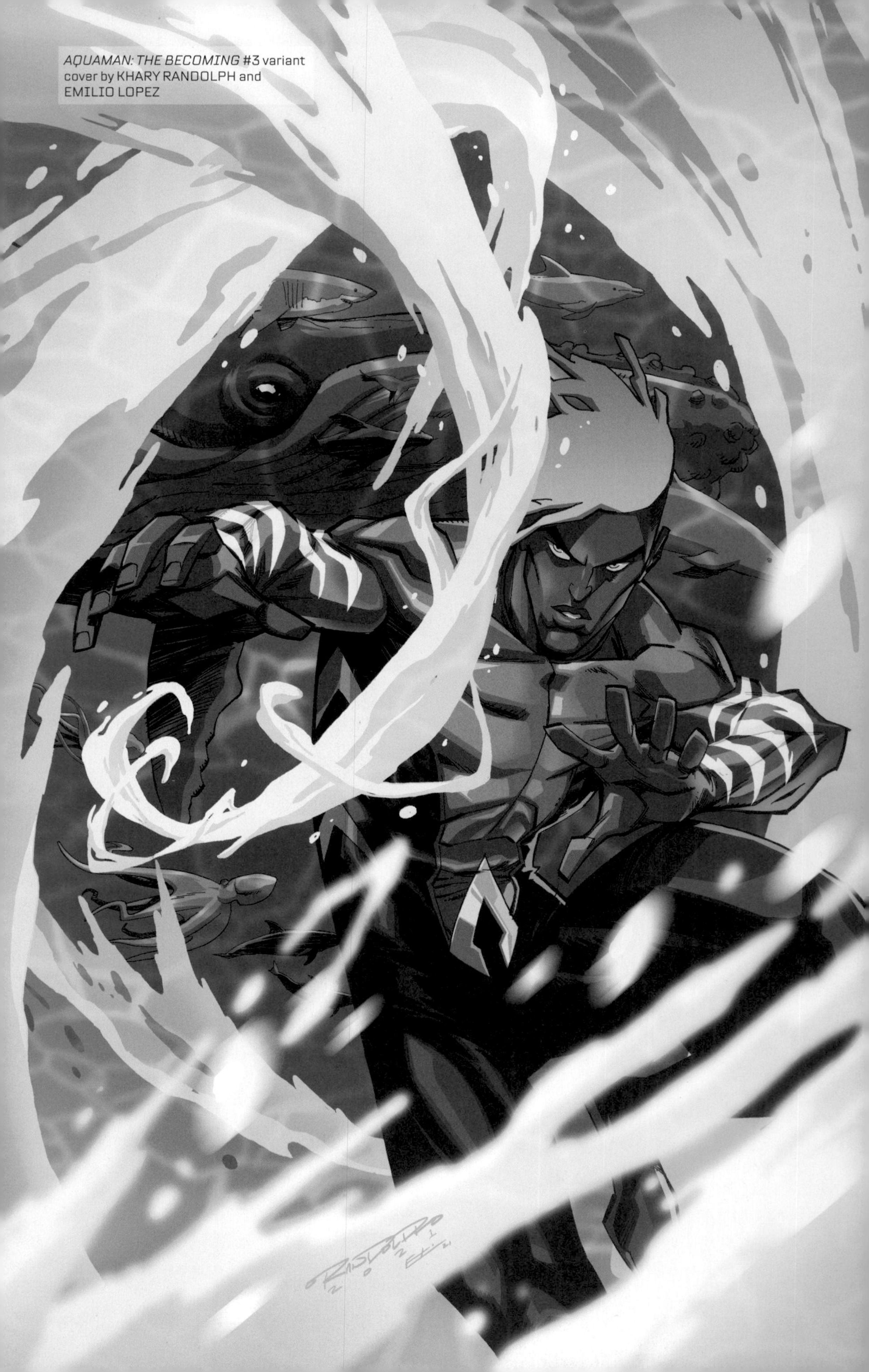

AQUAMAN: THE BECOMING #3 variant cover by KHARY RANDOLPH and EMILIO LOPEZ

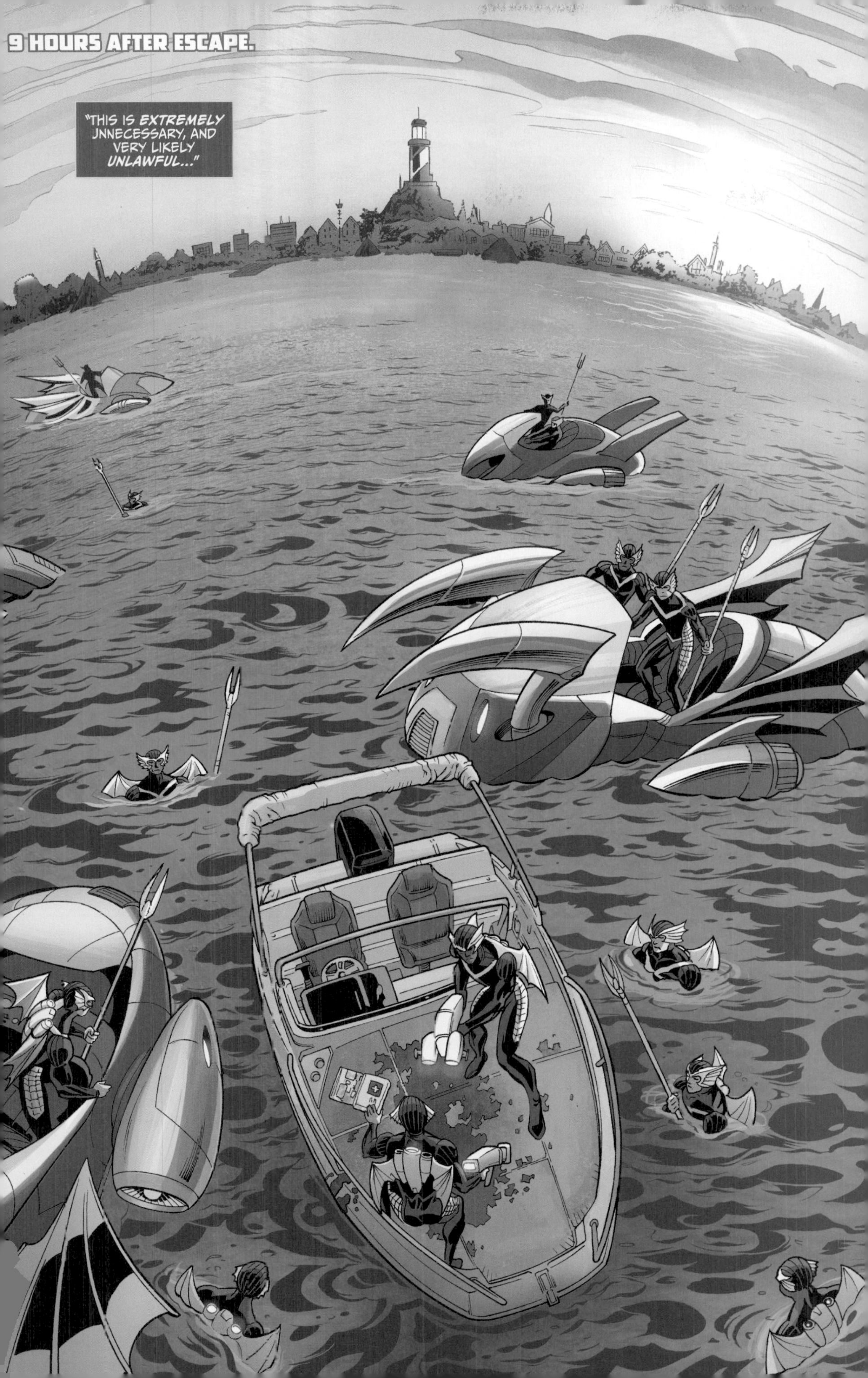
9 HOURS AFTER ESCAPE.
"THIS IS EXTREMELY JNNECESSARY, AND VERY LIKELY UNLAWFUL..."

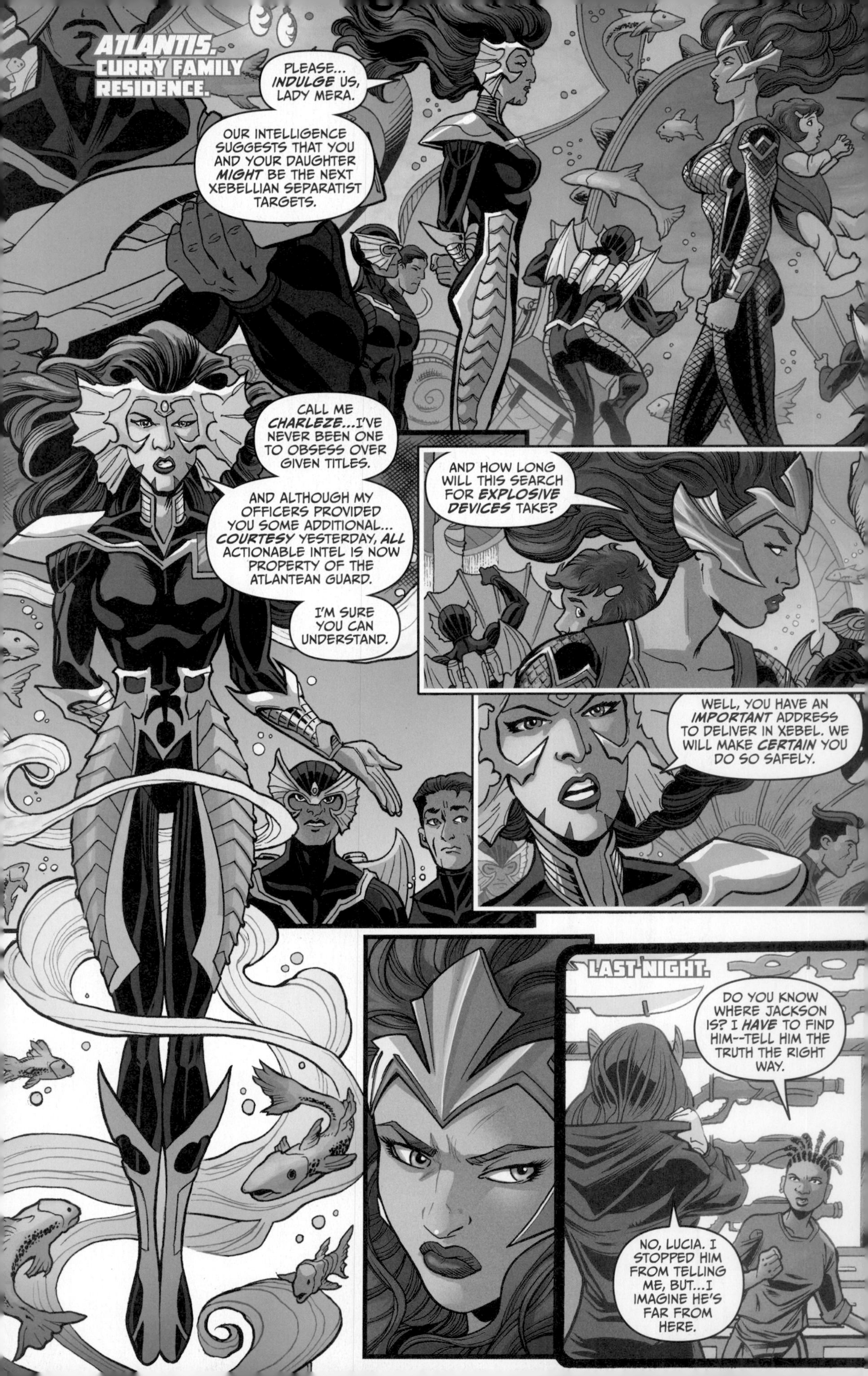
ATLANTIS. CURRY FAMILY RESIDENCE.
PLEASE... INDULGE US, LADY MERA.
OUR INTELLIGENCE SUGGESTS THAT YOU AND YOUR DAUGHTER MIGHT BE THE NEXT XEBELLIAN SEPARATIST TARGETS.
CALL ME CHARLEZE...I'VE NEVER BEEN ONE TO OBSESS OVER GIVEN TITLES.
AND ALTHOUGH MY OFFICERS PROVIDED YOU SOME ADDITIONAL... COURTESY YESTERDAY, ALL ACTIONABLE INTEL IS NOW PROPERTY OF THE ATLANTEAN GUARD.
I'M SURE YOU CAN UNDERSTAND.
AND HOW LONG WILL THIS SEARCH FOR EXPLOSIVE DEVICES TAKE?
WELL, YOU HAVE AN IMPORTANT ADDRESS TO DELIVER IN XEBEL. WE WILL MAKE CERTAIN YOU DO SO SAFELY.
LAST NIGHT.
DO YOU KNOW WHERE JACKSON IS? I HAVE TO FIND HIM--TELL HIM THE TRUTH THE RIGHT WAY.
NO, LUCIA. I STOPPED HIM FROM TELLING ME, BUT...I IMAGINE HE'S FAR FROM HERE.

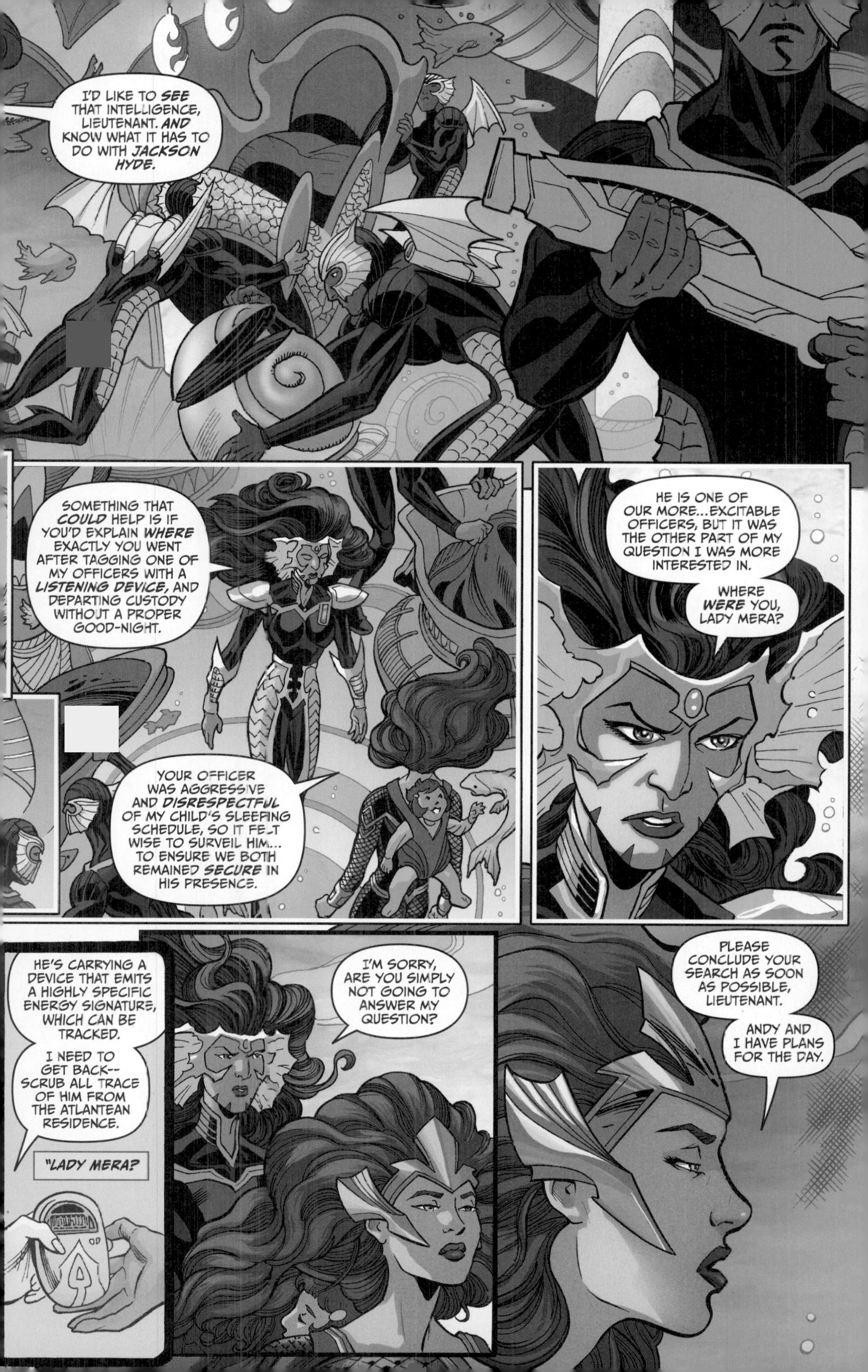
I'D LIKE TO SEE THAT INTELLIGENCE, LIEUTENANT. AND KNOW WHAT IT HAS TO DO WITH JACKSON HYDE.
SOMETHING THAT COULD HELP IS IF YOU'D EXPLAIN WHERE EXACTLY YOU WENT AFTER TAGGING ONE OF MY OFFICERS WITH A LISTENING DEVICE, AND DEPARTING CUSTODY WITHOUT A PROPER GOOD-NIGHT.
YOUR OFFICER WAS AGGRESSIVE AND DISRESPECTFUL OF MY CHILD'S SLEEPING SCHEDULE, SO IT FELT WISE TO SURVEIL HIM... TO ENSURE WE BOTH REMAINED SECURE IN HIS PRESENCE.
HE IS ONE OF OUR MORE...EXCITABLE OFFICERS, BUT IT WAS THE OTHER PART OF MY QUESTION I WAS MORE INTERESTED IN.
WHERE WERE YOU, LADY MERA?
HE'S CARRYING A DEVICE THAT EMITS A HIGHLY SPECIFIC ENERGY SIGNATURE, WHICH CAN BE TRACKED.
I NEED TO GET BACK-- SCRUB ALL TRACE OF HIM FROM THE ATLANTEAN RESIDENCE.
"LADY MERA?
I'M SORRY, ARE YOU SIMPLY NOT GOING TO ANSWER MY QUESTION?
PLEASE CONCLUDE YOUR SEARCH AS SOON AS POSSIBLE, LIEUTENANT.
ANDY AND I HAVE PLANS FOR THE DAY.

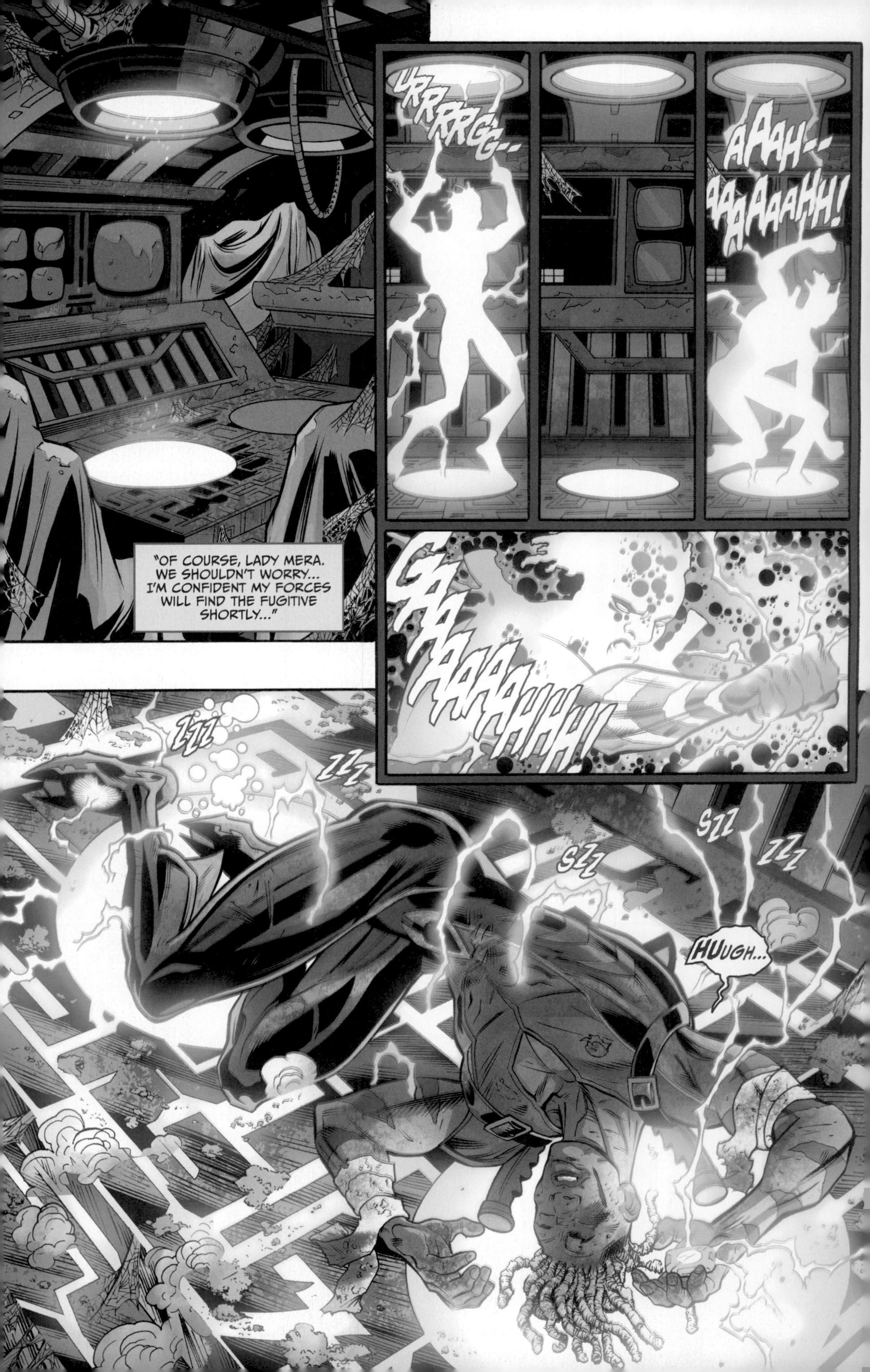
"OF COURSE, LADY MERA. WE SHOULDN'T WORRY... I'M CONFIDENT MY FORCES WILL FIND THE FUGITIVE SHORTLY..."
URRRRGG--
AAAH--AAAAAAHH!
GAAAAAAAAHHH!
ZZZ
ZZZ
SZZ
SZZ
ZZZ
HUUGH...

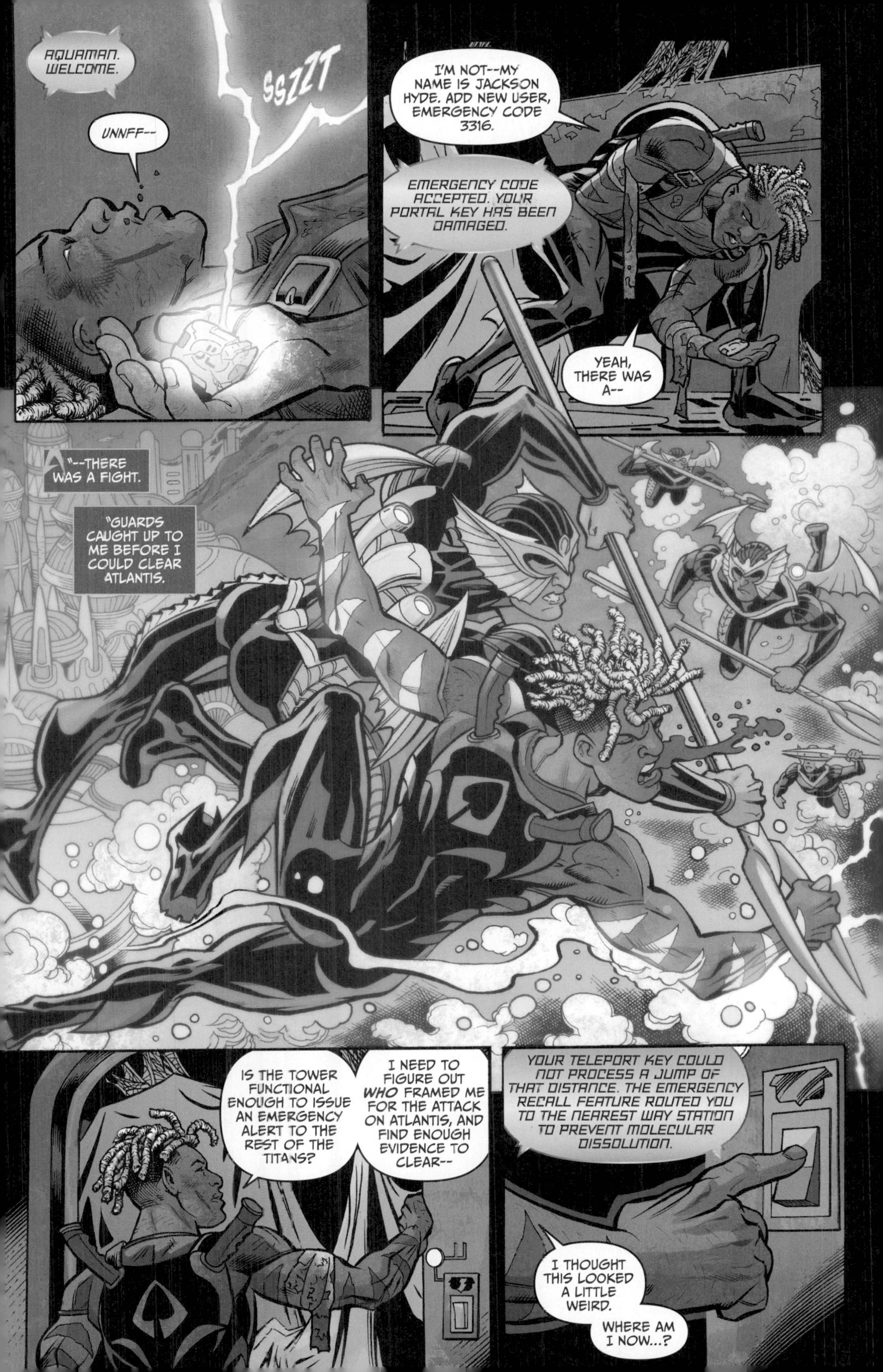
AQUAMAN. WELCOME.
UNNFF--
SSZZZT
I'M NOT--MY NAME IS JACKSON HYDE. ADD NEW USER, EMERGENCY CODE 3316.
EMERGENCY CODE ACCEPTED. YOUR PORTAL KEY HAS BEEN DAMAGED.
YEAH, THERE WAS A--
"--THERE WAS A FIGHT.
"GUARDS CAUGHT UP TO ME BEFORE I COULD CLEAR ATLANTIS.
IS THE TOWER FUNCTIONAL ENOUGH TO ISSUE AN EMERGENCY ALERT TO THE REST OF THE TITANS?
I NEED TO FIGURE OUT WHO FRAMED ME FOR THE ATTACK ON ATLANTIS, AND FIND ENOUGH EVIDENCE TO CLEAR--
YOUR TELEPORT KEY COULD NOT PROCESS A JUMP OF THAT DISTANCE. THE EMERGENCY RECALL FEATURE ROUTED YOU TO THE NEAREST WAY STATION TO PREVENT MOLECULAR DISSOLUTION.
I THOUGHT THIS LOOKED A LITTLE WEIRD.
WHERE AM I NOW...?

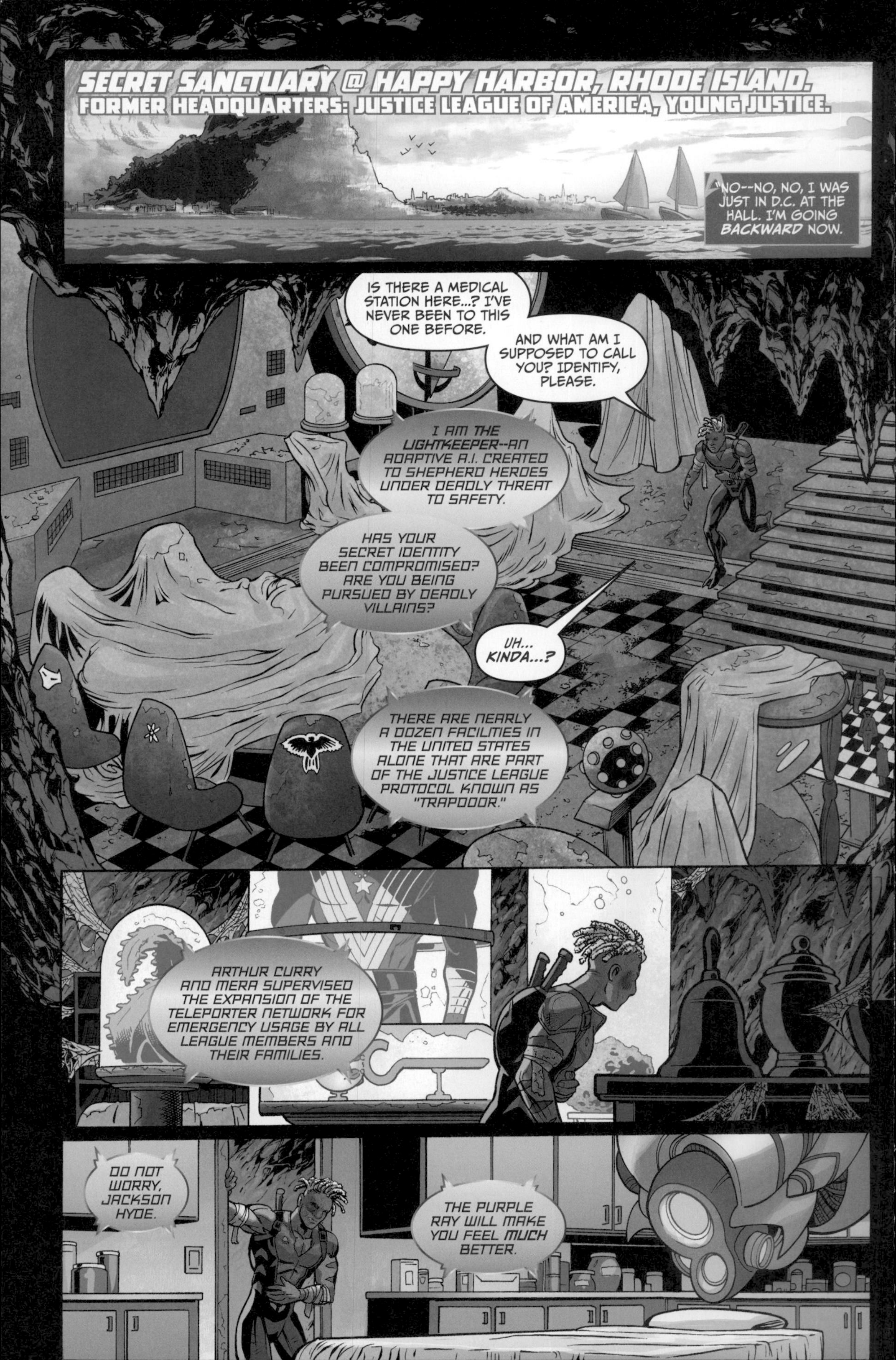
SECRET SANCTUARY @ HAPPY HARBOR, RHODE ISLAND.
FORMER HEADQUARTERS: JUSTICE LEAGUE OF AMERICA, YOUNG JUSTICE.
"NO--NO, NO, I WAS JUST IN D.C. AT THE HALL. I'M GOING *BACKWARD* NOW.
IS THERE A MEDICAL STATION HERE...? I'VE NEVER BEEN TO THIS ONE BEFORE.
AND WHAT AM I SUPPOSED TO CALL YOU? IDENTIFY, PLEASE.
I AM THE *LIGHTKEEPER*--AN ADAPTIVE A.I. CREATED TO SHEPHERD HEROES UNDER DEADLY THREAT TO SAFETY.
HAS YOUR SECRET IDENTITY BEEN COMPROMISED? ARE YOU BEING PURSUED BY DEADLY VILLAINS?
UH... KINDA...?
THERE ARE NEARLY A DOZEN FACILITIES IN THE UNITED STATES ALONE THAT ARE PART OF THE JUSTICE LEAGUE PROTOCOL KNOWN AS "TRAPDOOR."
ARTHUR CURRY AND MERA SUPERVISED THE EXPANSION OF THE TELEPORTER NETWORK FOR EMERGENCY USAGE BY ALL LEAGUE MEMBERS AND THEIR FAMILIES.
DO NOT WORRY, JACKSON HYDE.
THE PURPLE RAY WILL MAKE YOU FEEL *MUCH* BETTER.

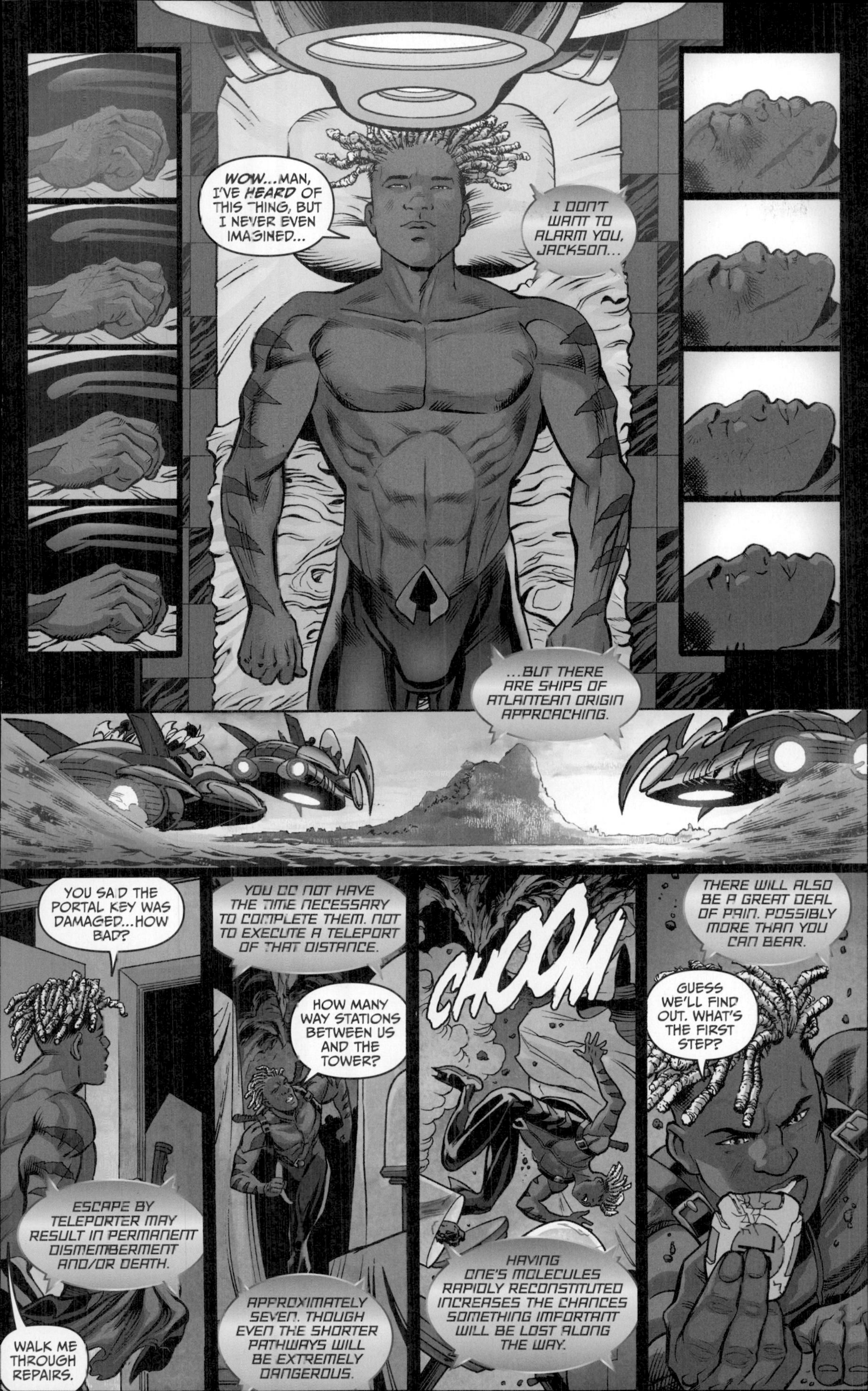
WOW...MAN, I'VE HEARD OF THIS THING, BUT I NEVER EVEN IMAGINED...
I DON'T WANT TO ALARM YOU, JACKSON...
...BUT THERE ARE SHIPS OF ATLANTEAN ORIGIN APPROACHING.
YOU SAID THE PORTAL KEY WAS DAMAGED...HOW BAD?
ESCAPE BY TELEPORTER MAY RESULT IN PERMANENT DISMEMBERMENT AND/OR DEATH.
WALK ME THROUGH REPAIRS.
YOU DO NOT HAVE THE TIME NECESSARY TO COMPLETE THEM. NOT TO EXECUTE A TELEPORT OF THAT DISTANCE.
HOW MANY WAY STATIONS BETWEEN US AND THE TOWER?
APPROXIMATELY SEVEN. THOUGH EVEN THE SHORTER PATHWAYS WILL BE EXTREMELY DANGEROUS.
CHOOM
HAVING ONE'S MOLECULES RAPIDLY RECONSTITUTED INCREASES THE CHANCES SOMETHING IMPORTANT WILL BE LOST ALONG THE WAY.
THERE WILL ALSO BE A GREAT DEAL OF PAIN. POSSIBLY MORE THAN YOU CAN BEAR.
GUESS WE'LL FIND OUT. WHAT'S THE FIRST STEP?

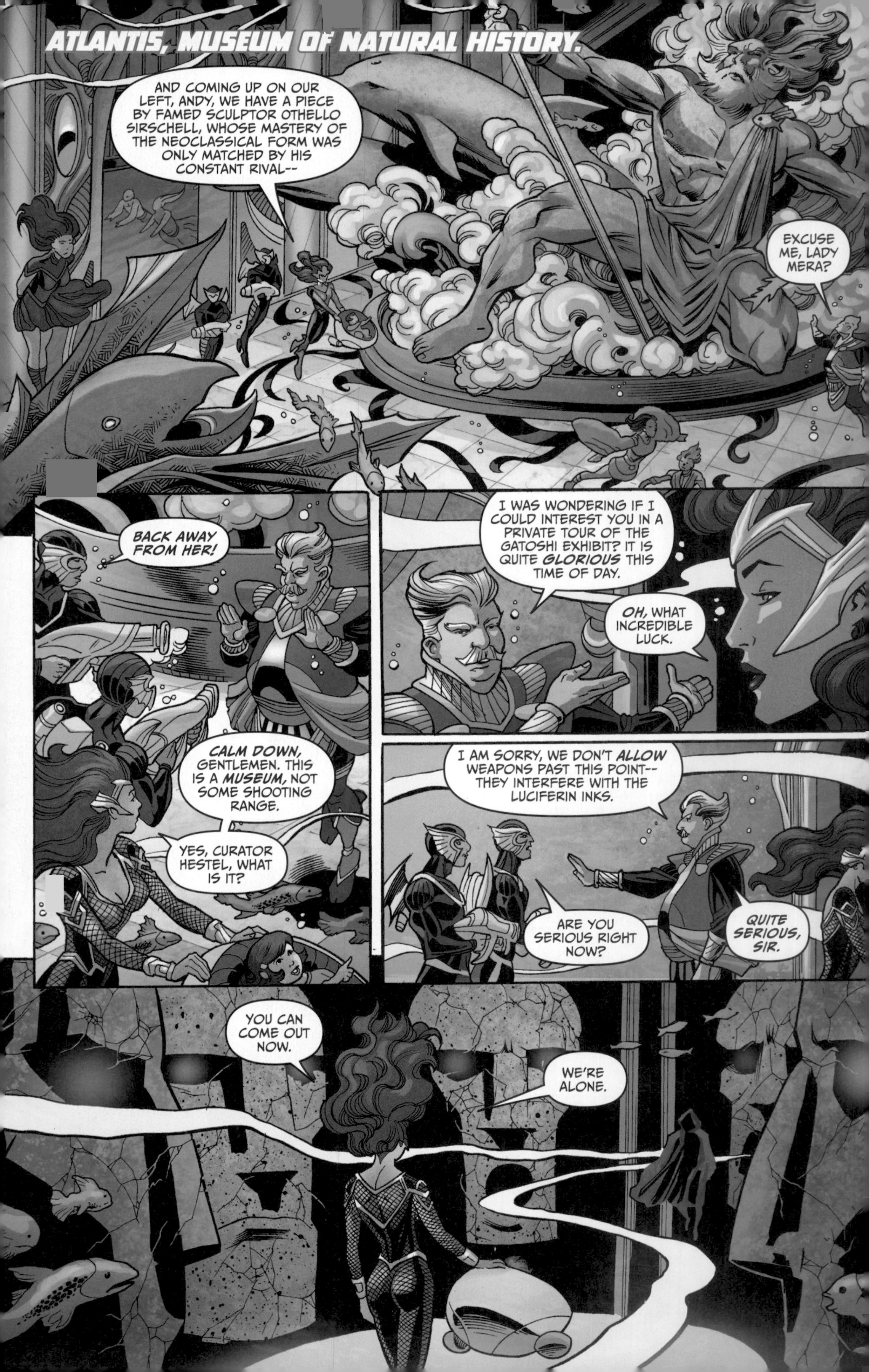
ATLANTIS, MUSEUM OF NATURAL HISTORY.
AND COMING UP ON OUR LEFT, ANDY, WE HAVE A PIECE BY FAMED SCULPTOR OTHELLO SIRSCHELL, WHOSE MASTERY OF THE NEOCLASSICAL FORM WAS ONLY MATCHED BY HIS CONSTANT RIVAL--
EXCUSE ME, LADY MERA?
BACK AWAY FROM HER!
CALM DOWN, GENTLEMEN. THIS IS A MUSEUM, NOT SOME SHOOTING RANGE.
YES, CURATOR HESTEL, WHAT IS IT?
I WAS WONDERING IF I COULD INTEREST YOU IN A PRIVATE TOUR OF THE GATOSHI EXHIBIT? IT IS QUITE GLORIOUS THIS TIME OF DAY.
OH, WHAT INCREDIBLE LUCK.
I AM SORRY, WE DON'T ALLOW WEAPONS PAST THIS POINT-- THEY INTERFERE WITH THE LUCIFERIN INKS.
ARE YOU SERIOUS RIGHT NOW?
QUITE SERIOUS, SIR.
YOU CAN COME OUT NOW.
WE'RE ALONE.

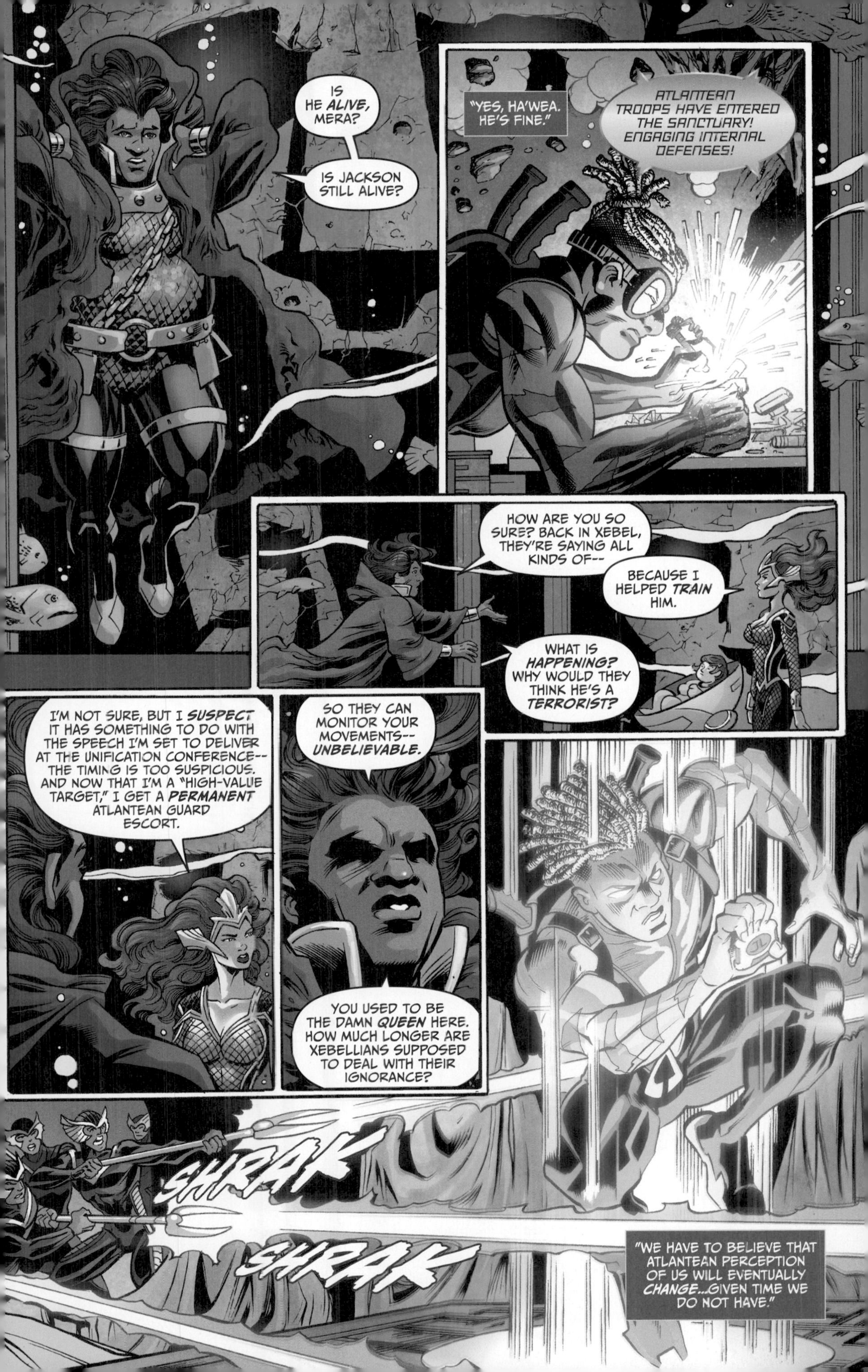
IS HE *ALIVE,* MERA?
IS JACKSON STILL ALIVE?
"YES, HA'WEA. HE'S FINE."
ATLANTEAN TROOPS HAVE ENTERED THE SANCTUARY! ENGAGING INTERNAL DEFENSES!
HOW ARE YOU SO SURE? BACK IN XEBEL, THEY'RE SAYING ALL KINDS OF--
BECAUSE I HELPED *TRAIN* HIM.
WHAT IS *HAPPENING?* WHY WOULD THEY THINK HE'S A *TERRORIST?*
I'M NOT SURE, BUT I *SUSPECT* IT HAS SOMETHING TO DO WITH THE SPEECH I'M SET TO DELIVER AT THE UNIFICATION CONFERENCE-- THE TIMING IS TOO SUSPICIOUS. AND NOW THAT I'M A "HIGH-VALUE TARGET," I GET A *PERMANENT* ATLANTEAN GUARD ESCORT.
SO THEY CAN MONITOR YOUR MOVEMENTS-- *UNBELIEVABLE.*
YOU USED TO BE THE DAMN *QUEEN* HERE. HOW MUCH LONGER ARE XEBELLIANS SUPPOSED TO DEAL WITH THEIR IGNORANCE?
SHRAK
SHRAK
"WE HAVE TO BELIEVE THAT ATLANTEAN PERCEPTION OF US WILL EVENTUALLY *CHANGE*...GIVEN TIME WE DO NOT HAVE."

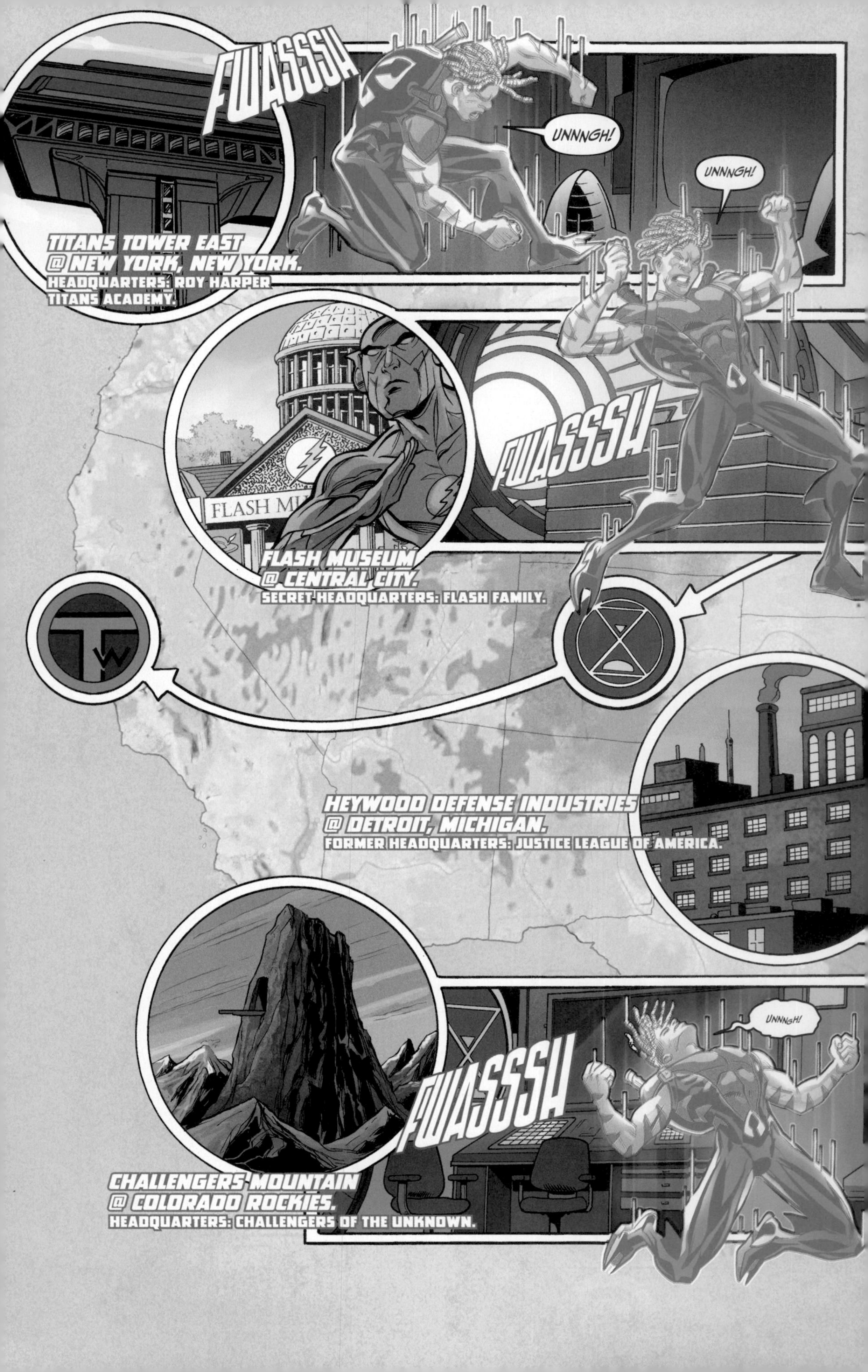
FWASSSH
UNNNGH!
UNNNGH!
TITANS TOWER EAST
@ NEW YORK, NEW YORK.
HEADQUARTERS: ROY HARPER
TITANS ACADEMY.
FLASH MU
FWASSSH
FLASH MUSEUM
@ CENTRAL CITY.
SECRET HEADQUARTERS: FLASH FAMILY.
HEYWOOD DEFENSE INDUSTRIES
@ DETROIT, MICHIGAN.
FORMER HEADQUARTERS: JUSTICE LEAGUE OF AMERICA.
UNNNGH!
FWASSSH
CHALLENGERS MOUNTAIN
@ COLORADO ROCKIES.
HEADQUARTERS: CHALLENGERS OF THE UNKNOWN.

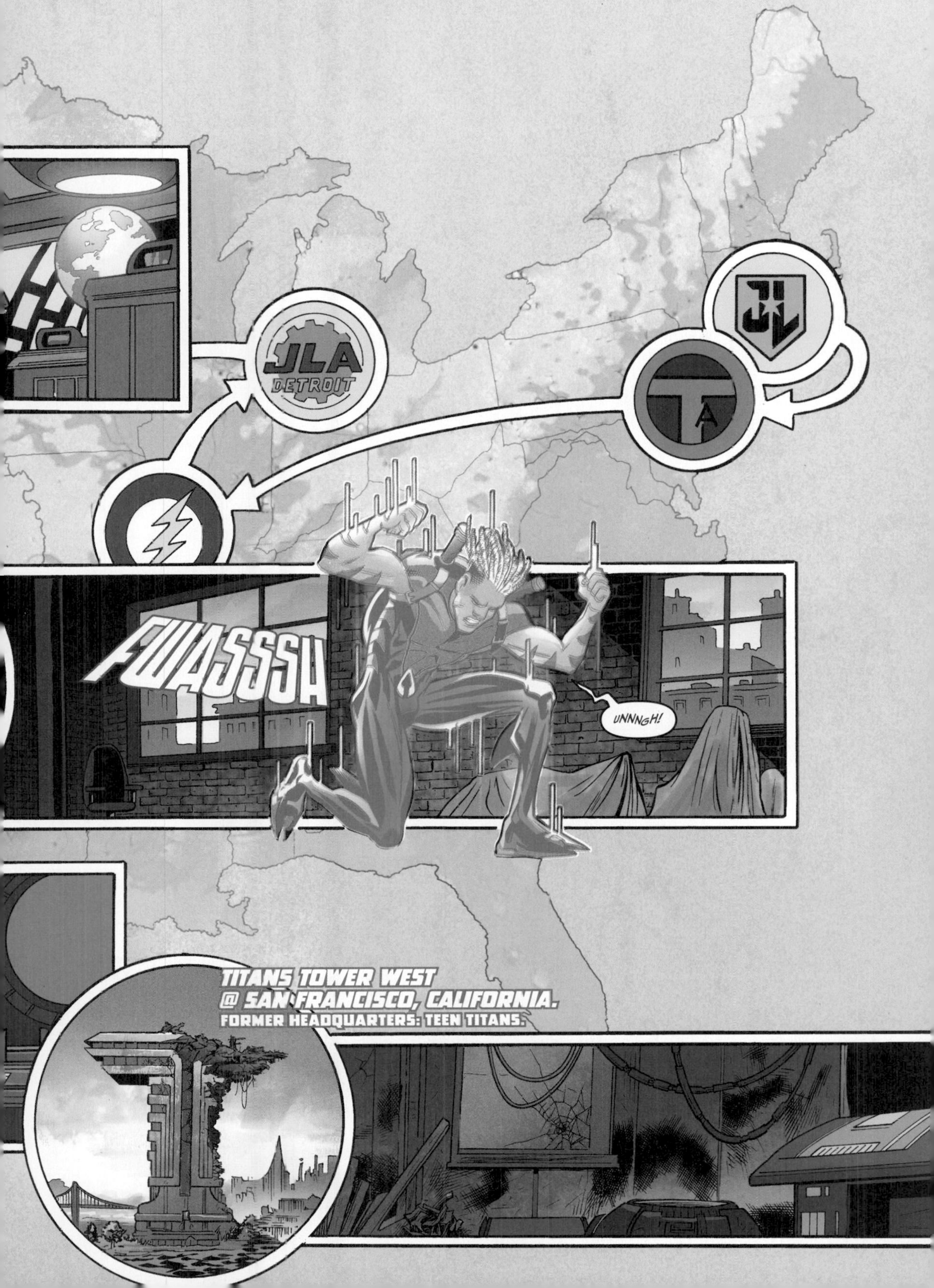
JLA
DETROIT
FWASSSH
UNNNGH!
TITANS TOWER WEST
@ SAN FRANCISCO, CALIFORNIA.
FORMER HEADQUARTERS: TEEN TITANS.

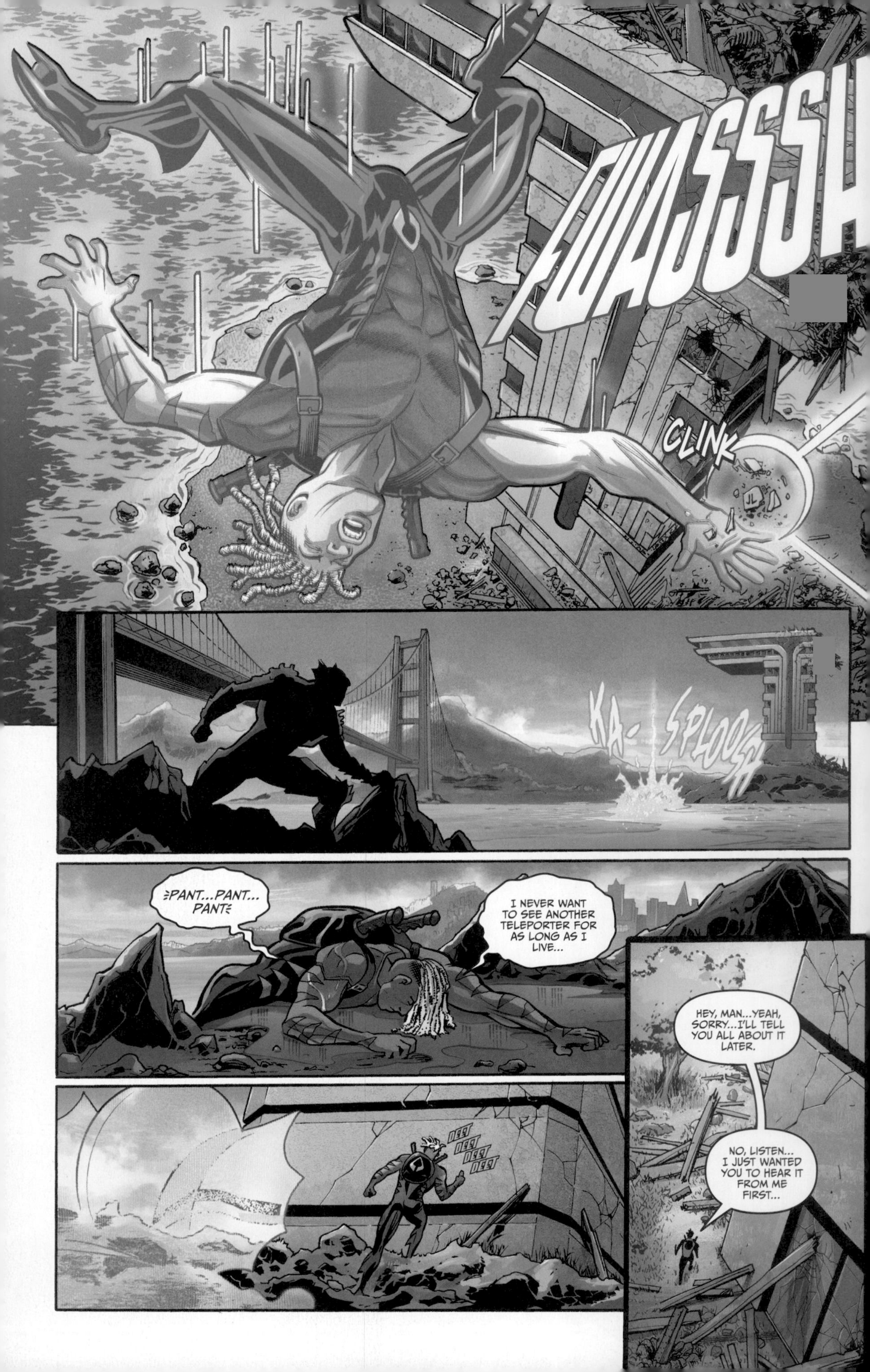
FWASSSH
CLINK
KA-SPLOOSH
PANT...PANT... PANT
I NEVER WANT TO SEE ANOTHER TELEPORTER FOR AS LONG AS I LIVE...
HEY, MAN...YEAH, SORRY...I'LL TELL YOU ALL ABOUT IT LATER.
NO, LISTEN... I JUST WANTED YOU TO HEAR IT FROM ME FIRST...

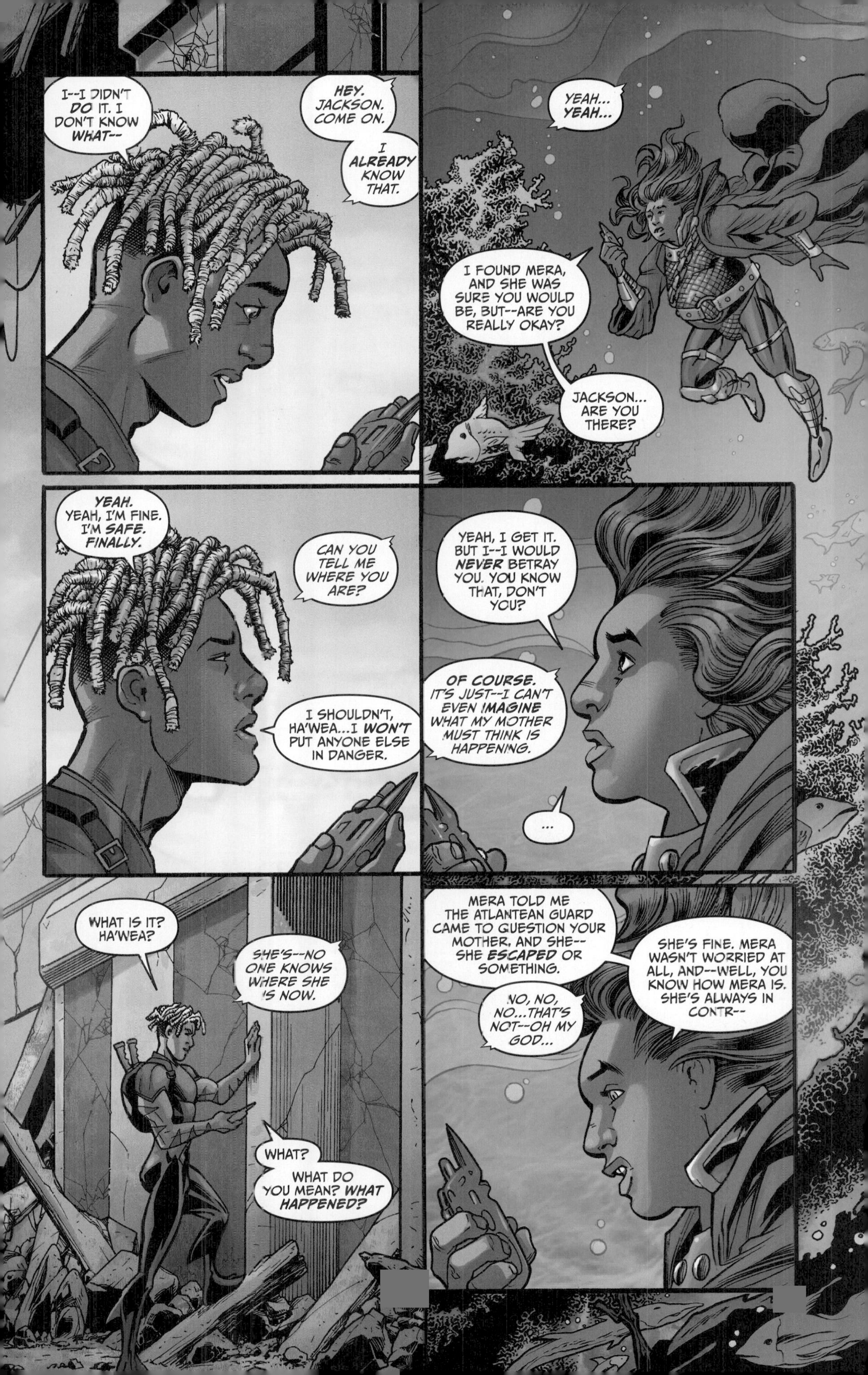
I--I DIDN'T DO IT. I DON'T KNOW WHAT--
HEY. JACKSON. COME ON.
I ALREADY KNOW THAT.
YEAH... YEAH...
I FOUND MERA, AND SHE WAS SURE YOU WOULD BE, BUT--ARE YOU REALLY OKAY?
JACKSON... ARE YOU THERE?
YEAH. YEAH, I'M FINE. I'M SAFE. FINALLY.
CAN YOU TELL ME WHERE YOU ARE?
I SHOULDN'T, HA'WEA...I WON'T PUT ANYONE ELSE IN DANGER.
YEAH, I GET IT. BUT I--I WOULD NEVER BETRAY YOU. YOU KNOW THAT, DON'T YOU?
OF COURSE. IT'S JUST--I CAN'T EVEN IMAGINE WHAT MY MOTHER MUST THINK IS HAPPENING.
...
WHAT IS IT? HA'WEA?
SHE'S--NO ONE KNOWS WHERE SHE IS NOW.
WHAT?
WHAT DO YOU MEAN? WHAT HAPPENED?
MERA TOLD ME THE ATLANTEAN GUARD CAME TO QUESTION YOUR MOTHER, AND SHE--SHE ESCAPED OR SOMETHING.
SHE'S FINE. MERA WASN'T WORRIED AT ALL, AND--WELL, YOU KNOW HOW MERA IS. SHE'S ALWAYS IN CONTR--
NO, NO, NO...THAT'S NOT--OH MY GOD...

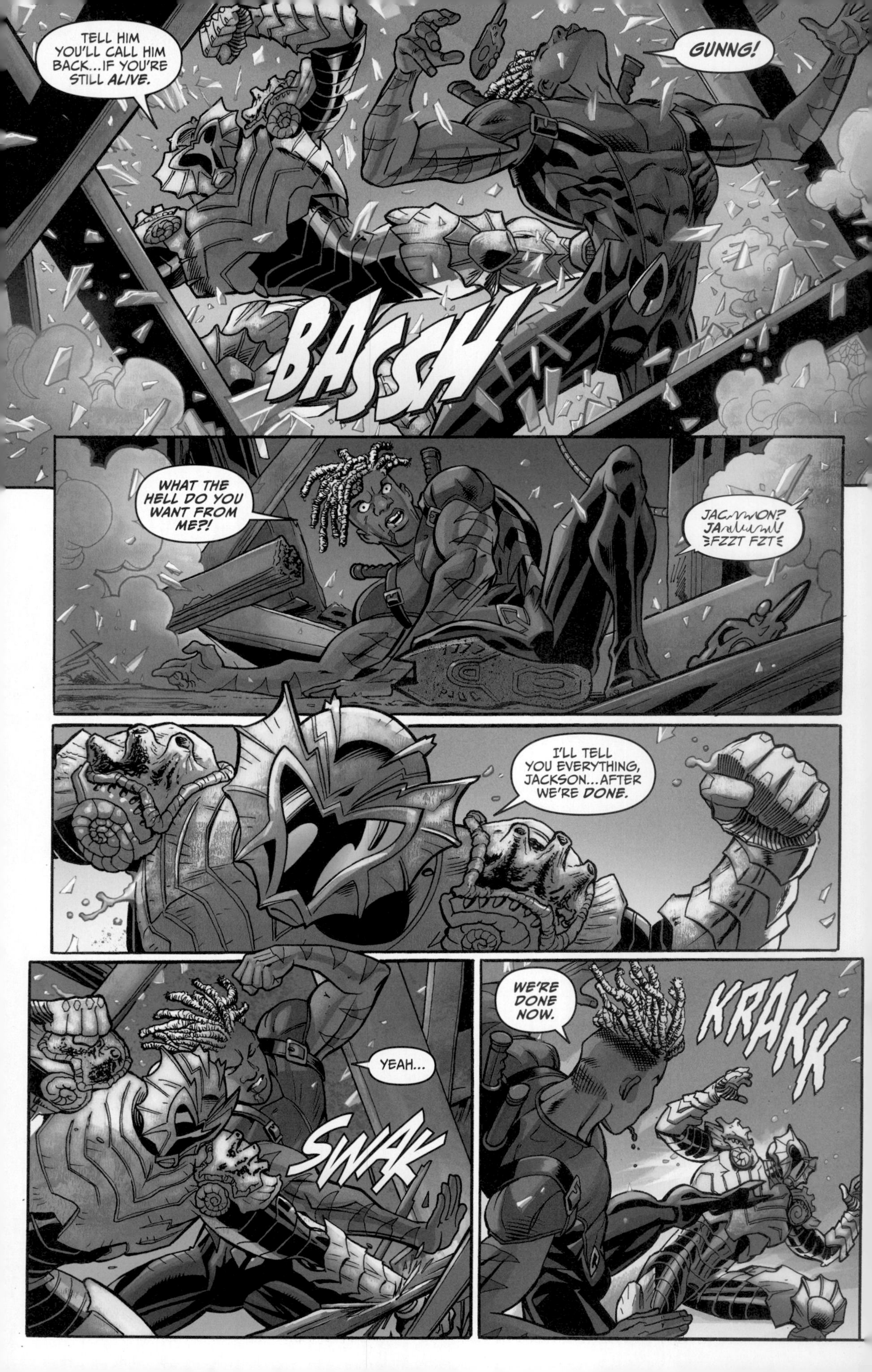

TELL HIM YOU'LL CALL HIM BACK...IF YOU'RE STILL ALIVE.
GUNNG!
BASSH
WHAT THE HELL DO YOU WANT FROM ME?!
FZZT FZT
I'LL TELL YOU EVERYTHING, JACKSON...AFTER WE'RE DONE.
YEAH...
SWAK
WE'RE DONE NOW.
KRAKK

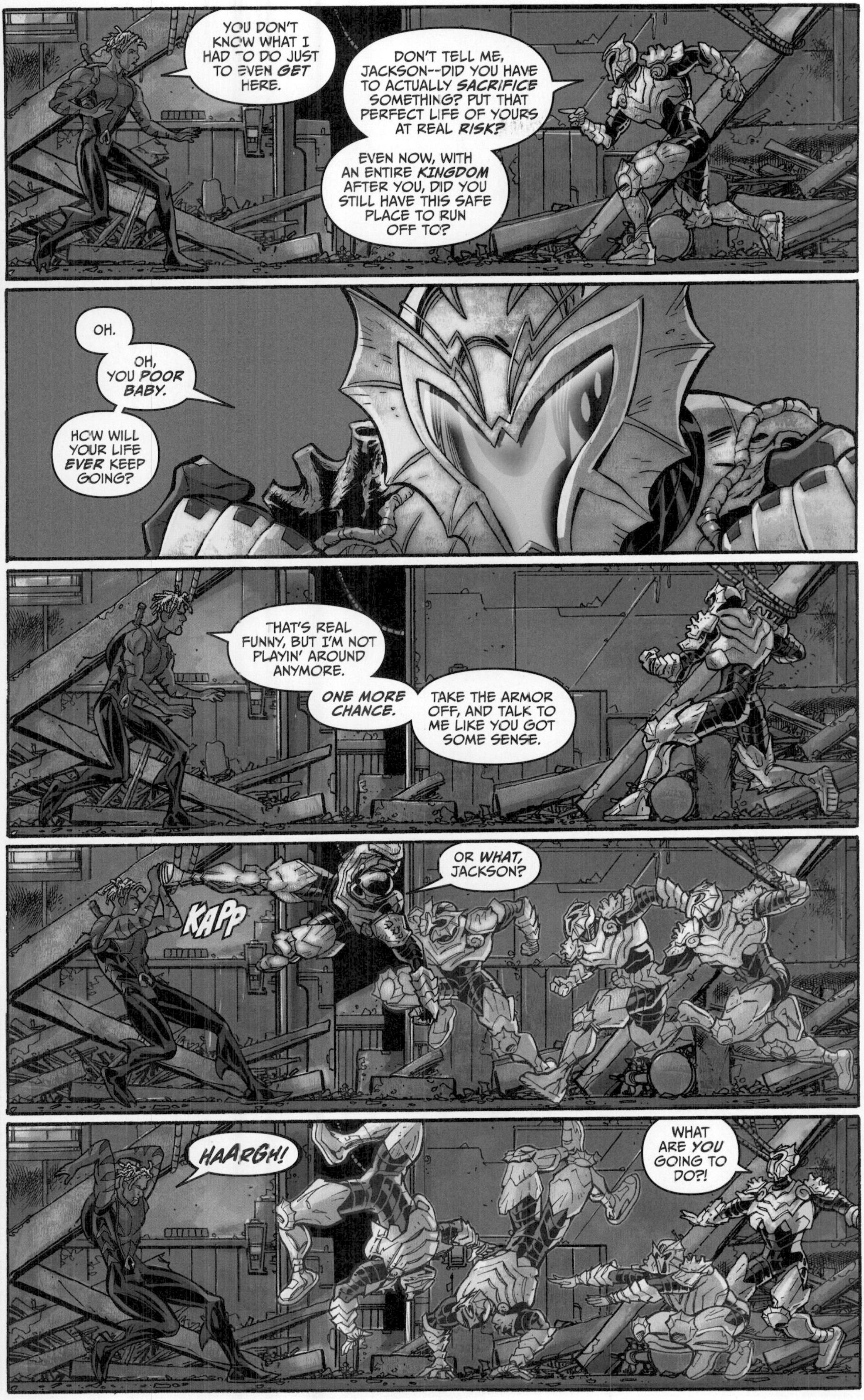
YOU DON'T KNOW WHAT I HAD TO DO JUST TO EVEN GET HERE.
DON'T TELL ME, JACKSON--DID YOU HAVE TO ACTUALLY SACRIFICE SOMETHING? PUT THAT PERFECT LIFE OF YOURS AT REAL RISK?
EVEN NOW, WITH AN ENTIRE KINGDOM AFTER YOU, DID YOU STILL HAVE THIS SAFE PLACE TO RUN OFF TO?
OH.
OH, YOU POOR BABY.
HOW WILL YOUR LIFE EVER KEEP GOING?
THAT'S REAL FUNNY, BUT I'M NOT PLAYIN' AROUND ANYMORE.
ONE MORE CHANCE.
TAKE THE ARMOR OFF, AND TALK TO ME LIKE YOU GOT SOME SENSE.
KAPP
OR WHAT, JACKSON?
HAARGH!
WHAT ARE YOU GOING TO DO?!

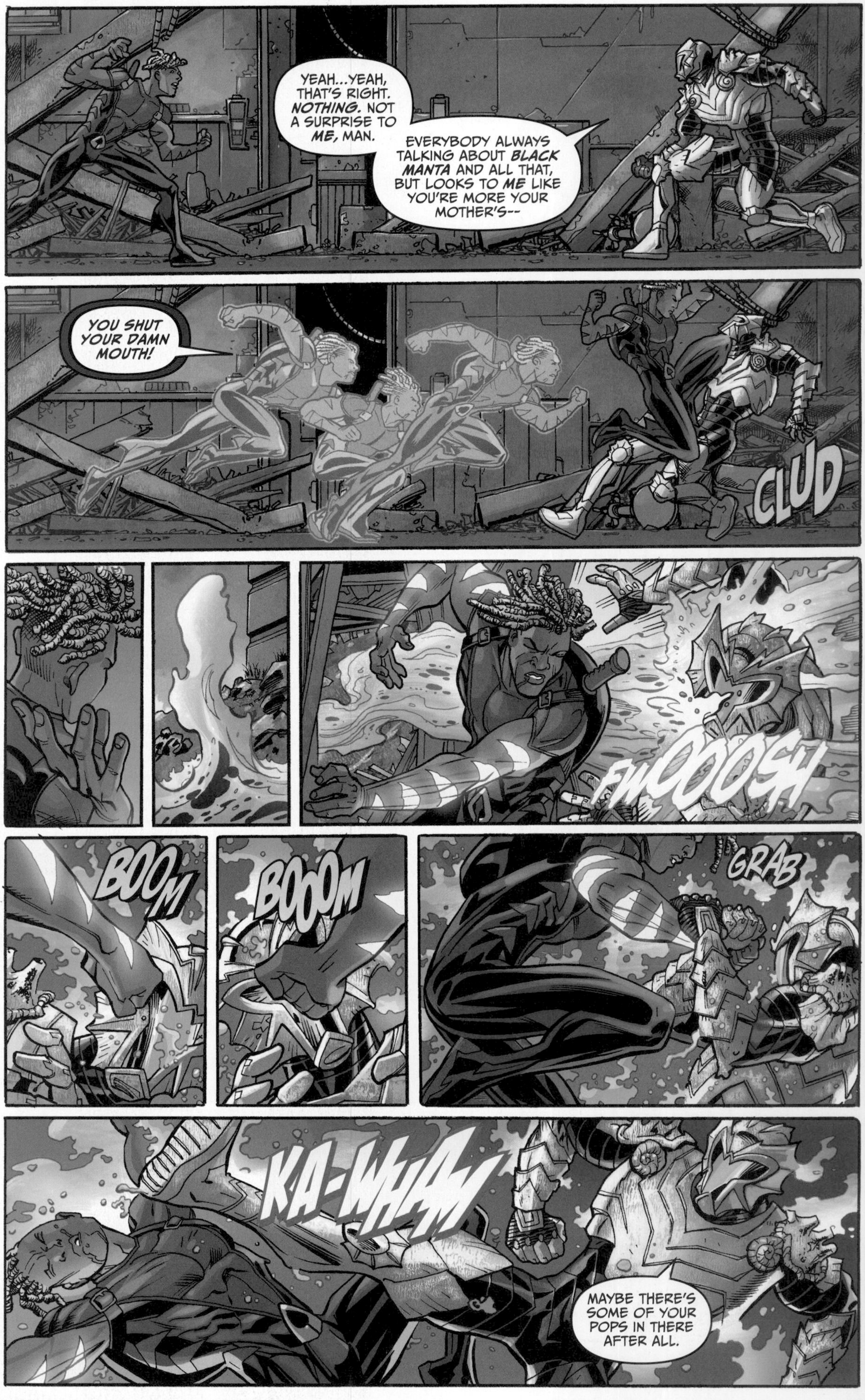
YEAH...YEAH, THAT'S RIGHT. NOTHING. NOT A SURPRISE TO ME, MAN.
EVERYBODY ALWAYS TALKING ABOUT BLACK MANTA AND ALL THAT, BUT LOOKS TO ME LIKE YOU'RE MORE YOUR MOTHER'S--
YOU SHUT YOUR DAMN MOUTH!
CLUD
FWOOOSH
BOOM
BOOOM
GRAB
KA-WHAM
MAYBE THERE'S SOME OF YOUR POPS IN THERE AFTER ALL.

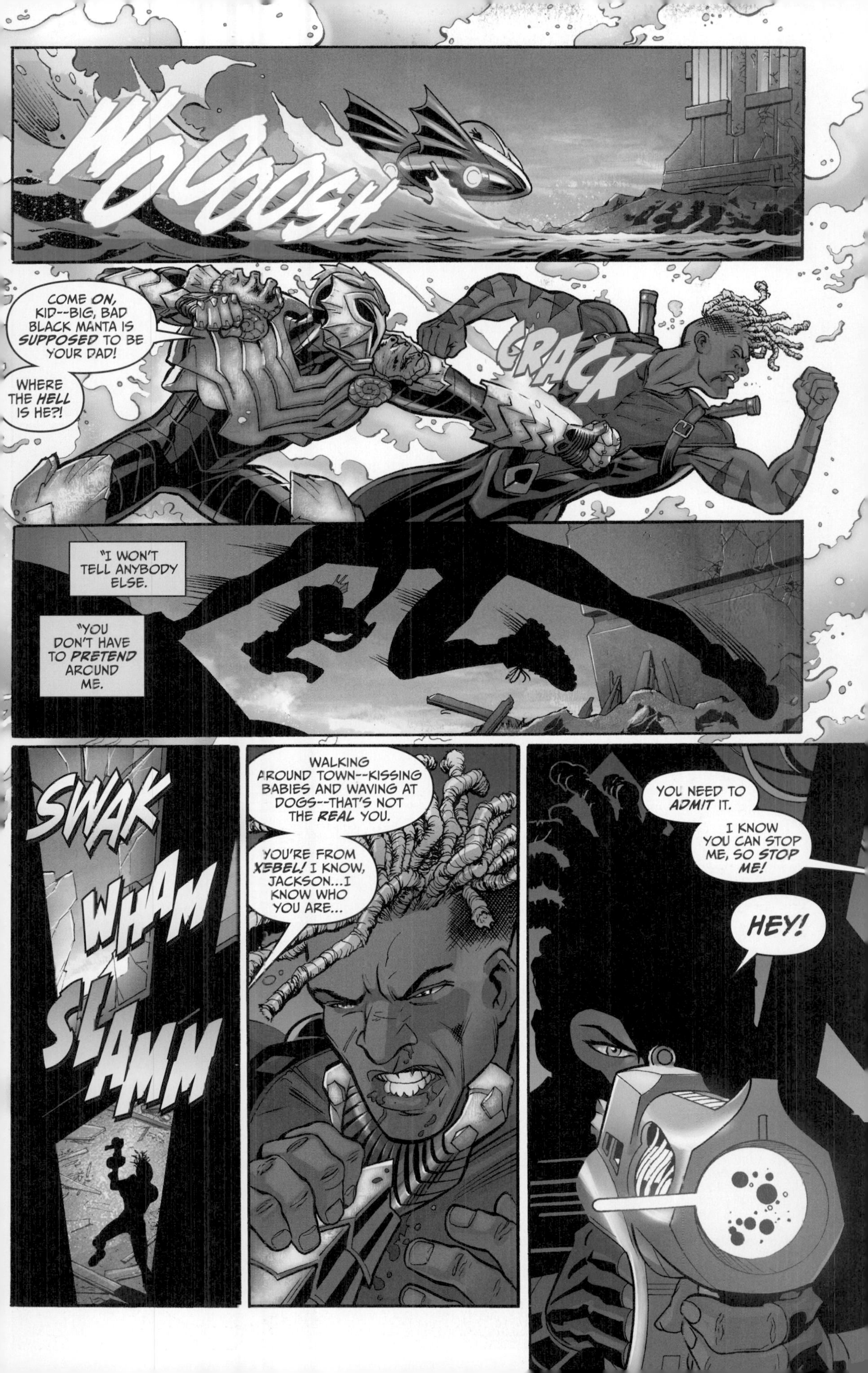
WOOOOSH
COME ON, KID--BIG, BAD BLACK MANTA IS SUPPOSED TO BE YOUR DAD!
WHERE THE HELL IS HE?!
CRACK
"I WON'T TELL ANYBODY ELSE.
"YOU DON'T HAVE TO PRETEND AROUND ME.
SWAK
WHAM
SLAMM
WALKING AROUND TOWN--KISSING BABIES AND WAVING AT DOGS--THAT'S NOT THE REAL YOU.
YOU'RE FROM XEBEL! I KNOW, JACKSON...I KNOW WHO YOU ARE...
YOU NEED TO ADMIT IT.
I KNOW YOU CAN STOP ME, SO STOP ME!
HEY!

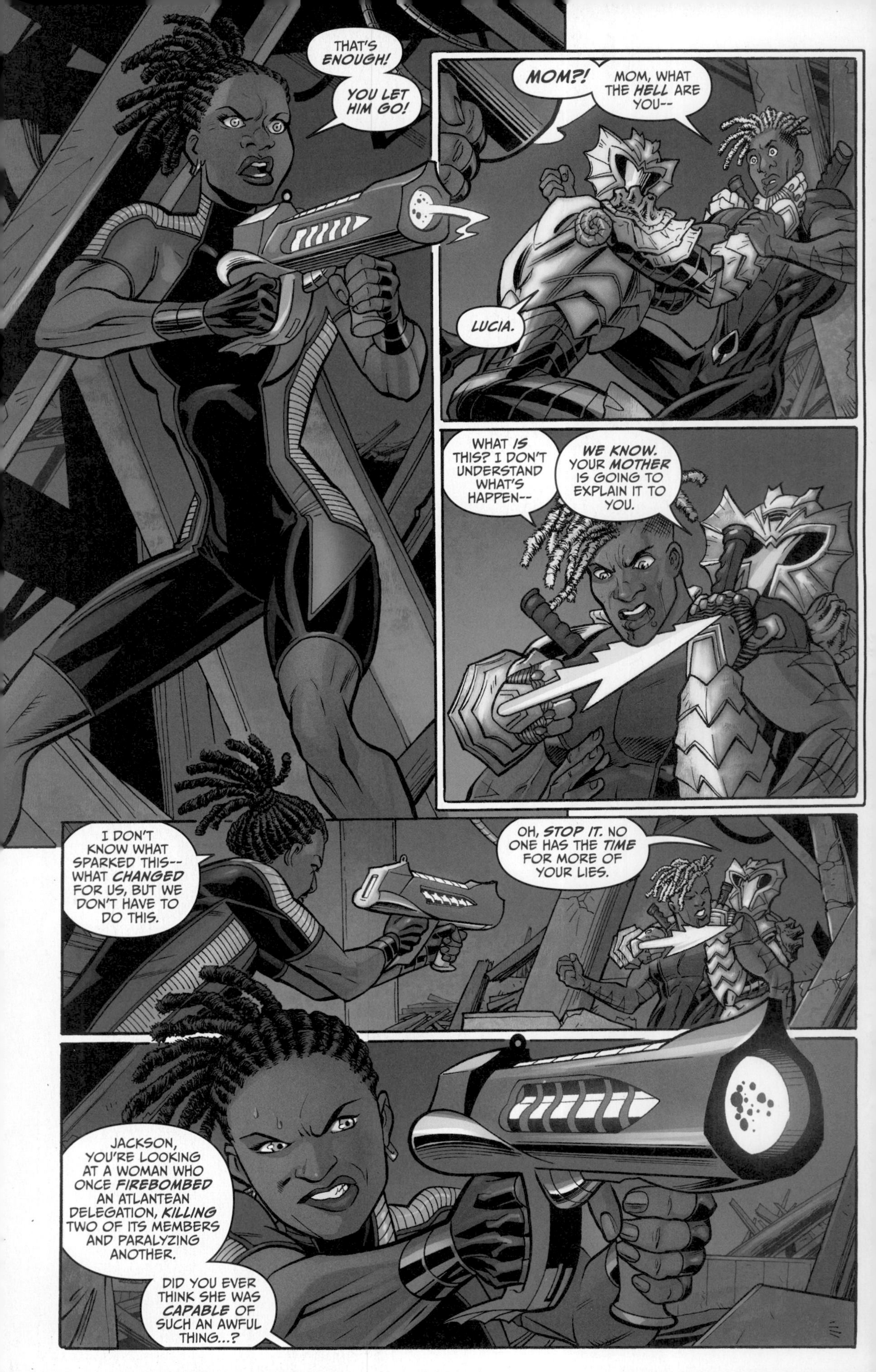

THAT'S ENOUGH!
YOU LET HIM GO!
MOM?!
MOM, WHAT THE HELL ARE YOU--
LUCIA.
WHAT IS THIS? I DON'T UNDERSTAND WHAT'S HAPPEN--
WE KNOW. YOUR MOTHER IS GOING TO EXPLAIN IT TO YOU.
I DON'T KNOW WHAT SPARKED THIS-- WHAT CHANGED FOR US, BUT WE DON'T HAVE TO DO THIS.
OH, STOP IT. NO ONE HAS THE TIME FOR MORE OF YOUR LIES.
JACKSON, YOU'RE LOOKING AT A WOMAN WHO ONCE FIREBOMBED AN ATLANTEAN DELEGATION, KILLING TWO OF ITS MEMBERS AND PARALYZING ANOTHER.
DID YOU EVER THINK SHE WAS CAPABLE OF SUCH AN AWFUL THING...?

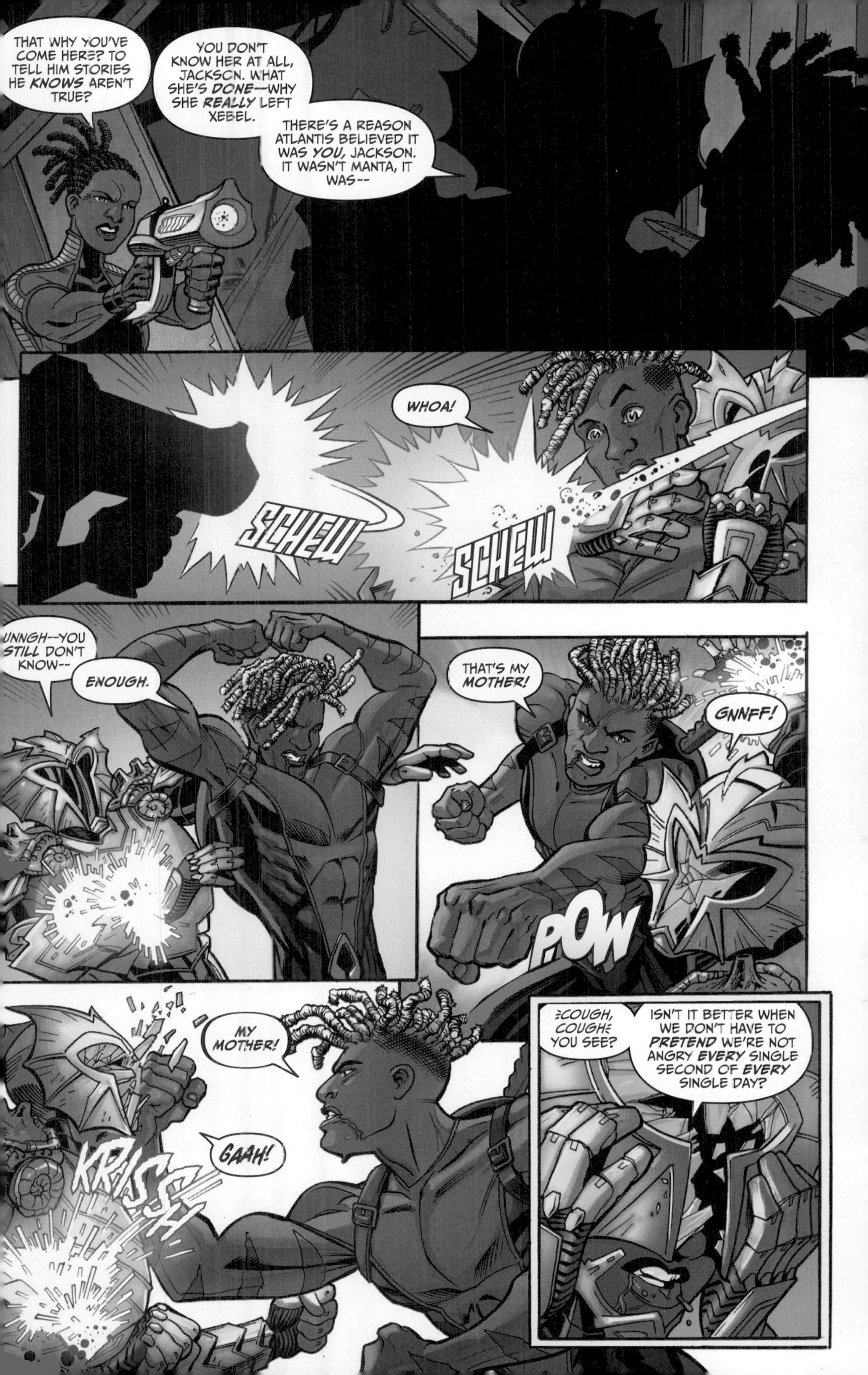
THAT WHY YOU'VE COME HERE? TO TELL HIM STORIES HE KNOWS AREN'T TRUE?
YOU DON'T KNOW HER AT ALL, JACKSON. WHAT SHE'S DONE--WHY SHE REALLY LEFT XEBEL.
THERE'S A REASON ATLANTIS BELIEVED IT WAS YOU, JACKSON. IT WASN'T MANTA, IT WAS--
WHOA!
SCHEW
SCHEW
UNNGH--YOU STILL DON'T KNOW--
ENOUGH.
THAT'S MY MOTHER!
GNNFF!
POW
MY MOTHER!
GAAH!
KRISSS
COUGH, COUGH YOU SEE?
ISN'T IT BETTER WHEN WE DON'T HAVE TO PRETEND WE'RE NOT ANGRY EVERY SINGLE SECOND OF EVERY SINGLE DAY?

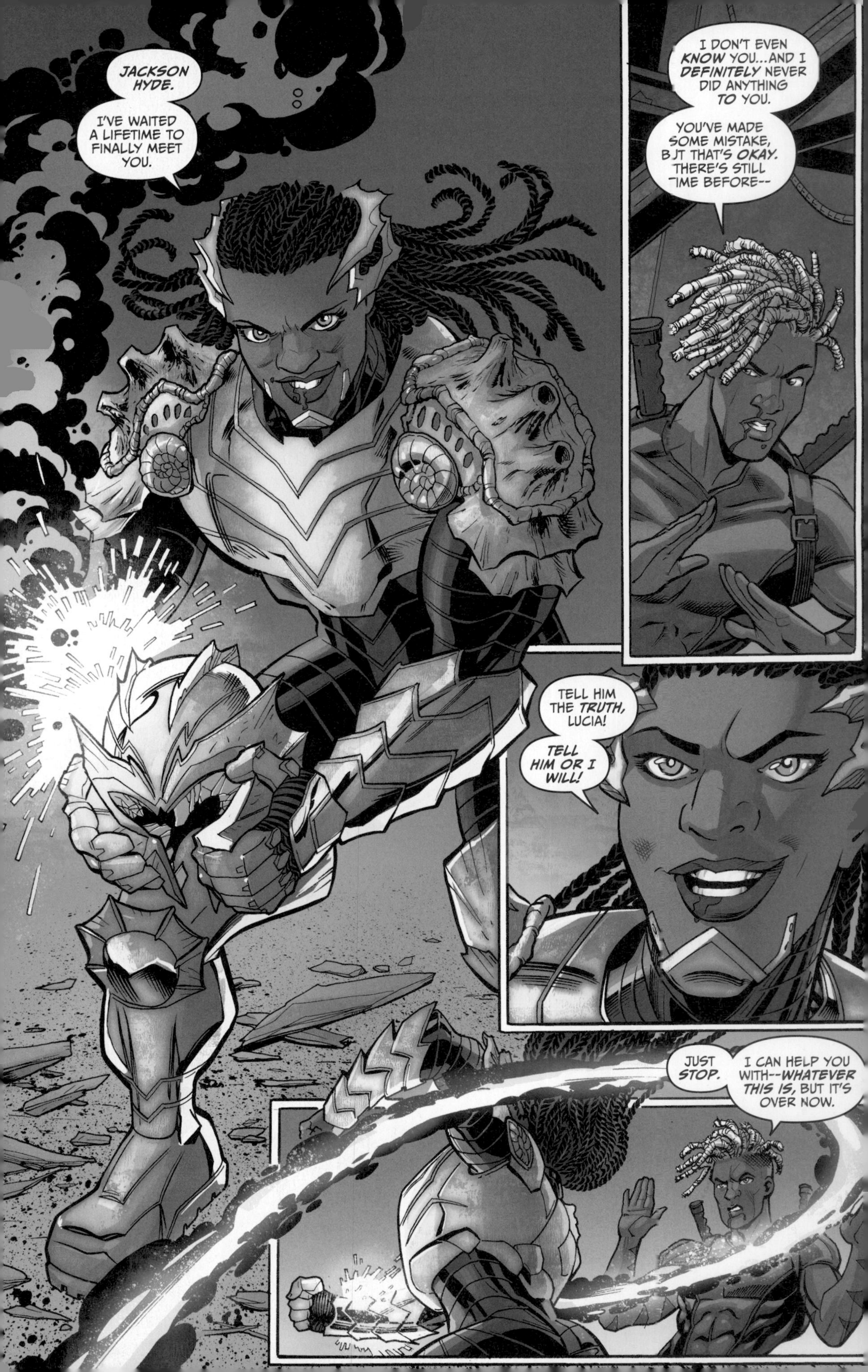
JACKSON HYDE.
I'VE WAITED A LIFETIME TO FINALLY MEET YOU.
I DON'T EVEN KNOW YOU...AND I DEFINITELY NEVER DID ANYTHING TO YOU.
YOU'VE MADE SOME MISTAKE, BUT THAT'S OKAY. THERE'S STILL TIME BEFORE--
TELL HIM THE TRUTH, LUCIA!
TELL HIM OR I WILL!
JUST STOP.
I CAN HELP YOU WITH--WHATEVER THIS IS, BUT IT'S OVER NOW.

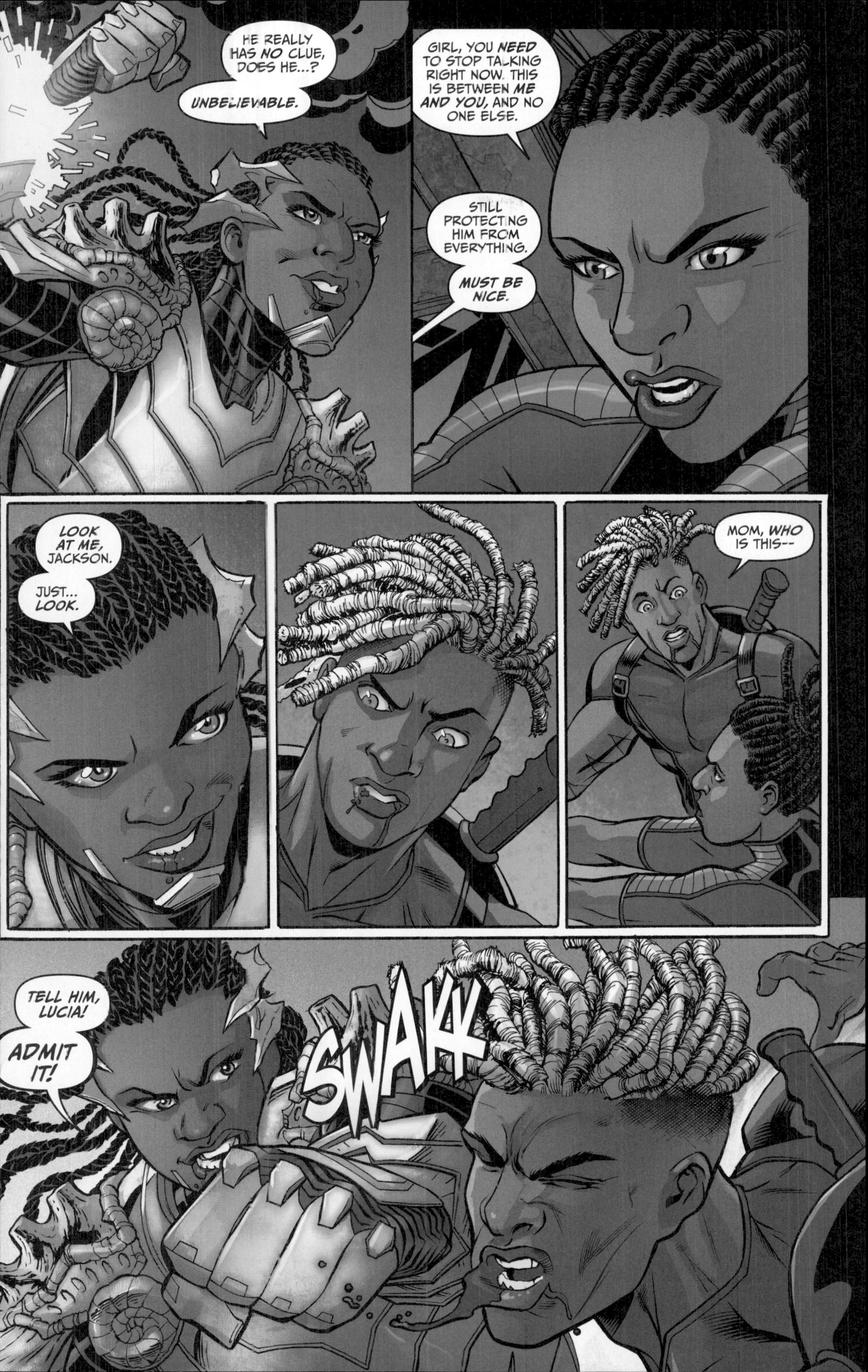
HE REALLY HAS NO CLUE, DOES HE...?
UNBELIEVABLE.
GIRL, YOU NEED TO STOP TALKING RIGHT NOW. THIS IS BETWEEN ME AND YOU, AND NO ONE ELSE.
STILL PROTECTING HIM FROM EVERYTHING.
MUST BE NICE.
LOOK AT ME, JACKSON.
JUST... LOOK.
MOM, WHO IS THIS--
TELL HIM, LUCIA!
ADMIT IT!
SWAKK

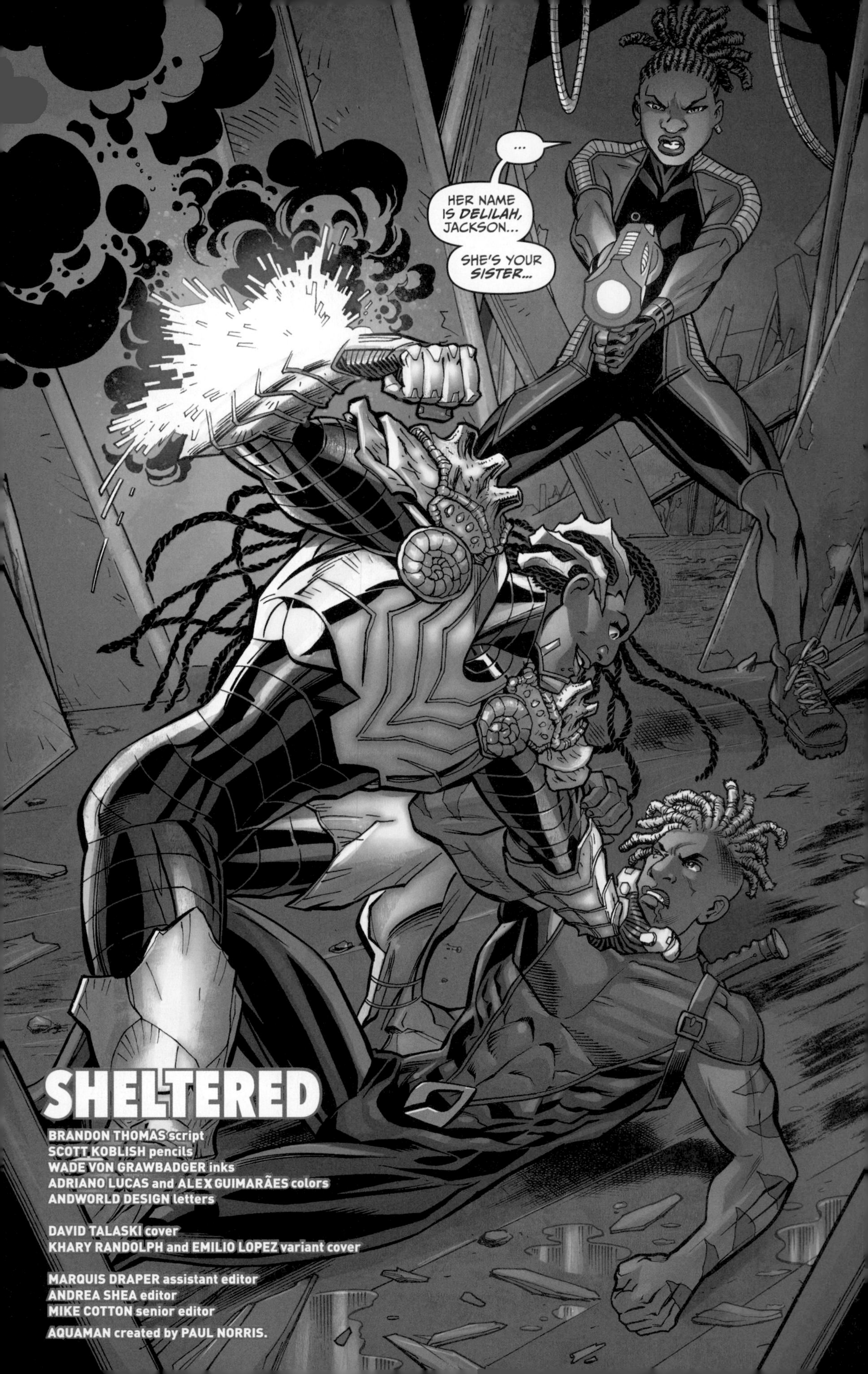
...
HER NAME IS DELILAH, JACKSON...
SHE'S YOUR SISTER...

SHELTERED

BRANDON THOMAS script
SCOTT KOBLISH pencils
WADE VON GRAWBADGER inks
ADRIANO LUCAS and **ALEX GUIMARÃES** colors
ANDWORLD DESIGN letters

DAVID TALASKI cover
KHARY RANDOLPH and **EMILIO LOPEZ** variant cover

MARQUIS DRAPER assistant editor
ANDREA SHEA editor
MIKE COTTON senior editor

AQUAMAN created by **PAUL NORRIS.**

AQUAMAN: THE BECOMING #4 cover by DAVID TALASKI

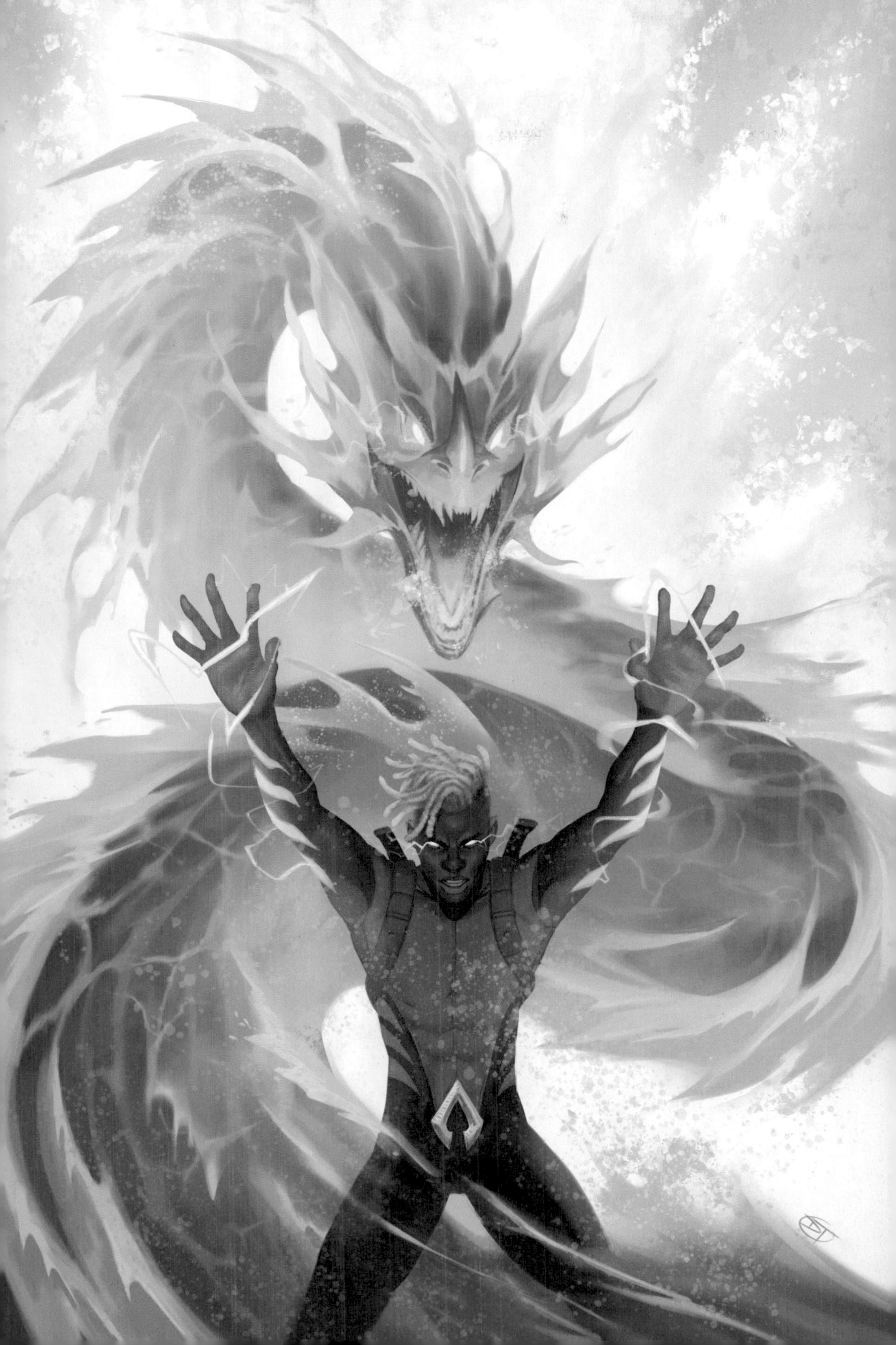

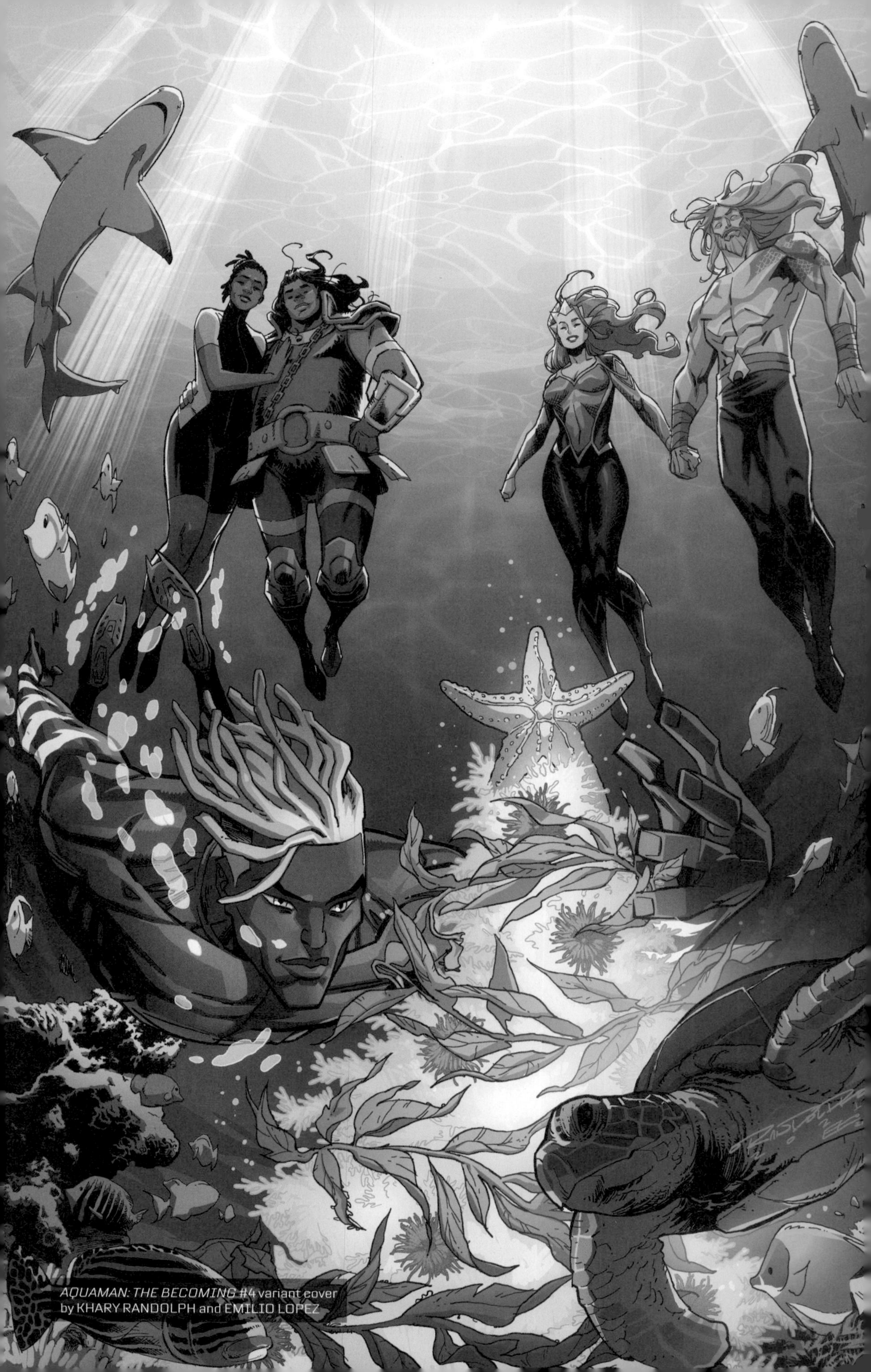
AQUAMAN: THE BECOMING #4 variant cover
by KHARY RANDOLPH and EMILIO LOPEZ

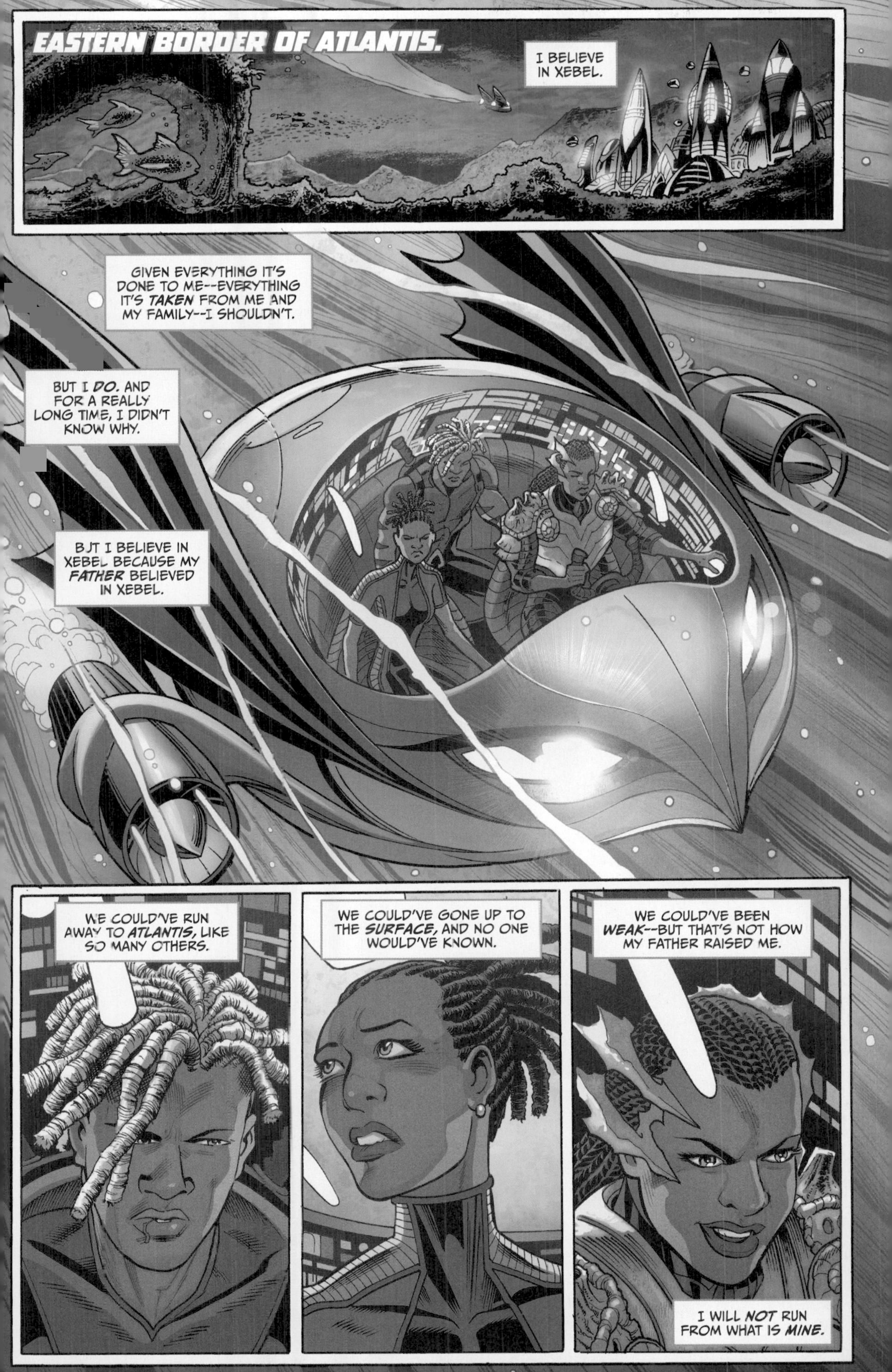
EASTERN BORDER OF ATLANTIS.
I BELIEVE IN XEBEL.
GIVEN EVERYTHING IT'S DONE TO ME--EVERYTHING IT'S TAKEN FROM ME AND MY FAMILY--I SHOULDN'T.
BUT I DO. AND FOR A REALLY LONG TIME, I DIDN'T KNOW WHY.
BUT I BELIEVE IN XEBEL BECAUSE MY FATHER BELIEVED IN XEBEL.
WE COULD'VE RUN AWAY TO ATLANTIS, LIKE SO MANY OTHERS.
WE COULD'VE GONE UP TO THE SURFACE, AND NO ONE WOULD'VE KNOWN.
WE COULD'VE BEEN WEAK--BUT THAT'S NOT HOW MY FATHER RAISED ME.
I WILL NOT RUN FROM WHAT IS MINE.

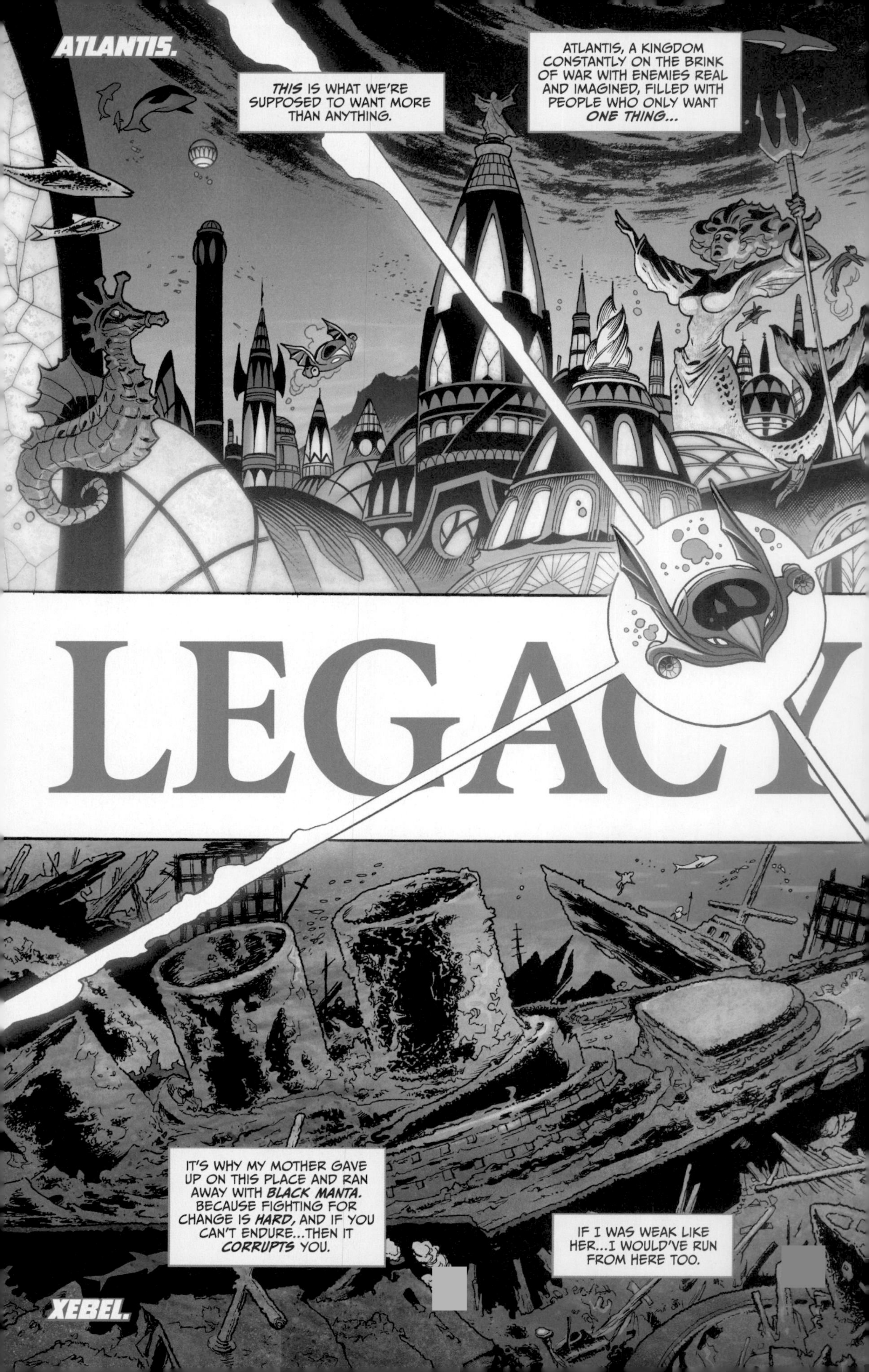
ATLANTIS.
THIS IS WHAT WE'RE SUPPOSED TO WANT MORE THAN ANYTHING.
ATLANTIS, A KINGDOM CONSTANTLY ON THE BRINK OF WAR WITH ENEMIES REAL AND IMAGINED, FILLED WITH PEOPLE WHO ONLY WANT ONE THING...
LEGACY
IT'S WHY MY MOTHER GAVE UP ON THIS PLACE AND RAN AWAY WITH BLACK MANTA. BECAUSE FIGHTING FOR CHANGE IS HARD, AND IF YOU CAN'T ENDURE...THEN IT CORRUPTS YOU.
IF I WAS WEAK LIKE HER...I WOULD'VE RUN FROM HERE TOO.
XEBEL.

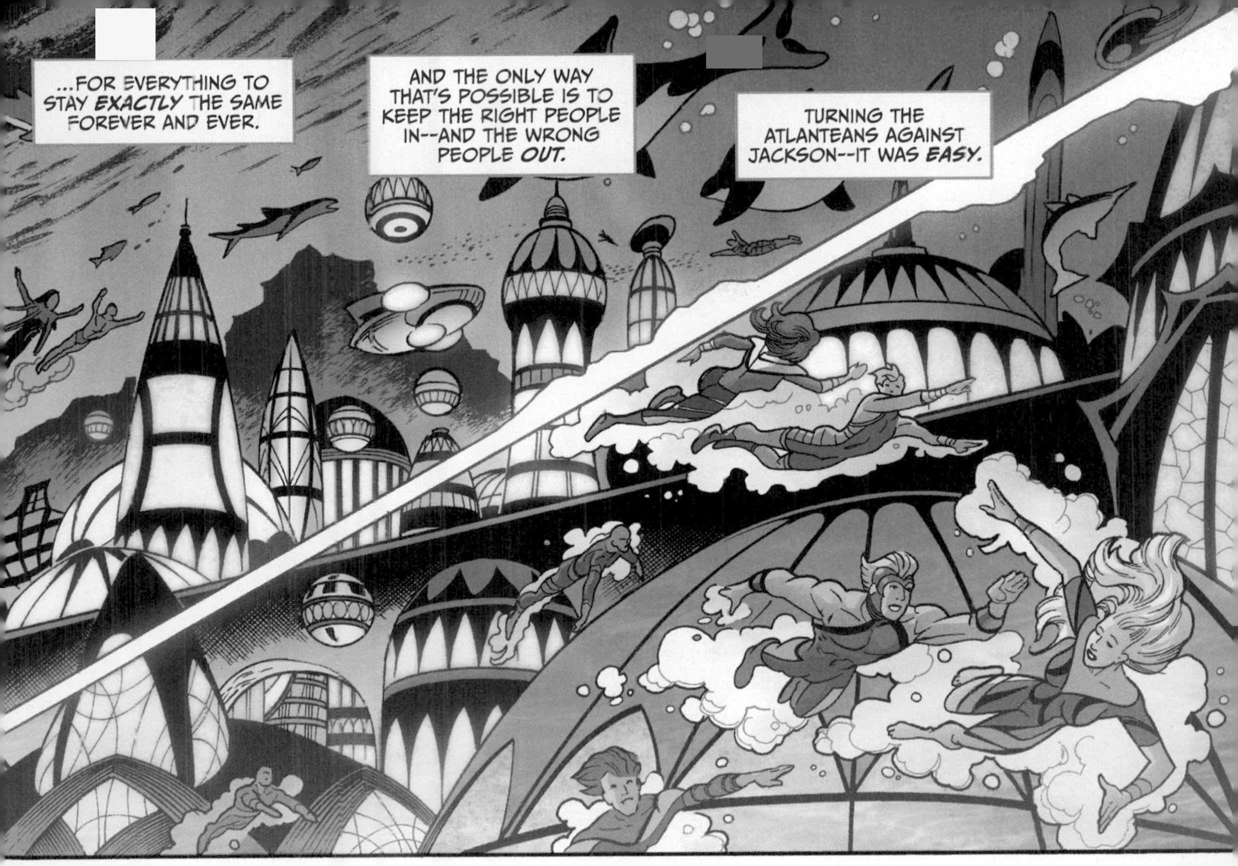
...FOR EVERYTHING TO STAY EXACTLY THE SAME FOREVER AND EVER.
AND THE ONLY WAY THAT'S POSSIBLE IS TO KEEP THE RIGHT PEOPLE IN--AND THE WRONG PEOPLE OUT.
TURNING THE ATLANTEANS AGAINST JACKSON--IT WAS EASY.

BRANDON THOMAS script **SCOTT KOBLISH** pencils
WADE VON GRAWBADGER inks **ADRIANO LUCAS** colors **ANDWORLD DESIGN** letters
DAVID TALASKI cover **KHARY RANDOLPH** and **EMILIO LOPEZ** variant cover
MARQUIS DRAPER assistant editor **ANDREA SHEA** editor
MIKE COTTON senior editor

AQUAMAN created by **PAUL NORRIS.**

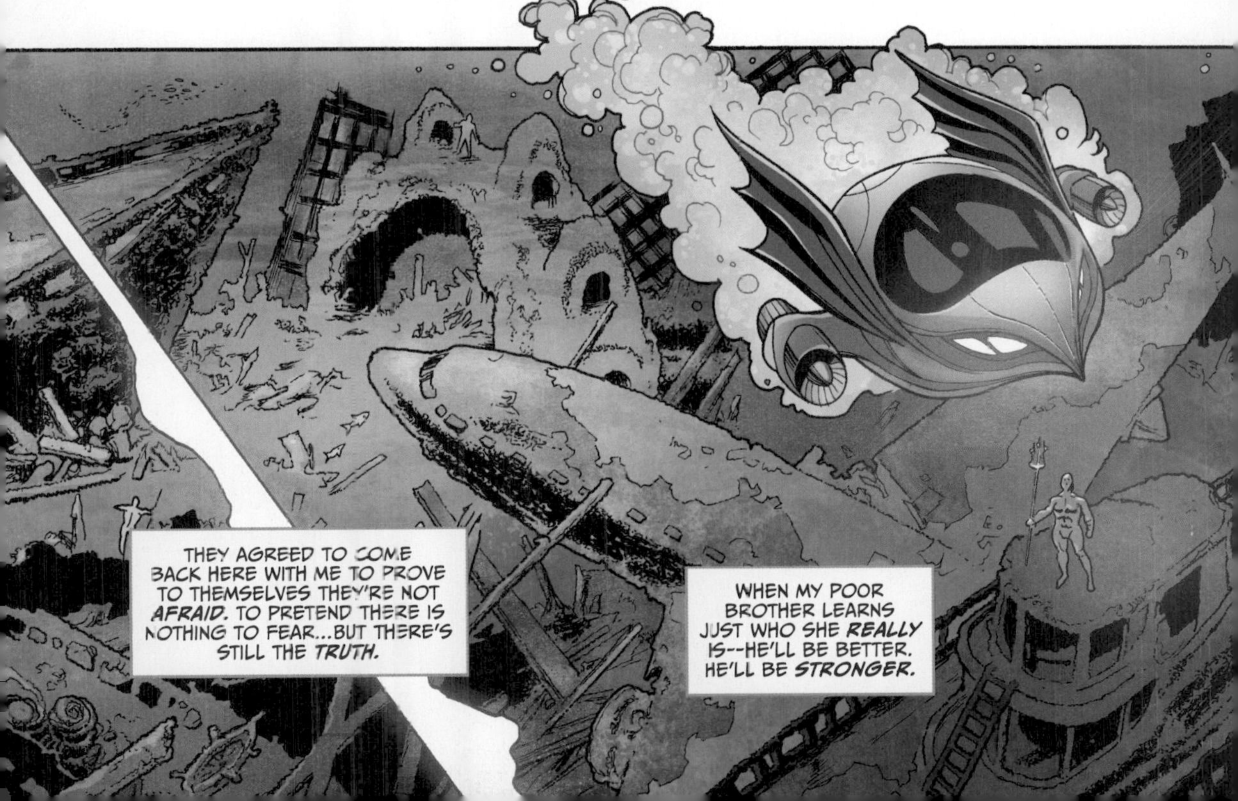
THEY AGREED TO COME BACK HERE WITH ME TO PROVE TO THEMSELVES THEY'RE NOT AFRAID. TO PRETEND THERE IS NOTHING TO FEAR...BUT THERE'S STILL THE TRUTH.
WHEN MY POOR BROTHER LEARNS JUST WHO SHE REALLY IS--HE'LL BE BETTER. HE'LL BE STRONGER.

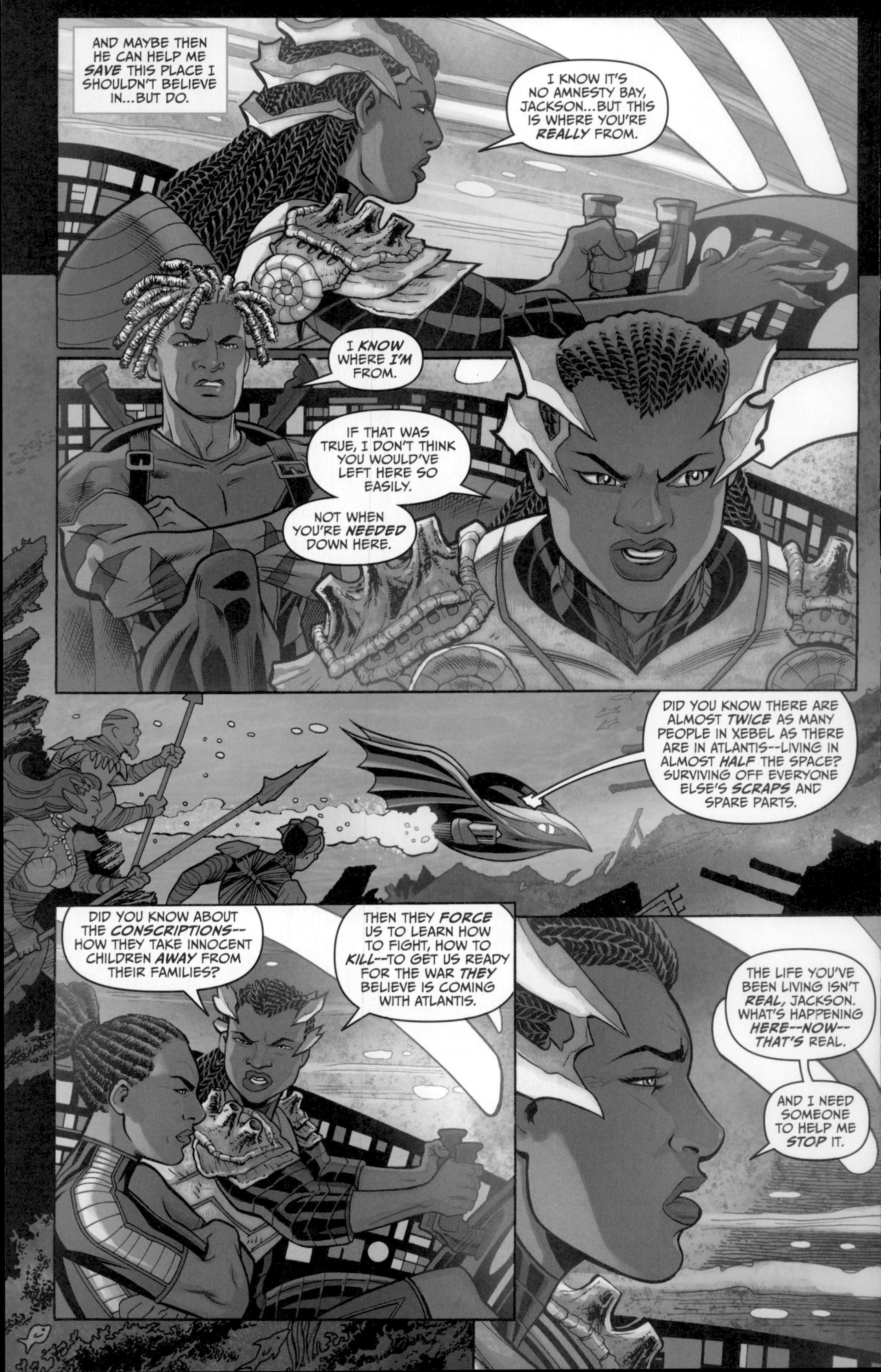
AND MAYBE THEN HE CAN HELP ME SAVE THIS PLACE I SHOULDN'T BELIEVE IN...BUT DO.
I KNOW IT'S NO AMNESTY BAY, JACKSON...BUT THIS IS WHERE YOU'RE REALLY FROM.
I KNOW WHERE I'M FROM.
IF THAT WAS TRUE, I DON'T THINK YOU WOULD'VE LEFT HERE SO EASILY.
NOT WHEN YOU'RE NEEDED DOWN HERE.
DID YOU KNOW THERE ARE ALMOST TWICE AS MANY PEOPLE IN XEBEL AS THERE ARE IN ATLANTIS--LIVING IN ALMOST HALF THE SPACE? SURVIVING OFF EVERYONE ELSE'S SCRAPS AND SPARE PARTS.
DID YOU KNOW ABOUT THE CONSCRIPTIONS--HOW THEY TAKE INNOCENT CHILDREN AWAY FROM THEIR FAMILIES?
THEN THEY FORCE US TO LEARN HOW TO FIGHT, HOW TO KILL--TO GET US READY FOR THE WAR THEY BELIEVE IS COMING WITH ATLANTIS.
THE LIFE YOU'VE BEEN LIVING ISN'T REAL, JACKSON. WHAT'S HAPPENING HERE--NOW--THAT'S REAL.
AND I NEED SOMEONE TO HELP ME STOP IT.

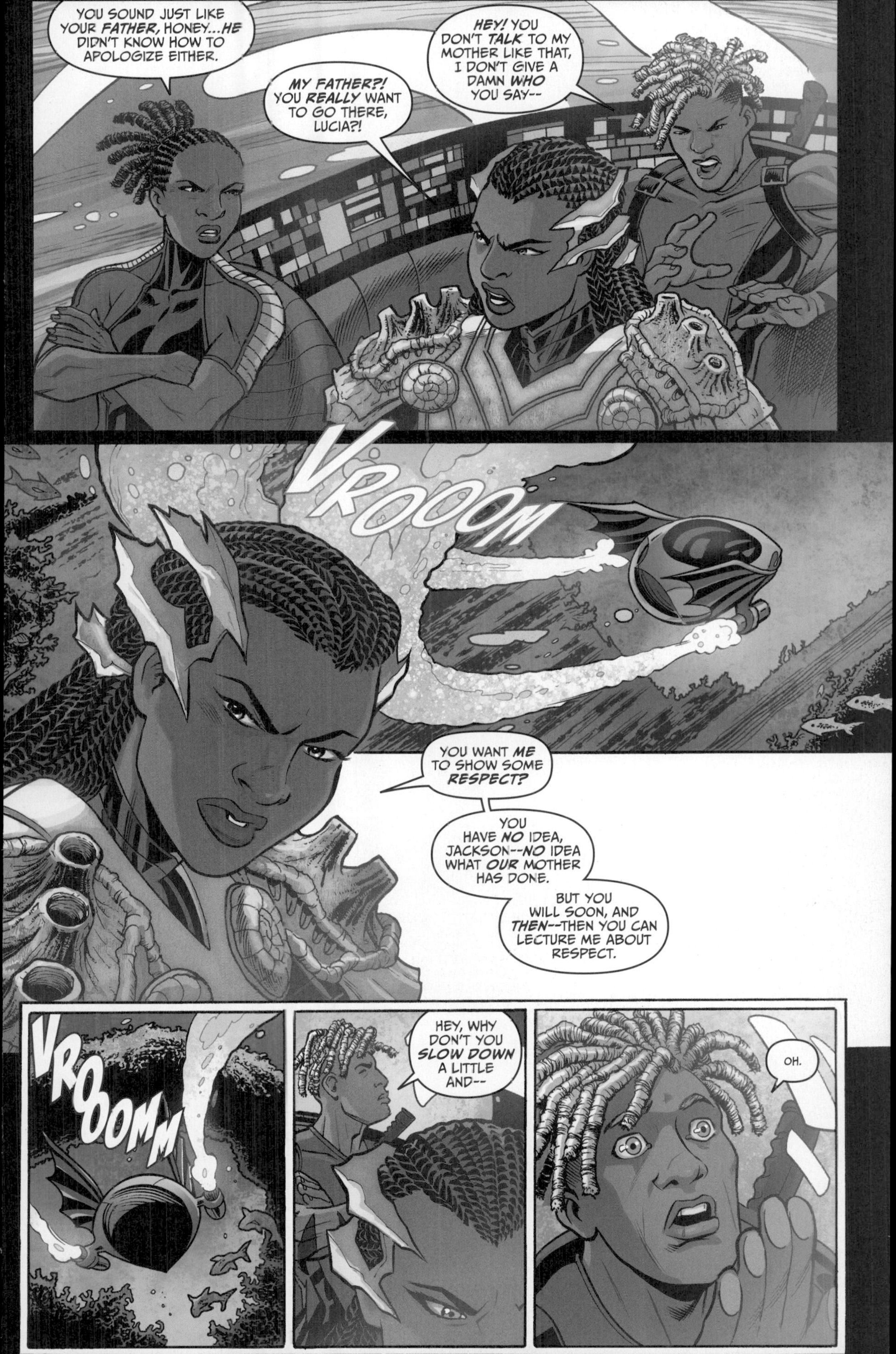
YOU SOUND JUST LIKE YOUR FATHER, HONEY...HE DIDN'T KNOW HOW TO APOLOGIZE EITHER.
MY FATHER?! YOU REALLY WANT TO GO THERE, LUCIA?!
HEY! YOU DON'T TALK TO MY MOTHER LIKE THAT, I DON'T GIVE A DAMN WHO YOU SAY--
VROOOM
YOU WANT ME TO SHOW SOME RESPECT?
YOU HAVE NO IDEA, JACKSON--NO IDEA WHAT OUR MOTHER HAS DONE.
BUT YOU WILL SOON, AND THEN--THEN YOU CAN LECTURE ME ABOUT RESPECT.
VROOOMM
HEY, WHY DON'T YOU SLOW DOWN A LITTLE AND--
OH.

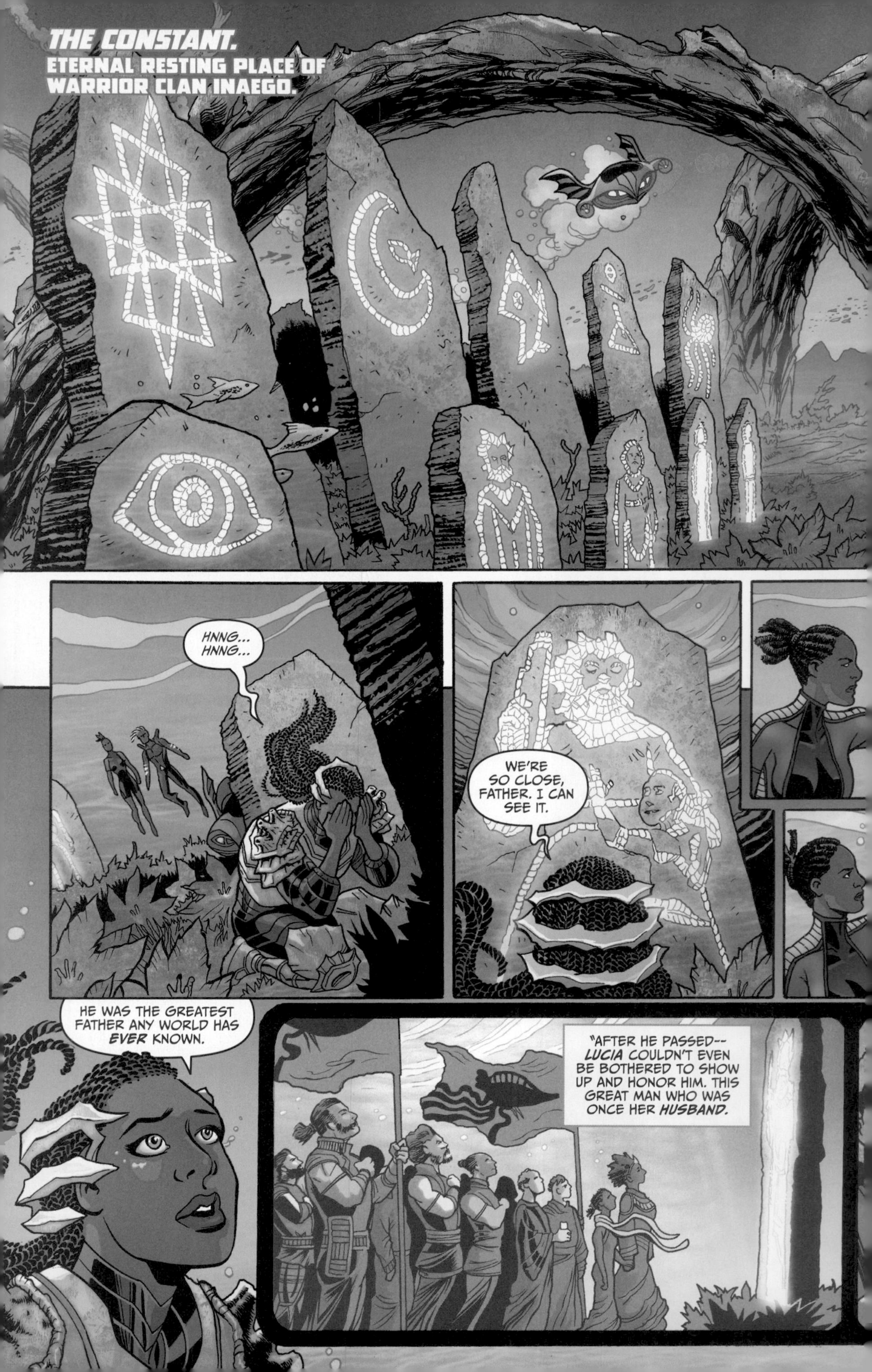
THE CONSTANT.
ETERNAL RESTING PLACE OF WARRIOR CLAN INAEGO.
HNNG... HNNG...
WE'RE SO CLOSE, FATHER. I CAN SEE IT.
HE WAS THE GREATEST FATHER ANY WORLD HAS *EVER* KNOWN.
"AFTER HE PASSED-- *LUCIA* COULDN'T EVEN BE BOTHERED TO SHOW UP AND HONOR HIM. THIS GREAT MAN WHO WAS ONCE HER *HUSBAND.*

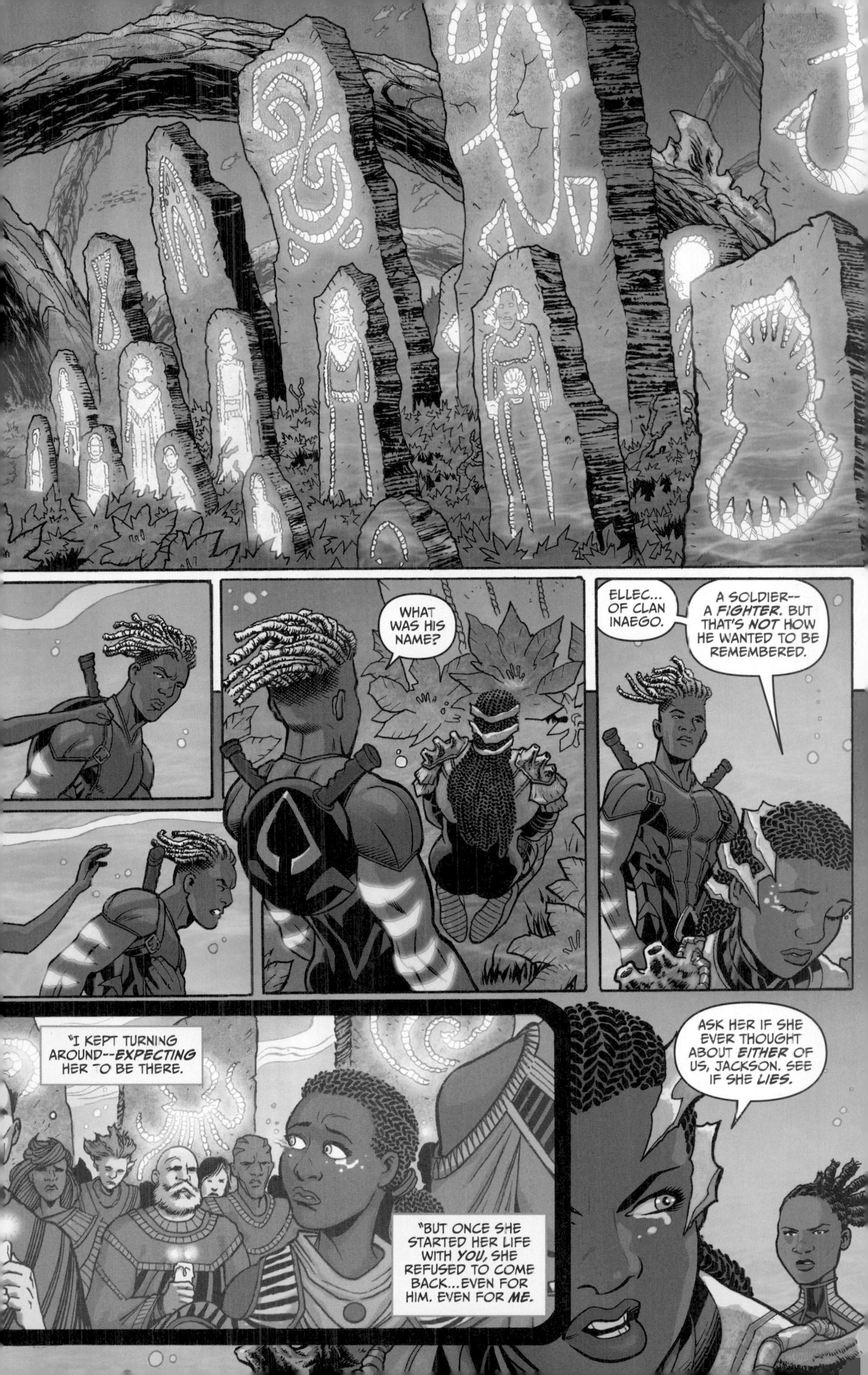
WHAT WAS HIS NAME?
ELLEC... OF CLAN INAEGO.
A SOLDIER-- A FIGHTER. BUT THAT'S NOT HOW HE WANTED TO BE REMEMBERED.
"I KEPT TURNING AROUND--EXPECTING HER TO BE THERE.
"BUT ONCE SHE STARTED HER LIFE WITH YOU, SHE REFUSED TO COME BACK...EVEN FOR HIM. EVEN FOR ME.
ASK HER IF SHE EVER THOUGHT ABOUT EITHER OF US, JACKSON. SEE IF SHE LIES.

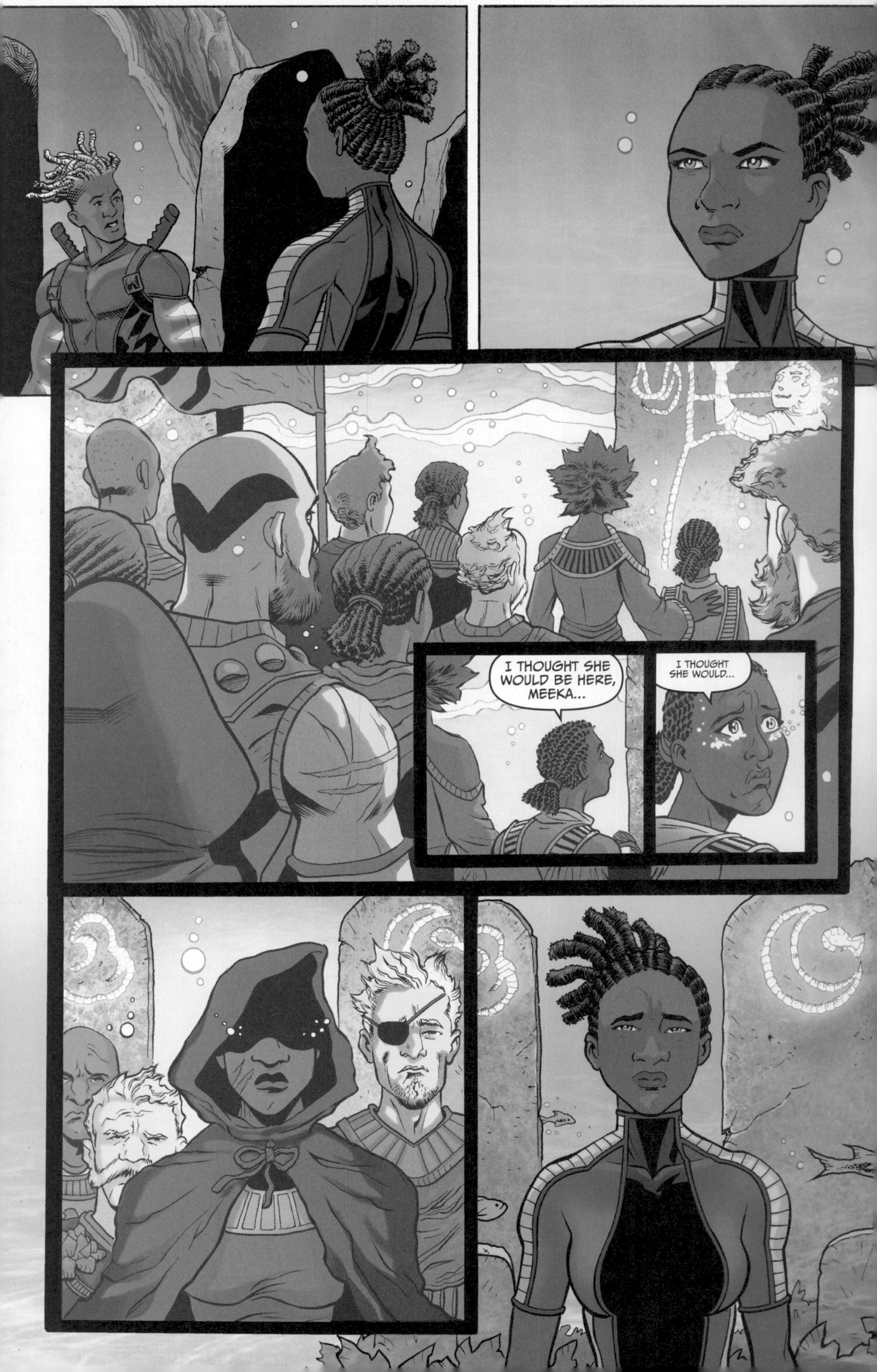
I THOUGHT SHE WOULD BE HERE, MEEKA...
I THOUGHT SHE WOULD...

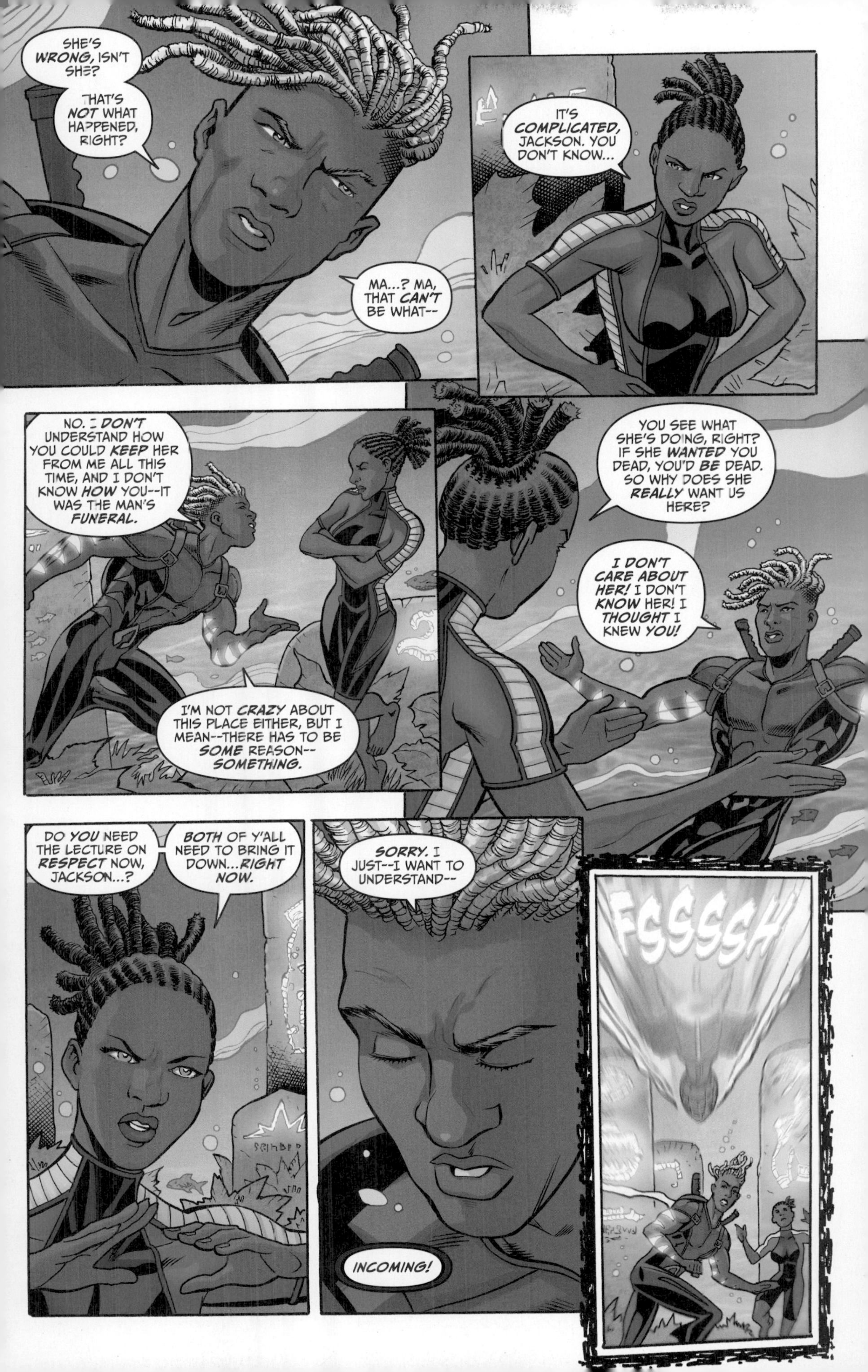

SHE'S WRONG, ISN'T SHE?
THAT'S NOT WHAT HAPPENED, RIGHT?
MA...? MA, THAT CAN'T BE WHAT--
IT'S COMPLICATED, JACKSON. YOU DON'T KNOW...
NO. I DON'T UNDERSTAND HOW YOU COULD KEEP HER FROM ME ALL THIS TIME, AND I DON'T KNOW HOW YOU--IT WAS THE MAN'S FUNERAL.
I'M NOT CRAZY ABOUT THIS PLACE EITHER, BUT I MEAN--THERE HAS TO BE SOME REASON--SOMETHING.
YOU SEE WHAT SHE'S DOING, RIGHT? IF SHE WANTED YOU DEAD, YOU'D BE DEAD. SO WHY DOES SHE REALLY WANT US HERE?
I DON'T CARE ABOUT HER! I DON'T KNOW HER! I THOUGHT I KNEW YOU!
DO YOU NEED THE LECTURE ON RESPECT NOW, JACKSON...?
BOTH OF Y'ALL NEED TO BRING IT DOWN...RIGHT NOW.
SORRY. I JUST--I WANT TO UNDERSTAND--
INCOMING!
FSSSSH

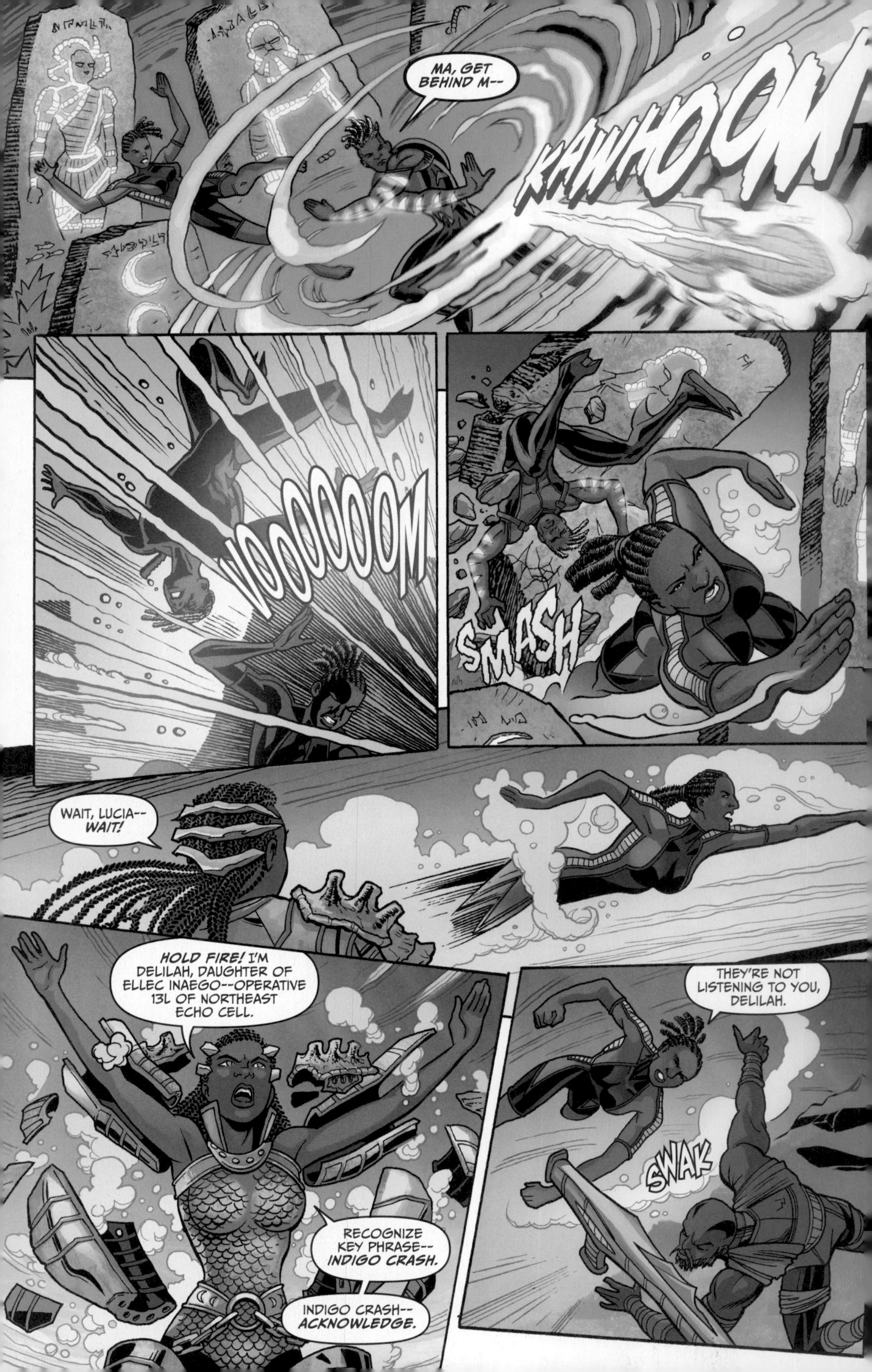
MA, GET BEHIND M--
KAWHOOOM
VOOOOOOM
SMASH
WAIT, LUCIA-- WAIT!
HOLD FIRE! I'M DELILAH, DAUGHTER OF ELLEC INAEGO--OPERATIVE 13L OF NORTHEAST ECHO CELL.
RECOGNIZE KEY PHRASE-- INDIGO CRASH.
INDIGO CRASH-- ACKNOWLEDGE.
THEY'RE NOT LISTENING TO YOU, DELILAH.
SWAK

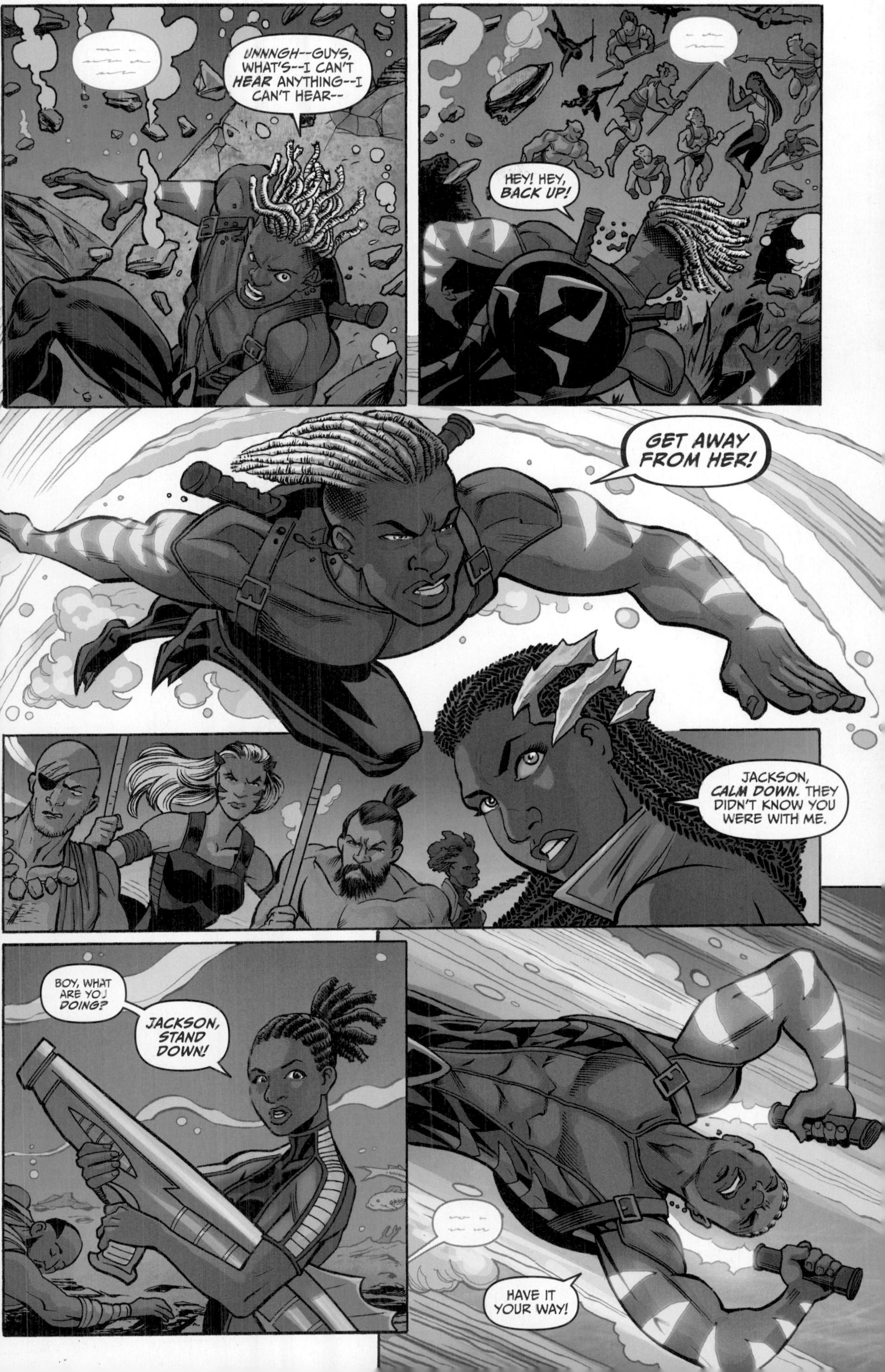
UNNNGH--GUYS, WHAT'S--I CAN'T HEAR ANYTHING--I CAN'T HEAR--
HEY! HEY, BACK UP!
GET AWAY FROM HER!
JACKSON, CALM DOWN. THEY DIDN'T KNOW YOU WERE WITH ME.
BOY, WHAT ARE YOU DOING?
JACKSON, STAND DOWN!
HAVE IT YOUR WAY!

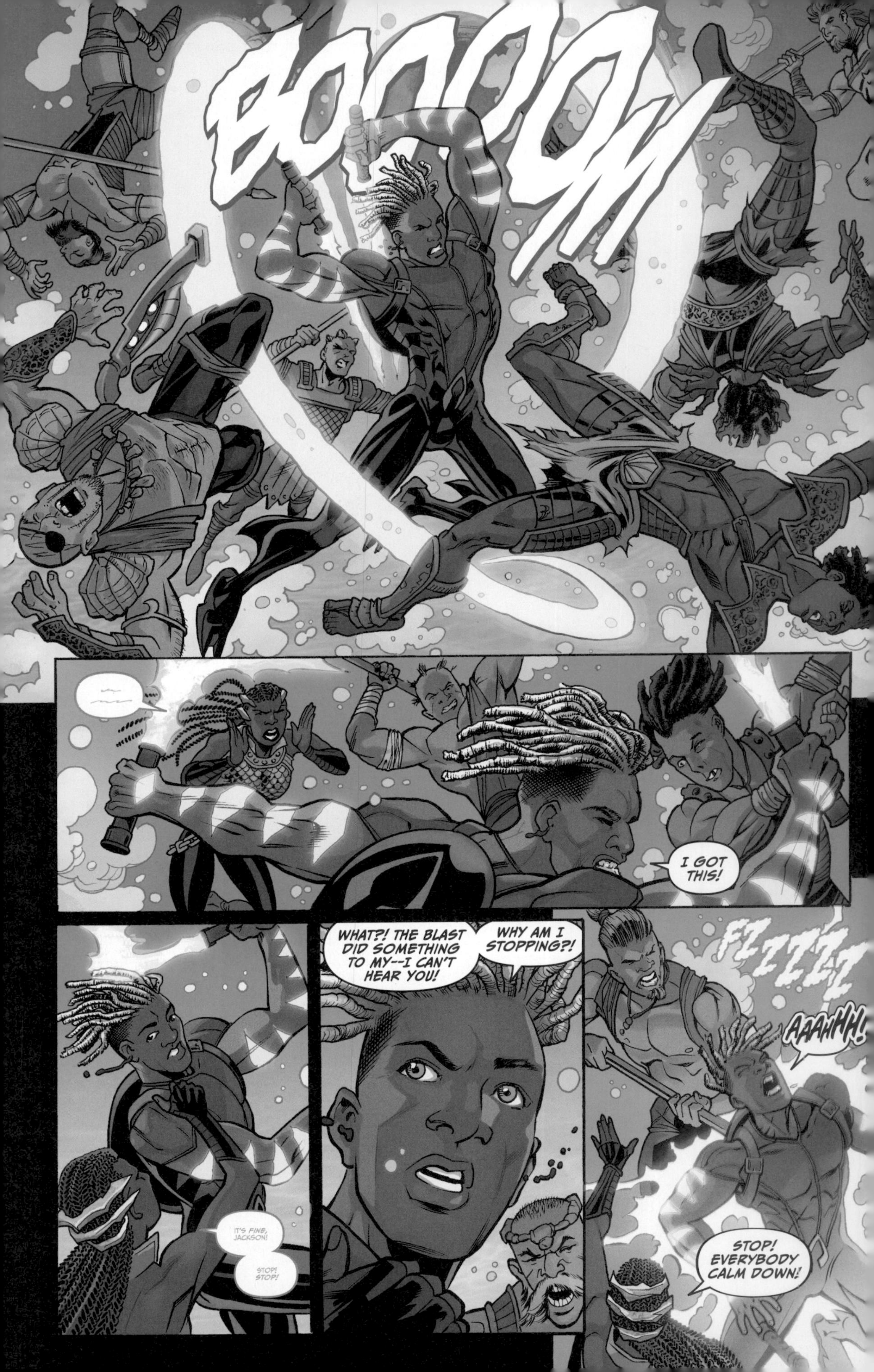
BOOOOM
I GOT THIS!
IT'S FINE, JACKSON!
STOP! STOP!
WHAT?! THE BLAST DID SOMETHING TO MY--I CAN'T HEAR YOU!
WHY AM I STOPPING?!
FZZZZZ
AAAHHH!
STOP! EVERYBODY CALM DOWN!

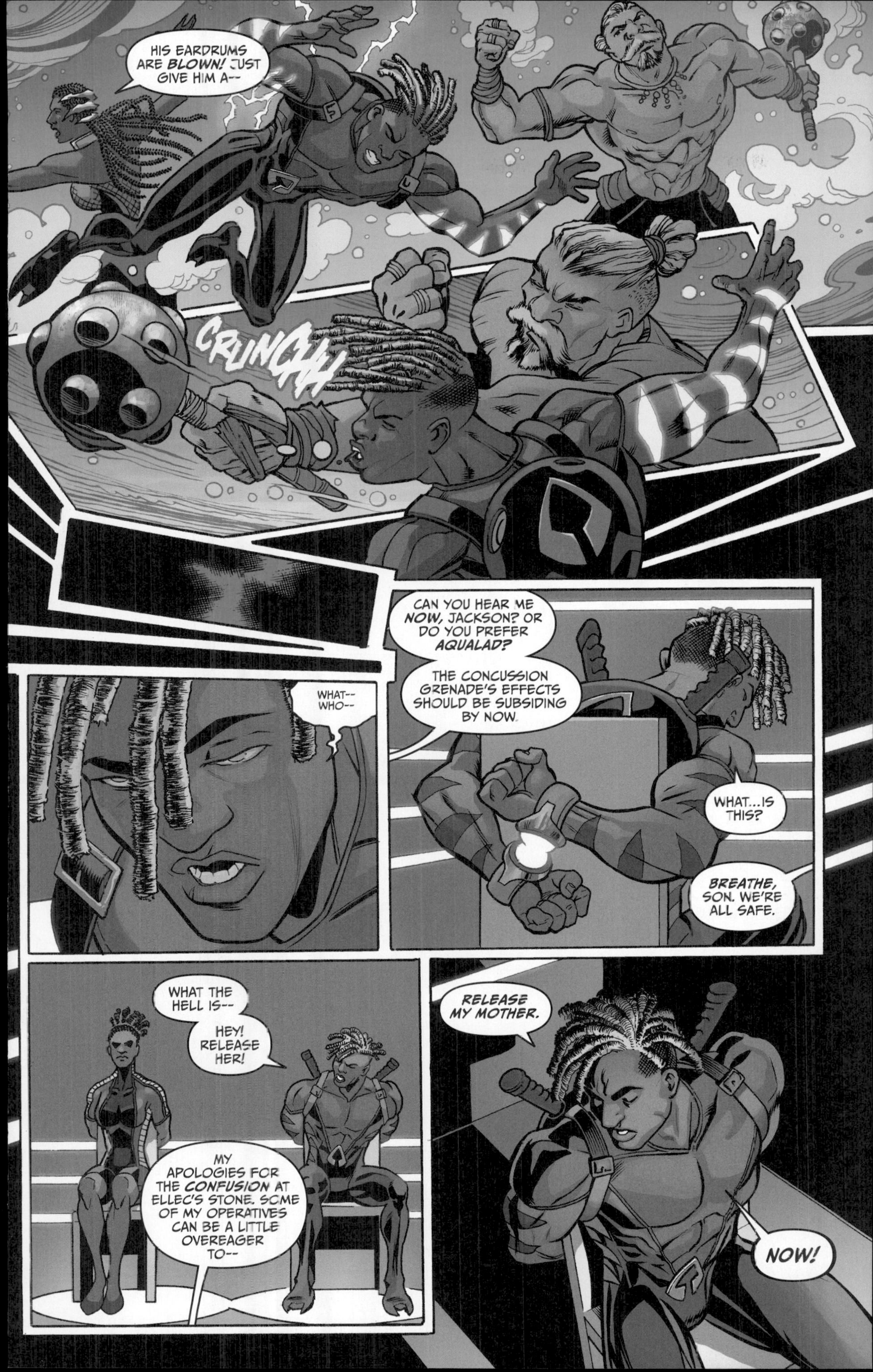
HIS EARDRUMS ARE BLOWN! JUST GIVE HIM A--
CRUNCHH
CAN YOU HEAR ME NOW, JACKSON? OR DO YOU PREFER AQUALAD?
THE CONCUSSION GRENADE'S EFFECTS SHOULD BE SUBSIDING BY NOW.
WHAT-- WHO--
WHAT...IS THIS?
BREATHE, SON. WE'RE ALL SAFE.
WHAT THE HELL IS--
HEY! RELEASE HER!
MY APOLOGIES FOR THE CONFUSION AT ELLEC'S STONE. SOME OF MY OPERATIVES CAN BE A LITTLE OVEREAGER TO--
RELEASE MY MOTHER.
NOW!

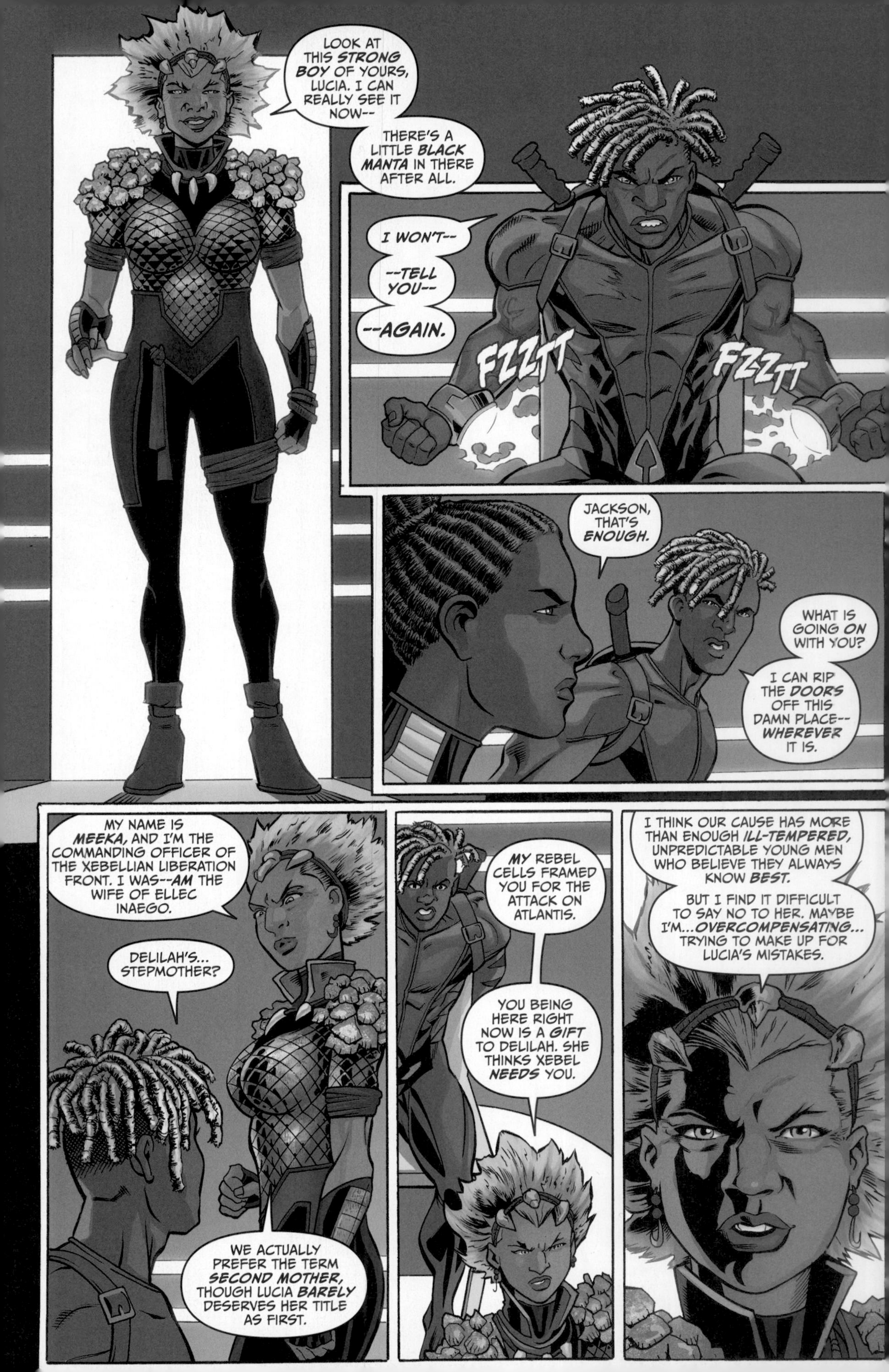

LOOK AT THIS STRONG BOY OF YOURS, LUCIA. I CAN REALLY SEE IT NOW--
THERE'S A LITTLE BLACK MANTA IN THERE AFTER ALL.
I WON'T--
--TELL YOU--
--AGAIN.
FZZTT
FZZTT
JACKSON, THAT'S ENOUGH.
WHAT IS GOING ON WITH YOU?
I CAN RIP THE DOORS OFF THIS DAMN PLACE-- WHEREVER IT IS.
MY NAME IS MEEKA, AND I'M THE COMMANDING OFFICER OF THE XEBELLIAN LIBERATION FRONT. I WAS--AM THE WIFE OF ELLEC INAEGO.
DELILAH'S... STEPMOTHER?
WE ACTUALLY PREFER THE TERM SECOND MOTHER, THOUGH LUCIA BARELY DESERVES HER TITLE AS FIRST.
MY REBEL CELLS FRAMED YOU FOR THE ATTACK ON ATLANTIS.
YOU BEING HERE RIGHT NOW IS A GIFT TO DELILAH. SHE THINKS XEBEL NEEDS YOU.
I THINK OUR CAUSE HAS MORE THAN ENOUGH ILL-TEMPERED, UNPREDICTABLE YOUNG MEN WHO BELIEVE THEY ALWAYS KNOW BEST.
BUT I FIND IT DIFFICULT TO SAY NO TO HER. MAYBE I'M...OVERCOMPENSATING... TRYING TO MAKE UP FOR LUCIA'S MISTAKES.

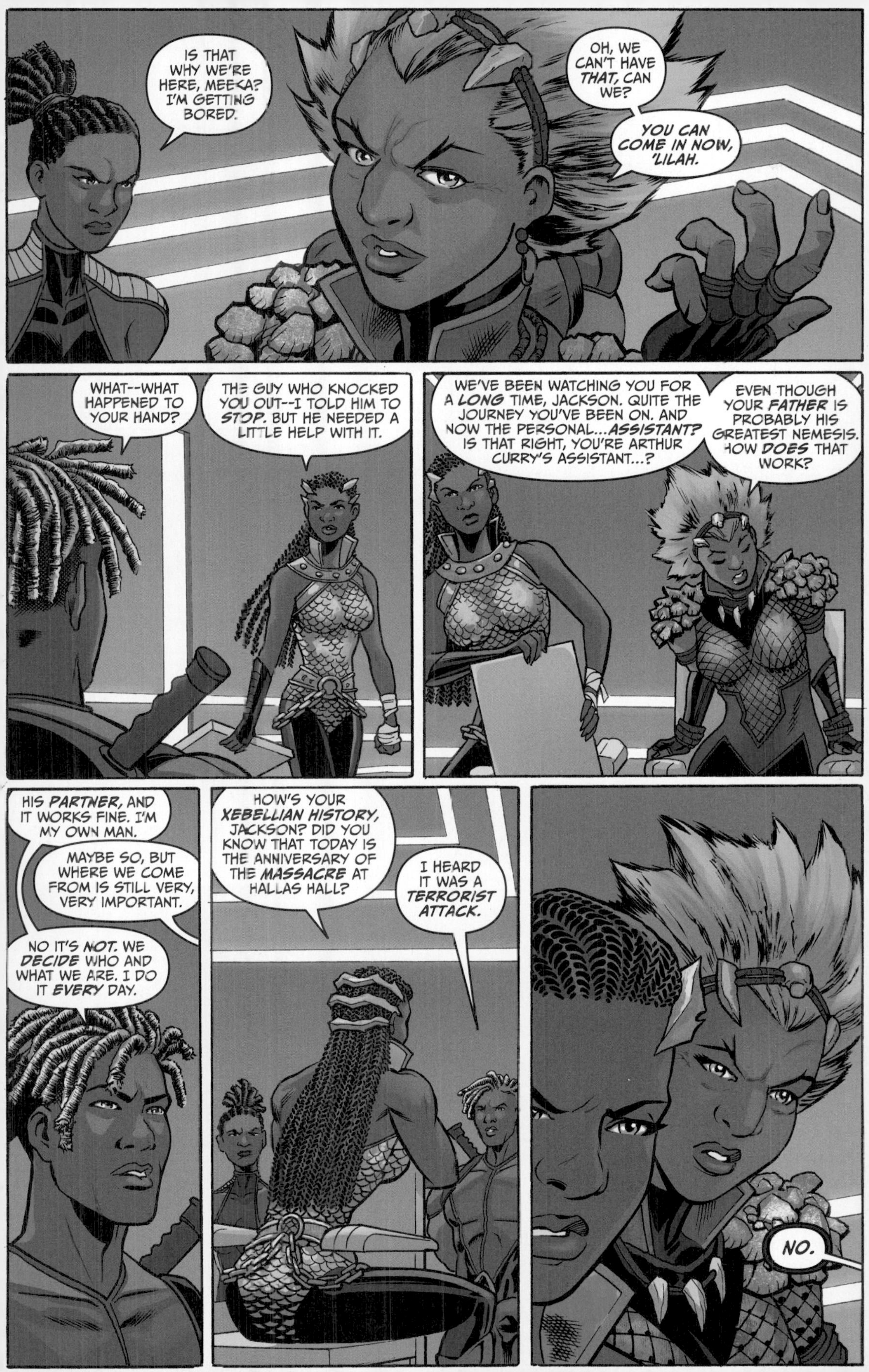
IS THAT WHY WE'RE HERE, MEEKA? I'M GETTING BORED.
OH, WE CAN'T HAVE THAT, CAN WE?
YOU CAN COME IN NOW, 'LILAH.
WHAT--WHAT HAPPENED TO YOUR HAND?
THE GUY WHO KNOCKED YOU OUT--I TOLD HIM TO STOP. BUT HE NEEDED A LITTLE HELP WITH IT.
WE'VE BEEN WATCHING YOU FOR A LONG TIME, JACKSON. QUITE THE JOURNEY YOU'VE BEEN ON. AND NOW THE PERSONAL...ASSISTANT? IS THAT RIGHT, YOU'RE ARTHUR CURRY'S ASSISTANT...?
EVEN THOUGH YOUR FATHER IS PROBABLY HIS GREATEST NEMESIS. HOW DOES THAT WORK?
HIS PARTNER, AND IT WORKS FINE. I'M MY OWN MAN.
MAYBE SO, BUT WHERE WE COME FROM IS STILL VERY, VERY IMPORTANT.
NO IT'S NOT. WE DECIDE WHO AND WHAT WE ARE. I DO IT EVERY DAY.
HOW'S YOUR XEBELLIAN HISTORY, JACKSON? DID YOU KNOW THAT TODAY IS THE ANNIVERSARY OF THE MASSACRE AT HALLAS HALL?
I HEARD IT WAS A TERRORIST ATTACK.
NO.

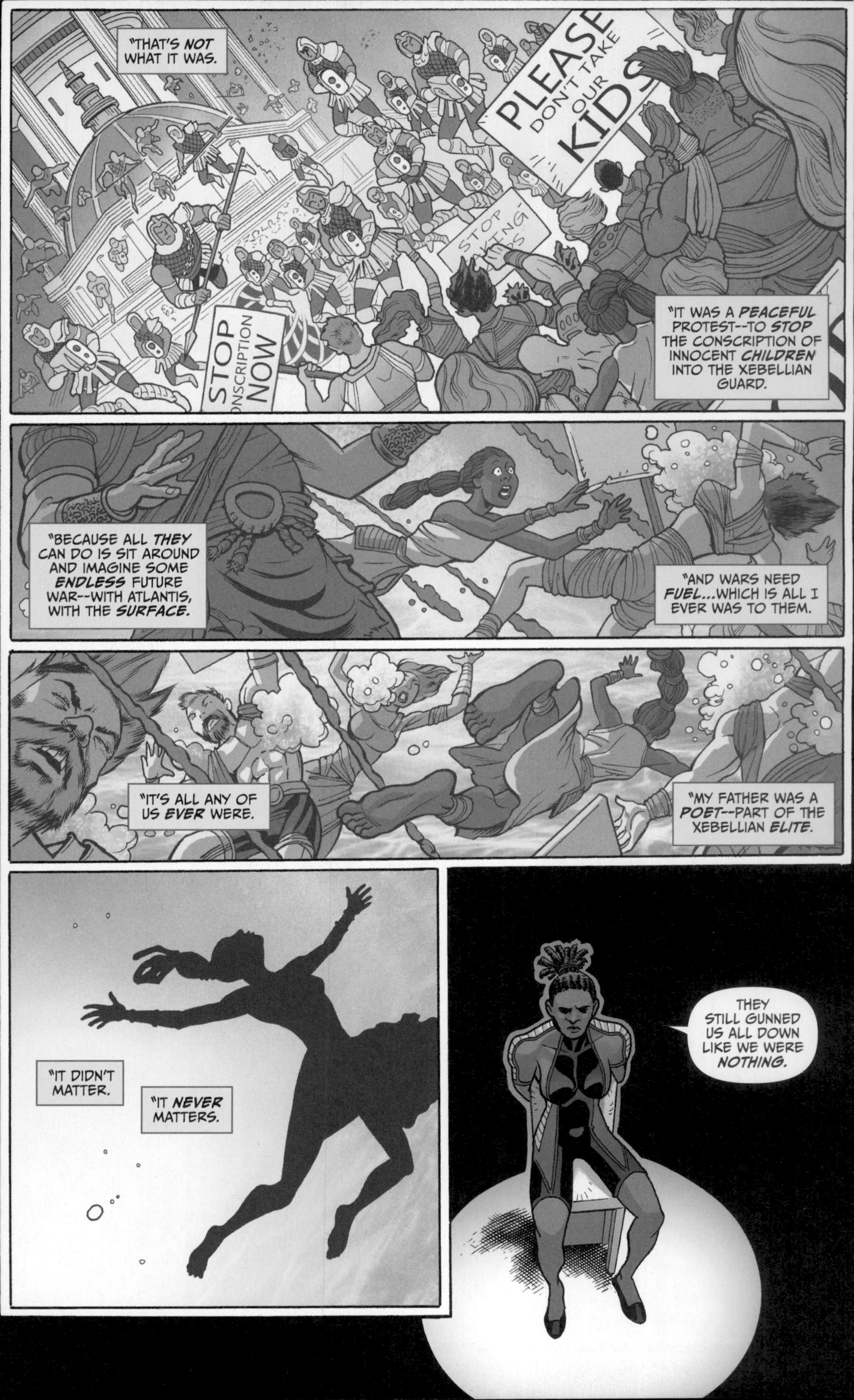

"THAT'S NOT WHAT IT WAS.
PLEASE DON'T TAKE OUR KIDS
STOP CONSCRIPTION NOW
"IT WAS A PEACEFUL PROTEST--TO STOP THE CONSCRIPTION OF INNOCENT CHILDREN INTO THE XEBELLIAN GUARD.
"BECAUSE ALL THEY CAN DO IS SIT AROUND AND IMAGINE SOME ENDLESS FUTURE WAR--WITH ATLANTIS, WITH THE SURFACE.
"AND WARS NEED FUEL...WHICH IS ALL I EVER WAS TO THEM.
"IT'S ALL ANY OF US EVER WERE.
"MY FATHER WAS A POET--PART OF THE XEBELLIAN ELITE.
"IT DIDN'T MATTER.
"IT NEVER MATTERS.
THEY STILL GUNNED US ALL DOWN LIKE WE WERE NOTHING.

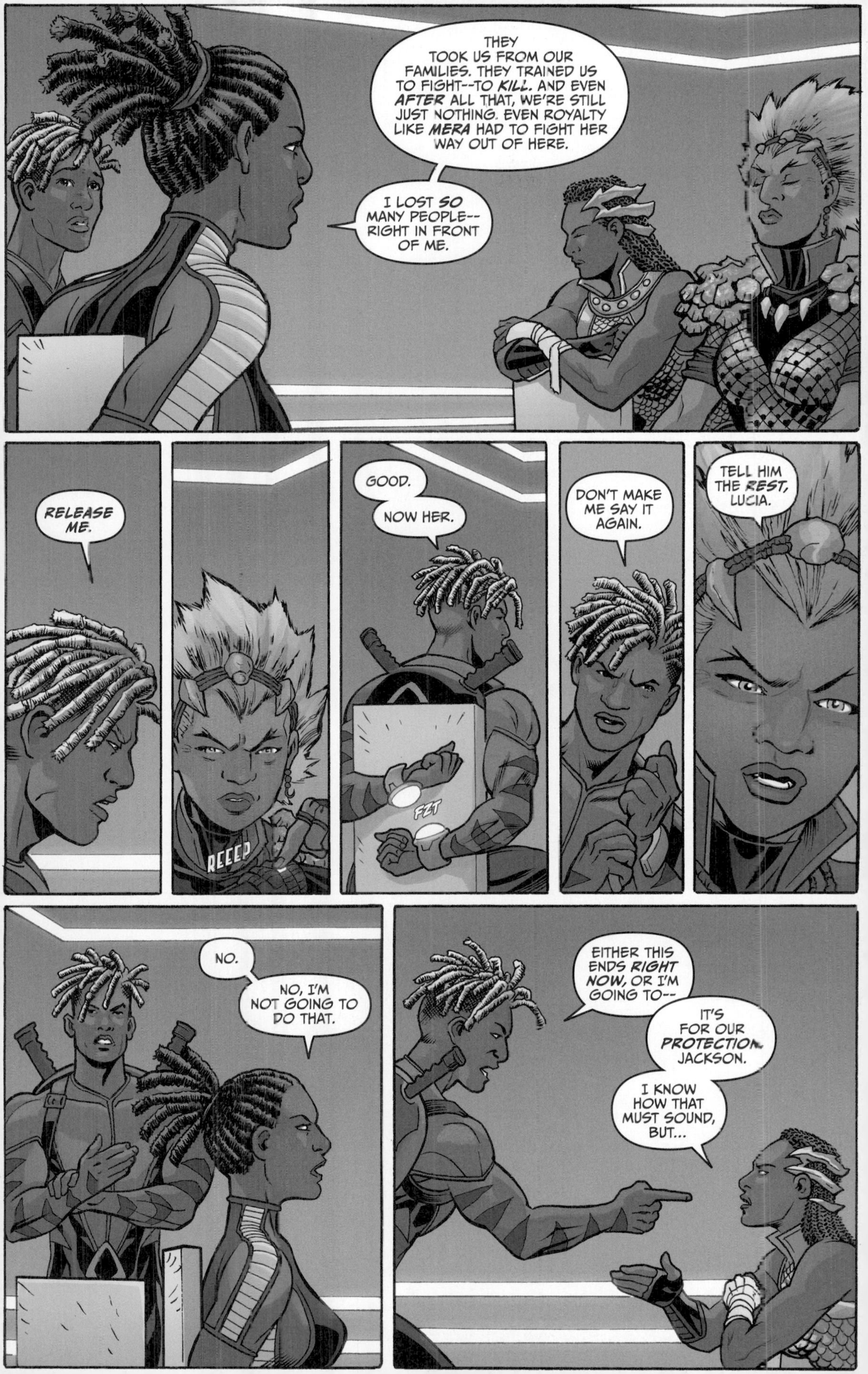

THEY TOOK US FROM OUR FAMILIES. THEY TRAINED US TO FIGHT--TO *KILL.* AND EVEN *AFTER* ALL THAT, WE'RE STILL JUST NOTHING. EVEN ROYALTY LIKE *MERA* HAD TO FIGHT HER WAY OUT OF HERE.
I LOST *SO* MANY PEOPLE-- RIGHT IN FRONT OF ME.
RELEASE ME.
REEEP
GOOD.
NOW HER.
FZT
DON'T MAKE ME SAY IT AGAIN.
TELL HIM THE *REST,* LUCIA.
NO.
NO, I'M NOT GOING TO DO THAT.
EITHER THIS ENDS *RIGHT NOW,* OR I'M GOING TO--
IT'S FOR OUR *PROTECTION,* JACKSON.
I KNOW HOW THAT MUST SOUND, BUT...

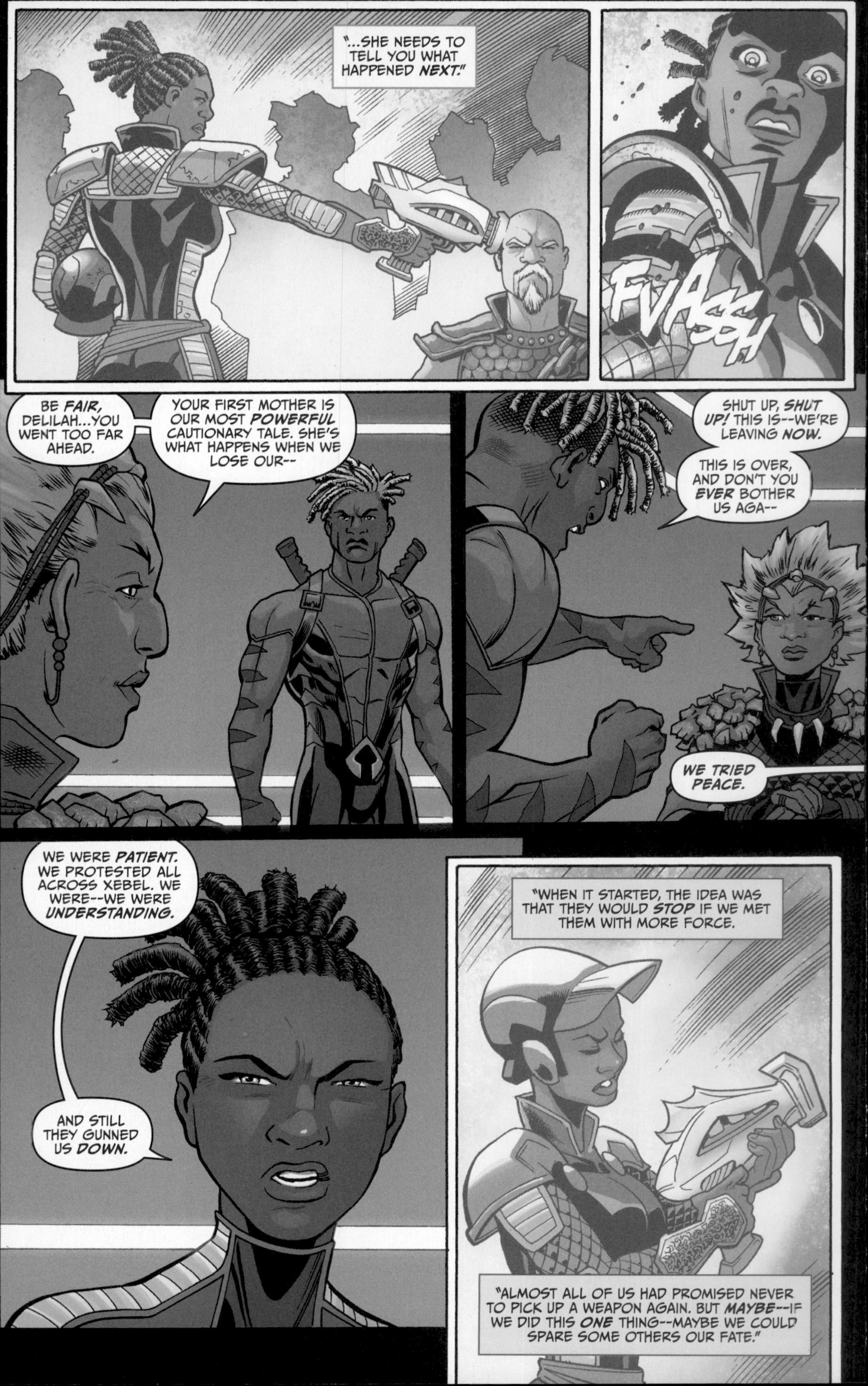
"...SHE NEEDS TO TELL YOU WHAT HAPPENED NEXT."
FVASSH
BE FAIR, DELILAH...YOU WENT TOO FAR AHEAD.
YOUR FIRST MOTHER IS OUR MOST POWERFUL CAUTIONARY TALE. SHE'S WHAT HAPPENS WHEN WE LOSE OUR--
SHUT UP, SHUT UP! THIS IS--WE'RE LEAVING NOW.
THIS IS OVER, AND DON'T YOU EVER BOTHER US AGA--
WE TRIED PEACE.
WE WERE PATIENT. WE PROTESTED ALL ACROSS XEBEL. WE WERE--WE WERE UNDERSTANDING.
AND STILL THEY GUNNED US DOWN.
"WHEN IT STARTED, THE IDEA WAS THAT THEY WOULD STOP IF WE MET THEM WITH MORE FORCE.
"ALMOST ALL OF US HAD PROMISED NEVER TO PICK UP A WEAPON AGAIN. BUT MAYBE--IF WE DID THIS ONE THING--MAYBE WE COULD SPARE SOME OTHERS OUR FATE."

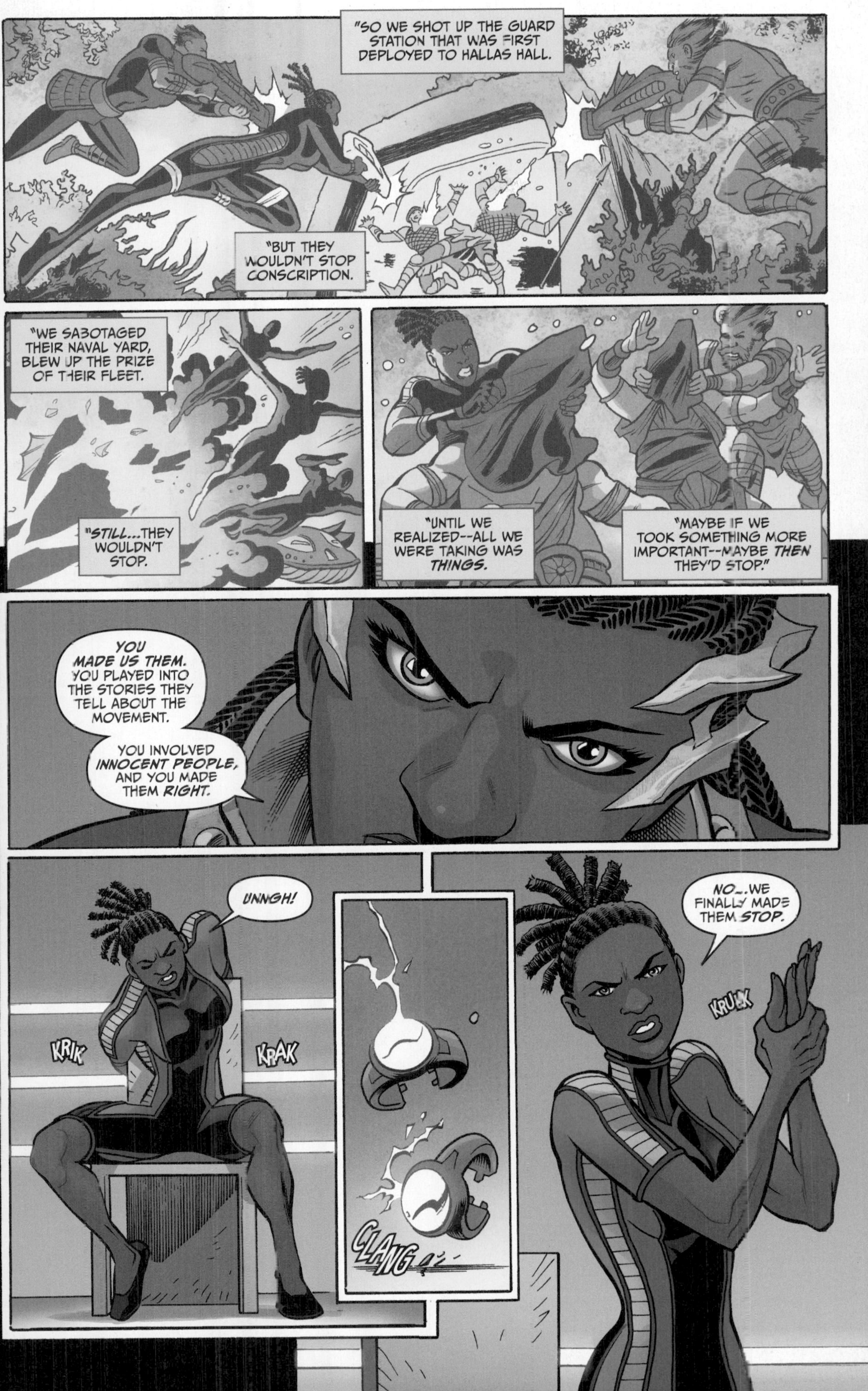
"SO WE SHOT UP THE GUARD STATION THAT WAS FIRST DEPLOYED TO HALLAS HALL.
"BUT THEY WOULDN'T STOP CONSCRIPTION.
"WE SABOTAGED THEIR NAVAL YARD, BLEW UP THE PRIZE OF THEIR FLEET.
"STILL...THEY WOULDN'T STOP.
"UNTIL WE REALIZED--ALL WE WERE TAKING WAS THINGS.
"MAYBE IF WE TOOK SOMETHING MORE IMPORTANT--MAYBE THEN THEY'D STOP."
YOU MADE US THEM. YOU PLAYED INTO THE STORIES THEY TELL ABOUT THE MOVEMENT.
YOU INVOLVED INNOCENT PEOPLE, AND YOU MADE THEM RIGHT.
UNNGH!
KRIK
KRAK
CLANG
NO...WE FINALLY MADE THEM STOP.
KRULK

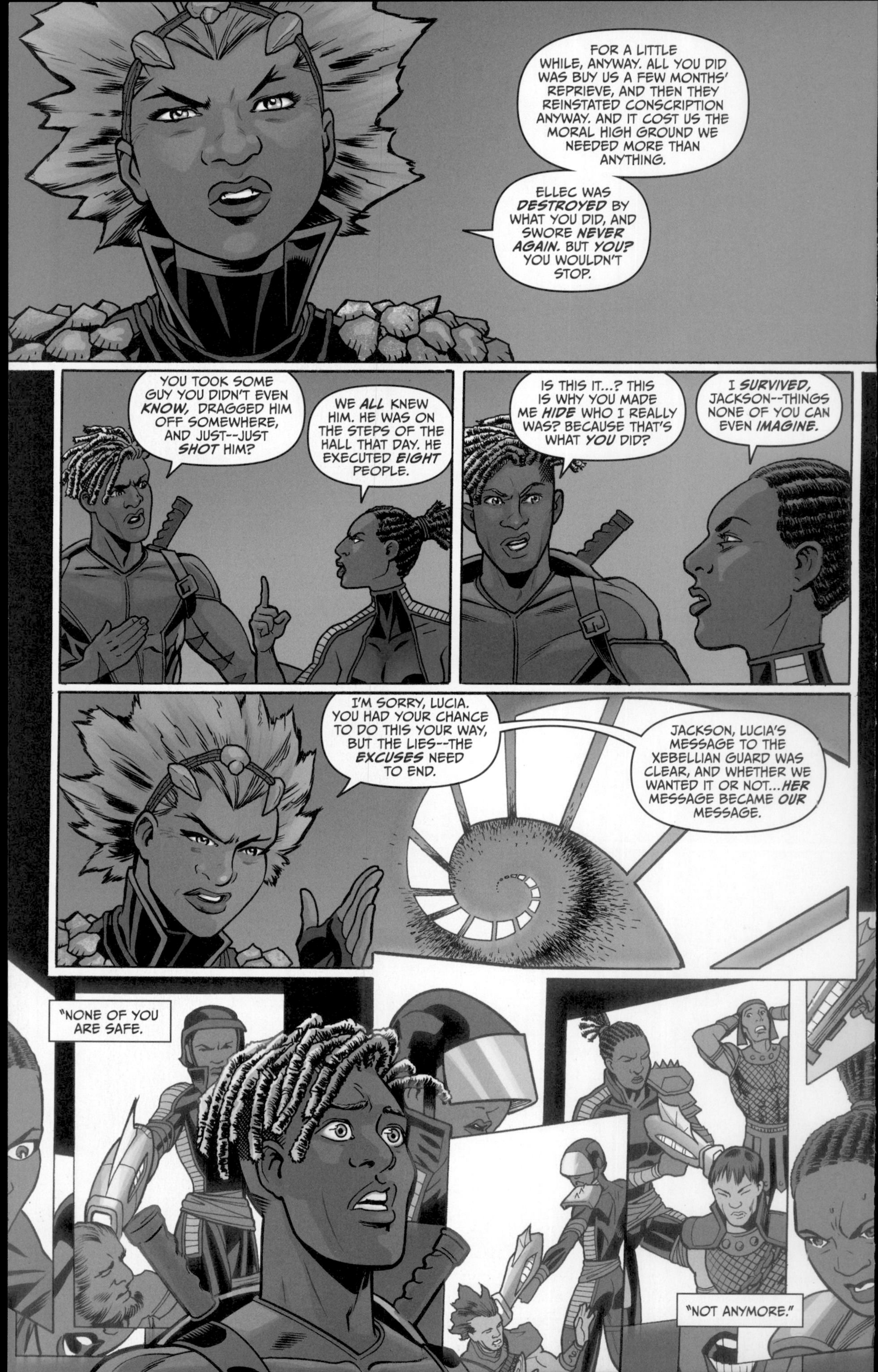
FOR A LITTLE WHILE, ANYWAY. ALL YOU DID WAS BUY US A FEW MONTHS' REPRIEVE, AND THEN THEY REINSTATED CONSCRIPTION ANYWAY. AND IT COST US THE MORAL HIGH GROUND WE NEEDED MORE THAN ANYTHING.
ELLEC WAS DESTROYED BY WHAT YOU DID, AND SWORE NEVER AGAIN. BUT YOU? YOU WOULDN'T STOP.
YOU TOOK SOME GUY YOU DIDN'T EVEN KNOW, DRAGGED HIM OFF SOMEWHERE, AND JUST--JUST SHOT HIM?
WE ALL KNEW HIM. HE WAS ON THE STEPS OF THE HALL THAT DAY. HE EXECUTED EIGHT PEOPLE.
IS THIS IT...? THIS IS WHY YOU MADE ME HIDE WHO I REALLY WAS? BECAUSE THAT'S WHAT YOU DID?
I SURVIVED, JACKSON--THINGS NONE OF YOU CAN EVEN IMAGINE.
I'M SORRY, LUCIA. YOU HAD YOUR CHANCE TO DO THIS YOUR WAY, BUT THE LIES--THE EXCUSES NEED TO END.
JACKSON, LUCIA'S MESSAGE TO THE XEBELLIAN GUARD WAS CLEAR, AND WHETHER WE WANTED IT OR NOT...HER MESSAGE BECAME OUR MESSAGE.
"NONE OF YOU ARE SAFE.
"NOT ANYMORE."

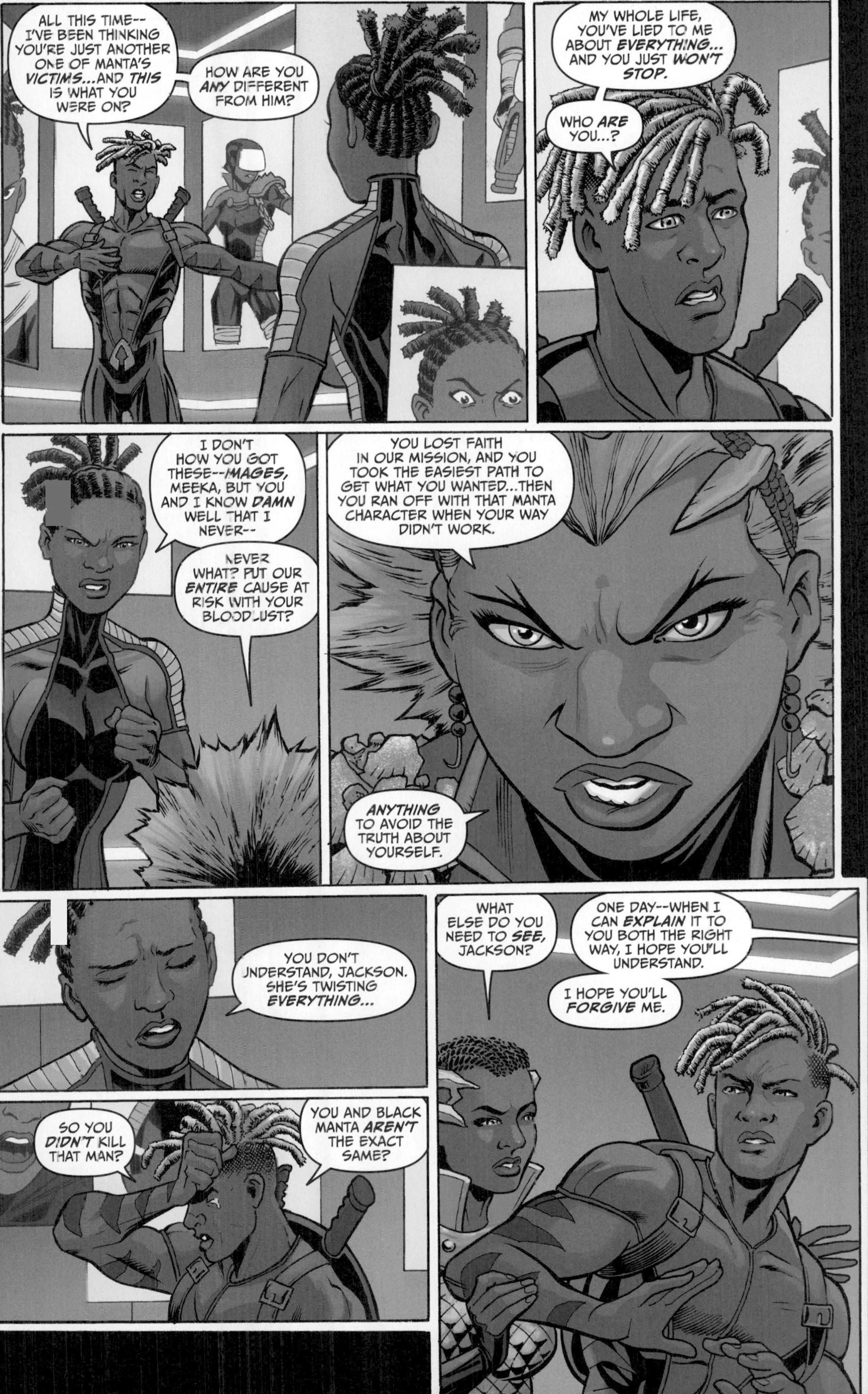

ALL THIS TIME-- I'VE BEEN THINKING YOU'RE JUST ANOTHER ONE OF MANTA'S VICTIMS...AND THIS IS WHAT YOU WERE ON?
HOW ARE YOU ANY DIFFERENT FROM HIM?
MY WHOLE LIFE, YOU'VE LIED TO ME ABOUT EVERYTHING... AND YOU JUST WON'T STOP.
WHO ARE YOU...?
I DON'T HOW YOU GOT THESE--IMAGES, MEEKA, BUT YOU AND I KNOW DAMN WELL THAT I NEVER--
NEVER WHAT? PUT OUR ENTIRE CAUSE AT RISK WITH YOUR BLOODLUST?
YOU LOST FAITH IN OUR MISSION, AND YOU TOOK THE EASIEST PATH TO GET WHAT YOU WANTED...THEN YOU RAN OFF WITH THAT MANTA CHARACTER WHEN YOUR WAY DIDN'T WORK.
ANYTHING TO AVOID THE TRUTH ABOUT YOURSELF.
YOU DON'T UNDERSTAND, JACKSON. SHE'S TWISTING EVERYTHING...
SO YOU DIDN'T KILL THAT MAN?
YOU AND BLACK MANTA AREN'T THE EXACT SAME?
WHAT ELSE DO YOU NEED TO SEE, JACKSON?
ONE DAY--WHEN I CAN EXPLAIN IT TO YOU BOTH THE RIGHT WAY, I HOPE YOU'LL UNDERSTAND.
I HOPE YOU'LL FORGIVE ME.

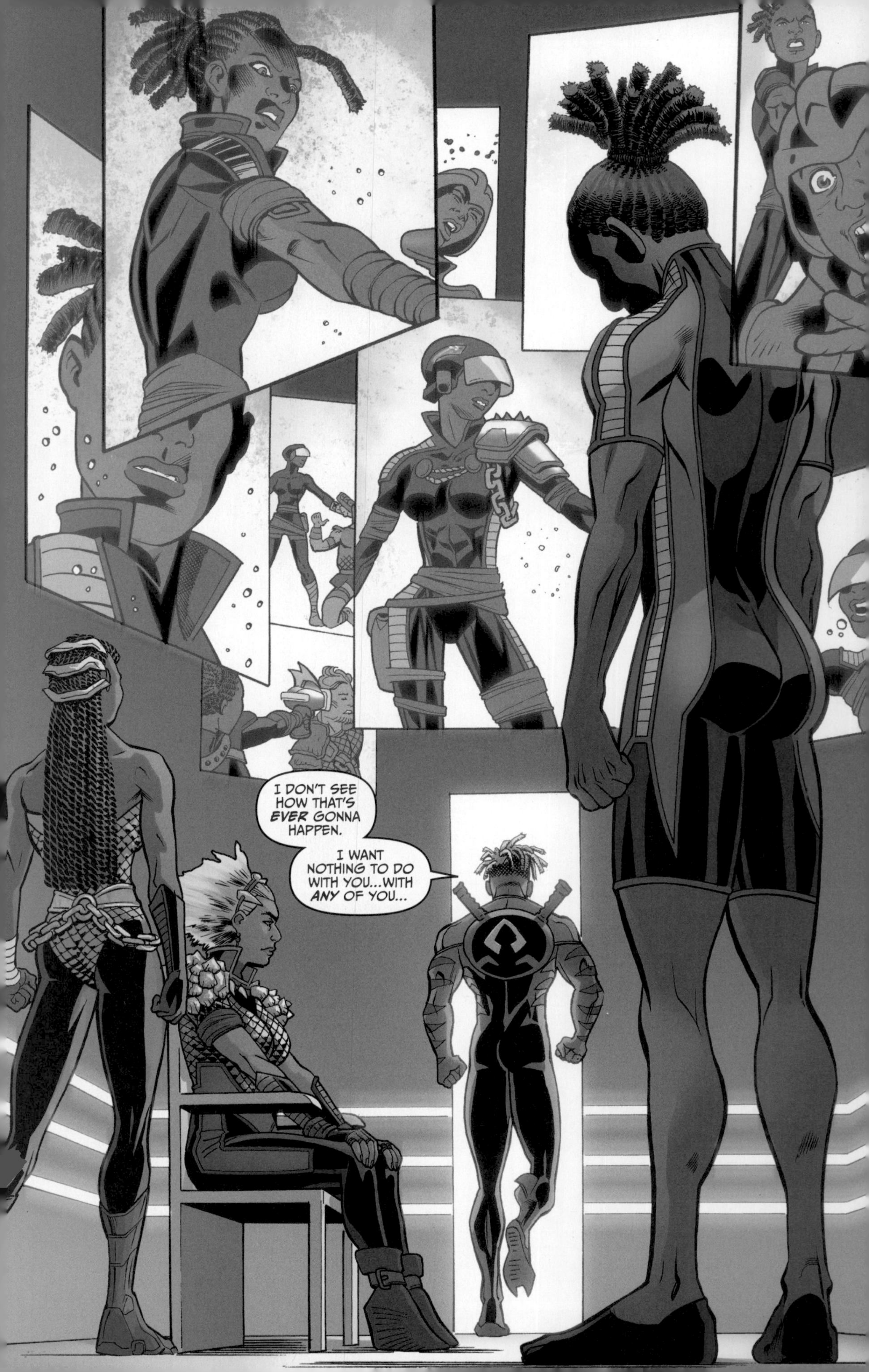
I DON'T SEE HOW THAT'S *EVER* GONNA HAPPEN.
I WANT NOTHING TO DO WITH YOU...WITH *ANY* OF YOU...

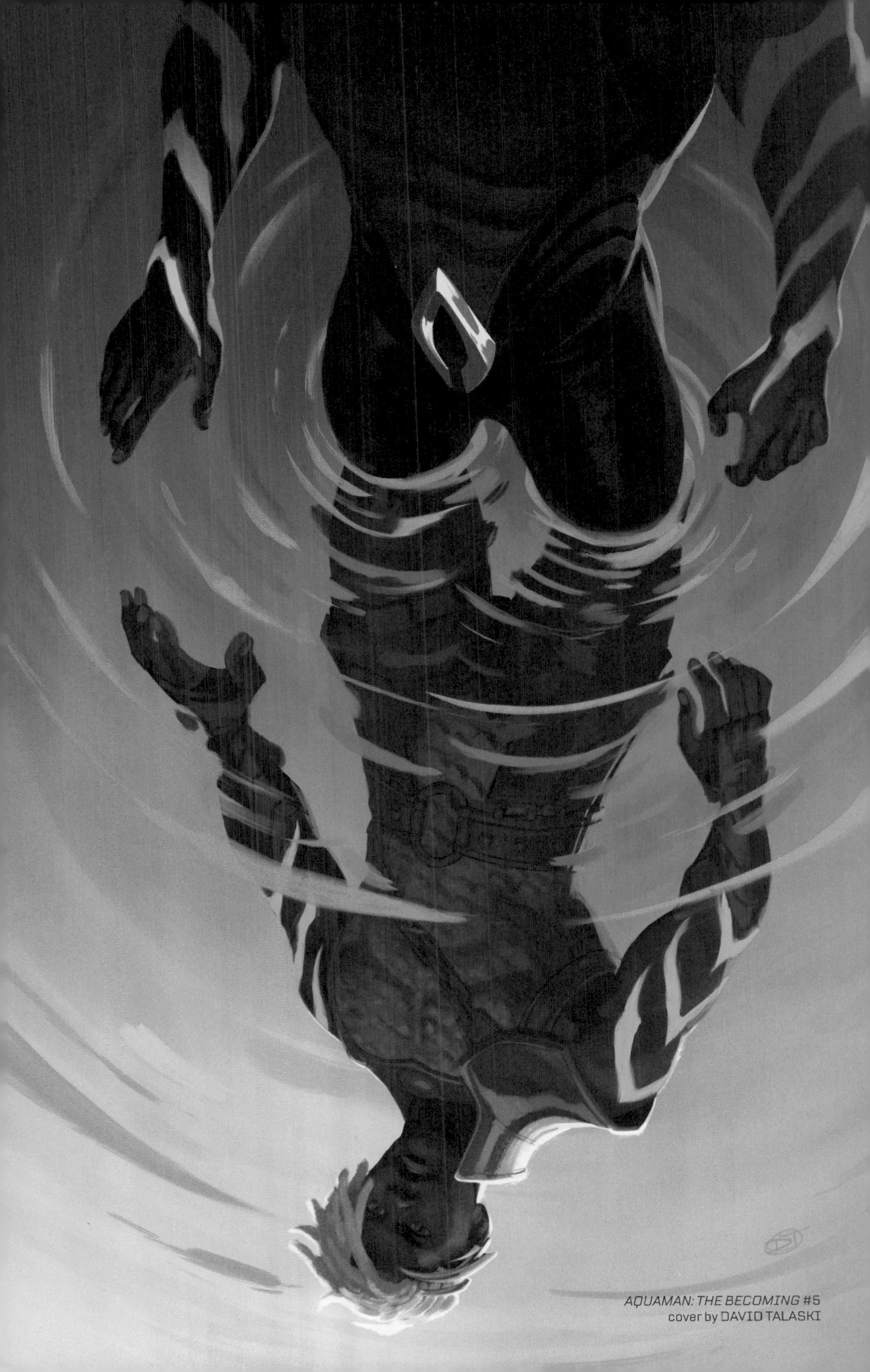

AQUAMAN: THE BECOMING #5
cover by DAVID TALASKI

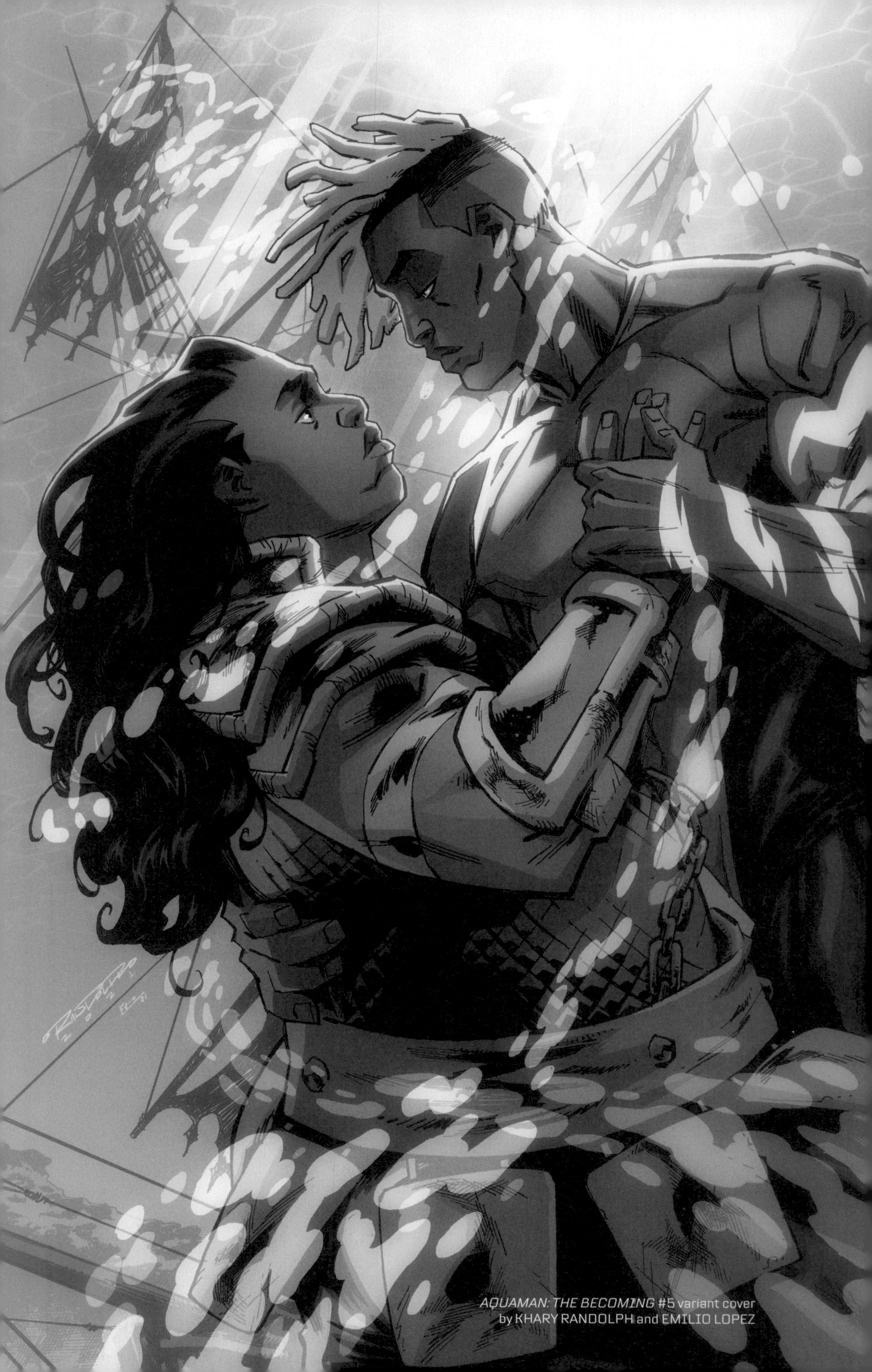

AQUAMAN: THE BECOMING #5 variant cover
by KHARY RANDOLPH and EMILIO LOPEZ

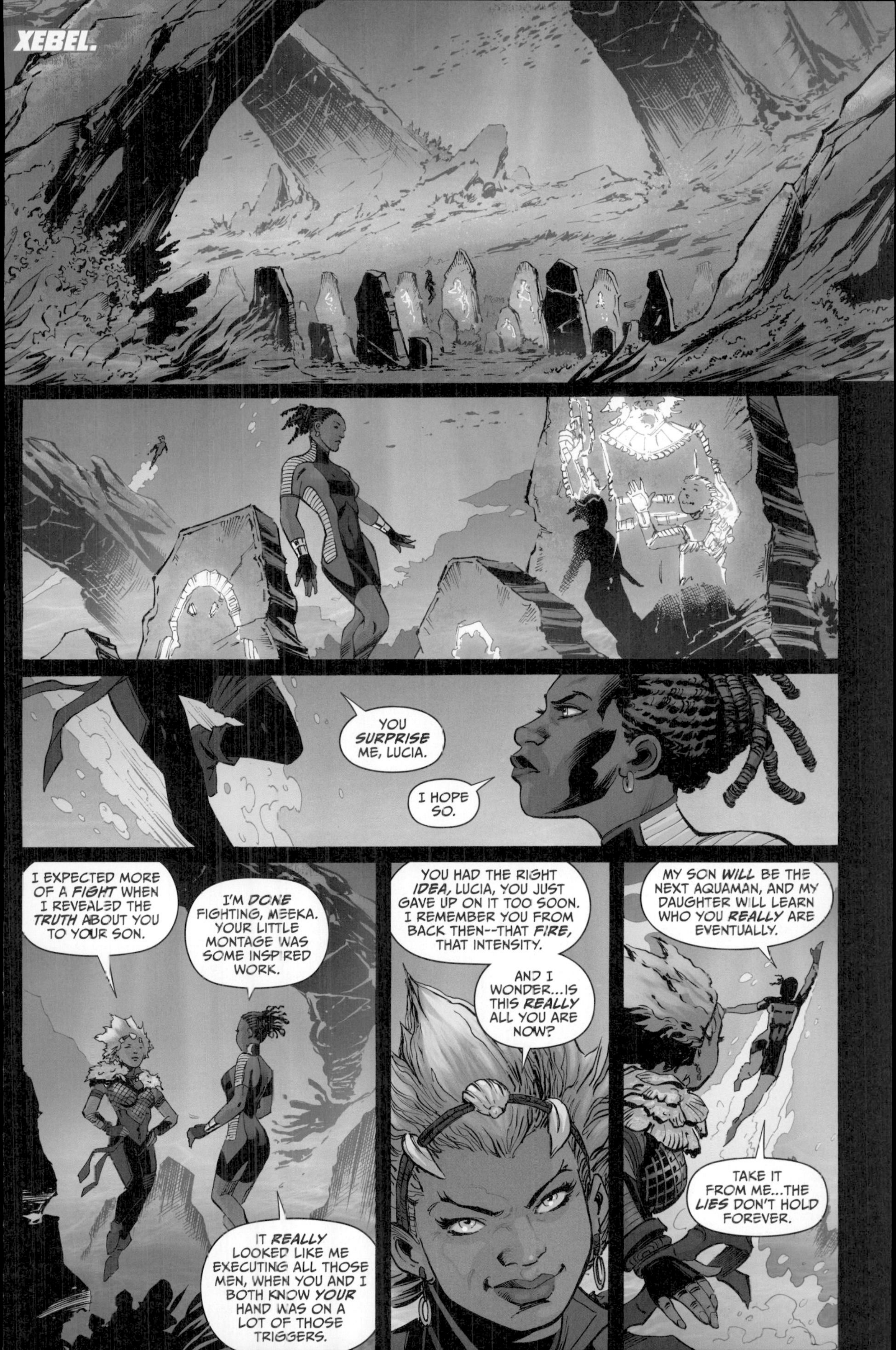
XEBEL.
YOU SURPRISE ME, LUCIA.
I HOPE SO.
I EXPECTED MORE OF A FIGHT WHEN I REVEALED THE TRUTH ABOUT YOU TO YOUR SON.
I'M DONE FIGHTING, MEEKA. YOUR LITTLE MONTAGE WAS SOME INSPIRED WORK.
IT REALLY LOOKED LIKE ME EXECUTING ALL THOSE MEN, WHEN YOU AND I BOTH KNOW YOUR HAND WAS ON A LOT OF THOSE TRIGGERS.
YOU HAD THE RIGHT IDEA, LUCIA, YOU JUST GAVE UP ON IT TOO SOON. I REMEMBER YOU FROM BACK THEN--THAT FIRE, THAT INTENSITY.
AND I WONDER...IS THIS REALLY ALL YOU ARE NOW?
MY SON WILL BE THE NEXT AQUAMAN, AND MY DAUGHTER WILL LEARN WHO YOU REALLY ARE EVENTUALLY.
TAKE IT FROM ME...THE LIES DON'T HOLD FOREVER.

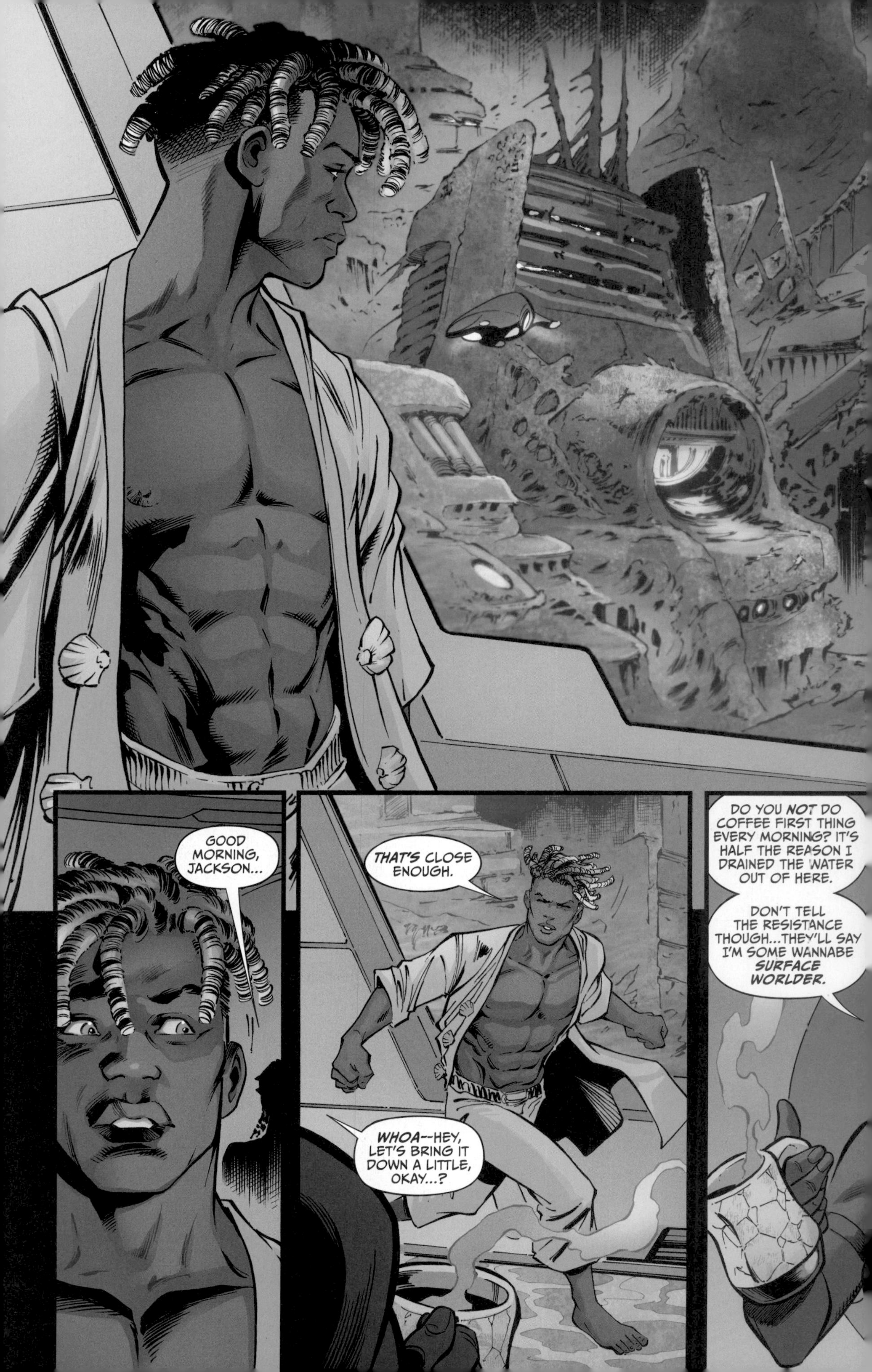

GOOD MORNING, JACKSON...
THAT'S CLOSE ENOUGH.
WHOA--HEY, LET'S BRING IT DOWN A LITTLE, OKAY...?
DO YOU *NOT* DO COFFEE FIRST THING EVERY MORNING? IT'S HALF THE REASON I DRAINED THE WATER OUT OF HERE.
DON'T TELL THE RESISTANCE THOUGH...THEY'LL SAY I'M SOME WANNABE ***SURFACE WORLDER.***

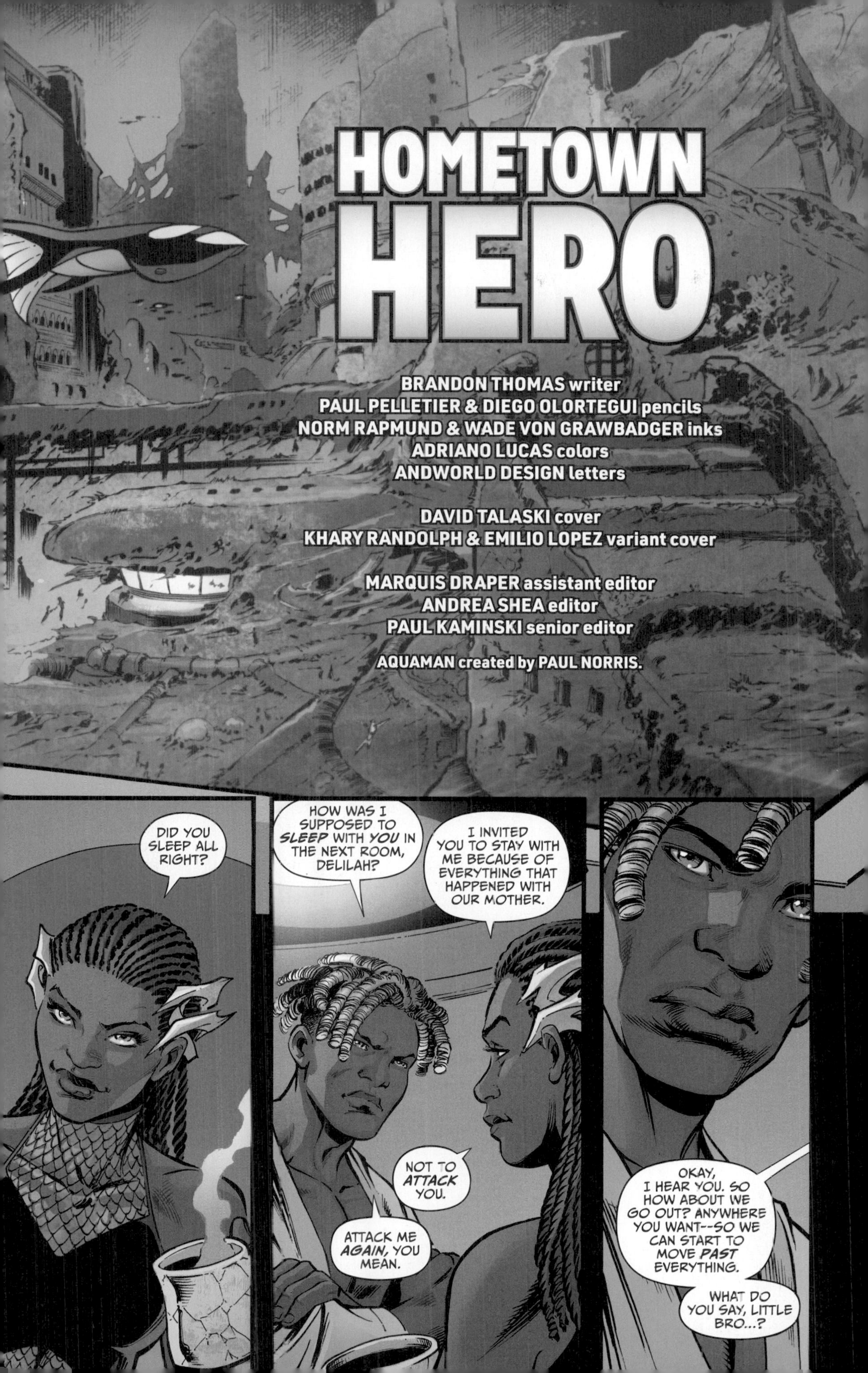
HOMETOWN HERO
BRANDON THOMAS writer
PAUL PELLETIER & DIEGO OLORTEGUI pencils
NORM RAPMUND & WADE VON GRAWBADGER inks
ADRIANO LUCAS colors
ANDWORLD DESIGN letters
DAVID TALASKI cover
KHARY RANDOLPH & EMILIO LOPEZ variant cover
MARQUIS DRAPER assistant editor
ANDREA SHEA editor
PAUL KAMINSKI senior editor
AQUAMAN created by PAUL NORRIS.
DID YOU SLEEP ALL RIGHT?
HOW WAS I SUPPOSED TO SLEEP WITH YOU IN THE NEXT ROOM, DELILAH?
I INVITED YOU TO STAY WITH ME BECAUSE OF EVERYTHING THAT HAPPENED WITH OUR MOTHER.
NOT TO ATTACK YOU.
ATTACK ME AGAIN, YOU MEAN.
OKAY, I HEAR YOU. SO HOW ABOUT WE GO OUT? ANYWHERE YOU WANT--SO WE CAN START TO MOVE PAST EVERYTHING.
WHAT DO YOU SAY, LITTLE BRO...?

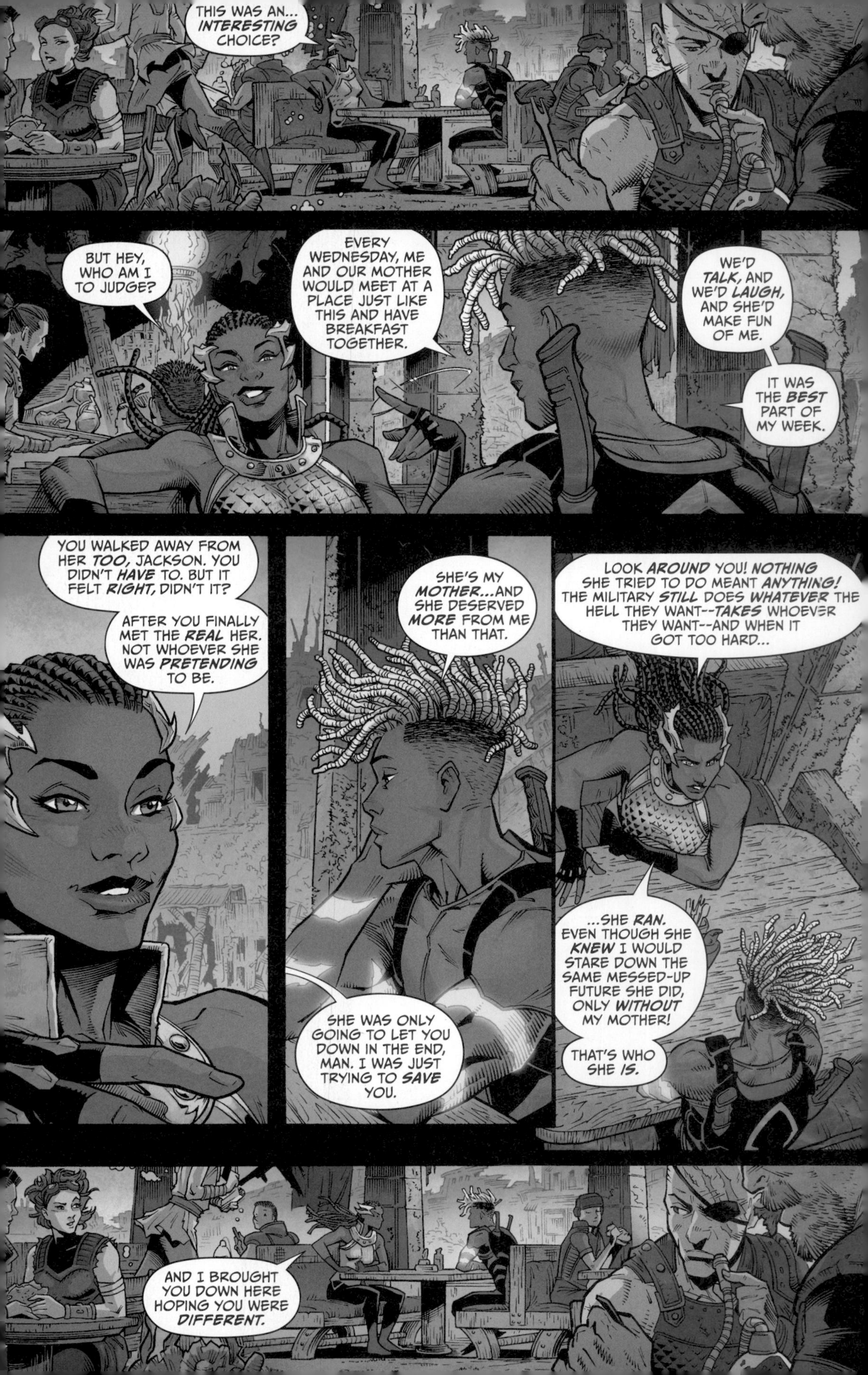
THIS WAS AN... INTERESTING CHOICE?
BUT HEY, WHO AM I TO JUDGE?
EVERY WEDNESDAY, ME AND OUR MOTHER WOULD MEET AT A PLACE JUST LIKE THIS AND HAVE BREAKFAST TOGETHER.
WE'D TALK, AND WE'D LAUGH, AND SHE'D MAKE FUN OF ME.
IT WAS THE BEST PART OF MY WEEK.
YOU WALKED AWAY FROM HER TOO, JACKSON. YOU DIDN'T HAVE TO. BUT IT FELT RIGHT, DIDN'T IT?
AFTER YOU FINALLY MET THE REAL HER. NOT WHOEVER SHE WAS PRETENDING TO BE.
SHE'S MY MOTHER...AND SHE DESERVED MORE FROM ME THAN THAT.
SHE WAS ONLY GOING TO LET YOU DOWN IN THE END, MAN. I WAS JUST TRYING TO SAVE YOU.
LOOK AROUND YOU! NOTHING SHE TRIED TO DO MEANT ANYTHING! THE MILITARY STILL DOES WHATEVER THE HELL THEY WANT--TAKES WHOEVER THEY WANT--AND WHEN IT GOT TOO HARD...
...SHE RAN. EVEN THOUGH SHE KNEW I WOULD STARE DOWN THE SAME MESSED-UP FUTURE SHE DID, ONLY WITHOUT MY MOTHER!
THAT'S WHO SHE IS.
AND I BROUGHT YOU DOWN HERE HOPING YOU WERE DIFFERENT.

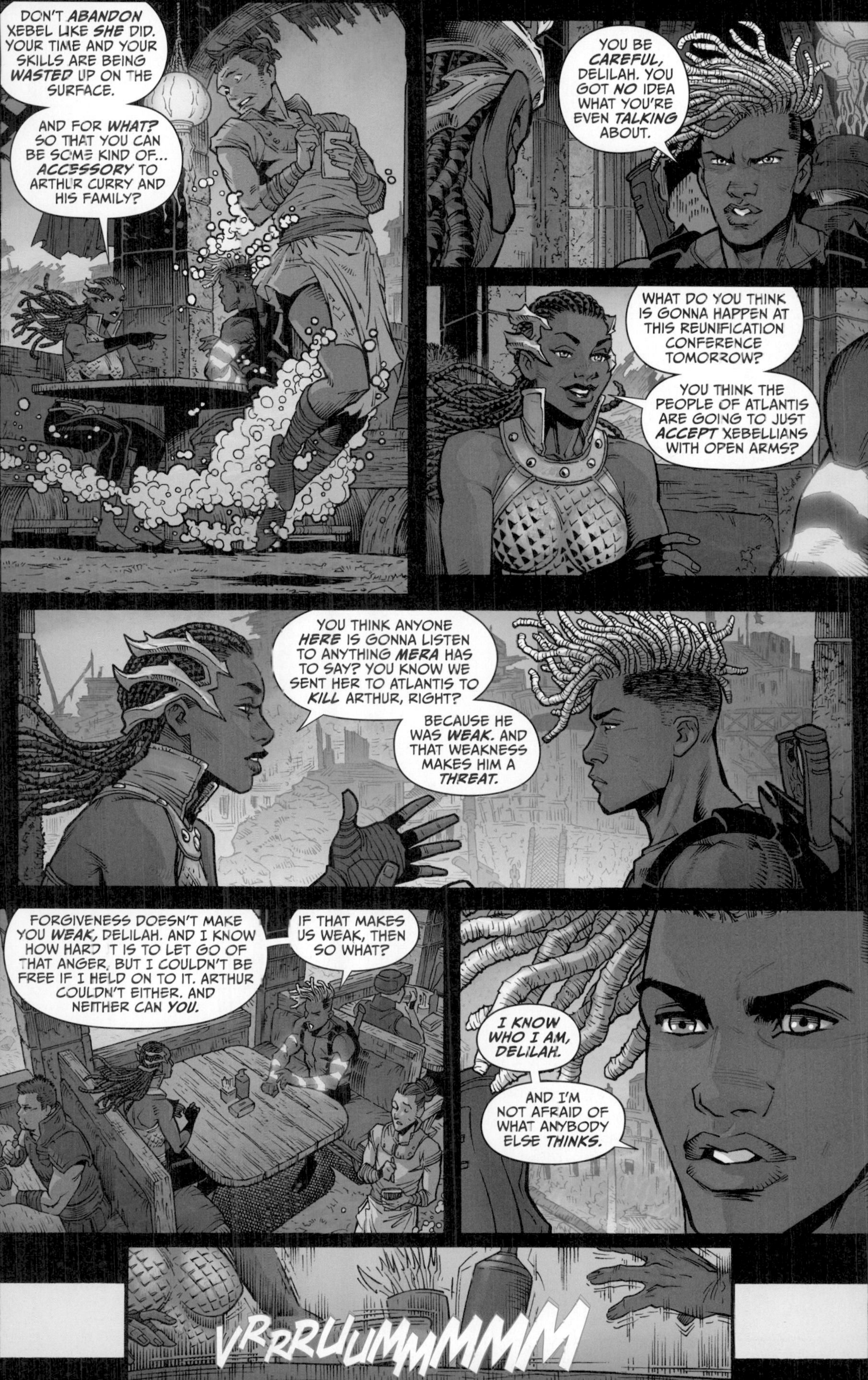
DON'T ABANDON XEBEL LIKE SHE DID. YOUR TIME AND YOUR SKILLS ARE BEING WASTED UP ON THE SURFACE.
AND FOR WHAT? SO THAT YOU CAN BE SOME KIND OF... ACCESSORY TO ARTHUR CURRY AND HIS FAMILY?
YOU BE CAREFUL, DELILAH. YOU GOT NO IDEA WHAT YOU'RE EVEN TALKING ABOUT.
WHAT DO YOU THINK IS GONNA HAPPEN AT THIS REUNIFICATION CONFERENCE TOMORROW?
YOU THINK THE PEOPLE OF ATLANTIS ARE GOING TO JUST ACCEPT XEBELLIANS WITH OPEN ARMS?
YOU THINK ANYONE HERE IS GONNA LISTEN TO ANYTHING MERA HAS TO SAY? YOU KNOW WE SENT HER TO ATLANTIS TO KILL ARTHUR, RIGHT?
BECAUSE HE WAS WEAK. AND THAT WEAKNESS MAKES HIM A THREAT.
FORGIVENESS DOESN'T MAKE YOU WEAK, DELILAH. AND I KNOW HOW HARD IT IS TO LET GO OF THAT ANGER. BUT I COULDN'T BE FREE IF I HELD ON TO IT. ARTHUR COULDN'T EITHER. AND NEITHER CAN YOU.
IF THAT MAKES US WEAK, THEN SO WHAT?
I KNOW WHO I AM, DELILAH.
AND I'M NOT AFRAID OF WHAT ANYBODY ELSE THINKS.
VRRRUUMMMMMM

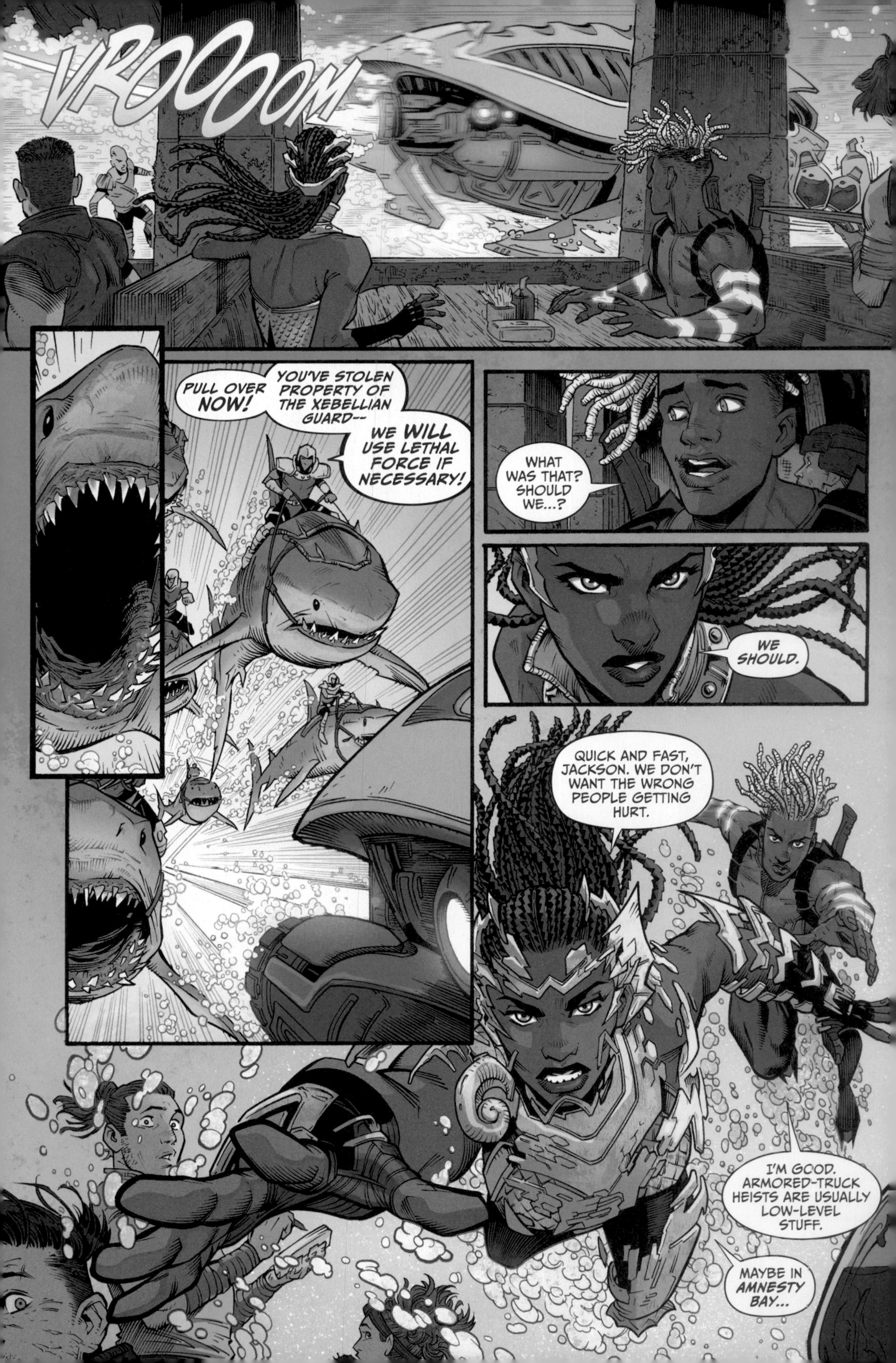
VROOOOM
PULL OVER NOW!
YOU'VE STOLEN PROPERTY OF THE XEBELLIAN GUARD--
WE WILL USE LETHAL FORCE IF NECESSARY!
WHAT WAS THAT? SHOULD WE...?
WE SHOULD.
QUICK AND FAST, JACKSON. WE DON'T WANT THE WRONG PEOPLE GETTING HURT.
I'M GOOD. ARMORED-TRUCK HEISTS ARE USUALLY LOW-LEVEL STUFF.
MAYBE IN AMNESTY BAY...

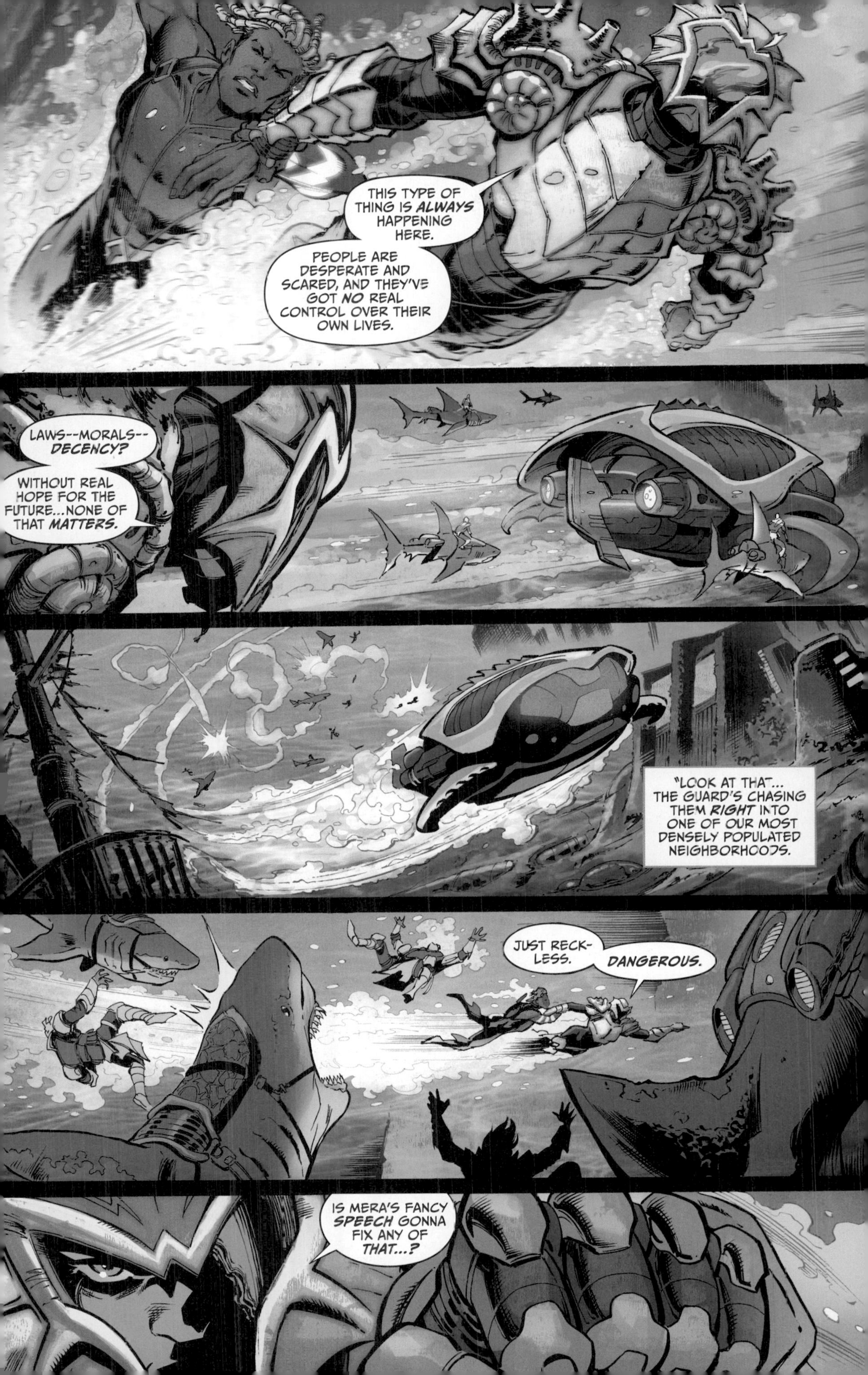
THIS TYPE OF THING IS *ALWAYS* HAPPENING HERE.
PEOPLE ARE DESPERATE AND SCARED, AND THEY'VE GOT *NO* REAL CONTROL OVER THEIR OWN LIVES.
LAWS--MORALS--*DECENCY?*
WITHOUT REAL HOPE FOR THE FUTURE...NONE OF THAT *MATTERS.*
"LOOK AT THAT... THE GUARD'S CHASING THEM *RIGHT* INTO ONE OF OUR MOST DENSELY POPULATED NEIGHBORHOODS.
JUST RECK-LESS.
DANGEROUS.
IS MERA'S FANCY *SPEECH* GONNA FIX ANY OF *THAT...?*

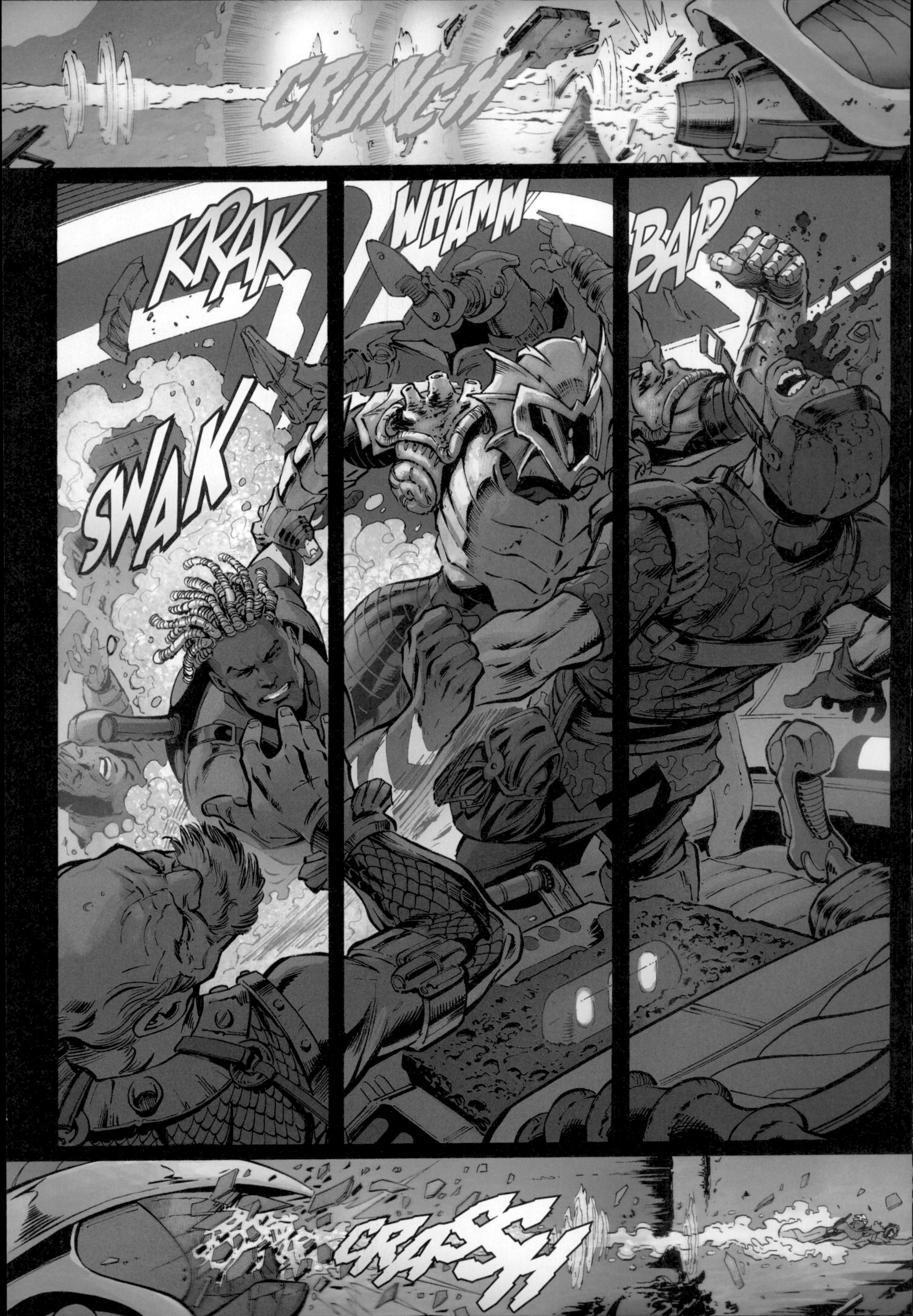
CRUNCH
KRAK
WHAMM
BAP
SWAK
CRASH

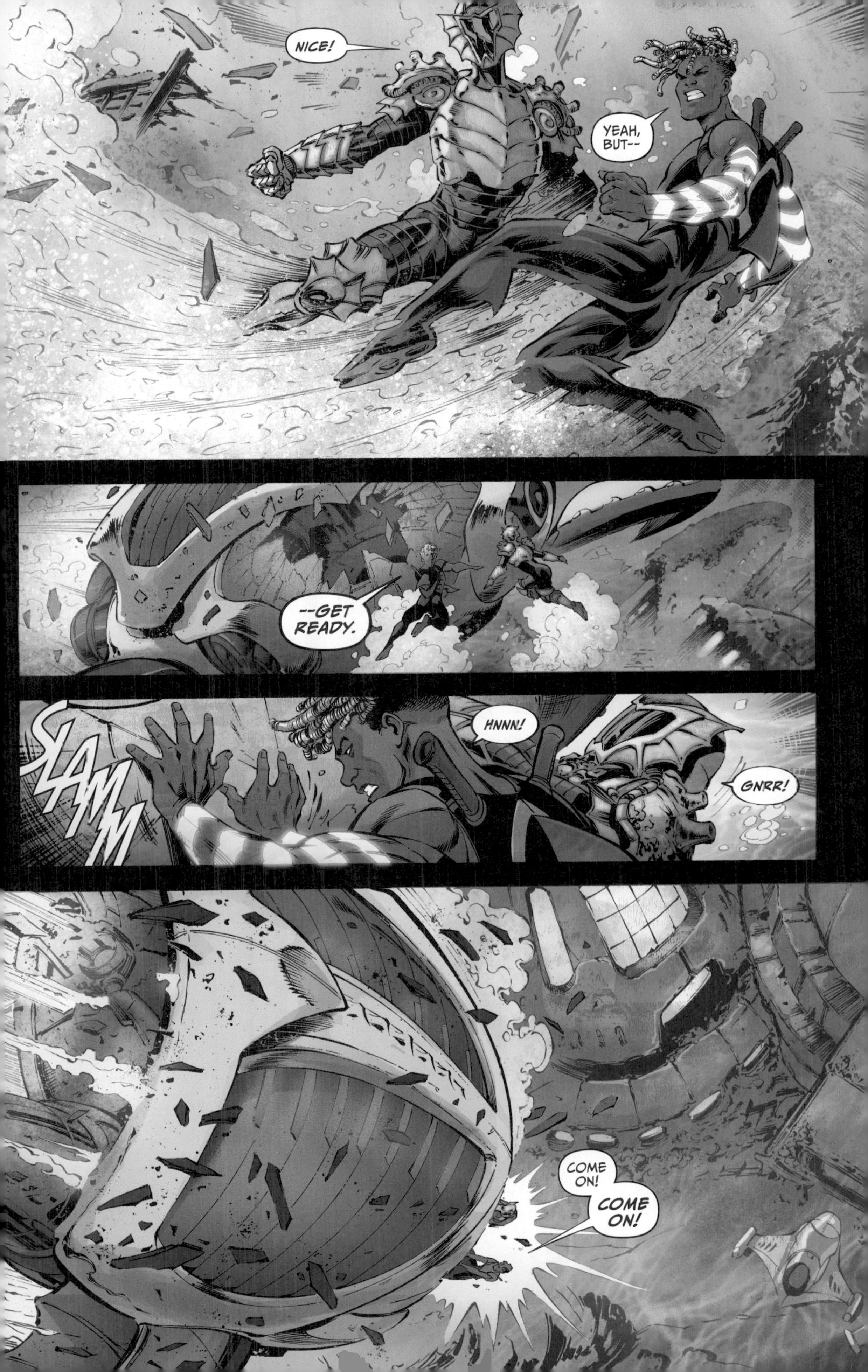
NICE!
YEAH, BUT--
--GET READY.
SLAMM
HNNN!
GNRR!
COME ON!
COME ON!

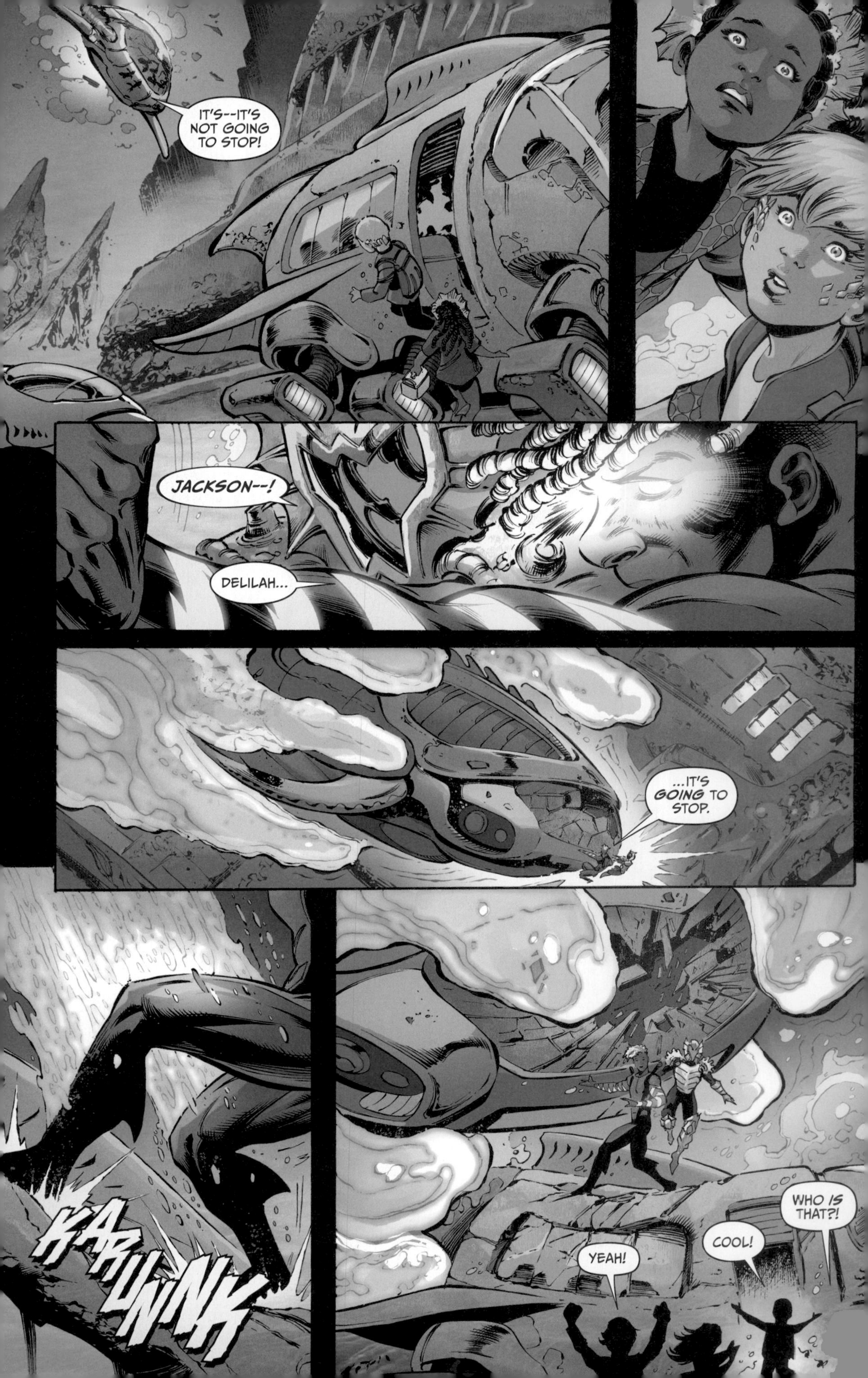
IT'S--IT'S NOT GOING TO STOP!
JACKSON--!
DELILAH...
...IT'S GOING TO STOP.
KARUNNK
YEAH!
COOL!
WHO IS THAT?!

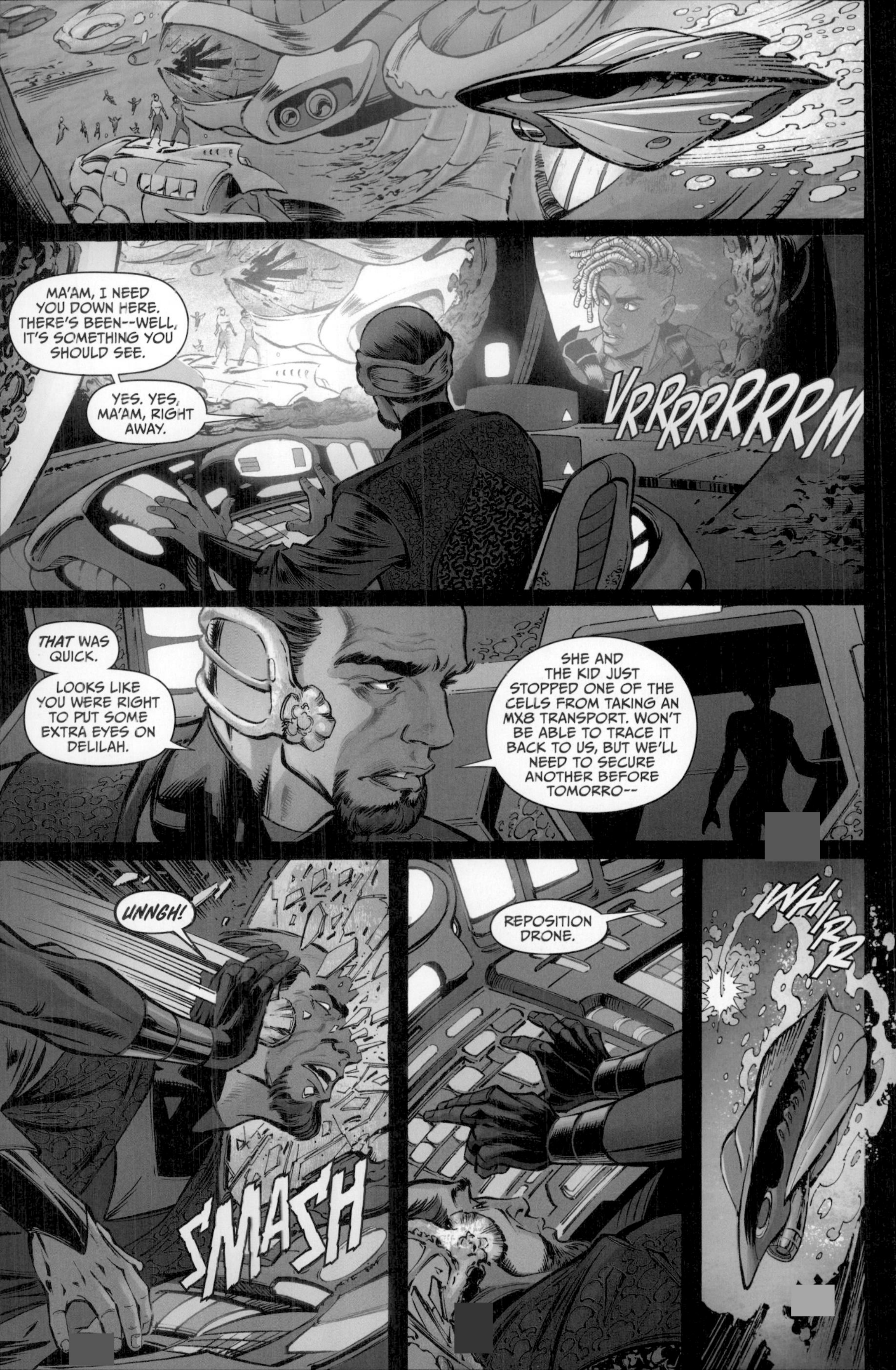
MA'AM, I NEED YOU DOWN HERE. THERE'S BEEN--WELL, IT'S SOMETHING YOU SHOULD SEE.
YES. YES, MA'AM, RIGHT AWAY.
VRRRRRRRRM
THAT WAS QUICK.
LOOKS LIKE YOU WERE RIGHT TO PUT SOME EXTRA EYES ON DELILAH.
SHE AND THE KID JUST STOPPED ONE OF THE CELLS FROM TAKING AN MX8 TRANSPORT. WON'T BE ABLE TO TRACE IT BACK TO US, BUT WE'LL NEED TO SECURE ANOTHER BEFORE TOMORRO--
UNNGH!
SMASH
REPOSITION DRONE.
WHIRR

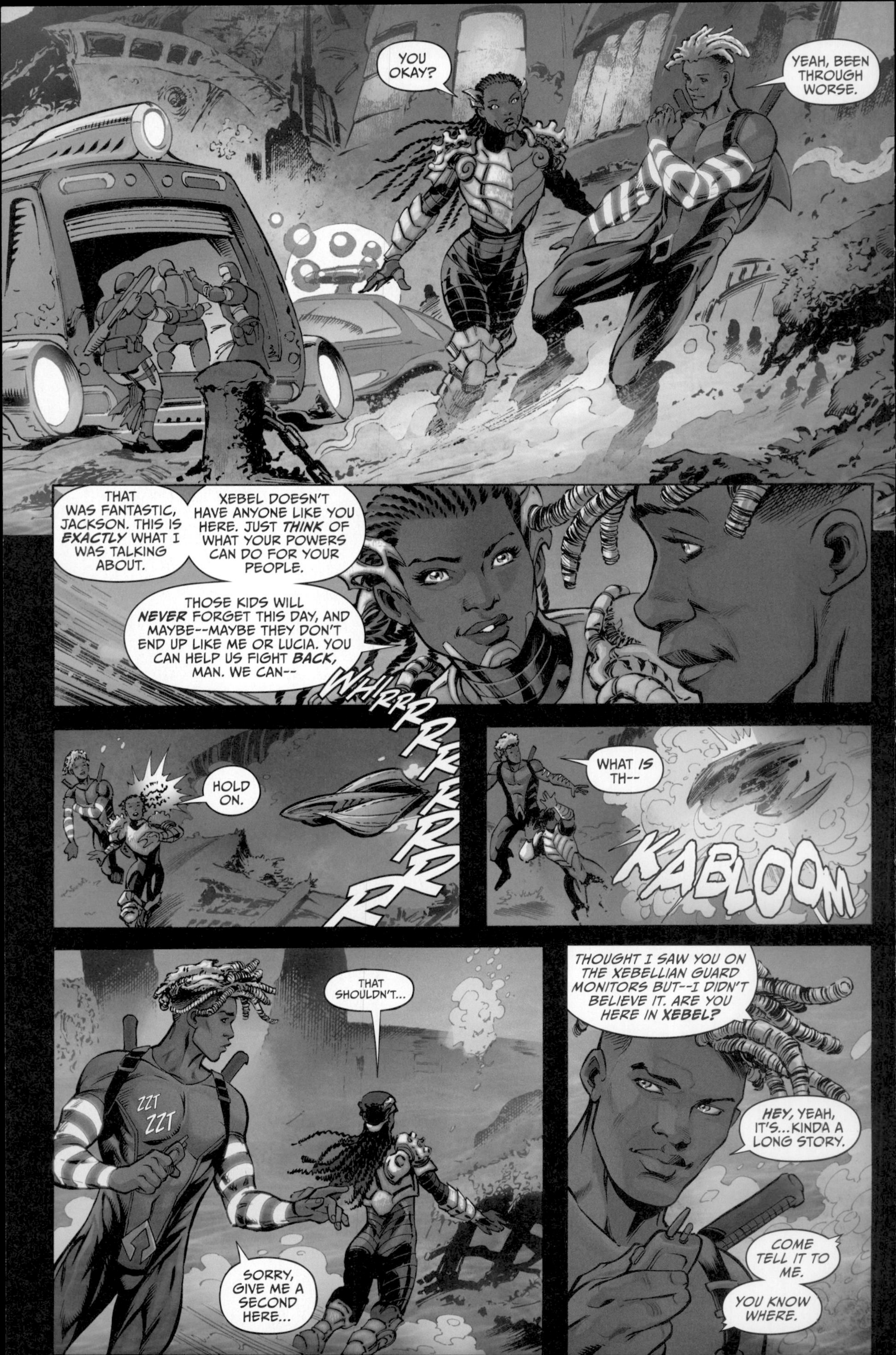
YOU OKAY?
YEAH, BEEN THROUGH WORSE.
THAT WAS FANTASTIC, JACKSON. THIS IS EXACTLY WHAT I WAS TALKING ABOUT.
XEBEL DOESN'T HAVE ANYONE LIKE YOU HERE. JUST THINK OF WHAT YOUR POWERS CAN DO FOR YOUR PEOPLE.
THOSE KIDS WILL NEVER FORGET THIS DAY, AND MAYBE--MAYBE THEY DON'T END UP LIKE ME OR LUCIA. YOU CAN HELP US FIGHT BACK, MAN. WE CAN--
WHIRRRRRRRRR
HOLD ON.
WHAT IS TH--
KABLOOM
ZZT ZZT
THAT SHOULDN'T...
SORRY, GIVE ME A SECOND HERE...
THOUGHT I SAW YOU ON THE XEBELLIAN GUARD MONITORS BUT--I DIDN'T BELIEVE IT. ARE YOU HERE IN XEBEL?
HEY, YEAH, IT'S...KINDA A LONG STORY.
COME TELL IT TO ME.
YOU KNOW WHERE.

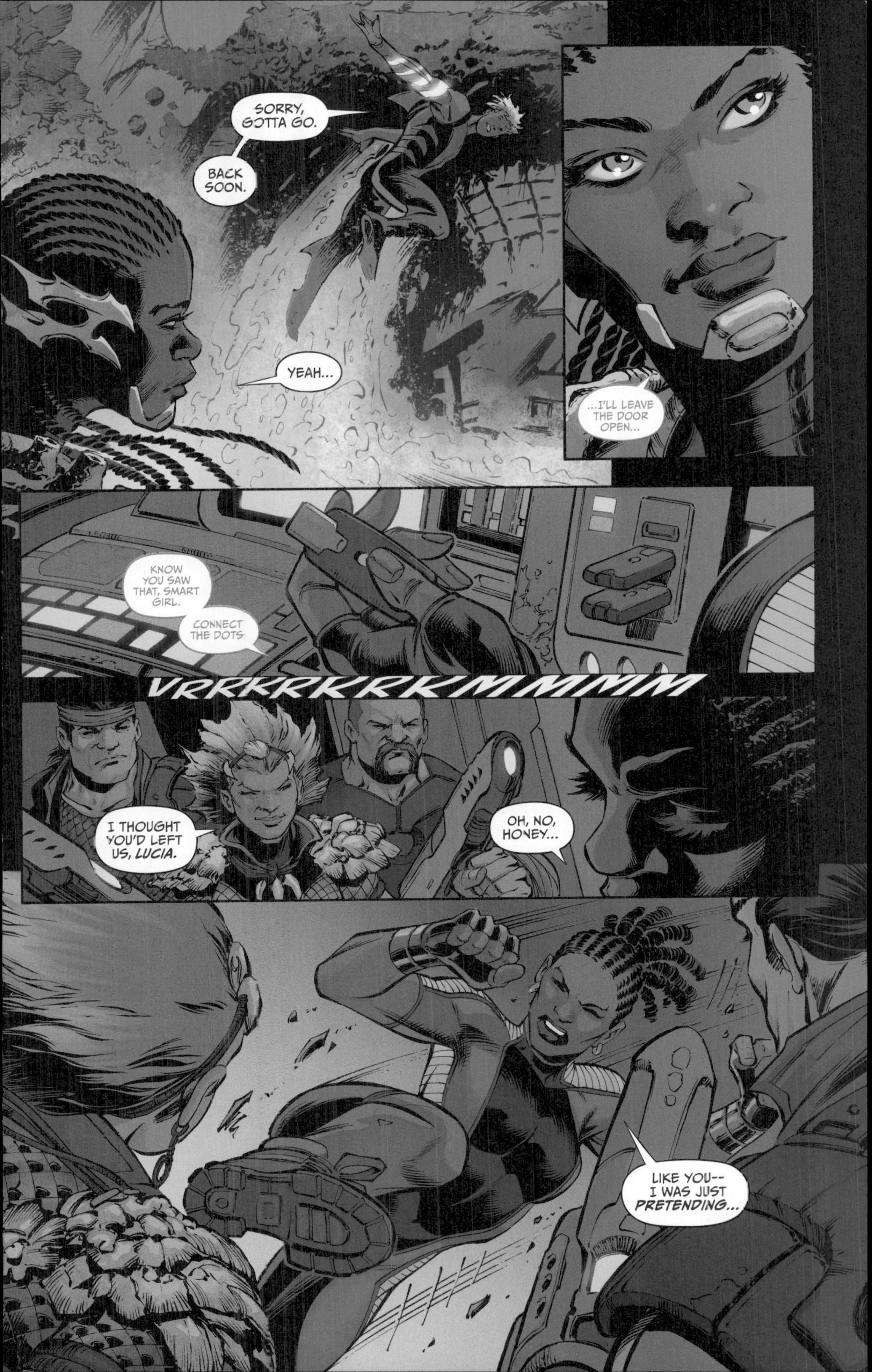
SORRY, GOTTA GO.
BACK SOON.
YEAH...
...I'LL LEAVE THE DOOR OPEN...
KNOW YOU SAW THAT, SMART GIRL.
CONNECT THE DOTS
VRRKRKRKRKMMMMM
I THOUGHT YOU'D LEFT US, *LUCIA.*
OH, NO, HONEY...
LIKE YOU-- I WAS JUST *PRETENDING*...

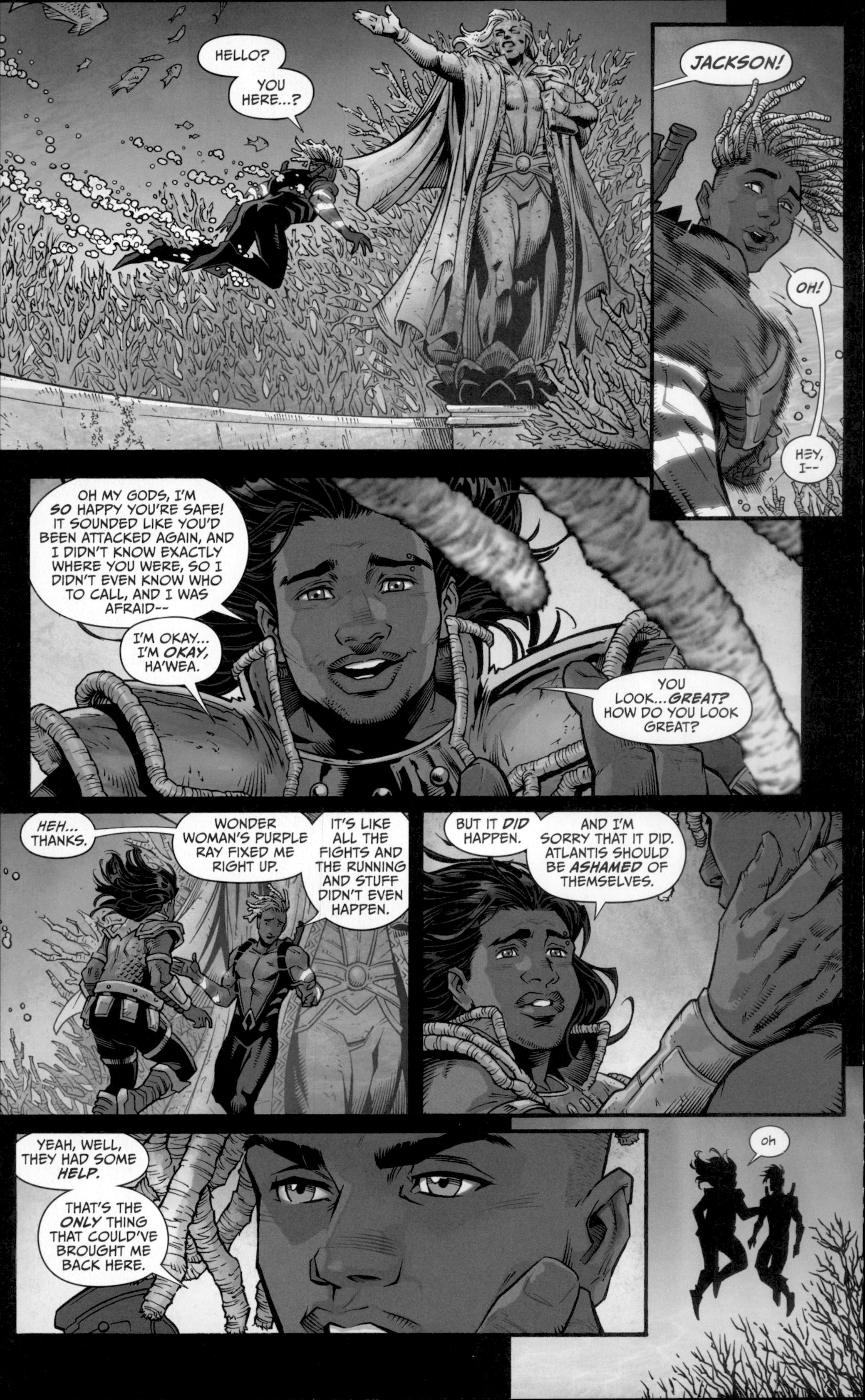
HELLO?
YOU HERE...?
JACKSON!
OH!
HEY, I--
OH MY GODS, I'M SO HAPPY YOU'RE SAFE! IT SOUNDED LIKE YOU'D BEEN ATTACKED AGAIN, AND I DIDN'T KNOW EXACTLY WHERE YOU WERE, SO I DIDN'T EVEN KNOW WHO TO CALL, AND I WAS AFRAID--
I'M OKAY... I'M OKAY, HA'WEA.
YOU LOOK...GREAT? HOW DO YOU LOOK GREAT?
HEH... THANKS.
WONDER WOMAN'S PURPLE RAY FIXED ME RIGHT UP.
IT'S LIKE ALL THE FIGHTS AND THE RUNNING AND STUFF DIDN'T EVEN HAPPEN.
BUT IT DID HAPPEN.
AND I'M SORRY THAT IT DID. ATLANTIS SHOULD BE ASHAMED OF THEMSELVES.
YEAH, WELL, THEY HAD SOME HELP.
THAT'S THE ONLY THING THAT COULD'VE BROUGHT ME BACK HERE.
oh

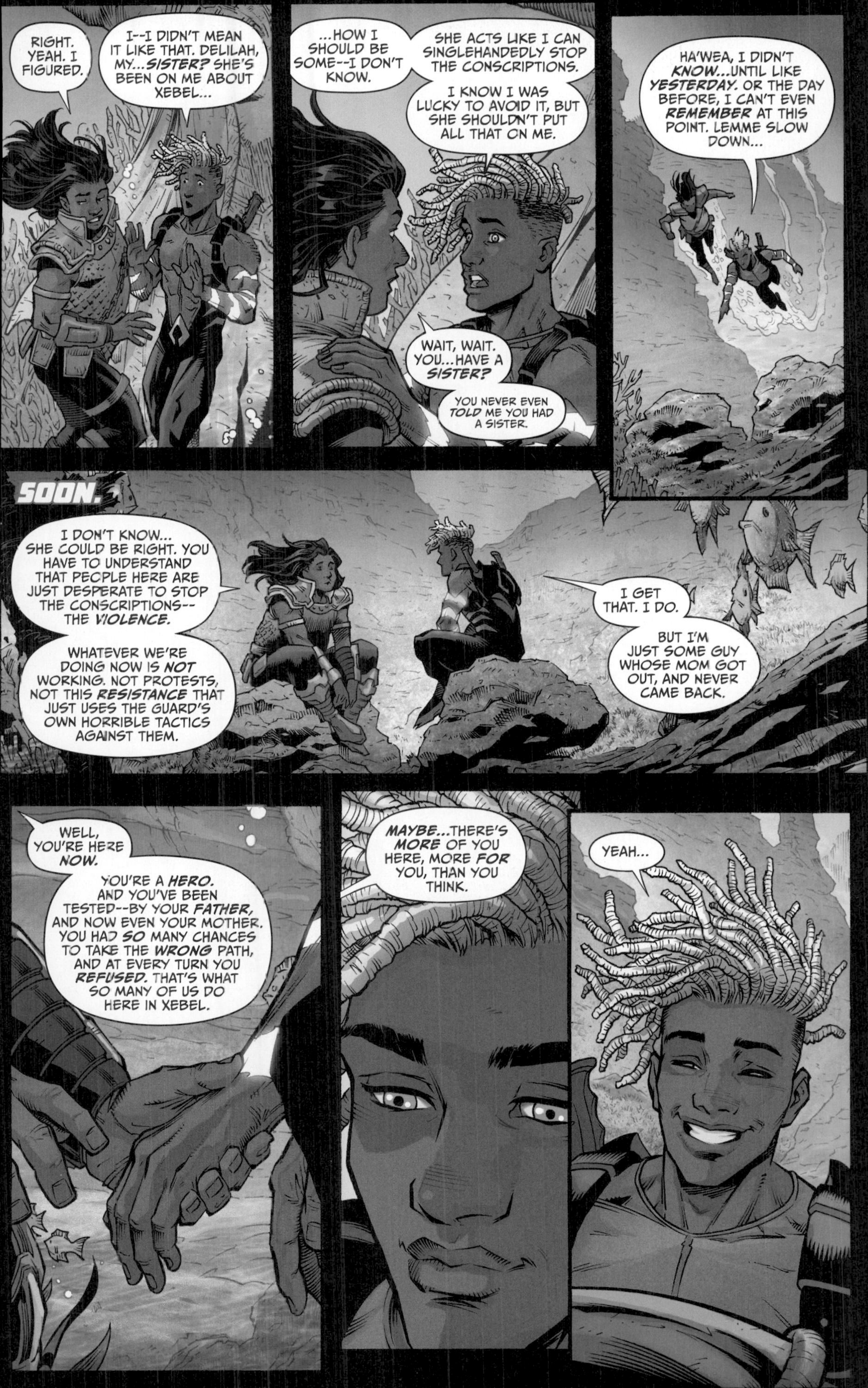

RIGHT. YEAH. I FIGURED.
I--I DIDN'T MEAN IT LIKE THAT. DELILAH, MY...SISTER? SHE'S BEEN ON ME ABOUT XEBEL...
...HOW I SHOULD BE SOME--I DON'T KNOW.
SHE ACTS LIKE I CAN SINGLEHANDEDLY STOP THE CONSCRIPTIONS.
I KNOW I WAS LUCKY TO AVOID IT, BUT SHE SHOULDN'T PUT ALL THAT ON ME.
WAIT, WAIT. YOU...HAVE A SISTER?
YOU NEVER EVEN TOLD ME YOU HAD A SISTER.
HA'WEA, I DIDN'T KNOW...UNTIL LIKE YESTERDAY. OR THE DAY BEFORE, I CAN'T EVEN REMEMBER AT THIS POINT. LEMME SLOW DOWN...
SOON.
I DON'T KNOW... SHE COULD BE RIGHT. YOU HAVE TO UNDERSTAND THAT PEOPLE HERE ARE JUST DESPERATE TO STOP THE CONSCRIPTIONS-- THE VIOLENCE.
WHATEVER WE'RE DOING NOW IS NOT WORKING. NOT PROTESTS, NOT THIS RESISTANCE THAT JUST USES THE GUARD'S OWN HORRIBLE TACTICS AGAINST THEM.
I GET THAT. I DO.
BUT I'M JUST SOME GUY WHOSE MOM GOT OUT, AND NEVER CAME BACK.
WELL, YOU'RE HERE NOW.
YOU'RE A HERO. AND YOU'VE BEEN TESTED--BY YOUR FATHER, AND NOW EVEN YOUR MOTHER. YOU HAD SO MANY CHANCES TO TAKE THE WRONG PATH, AND AT EVERY TURN YOU REFUSED. THAT'S WHAT SO MANY OF US DO HERE IN XEBEL.
MAYBE...THERE'S MORE OF YOU HERE, MORE FOR YOU, THAN YOU THINK.
YEAH...

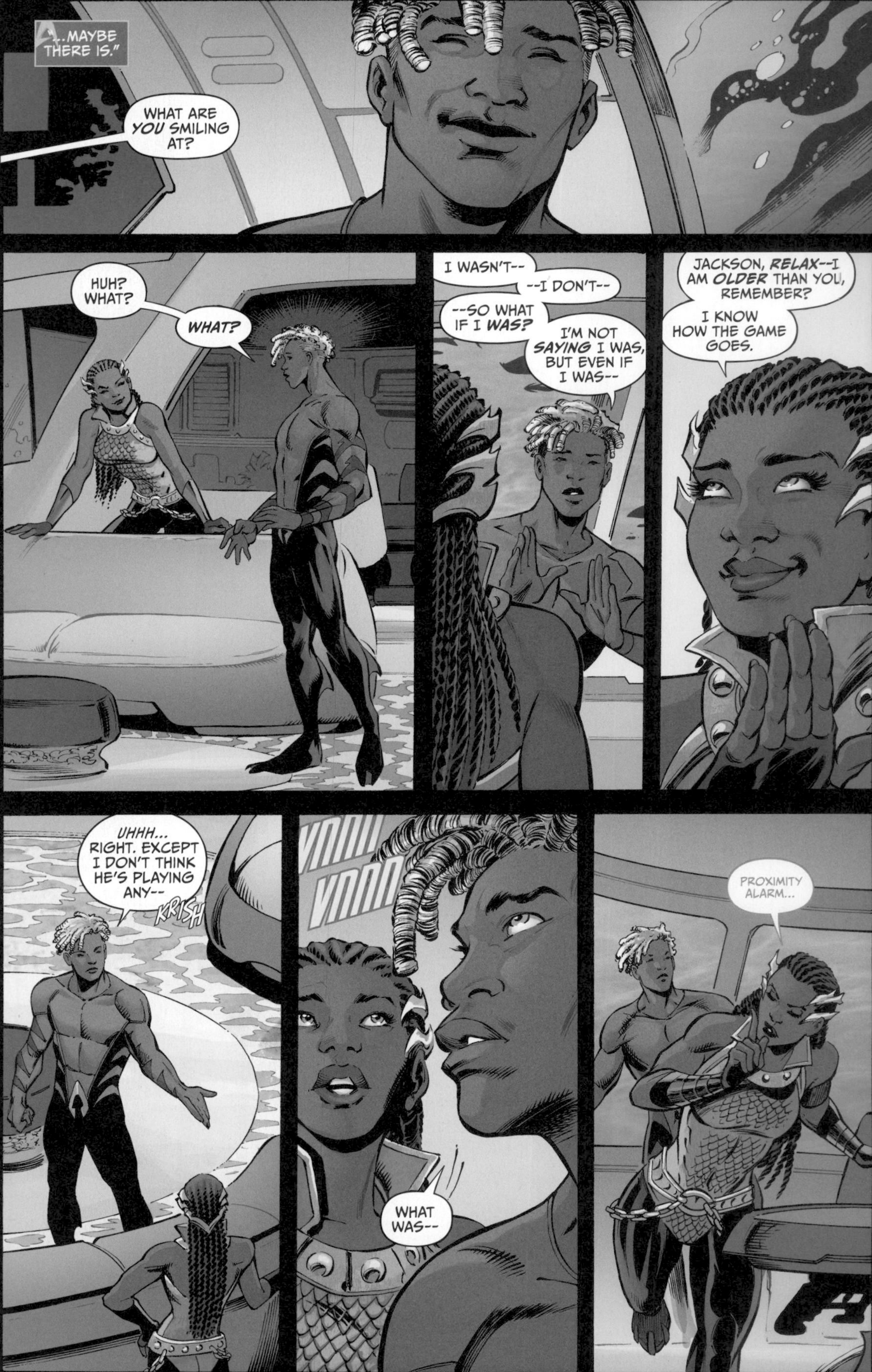
"...MAYBE THERE IS."
WHAT ARE *YOU* SMILING AT?
HUH? WHAT?
WHAT?
I WASN'T--
--I DON'T--
--SO WHAT IF I *WAS?*
I'M NOT *SAYING* I WAS, BUT EVEN IF I WAS--
JACKSON, *RELAX*--I AM *OLDER* THAN YOU, REMEMBER?
I KNOW HOW THE GAME GOES.
UHHH... RIGHT. EXCEPT I DON'T THINK HE'S PLAYING ANY--
KRISH
VNNN VNNN
WHAT WAS--
PROXIMITY ALARM...

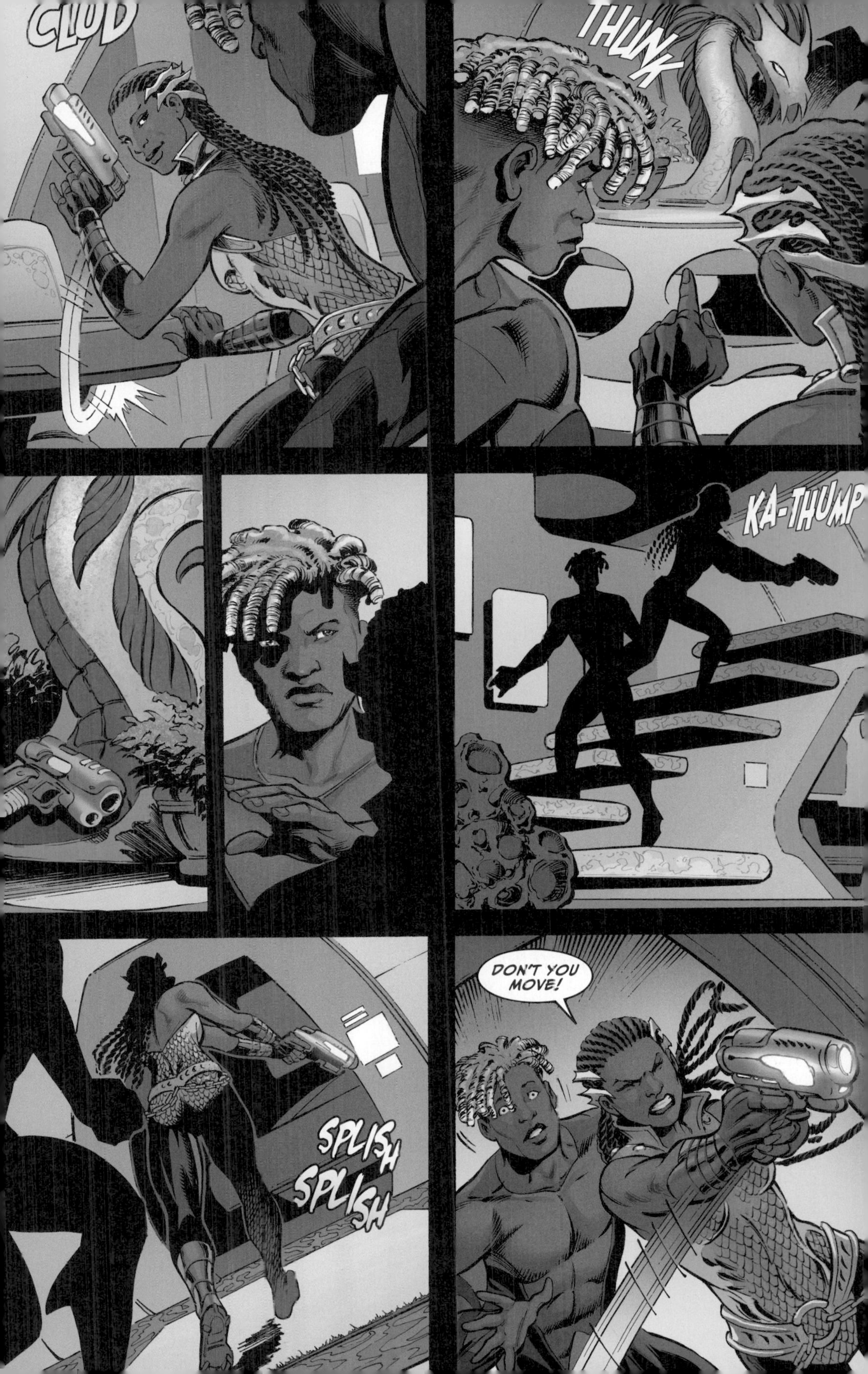
CLUD
THUNK
KA-THUMP
SPLISH
SPLISH
DON'T YOU MOVE!

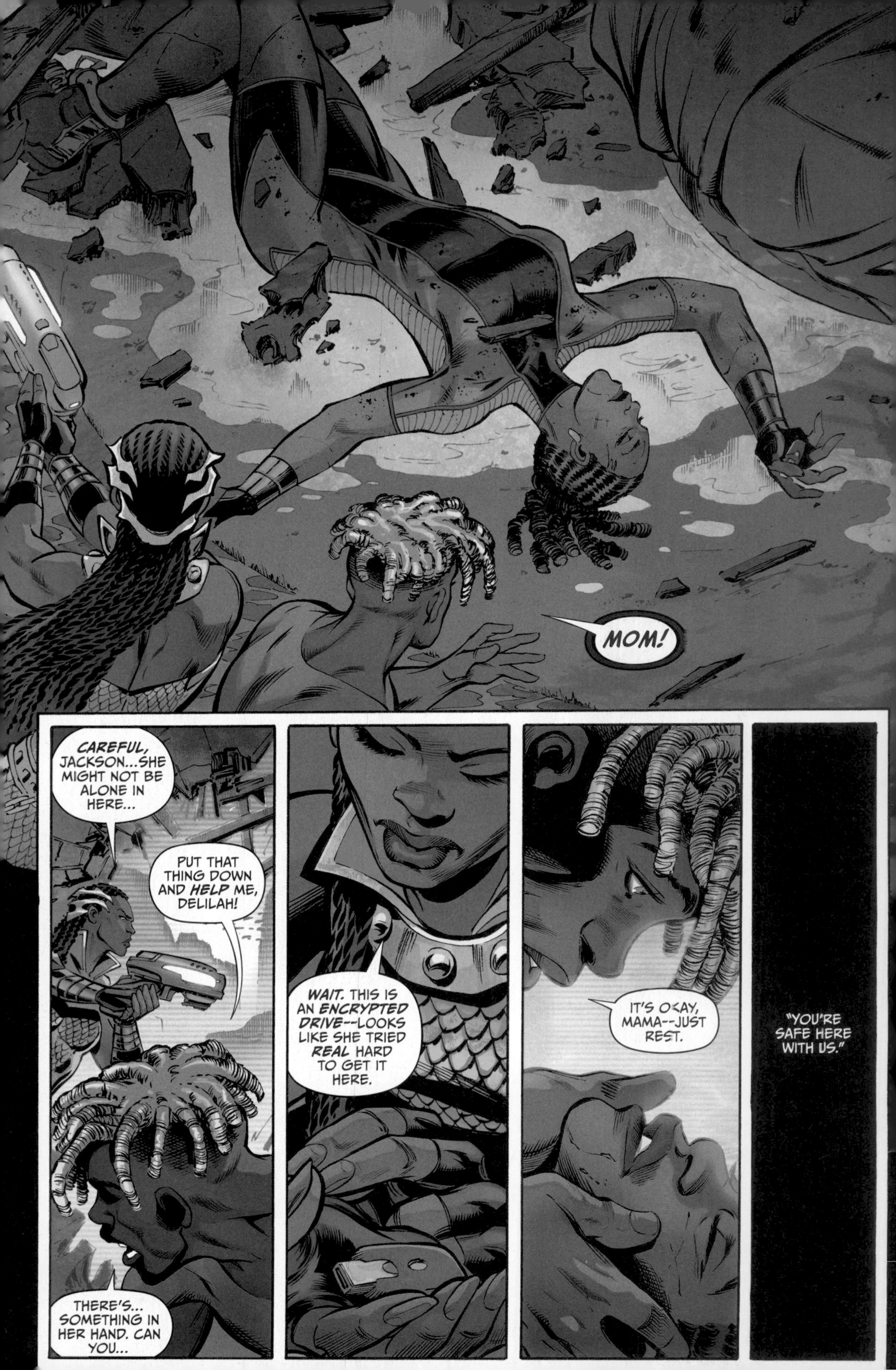
MOM!
CAREFUL, JACKSON...SHE MIGHT NOT BE ALONE IN HERE...
PUT THAT THING DOWN AND HELP ME, DELILAH!
THERE'S... SOMETHING IN HER HAND. CAN YOU...
WAIT. THIS IS AN ENCRYPTED DRIVE--LOOKS LIKE SHE TRIED REAL HARD TO GET IT HERE.
IT'S OKAY, MAMA--JUST REST.
"YOU'RE SAFE HERE WITH US."

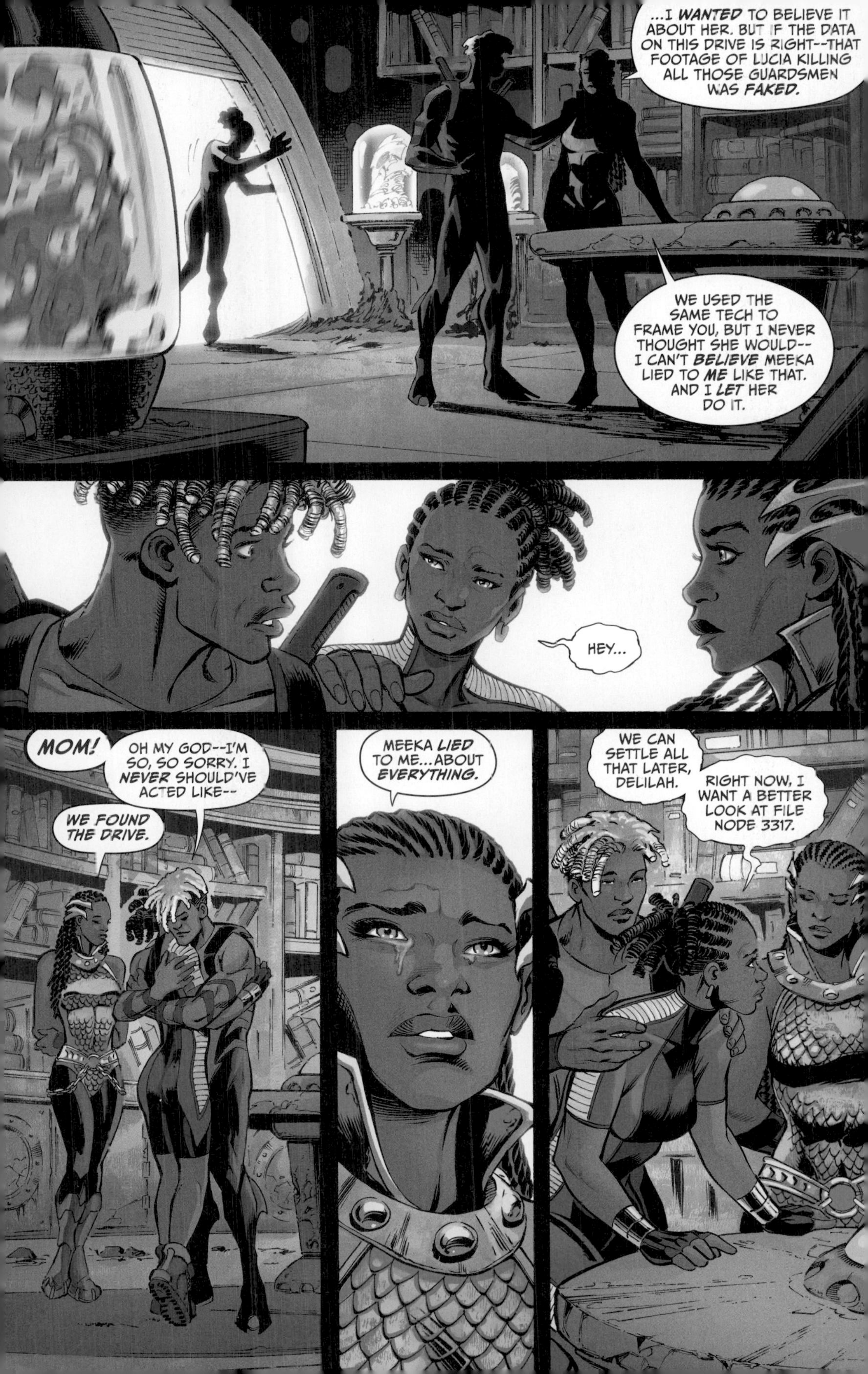
...I WANTED TO BELIEVE IT ABOUT HER. BUT IF THE DATA ON THIS DRIVE IS RIGHT--THAT FOOTAGE OF LUCIA KILLING ALL THOSE GUARDSMEN WAS FAKED.
WE USED THE SAME TECH TO FRAME YOU, BUT I NEVER THOUGHT SHE WOULD-- I CAN'T BELIEVE MEEKA LIED TO ME LIKE THAT. AND I LET HER DO IT.
HEY...
MOM!
OH MY GOD--I'M SO, SO SORRY. I NEVER SHOULD'VE ACTED LIKE--
WE FOUND THE DRIVE.
MEEKA LIED TO ME...ABOUT EVERYTHING.
WE CAN SETTLE ALL THAT LATER, DELILAH.
RIGHT NOW, I WANT A BETTER LOOK AT FILE NODE 3317.

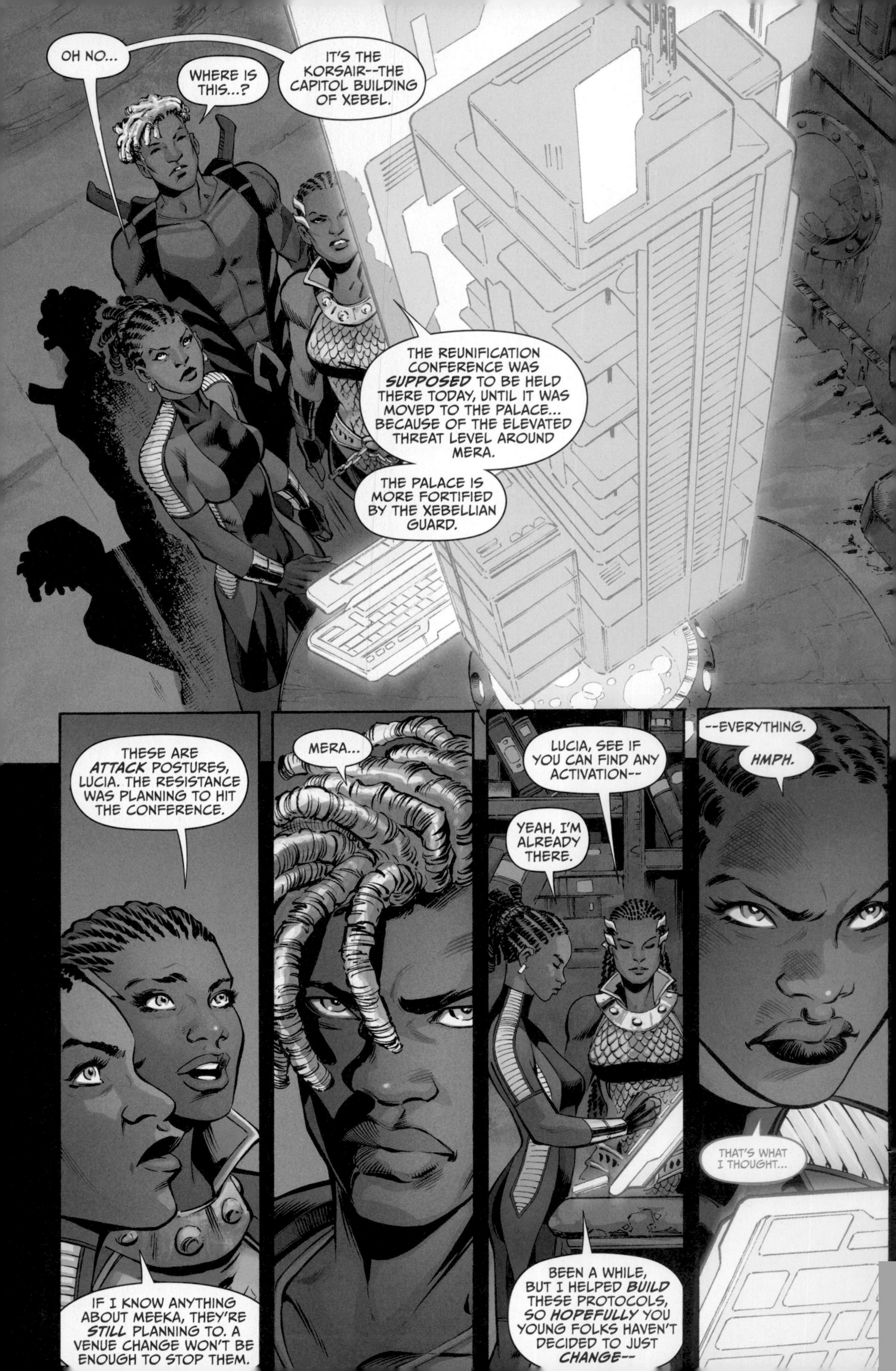
OH NO...
WHERE IS THIS...?
IT'S THE KORSAIR--THE CAPITOL BUILDING OF XEBEL.
THE REUNIFICATION CONFERENCE WAS SUPPOSED TO BE HELD THERE TODAY, UNTIL IT WAS MOVED TO THE PALACE... BECAUSE OF THE ELEVATED THREAT LEVEL AROUND MERA.
THE PALACE IS MORE FORTIFIED BY THE XEBELLIAN GUARD.
THESE ARE ATTACK POSTURES, LUCIA. THE RESISTANCE WAS PLANNING TO HIT THE CONFERENCE.
IF I KNOW ANYTHING ABOUT MEEKA, THEY'RE STILL PLANNING TO. A VENUE CHANGE WON'T BE ENOUGH TO STOP THEM.
MERA...
LUCIA, SEE IF YOU CAN FIND ANY ACTIVATION--
YEAH, I'M ALREADY THERE.
BEEN A WHILE, BUT I HELPED BUILD THESE PROTOCOLS, SO HOPEFULLY YOU YOUNG FOLKS HAVEN'T DECIDED TO JUST CHANGE--
--EVERYTHING.
HMPH.
THAT'S WHAT I THOUGHT...

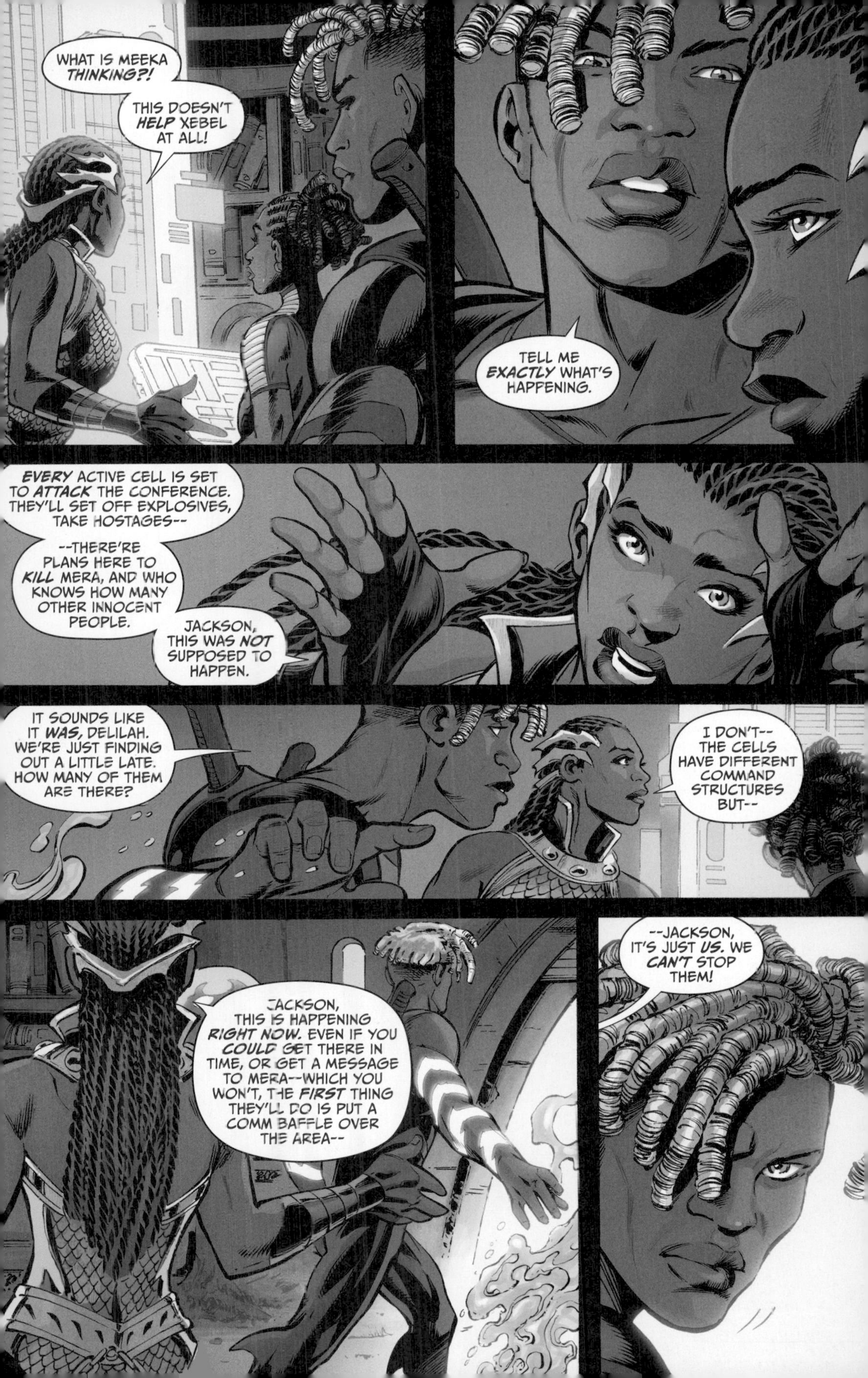
WHAT IS MEEKA THINKING?!
THIS DOESN'T HELP XEBEL AT ALL!
TELL ME EXACTLY WHAT'S HAPPENING.
EVERY ACTIVE CELL IS SET TO ATTACK THE CONFERENCE. THEY'LL SET OFF EXPLOSIVES, TAKE HOSTAGES--
--THERE'RE PLANS HERE TO KILL MERA, AND WHO KNOWS HOW MANY OTHER INNOCENT PEOPLE.
JACKSON, THIS WAS NOT SUPPOSED TO HAPPEN.
IT SOUNDS LIKE IT WAS, DELILAH. WE'RE JUST FINDING OUT A LITTLE LATE. HOW MANY OF THEM ARE THERE?
I DON'T-- THE CELLS HAVE DIFFERENT COMMAND STRUCTURES BUT--
JACKSON, THIS IS HAPPENING RIGHT NOW. EVEN IF YOU COULD GET THERE IN TIME, OR GET A MESSAGE TO MERA--WHICH YOU WON'T, THE FIRST THING THEY'LL DO IS PUT A COMM BAFFLE OVER THE AREA--
--JACKSON, IT'S JUST US. WE CAN'T STOP THEM!

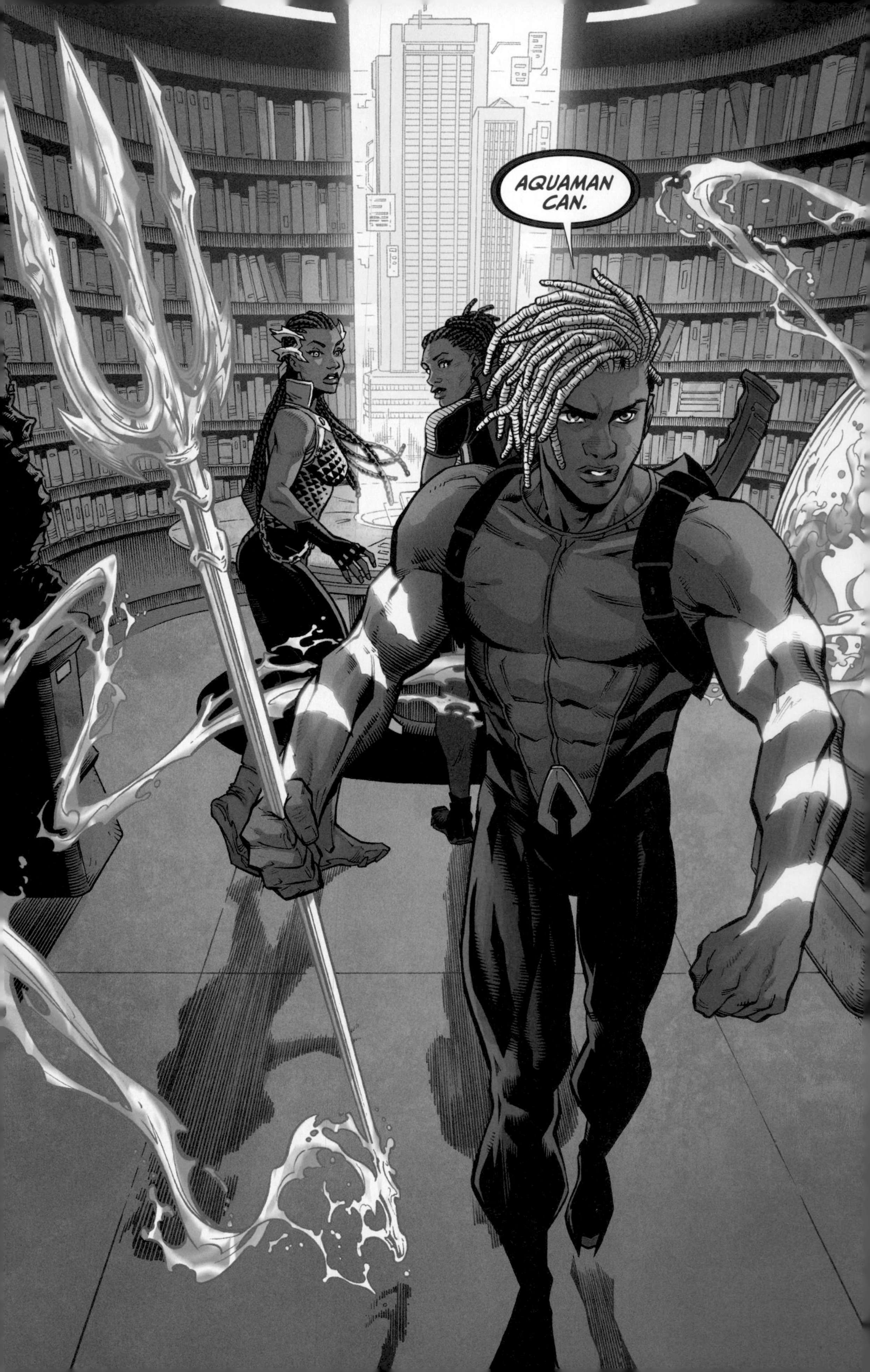
AQUAMAN CAN.

AQUAMAN: THE BECOMING #6
cover by DAVID TALASKI

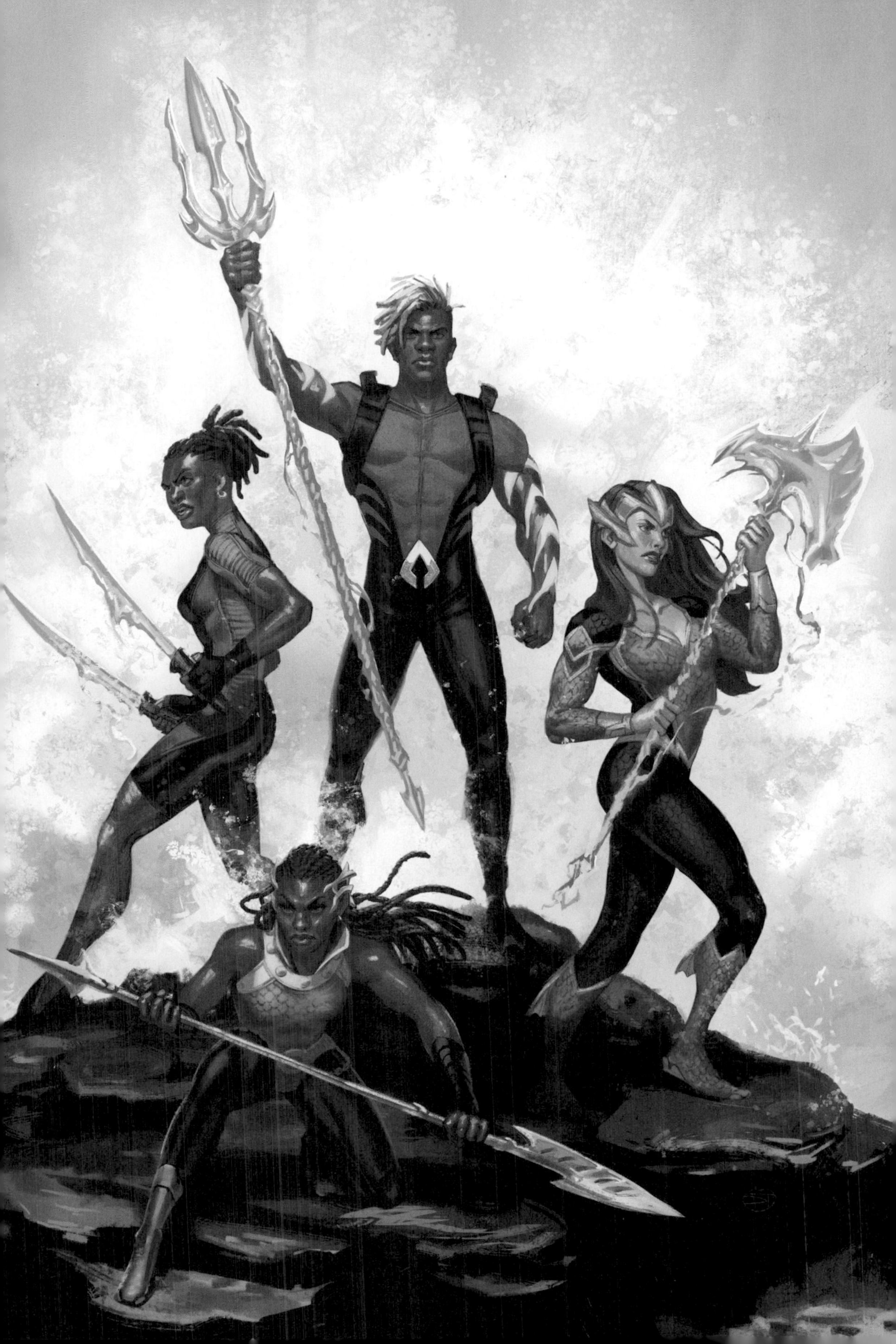

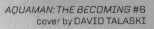

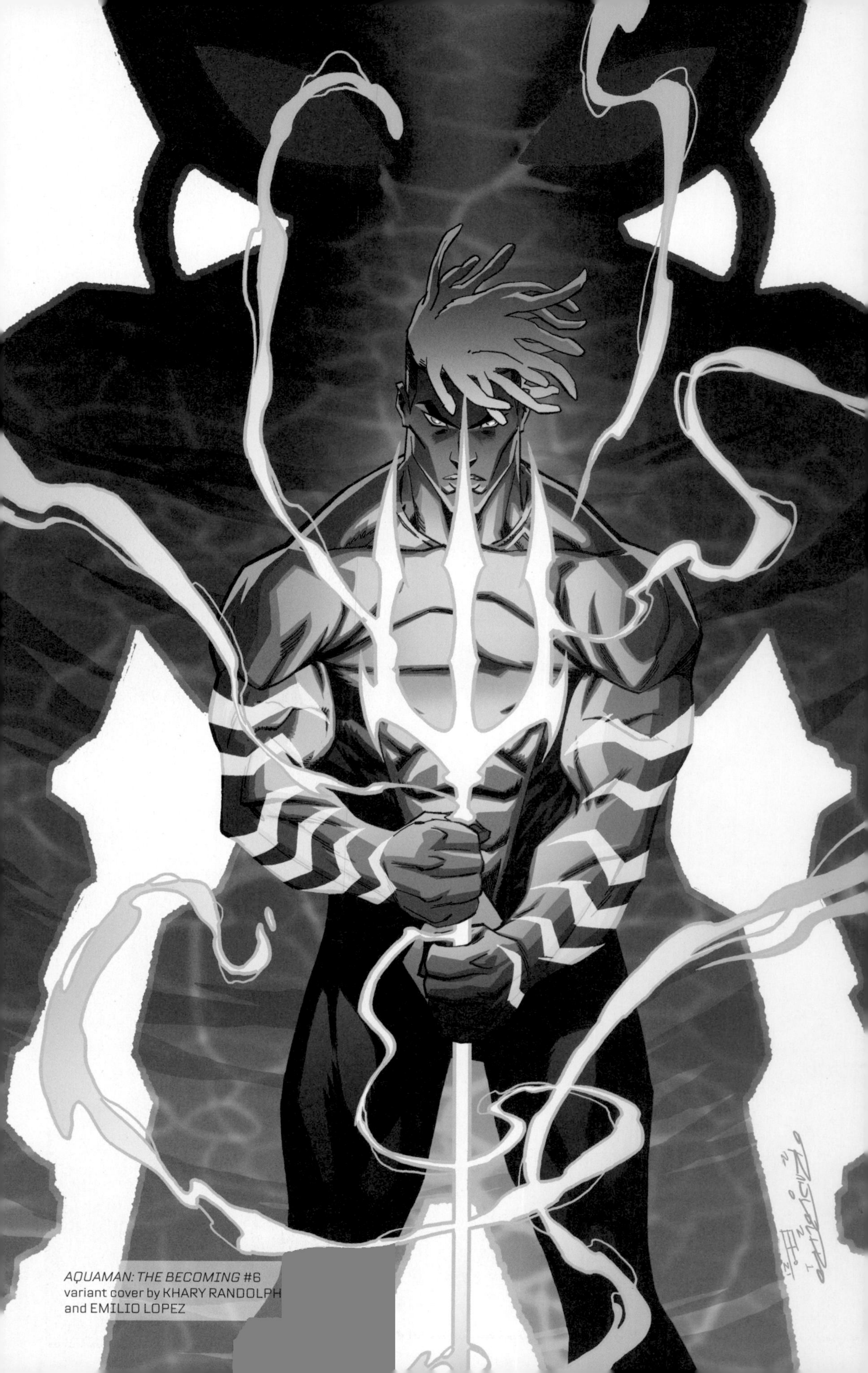

AQUAMAN: THE BECOMING #6
variant cover by KHARY RANDOLPH
and EMILIO LOPEZ

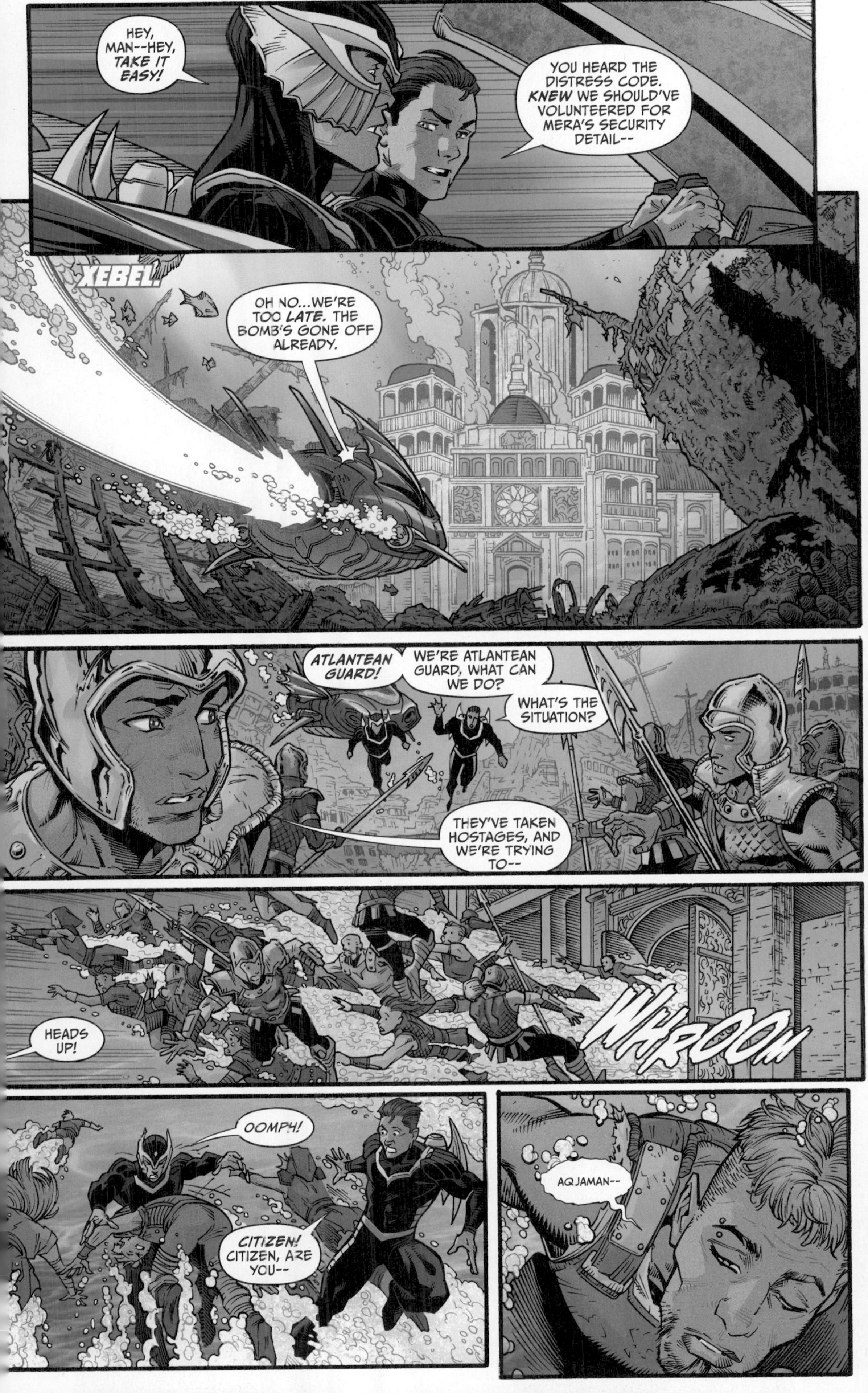
HEY, MAN--HEY, TAKE IT EASY!
YOU HEARD THE DISTRESS CODE. KNEW WE SHOULD'VE VOLUNTEERED FOR MERA'S SECURITY DETAIL--
XEBEL.
OH NO...WE'RE TOO LATE. THE BOMB'S GONE OFF ALREADY.
ATLANTEAN GUARD!
WE'RE ATLANTEAN GUARD, WHAT CAN WE DO?
WHAT'S THE SITUATION?
THEY'VE TAKEN HOSTAGES, AND WE'RE TRYING TO--
HEADS UP!
WHROOM
OOMPH!
CITIZEN! CITIZEN, ARE YOU--
AQUAMAN--

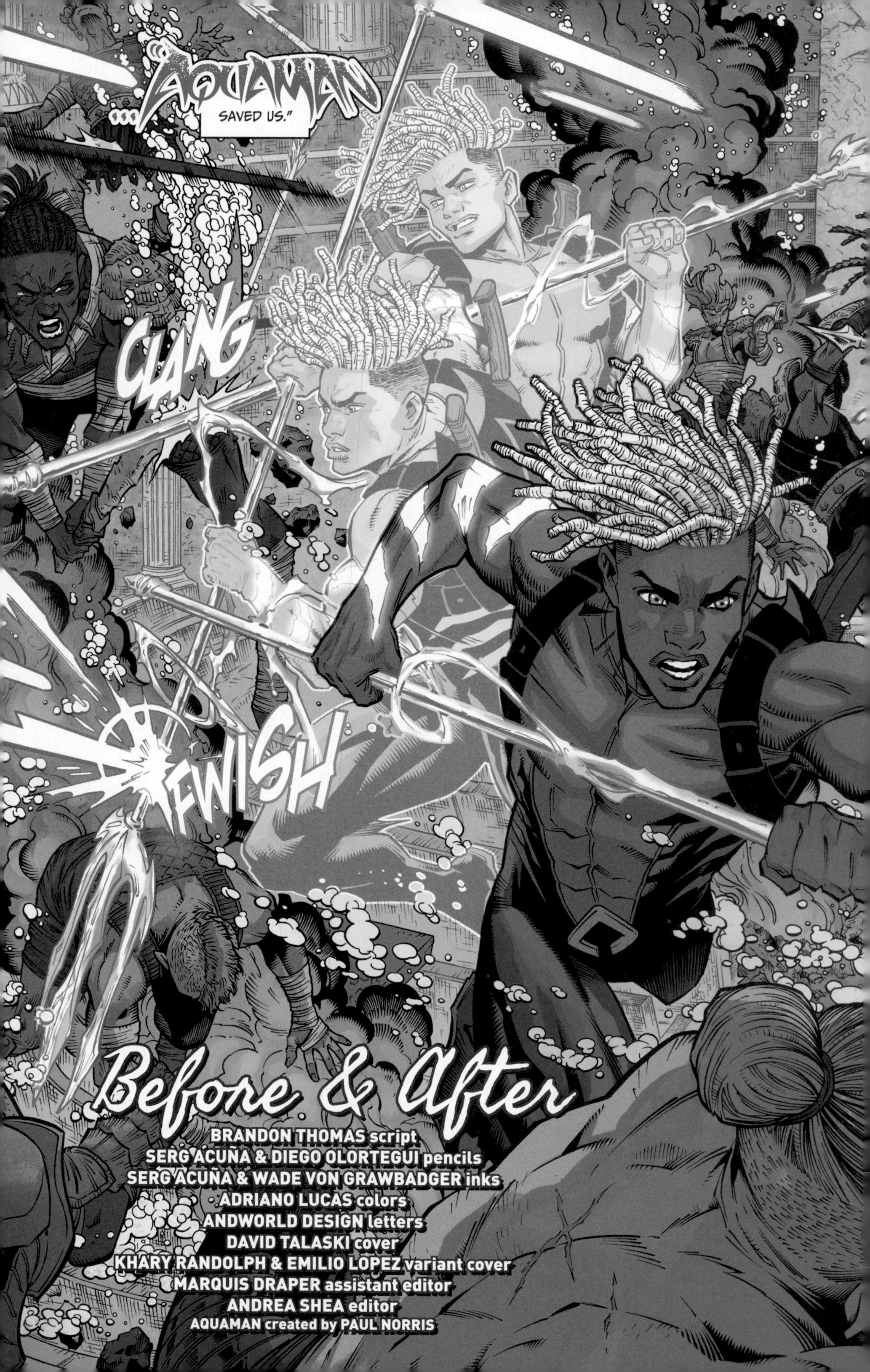
...AQUAMAN SAVED US."
CLANG
FWISH
Before & After
BRANDON THOMAS script
SERG ACUÑA & DIEGO OLORTEGUI pencils
SERG ACUÑA & WADE VON GRAWBADGER inks
ADRIANO LUCAS colors
ANDWORLD DESIGN letters
DAVID TALASKI cover
KHARY RANDOLPH & EMILIO LOPEZ variant cover
MARQUIS DRAPER assistant editor
ANDREA SHEA editor
AQUAMAN created by PAUL NORRIS

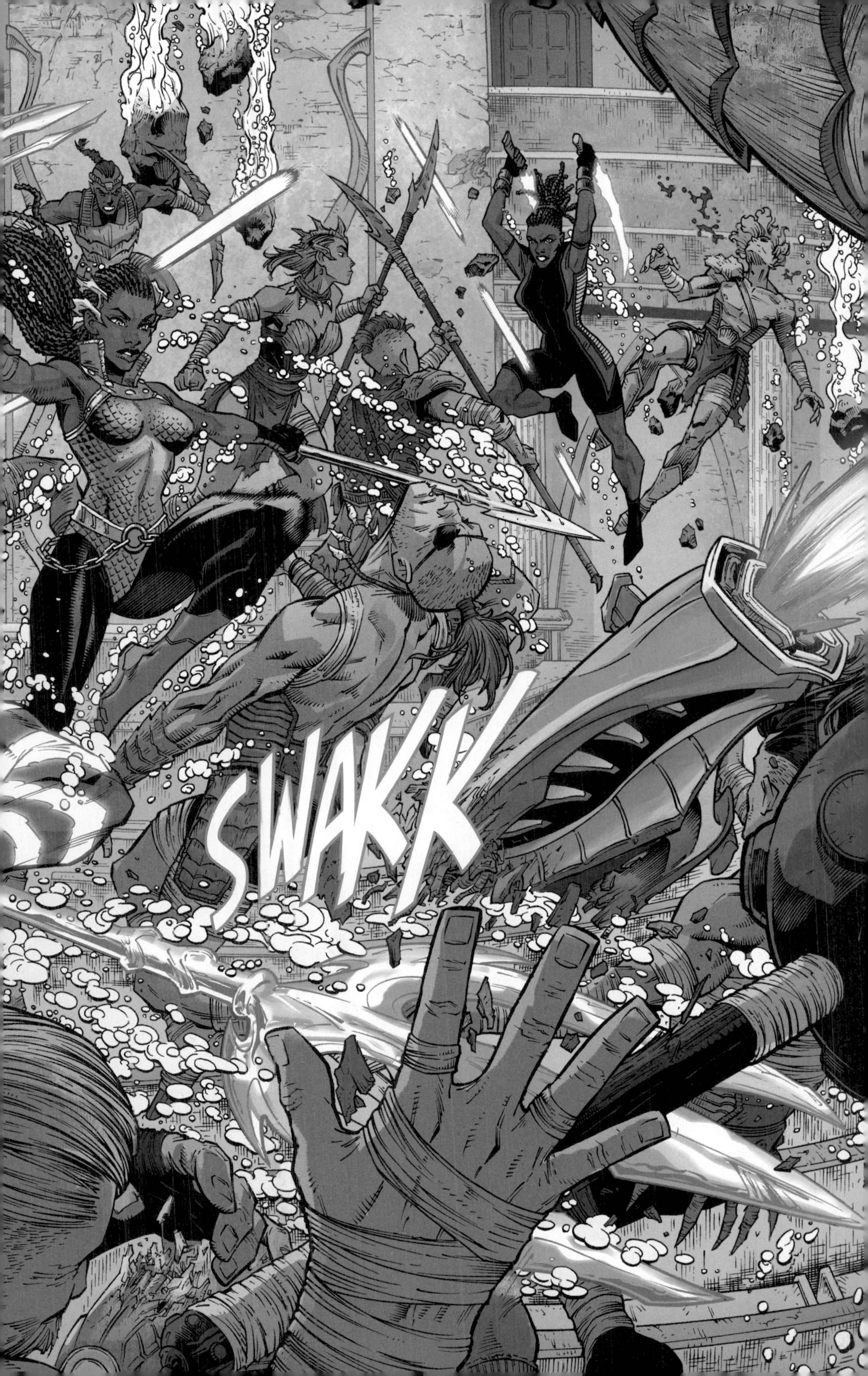
SWAKK

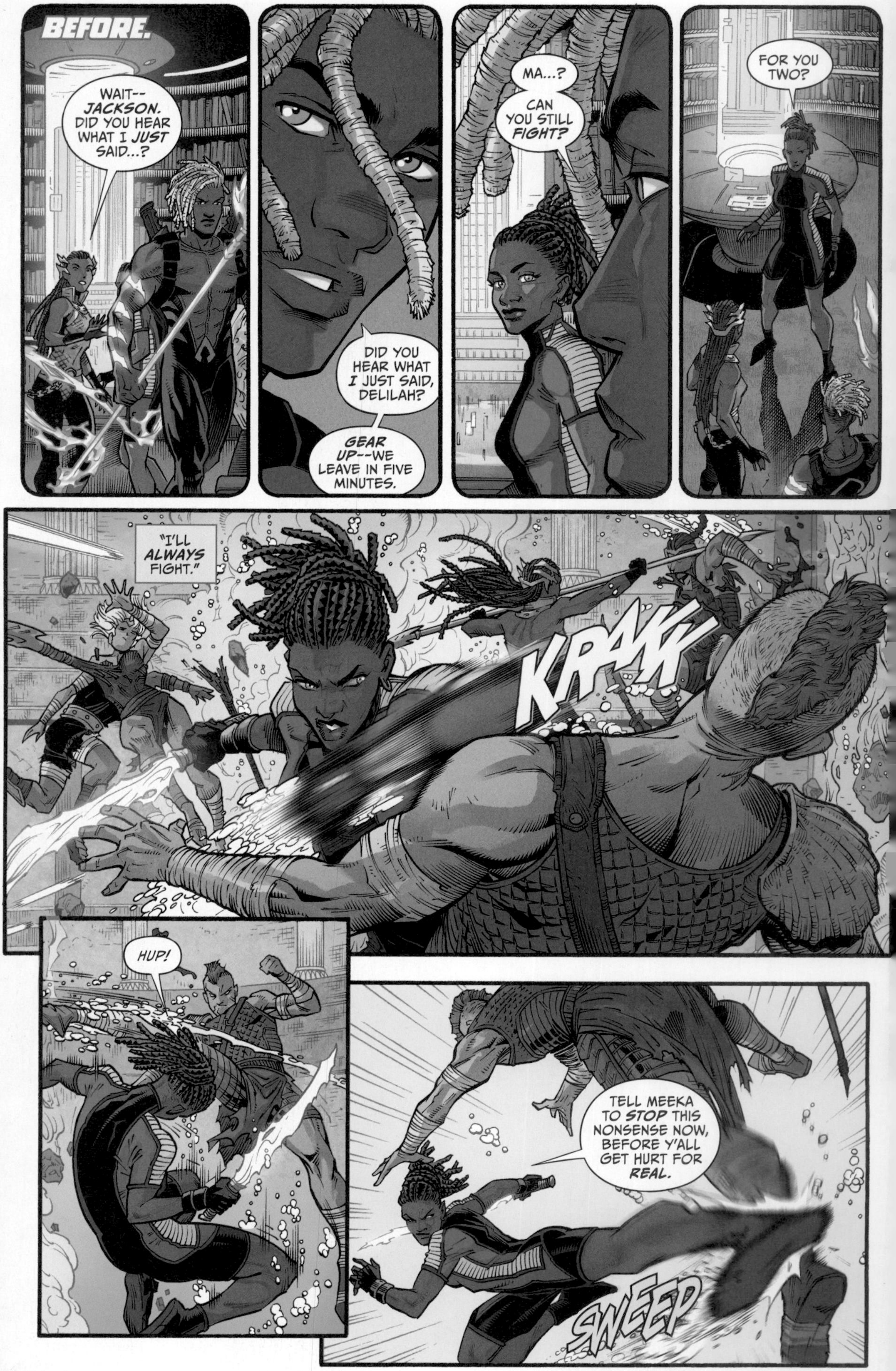
BEFORE.
WAIT-- JACKSON. DID YOU HEAR WHAT I JUST SAID...?
DID YOU HEAR WHAT I JUST SAID, DELILAH?
GEAR UP--WE LEAVE IN FIVE MINUTES.
MA...?
CAN YOU STILL FIGHT?
FOR YOU TWO?
"I'LL ALWAYS FIGHT."
KRAKK
HUP!
TELL MEEKA TO STOP THIS NONSENSE NOW, BEFORE Y'ALL GET HURT FOR REAL.
SWEEP

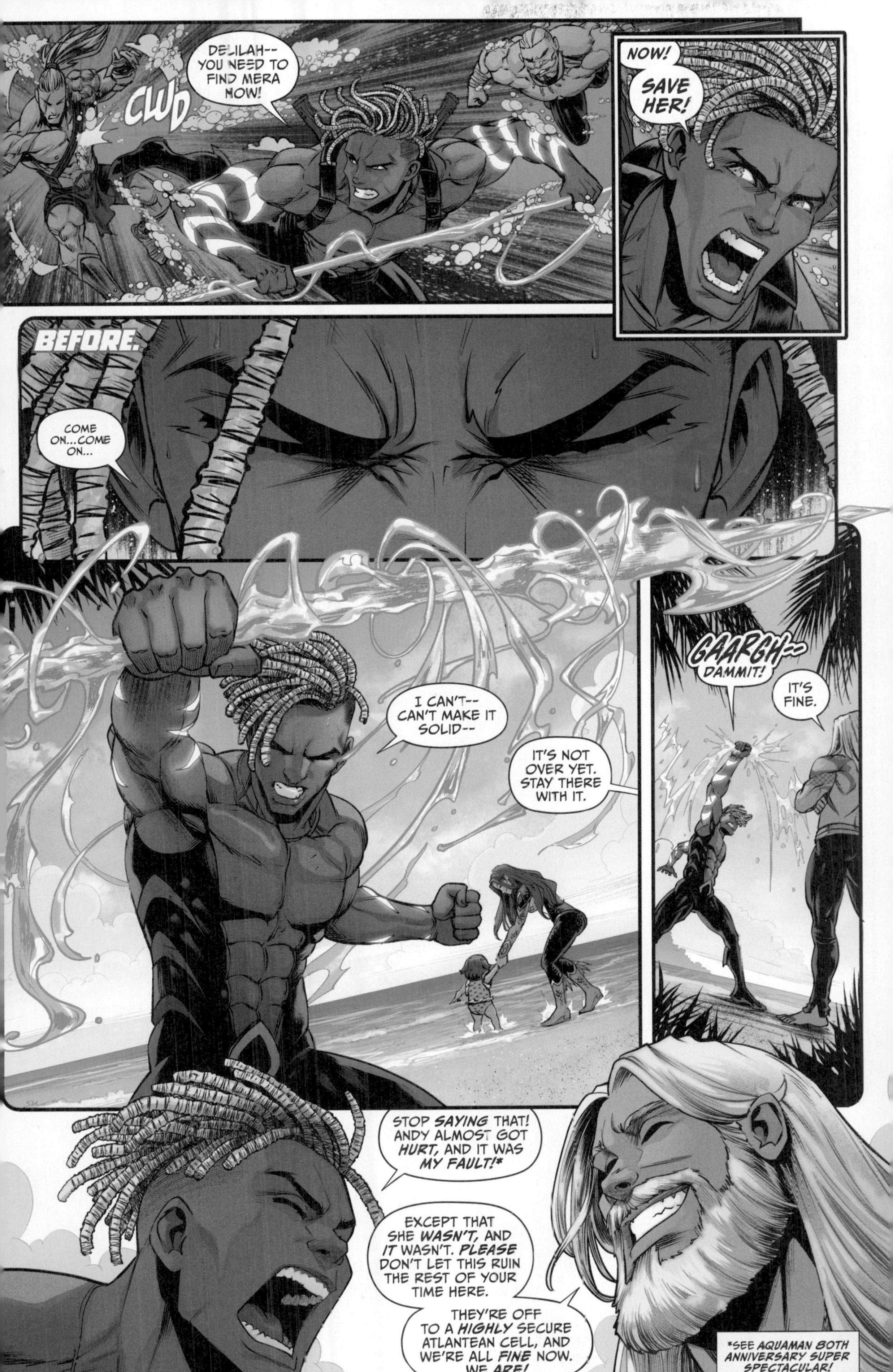
DELILAH-- YOU NEED TO FIND MERA NOW!
CLUD
NOW!
SAVE HER!
BEFORE.
COME ON...COME ON...
I CAN'T-- CAN'T MAKE IT SOLID--
IT'S NOT OVER YET. STAY THERE WITH IT.
GAARGH-- DAMMIT!
IT'S FINE.
STOP SAYING THAT! ANDY ALMOST GOT HURT, AND IT WAS MY FAULT!*
EXCEPT THAT SHE WASN'T, AND IT WASN'T. PLEASE DON'T LET THIS RUIN THE REST OF YOUR TIME HERE.
THEY'RE OFF TO A HIGHLY SECURE ATLANTEAN CELL, AND WE'RE ALL FINE NOW. WE ARE!
*SEE AQUAMAN 80TH ANNIVERSARY SUPER SPECTACULAR!

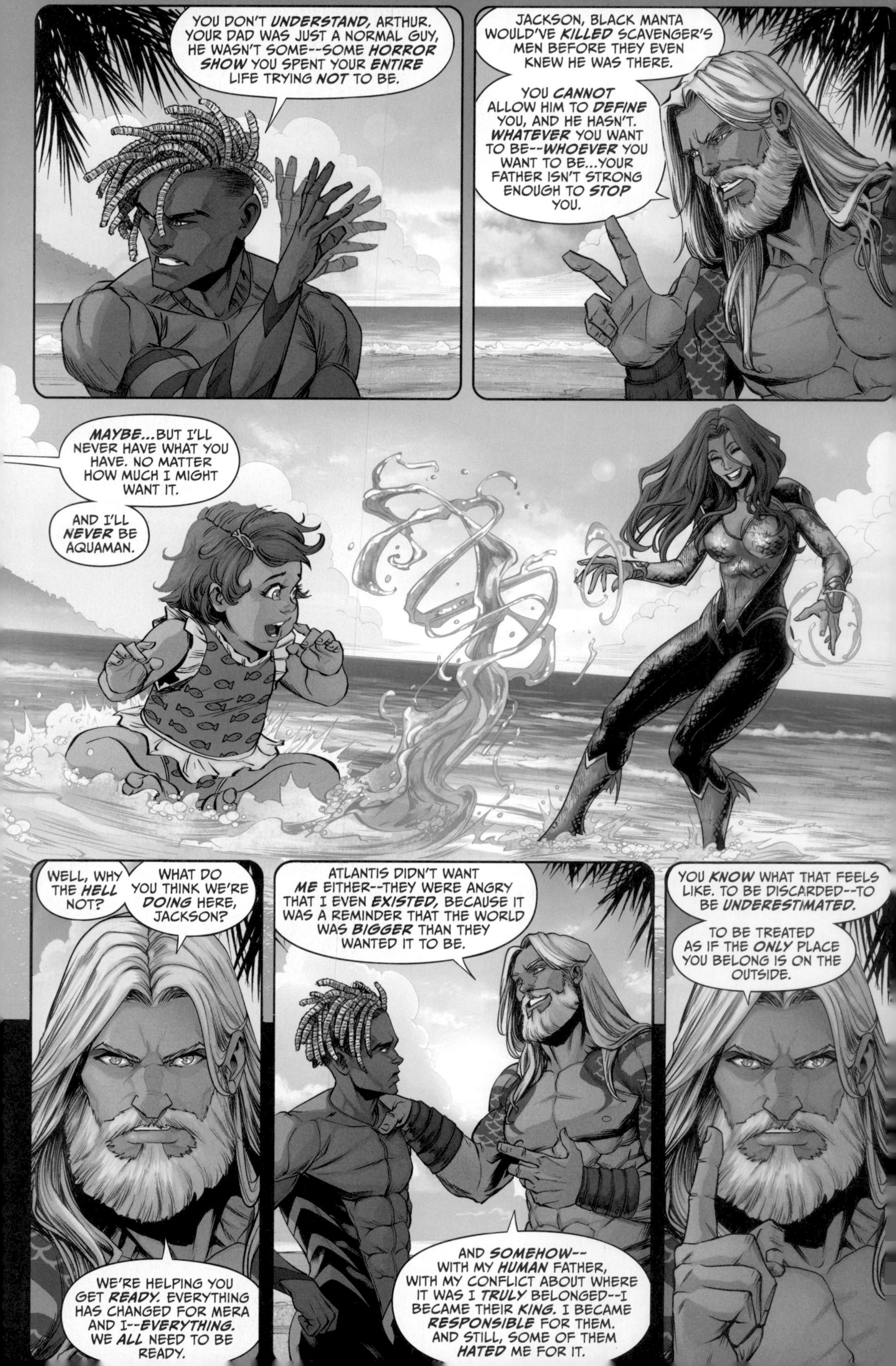
YOU DON'T UNDERSTAND, ARTHUR. YOUR DAD WAS JUST A NORMAL GUY, HE WASN'T SOME--SOME HORROR SHOW YOU SPENT YOUR ENTIRE LIFE TRYING NOT TO BE.
JACKSON, BLACK MANTA WOULD'VE KILLED SCAVENGER'S MEN BEFORE THEY EVEN KNEW HE WAS THERE.
YOU CANNOT ALLOW HIM TO DEFINE YOU, AND HE HASN'T. WHATEVER YOU WANT TO BE--WHOEVER YOU WANT TO BE...YOUR FATHER ISN'T STRONG ENOUGH TO STOP YOU.
MAYBE...BUT I'LL NEVER HAVE WHAT YOU HAVE. NO MATTER HOW MUCH I MIGHT WANT IT.
AND I'LL NEVER BE AQUAMAN.
WELL, WHY THE HELL NOT?
WHAT DO YOU THINK WE'RE DOING HERE, JACKSON?
WE'RE HELPING YOU GET READY. EVERYTHING HAS CHANGED FOR MERA AND I--EVERYTHING. WE ALL NEED TO BE READY.
ATLANTIS DIDN'T WANT ME EITHER--THEY WERE ANGRY THAT I EVEN EXISTED, BECAUSE IT WAS A REMINDER THAT THE WORLD WAS BIGGER THAN THEY WANTED IT TO BE.
AND SOMEHOW-- WITH MY HUMAN FATHER, WITH MY CONFLICT ABOUT WHERE IT WAS I TRULY BELONGED--I BECAME THEIR KING. I BECAME RESPONSIBLE FOR THEM. AND STILL, SOME OF THEM HATED ME FOR IT.
YOU KNOW WHAT THAT FEELS LIKE. TO BE DISCARDED--TO BE UNDERESTIMATED.
TO BE TREATED AS IF THE ONLY PLACE YOU BELONG IS ON THE OUTSIDE.

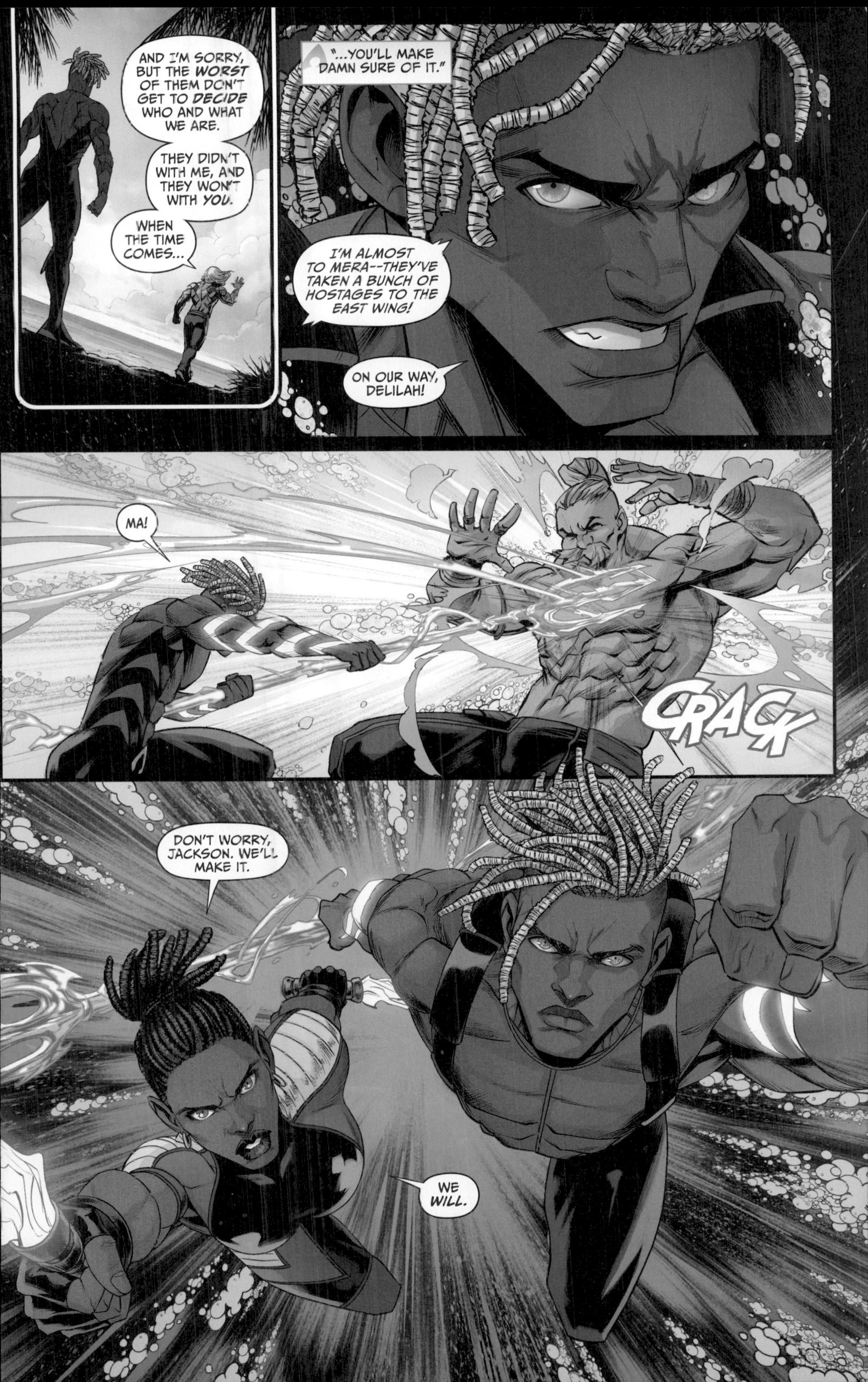
AND I'M SORRY, BUT THE WORST OF THEM DON'T GET TO DECIDE WHO AND WHAT WE ARE.
THEY DIDN'T WITH ME, AND THEY WON'T WITH YOU.
WHEN THE TIME COMES...
"...YOU'LL MAKE DAMN SURE OF IT."
I'M ALMOST TO MERA--THEY'VE TAKEN A BUNCH OF HOSTAGES TO THE EAST WING!
ON OUR WAY, DELILAH!
MA!
CRACK
DON'T WORRY, JACKSON. WE'LL MAKE IT.
WE WILL.

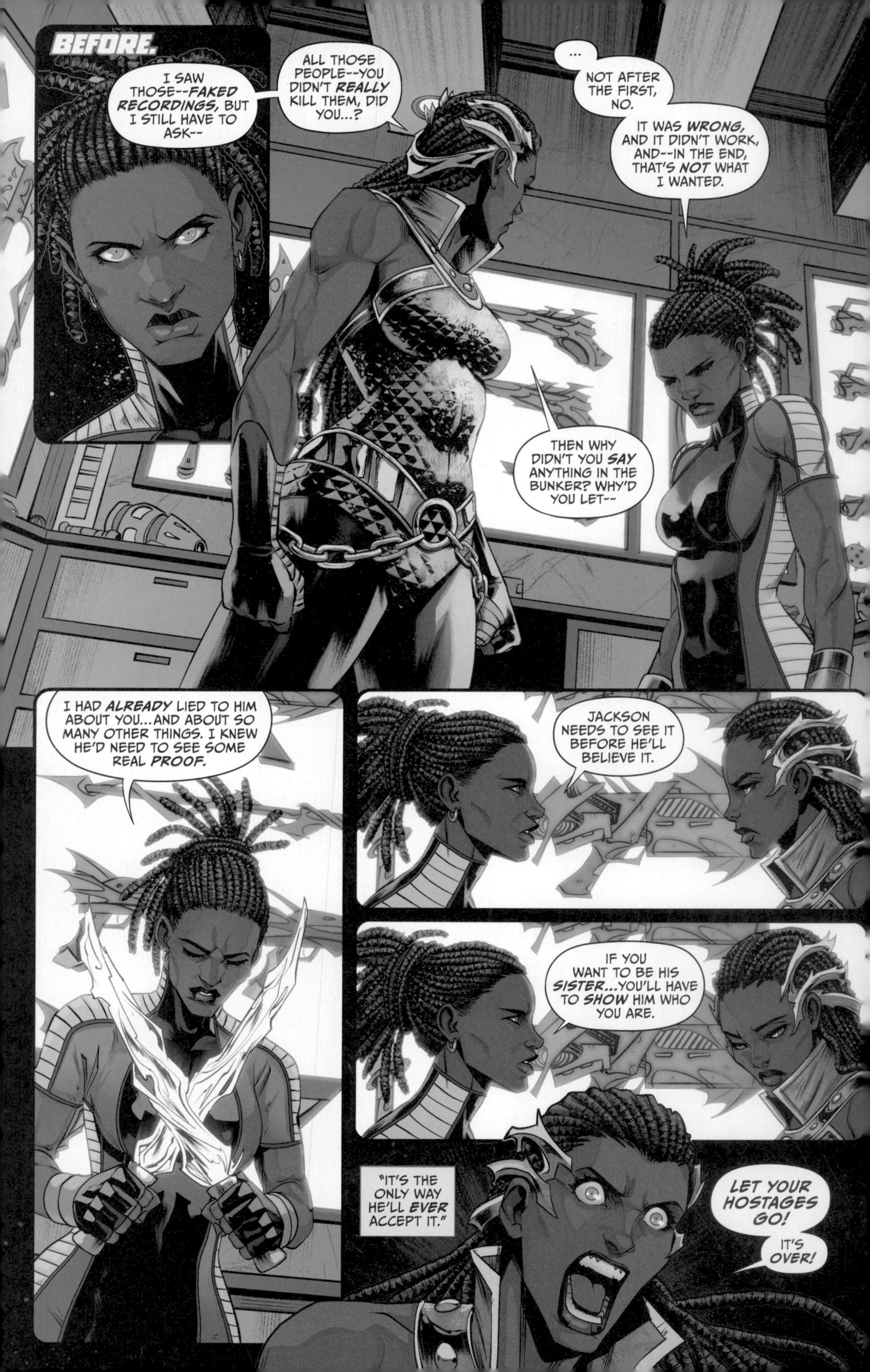
BEFORE.
I SAW THOSE--FAKED RECORDINGS, BUT I STILL HAVE TO ASK--
ALL THOSE PEOPLE--YOU DIDN'T REALLY KILL THEM, DID YOU...?
...
NOT AFTER THE FIRST, NO.
IT WAS WRONG, AND IT DIDN'T WORK, AND--IN THE END, THAT'S NOT WHAT I WANTED.
THEN WHY DIDN'T YOU SAY ANYTHING IN THE BUNKER? WHY'D YOU LET--
I HAD ALREADY LIED TO HIM ABOUT YOU...AND ABOUT SO MANY OTHER THINGS. I KNEW HE'D NEED TO SEE SOME REAL PROOF.
JACKSON NEEDS TO SEE IT BEFORE HE'LL BELIEVE IT.
IF YOU WANT TO BE HIS SISTER...YOU'LL HAVE TO SHOW HIM WHO YOU ARE.
"IT'S THE ONLY WAY HE'LL EVER ACCEPT IT."
LET YOUR HOSTAGES GO!
IT'S OVER!

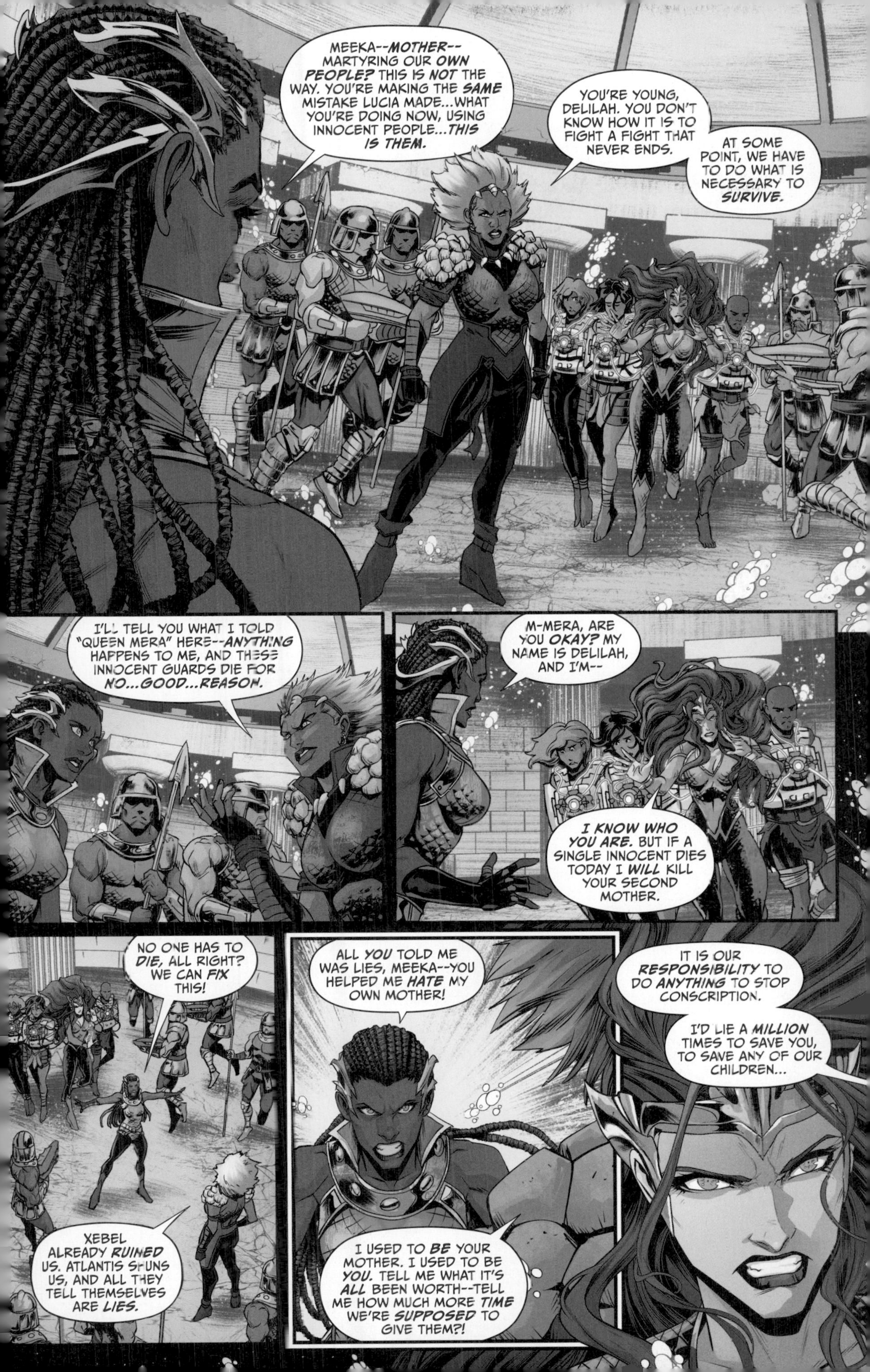
MEEKA--MOTHER--MARTYRING OUR OWN PEOPLE? THIS IS NOT THE WAY. YOU'RE MAKING THE SAME MISTAKE LUCIA MADE...WHAT YOU'RE DOING NOW, USING INNOCENT PEOPLE...THIS IS THEM.
YOU'RE YOUNG, DELILAH. YOU DON'T KNOW HOW IT IS TO FIGHT A FIGHT THAT NEVER ENDS.
AT SOME POINT, WE HAVE TO DO WHAT IS NECESSARY TO SURVIVE.
I'LL TELL YOU WHAT I TOLD "QUEEN MERA" HERE--ANYTHING HAPPENS TO ME, AND THESE INNOCENT GUARDS DIE FOR NO...GOOD...REASON.
M-MERA, ARE YOU OKAY? MY NAME IS DELILAH, AND I'M--
I KNOW WHO YOU ARE. BUT IF A SINGLE INNOCENT DIES TODAY I WILL KILL YOUR SECOND MOTHER.
NO ONE HAS TO DIE, ALL RIGHT? WE CAN FIX THIS!
XEBEL ALREADY RUINED US. ATLANTIS SHUNS US, AND ALL THEY TELL THEMSELVES ARE LIES.
ALL YOU TOLD ME WAS LIES, MEEKA--YOU HELPED ME HATE MY OWN MOTHER!
I USED TO BE YOUR MOTHER. I USED TO BE YOU. TELL ME WHAT IT'S ALL BEEN WORTH--TELL ME HOW MUCH MORE TIME WE'RE SUPPOSED TO GIVE THEM?!
IT IS OUR RESPONSIBILITY TO DO ANYTHING TO STOP CONSCRIPTION.
I'D LIE A MILLION TIMES TO SAVE YOU, TO SAVE ANY OF OUR CHILDREN...

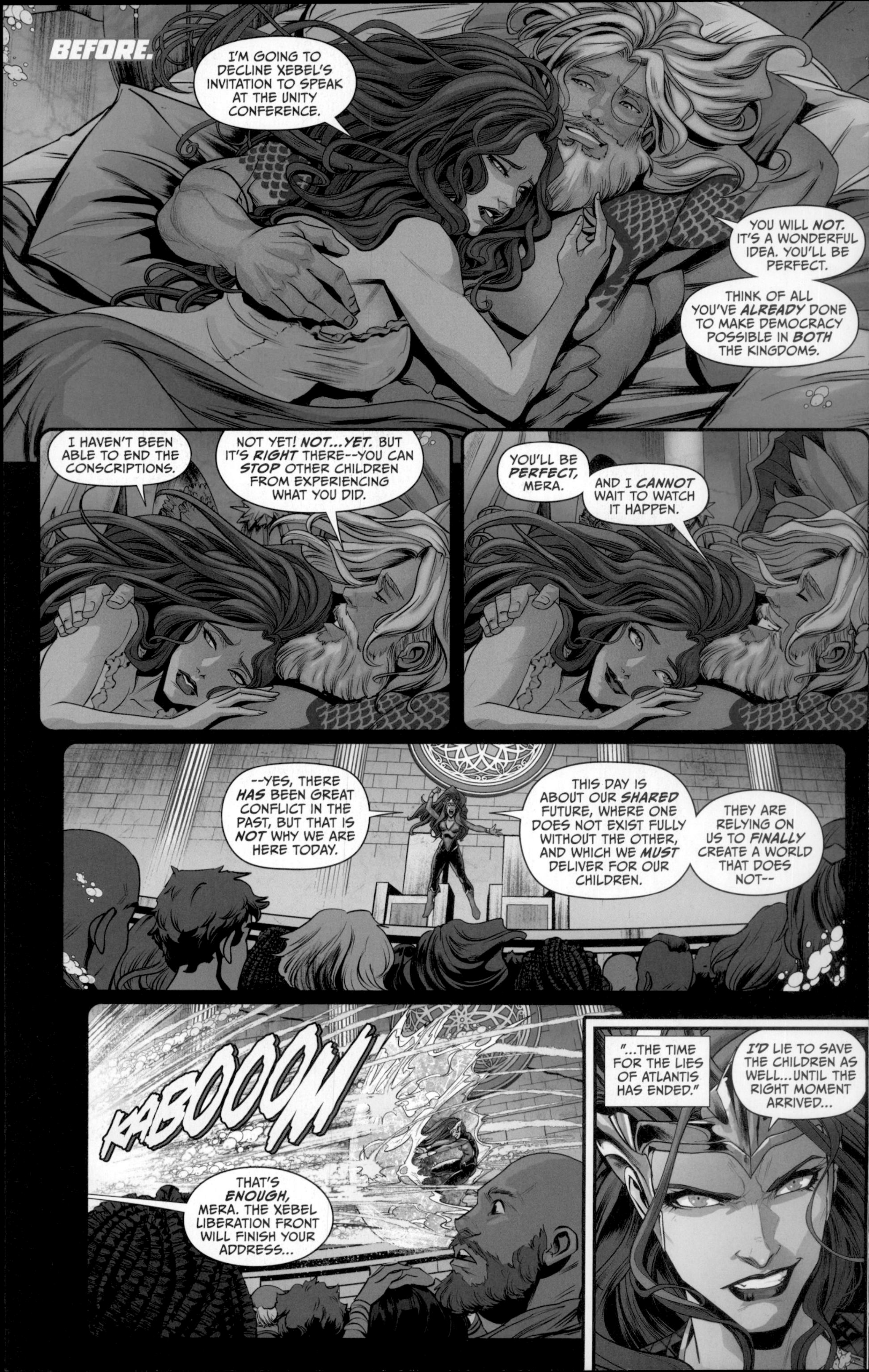
BEFORE.
I'M GOING TO DECLINE XEBEL'S INVITATION TO SPEAK AT THE UNITY CONFERENCE.
YOU WILL *NOT.* IT'S A WONDERFUL IDEA. YOU'LL BE PERFECT.
THINK OF ALL YOU'VE *ALREADY* DONE TO MAKE DEMOCRACY POSSIBLE IN *BOTH* THE KINGDOMS.
I HAVEN'T BEEN ABLE TO END THE CONSCRIPTIONS.
NOT YET! *NOT...YET.* BUT IT'S *RIGHT* THERE--YOU CAN *STOP* OTHER CHILDREN FROM EXPERIENCING WHAT YOU DID.
YOU'LL BE *PERFECT,* MERA.
AND I *CANNOT* WAIT TO WATCH IT HAPPEN.
--YES, THERE *HAS* BEEN GREAT CONFLICT IN THE PAST, BUT THAT IS *NOT* WHY WE ARE HERE TODAY.
THIS DAY IS ABOUT OUR *SHARED* FUTURE, WHERE ONE DOES NOT EXIST FULLY WITHOUT THE OTHER, AND WHICH WE *MUST* DELIVER FOR OUR CHILDREN.
THEY ARE RELYING ON US TO *FINALLY* CREATE A WORLD THAT DOES NOT--
KABOOOM
THAT'S *ENOUGH,* MERA. THE XEBEL LIBERATION FRONT WILL FINISH YOUR ADDRESS...
"...THE TIME FOR THE LIES OF ATLANTIS HAS ENDED."
I'D LIE TO SAVE THE CHILDREN AS WELL...UNTIL THE RIGHT MOMENT ARRIVED...

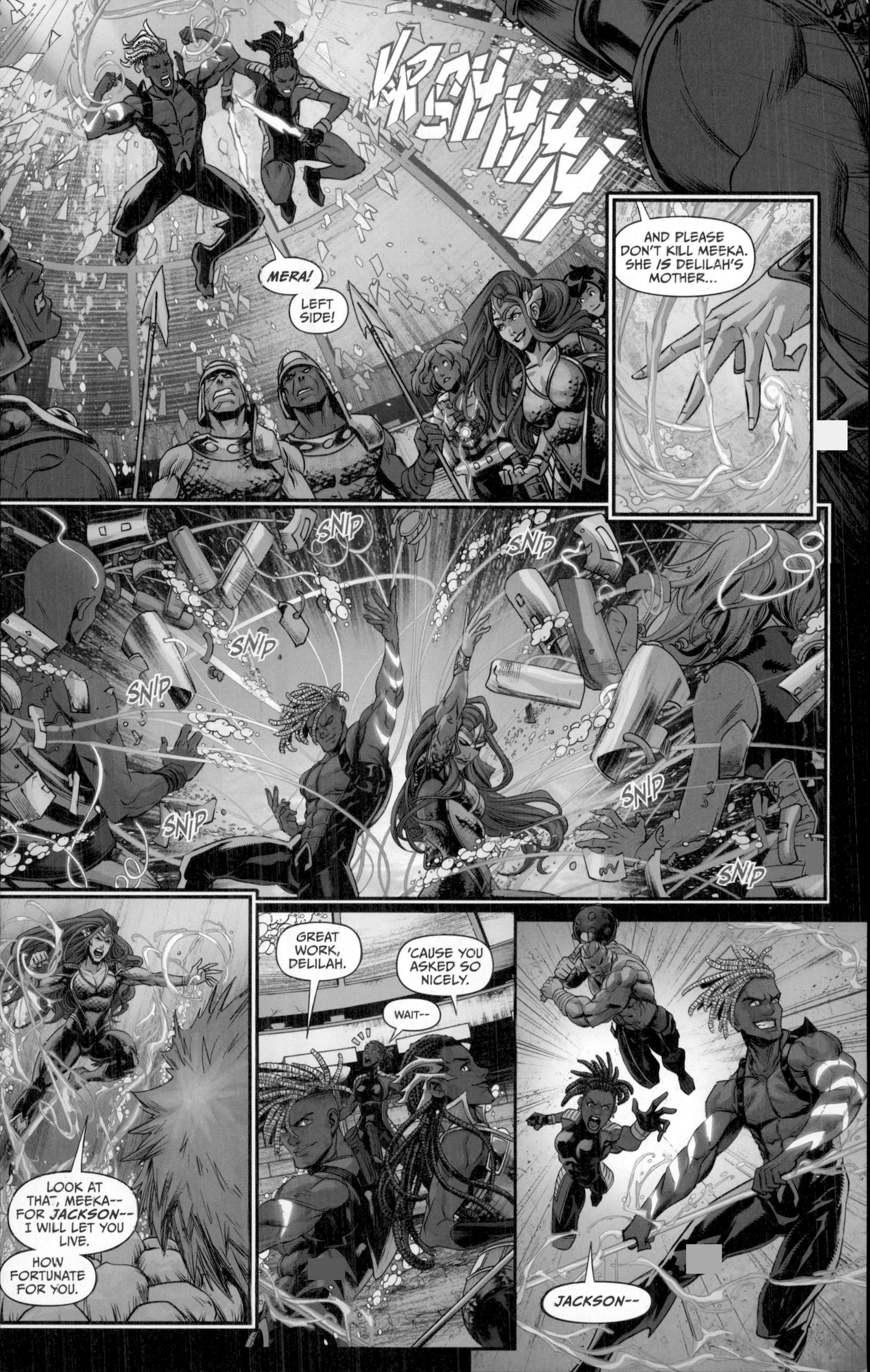
KRSSHHH
MERA!
LEFT SIDE!
AND PLEASE DON'T KILL MEEKA. SHE IS DELILAH'S MOTHER...
SNIP
SNIP
SNIP
SNIP
SNIP
SNIP
LOOK AT THAT, MEEKA-- FOR JACKSON-- I WILL LET YOU LIVE.
HOW FORTUNATE FOR YOU.
GREAT WORK, DELILAH.
'CAUSE YOU ASKED SO NICELY.
WAIT--
JACKSON--

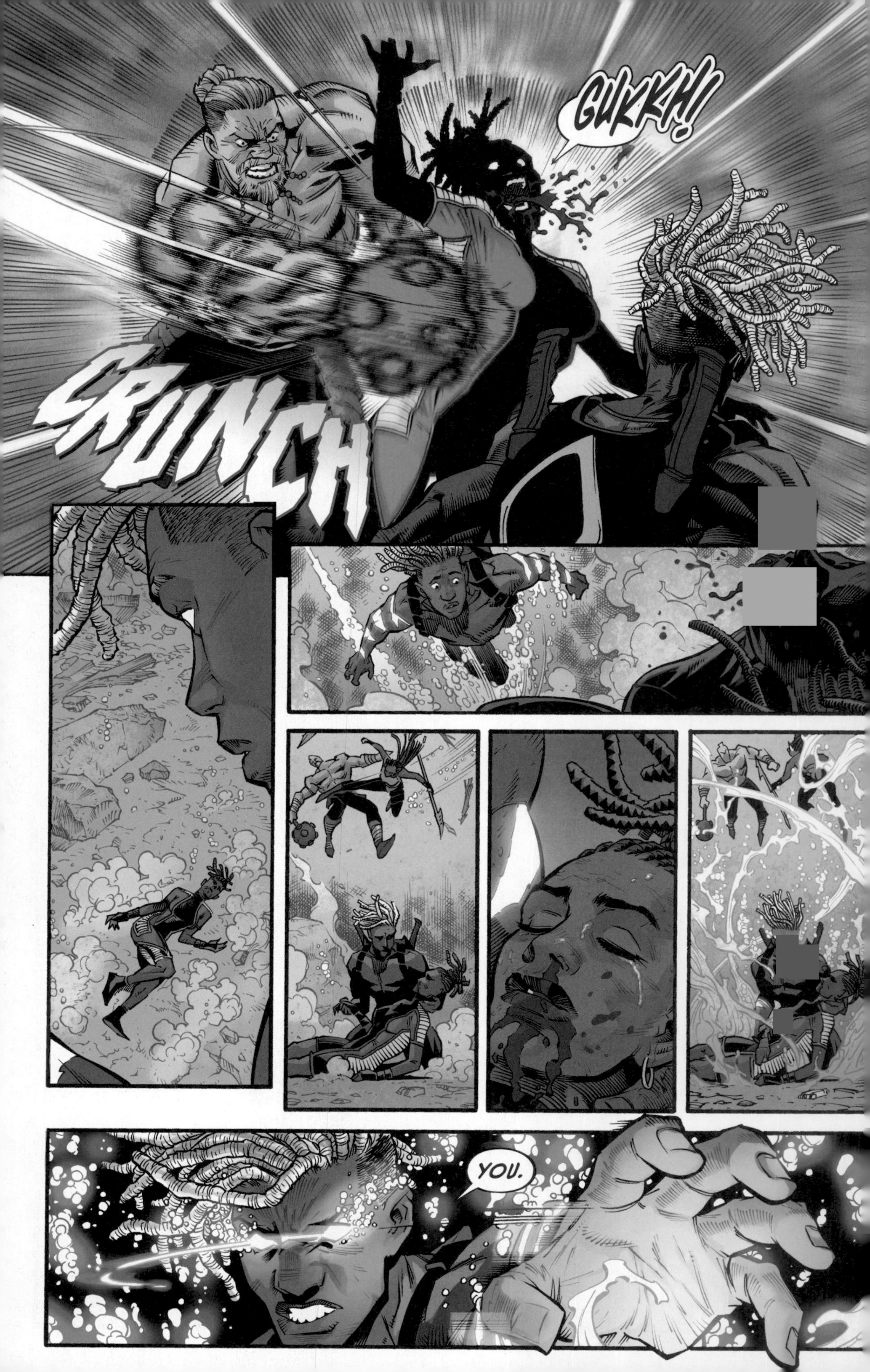
GUKKH!
CRUNCH
YOU.

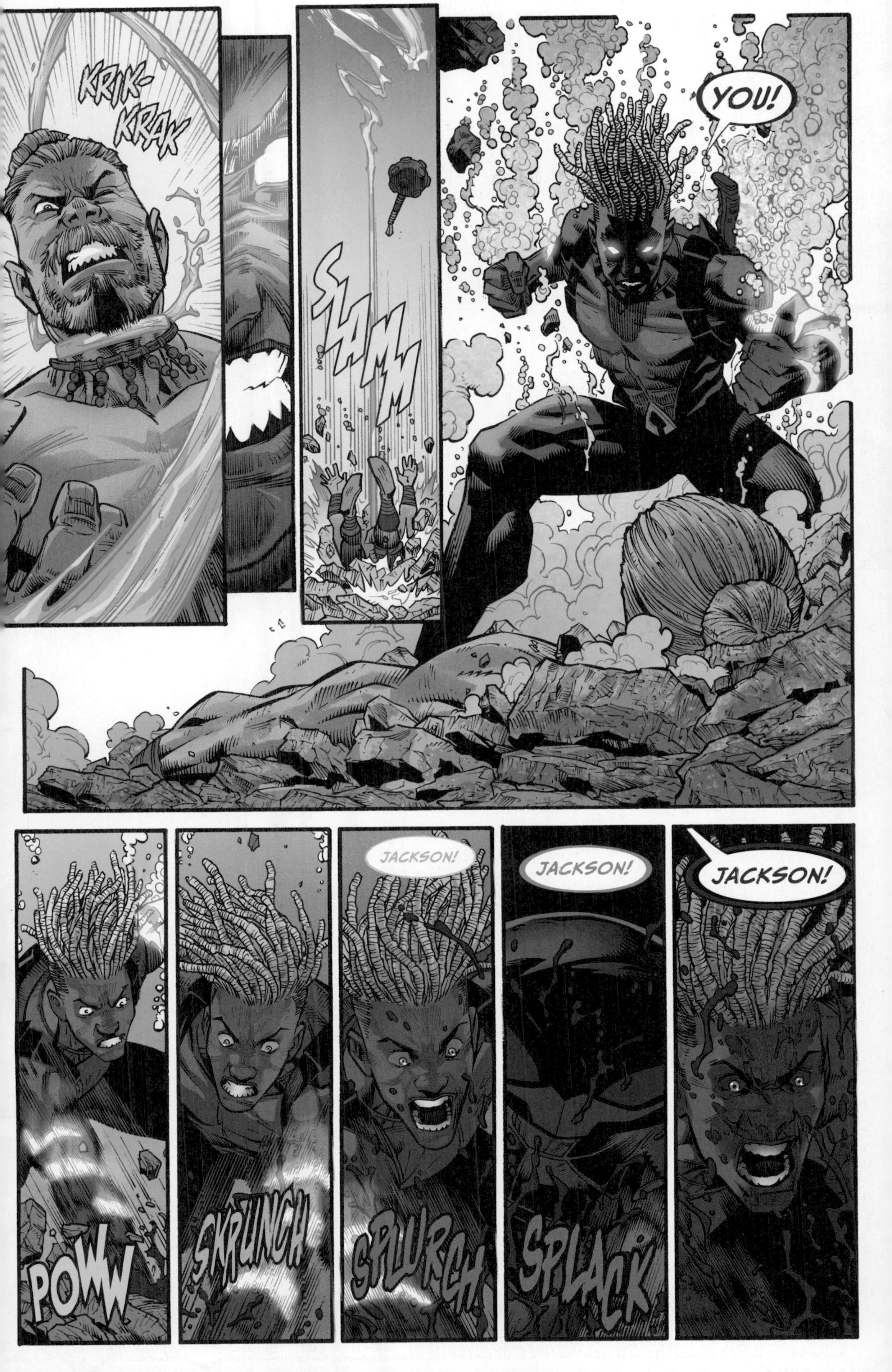
KRIK-
KRAK
SLAMM
YOU!
POWW
SKRUNCH
JACKSON!
SPLURCH
JACKSON!
SPLACK
JACKSON!

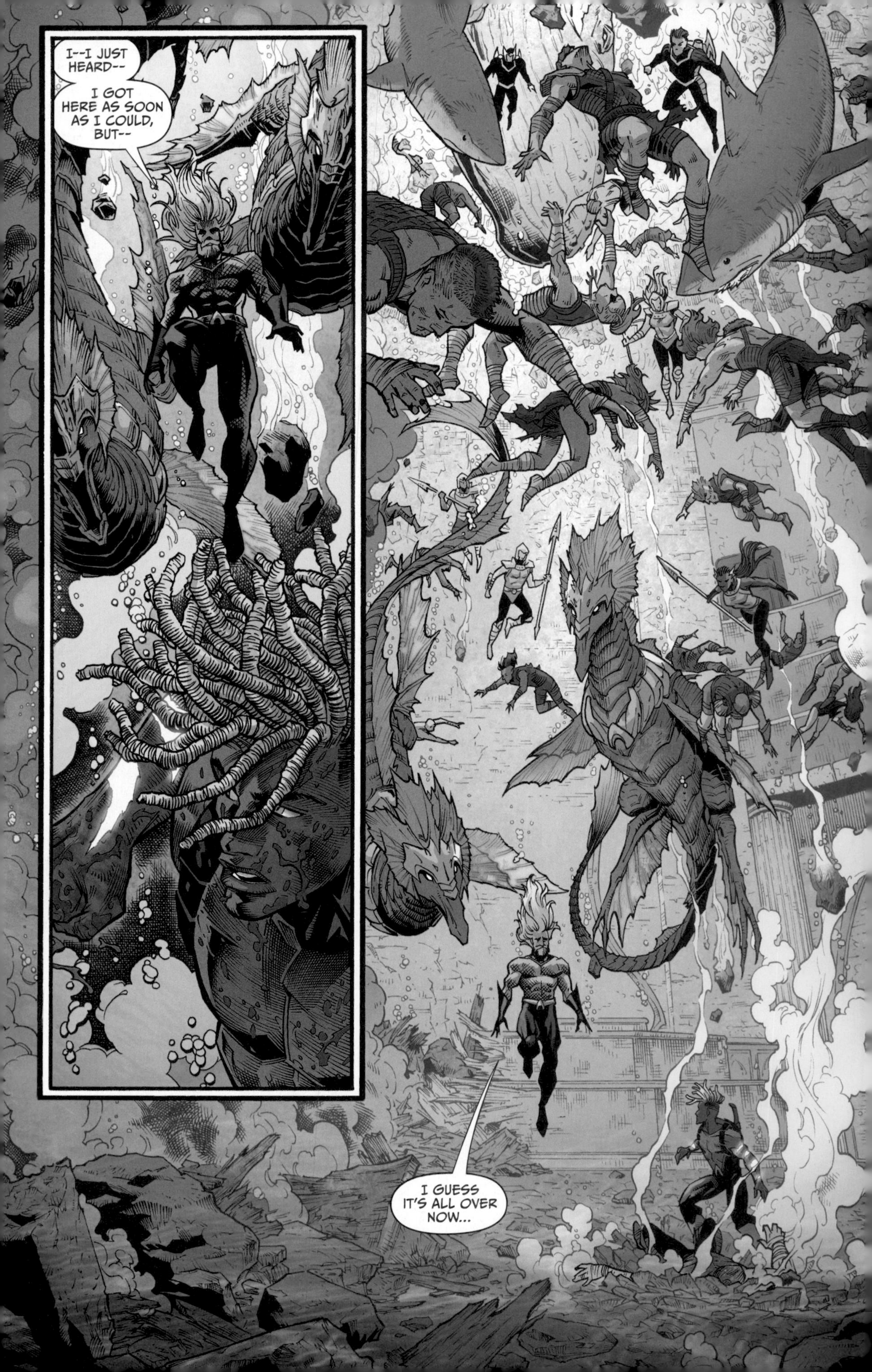
I--I JUST HEARD--
I GOT HERE AS SOON AS I COULD, BUT--
I GUESS IT'S ALL OVER NOW...

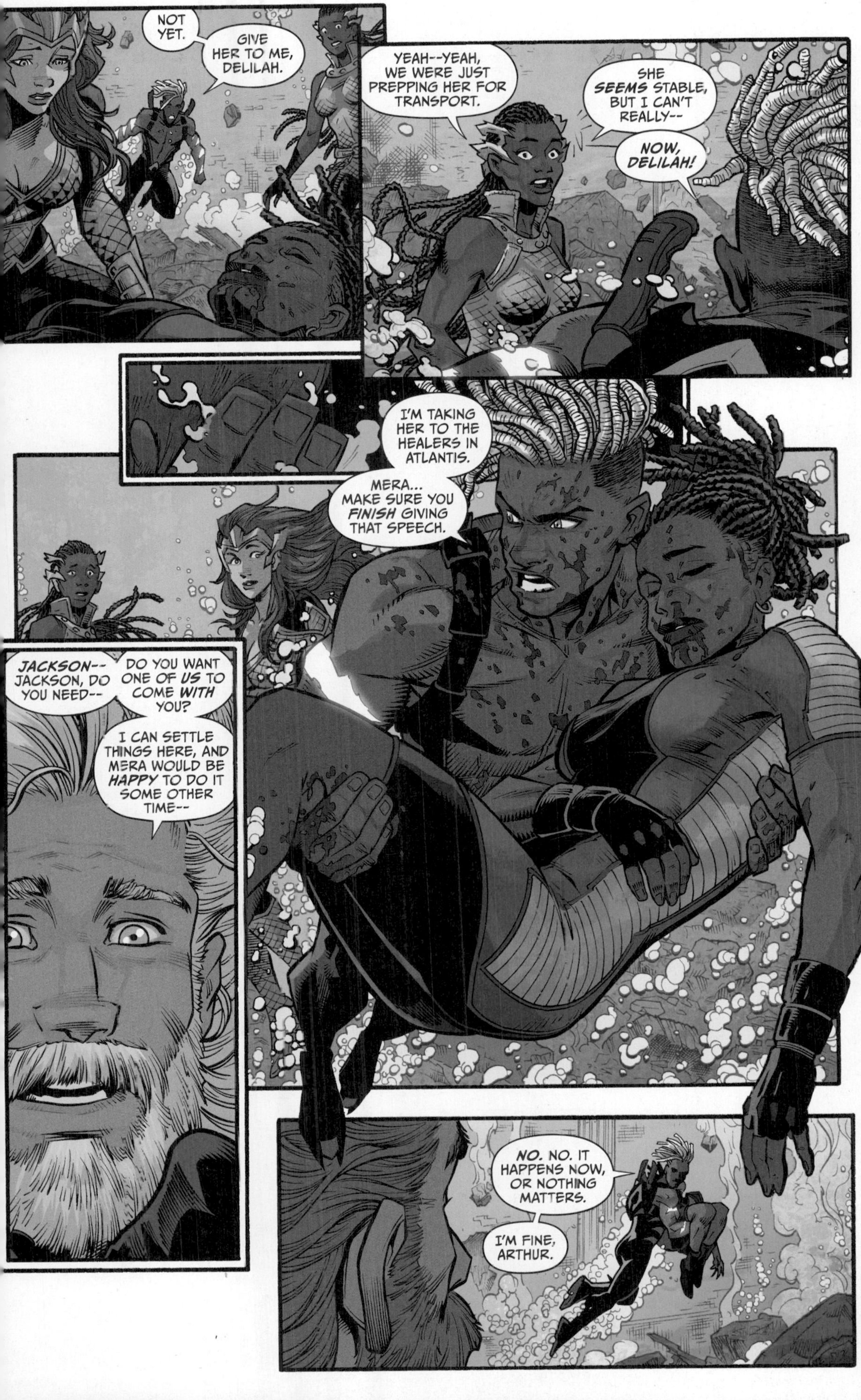
NOT YET.
GIVE HER TO ME, DELILAH.
YEAH--YEAH, WE WERE JUST PREPPING HER FOR TRANSPORT.
SHE SEEMS STABLE, BUT I CAN'T REALLY--
NOW, DELILAH!
I'M TAKING HER TO THE HEALERS IN ATLANTIS.
MERA... MAKE SURE YOU FINISH GIVING THAT SPEECH.
JACKSON-- JACKSON, DO YOU NEED--
DO YOU WANT ONE OF US TO COME WITH YOU?
I CAN SETTLE THINGS HERE, AND MERA WOULD BE HAPPY TO DO IT SOME OTHER TIME--
NO. NO. IT HAPPENS NOW, OR NOTHING MATTERS.
I'M FINE, ARTHUR.

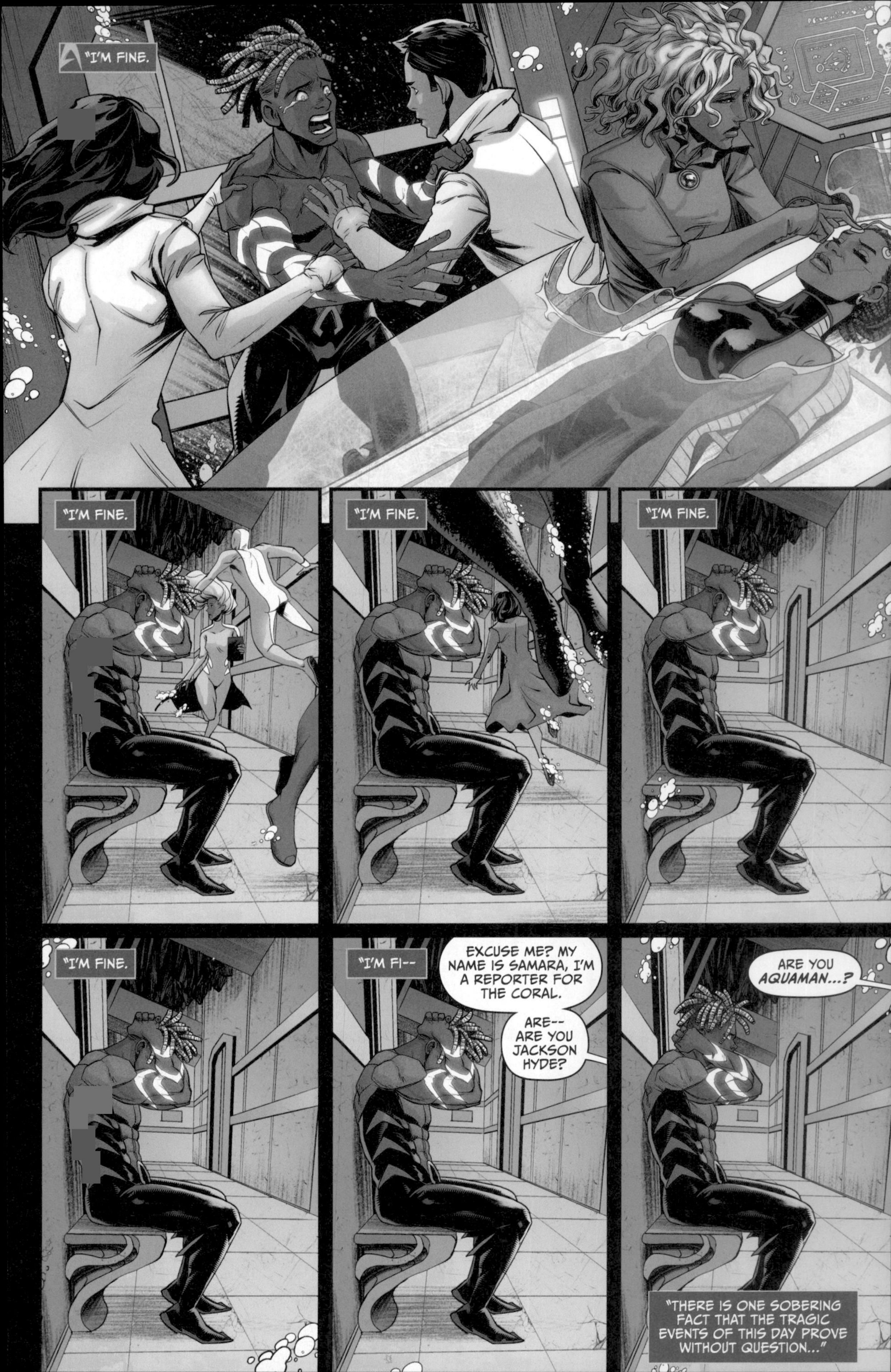
"I'M FINE.
"I'M FINE.
"I'M FINE.
"I'M FINE.
"I'M FINE.
"I'M FI--
EXCUSE ME? MY NAME IS SAMARA, I'M A REPORTER FOR THE CORAL.
ARE-- ARE YOU JACKSON HYDE?
ARE YOU AQUAMAN...?
"THERE IS ONE SOBERING FACT THAT THE TRAGIC EVENTS OF THIS DAY PROVE WITHOUT QUESTION..."

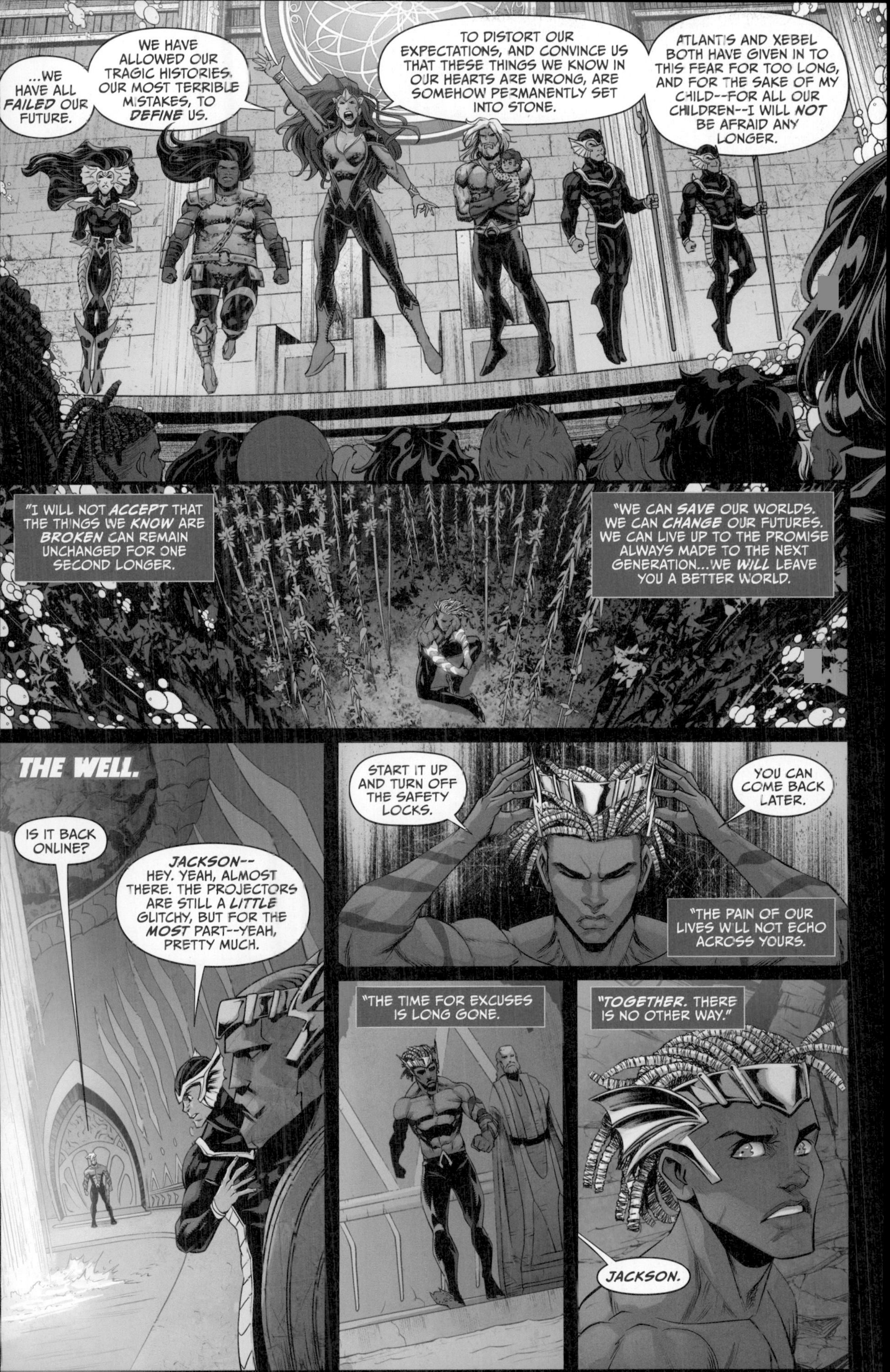
...WE HAVE ALL FAILED OUR FUTURE.
WE HAVE ALLOWED OUR TRAGIC HISTORIES, OUR MOST TERRIBLE MISTAKES, TO DEFINE US.
TO DISTORT OUR EXPECTATIONS, AND CONVINCE US THAT THESE THINGS WE KNOW IN OUR HEARTS ARE WRONG, ARE SOMEHOW PERMANENTLY SET INTO STONE.
ATLANTIS AND XEBEL BOTH HAVE GIVEN IN TO THIS FEAR FOR TOO LONG, AND FOR THE SAKE OF MY CHILD--FOR ALL OUR CHILDREN--I WILL NOT BE AFRAID ANY LONGER.
"I WILL NOT ACCEPT THAT THE THINGS WE KNOW ARE BROKEN CAN REMAIN UNCHANGED FOR ONE SECOND LONGER.
"WE CAN SAVE OUR WORLDS. WE CAN CHANGE OUR FUTURES. WE CAN LIVE UP TO THE PROMISE ALWAYS MADE TO THE NEXT GENERATION...WE WILL LEAVE YOU A BETTER WORLD.
THE WELL.
IS IT BACK ONLINE?
JACKSON-- HEY. YEAH, ALMOST THERE. THE PROJECTORS ARE STILL A LITTLE GLITCHY, BUT FOR THE MOST PART--YEAH, PRETTY MUCH.
START IT UP AND TURN OFF THE SAFETY LOCKS.
YOU CAN COME BACK LATER.
"THE PAIN OF OUR LIVES WILL NOT ECHO ACROSS YOURS.
"THE TIME FOR EXCUSES IS LONG GONE.
"TOGETHER. THERE IS NO OTHER WAY."
JACKSON.

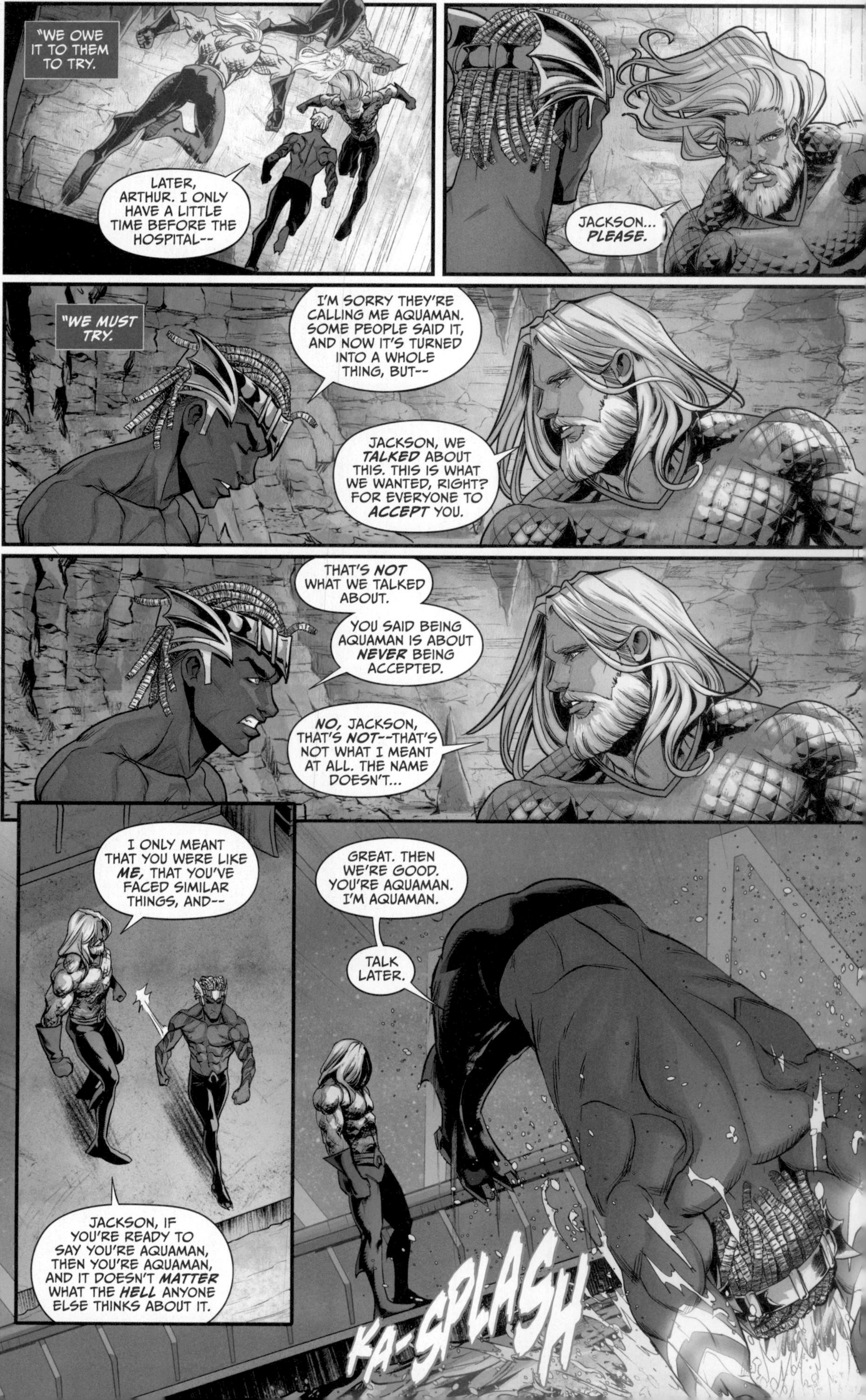
"WE OWE IT TO THEM TO TRY.
LATER, ARTHUR. I ONLY HAVE A LITTLE TIME BEFORE THE HOSPITAL--
JACKSON... PLEASE.
"WE MUST TRY.
I'M SORRY THEY'RE CALLING ME AQUAMAN. SOME PEOPLE SAID IT, AND NOW IT'S TURNED INTO A WHOLE THING, BUT--
JACKSON, WE TALKED ABOUT THIS. THIS IS WHAT WE WANTED, RIGHT? FOR EVERYONE TO ACCEPT YOU.
THAT'S NOT WHAT WE TALKED ABOUT.
YOU SAID BEING AQUAMAN IS ABOUT NEVER BEING ACCEPTED.
NO, JACKSON, THAT'S NOT--THAT'S NOT WHAT I MEANT AT ALL. THE NAME DOESN'T...
I ONLY MEANT THAT YOU WERE LIKE ME, THAT YOU'VE FACED SIMILAR THINGS, AND--
JACKSON, IF YOU'RE READY TO SAY YOU'RE AQUAMAN, THEN YOU'RE AQUAMAN, AND IT DOESN'T MATTER WHAT THE HELL ANYONE ELSE THINKS ABOUT IT.
GREAT. THEN WE'RE GOOD. YOU'RE AQUAMAN. I'M AQUAMAN.
TALK LATER.
KA-SPLASH

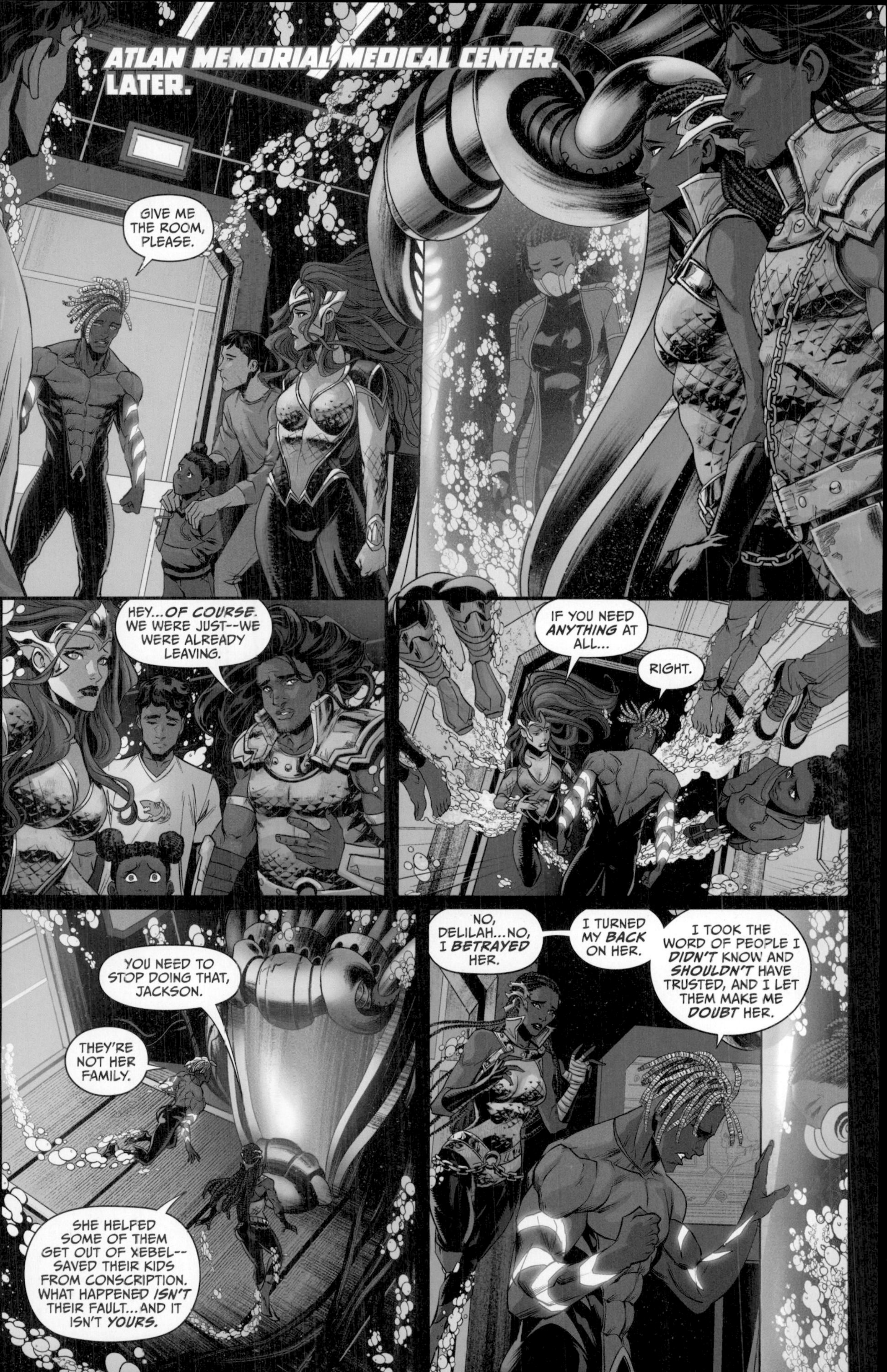
ATLAN MEMORIAL MEDICAL CENTER. LATER.
GIVE ME THE ROOM, PLEASE.
HEY...OF COURSE. WE WERE JUST--WE WERE ALREADY LEAVING.
IF YOU NEED ANYTHING AT ALL...
RIGHT.
YOU NEED TO STOP DOING THAT, JACKSON.
THEY'RE NOT HER FAMILY.
SHE HELPED SOME OF THEM GET OUT OF XEBEL--SAVED THEIR KIDS FROM CONSCRIPTION. WHAT HAPPENED ISN'T THEIR FAULT...AND IT ISN'T YOURS.
NO, DELILAH...NO, I BETRAYED HER.
I TURNED MY BACK ON HER.
I TOOK THE WORD OF PEOPLE I DIDN'T KNOW AND SHOULDN'T HAVE TRUSTED, AND I LET THEM MAKE ME DOUBT HER.

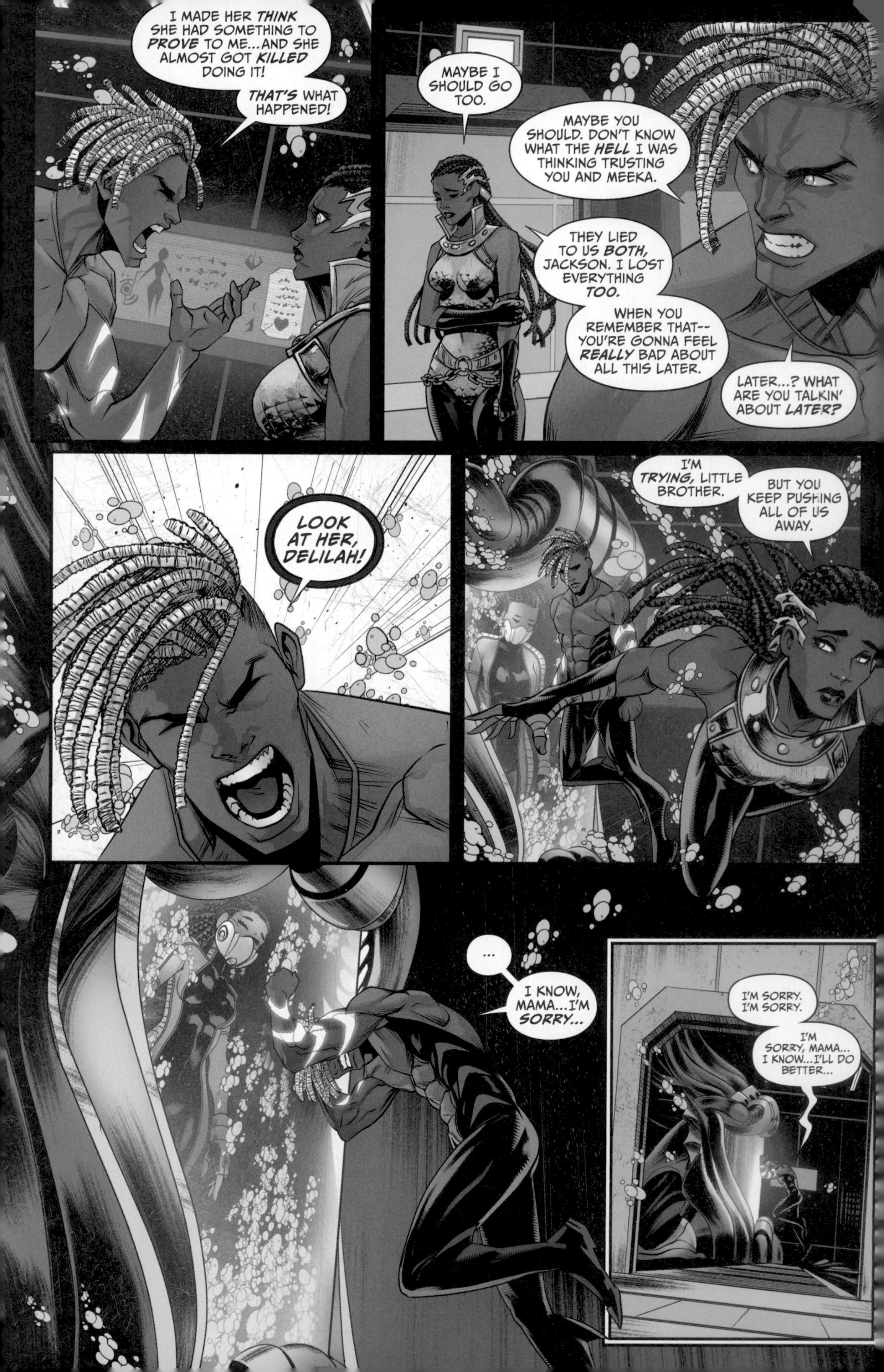
I MADE HER *THINK* SHE HAD SOMETHING TO *PROVE* TO ME...AND SHE ALMOST GOT *KILLED* DOING IT!
THAT'S WHAT HAPPENED!
MAYBE I SHOULD GO TOO.
MAYBE YOU SHOULD. DON'T KNOW WHAT THE *HELL* I WAS THINKING TRUSTING YOU AND MEEKA.
THEY LIED TO US *BOTH*, JACKSON. I LOST EVERYTHING *TOO*.
WHEN YOU REMEMBER THAT-- YOU'RE GONNA FEEL *REALLY* BAD ABOUT ALL THIS LATER.
LATER...? WHAT ARE YOU TALKIN' ABOUT *LATER?*
LOOK AT HER, DELILAH!
I'M *TRYING*, LITTLE BROTHER.
BUT YOU KEEP PUSHING ALL OF US AWAY.
...
I KNOW, MAMA...I'M *SORRY*...
I'M SORRY. I'M SORRY.
I'M SORRY, MAMA... I KNOW...I'LL DO BETTER...

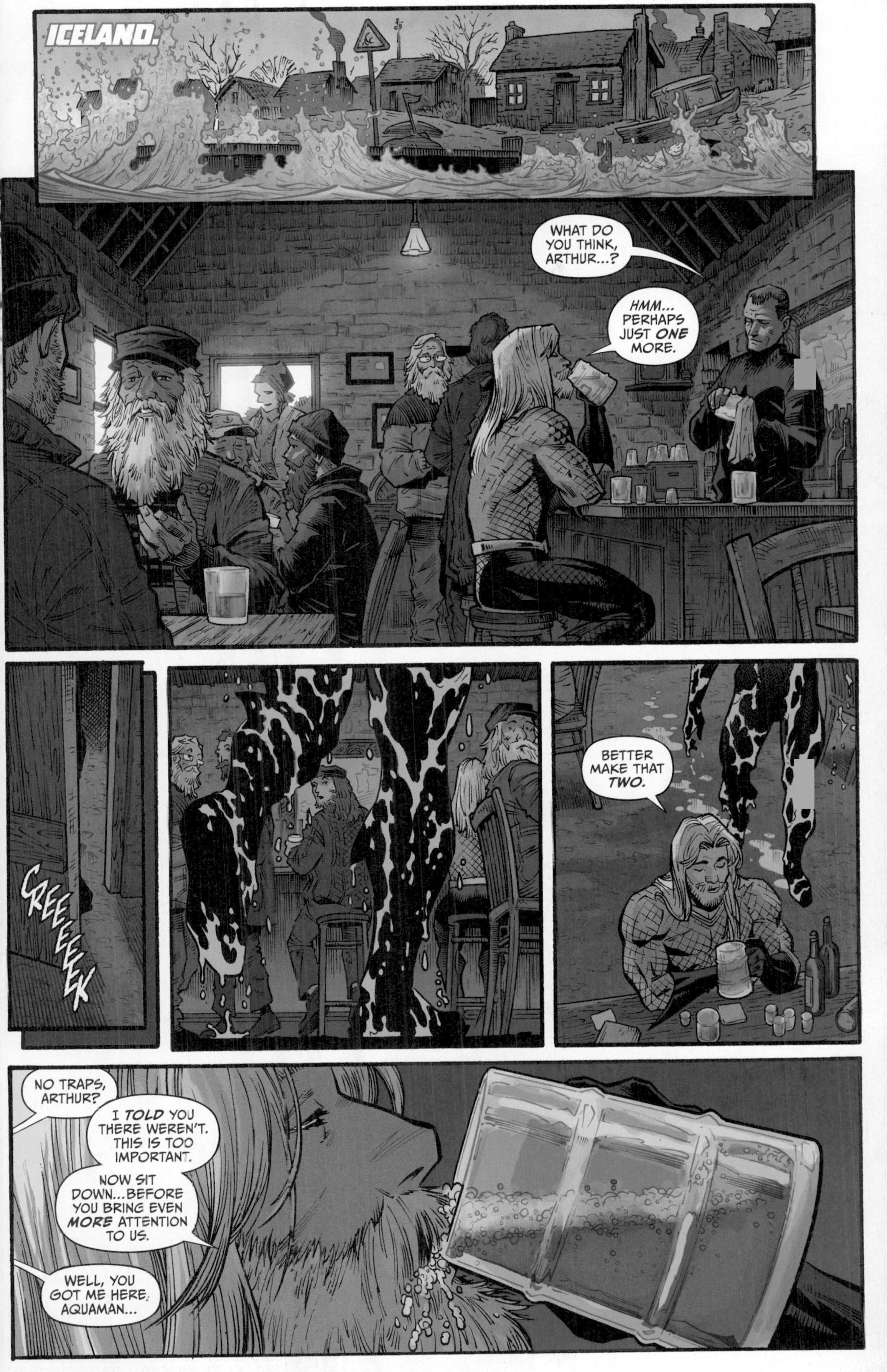
ICELAND.
WHAT DO YOU THINK, ARTHUR...?
HMM... PERHAPS JUST ONE MORE.
CREEEEEEK
BETTER MAKE THAT TWO.
NO TRAPS, ARTHUR?
I TOLD YOU THERE WEREN'T. THIS IS TOO IMPORTANT.
NOW SIT DOWN...BEFORE YOU BRING EVEN MORE ATTENTION TO US.
WELL, YOU GOT ME HERE, AQUAMAN...

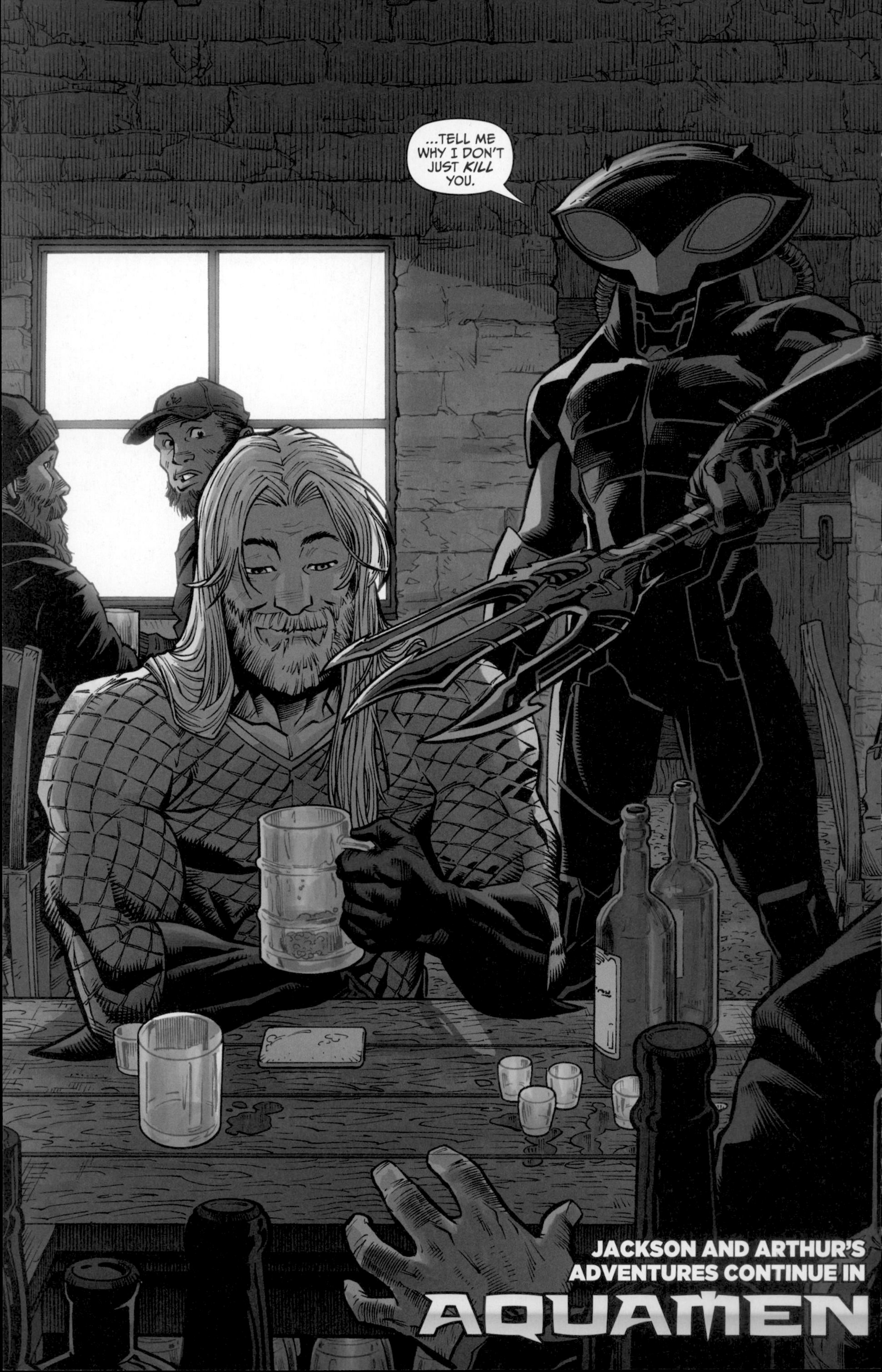
...TELL ME WHY I DON'T JUST KILL YOU.
JACKSON AND ARTHUR'S ADVENTURES CONTINUE IN
AQUAMEN

FUTURE STATE: AQUAMAN #1
cover by DANIEL SAMPERE and ADRIANO LUCAS

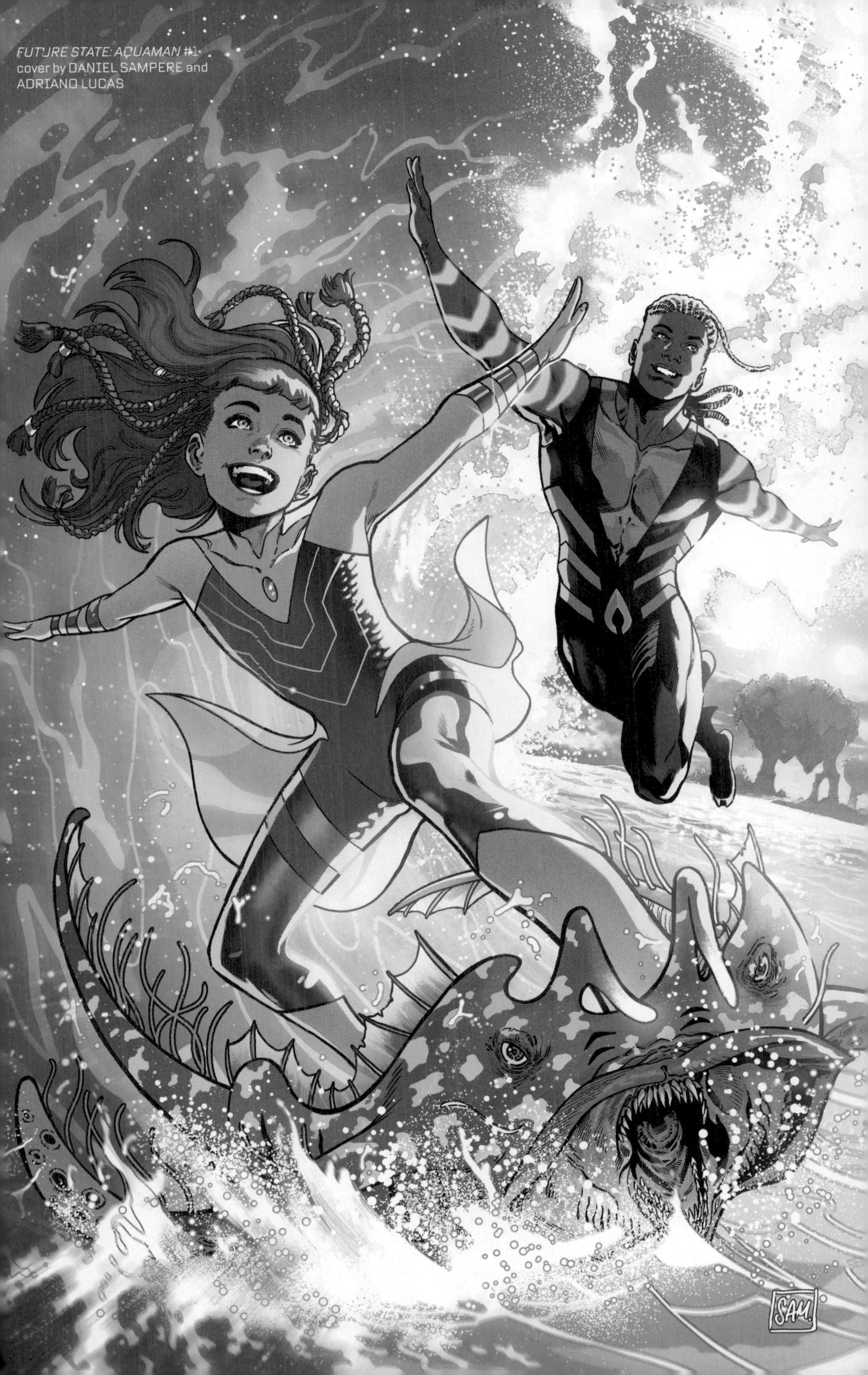
SAM.

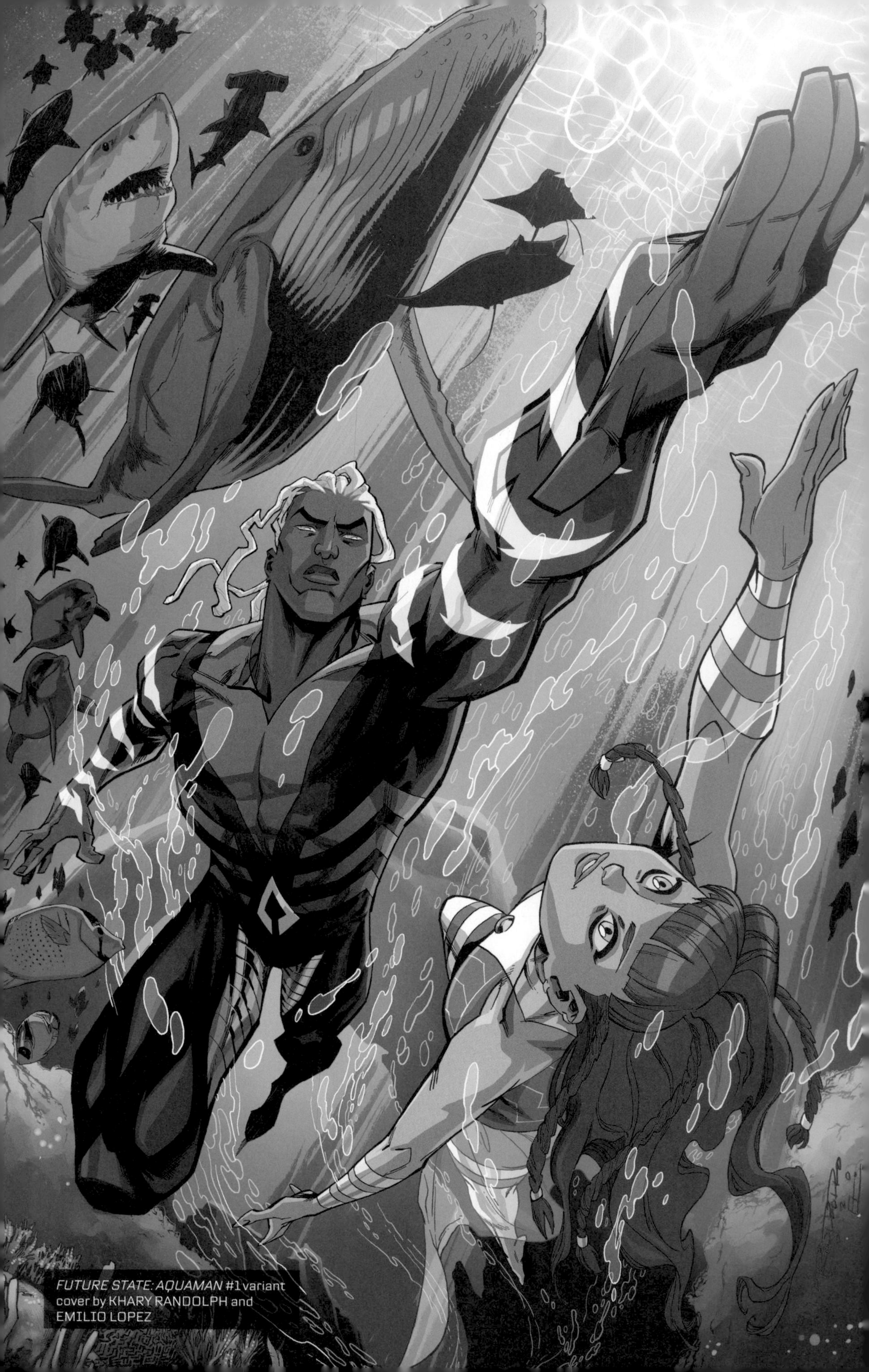

FUTURE STATE: AQUAMAN #1 variant cover by KHARY RANDOLPH and EMILIO LOPEZ

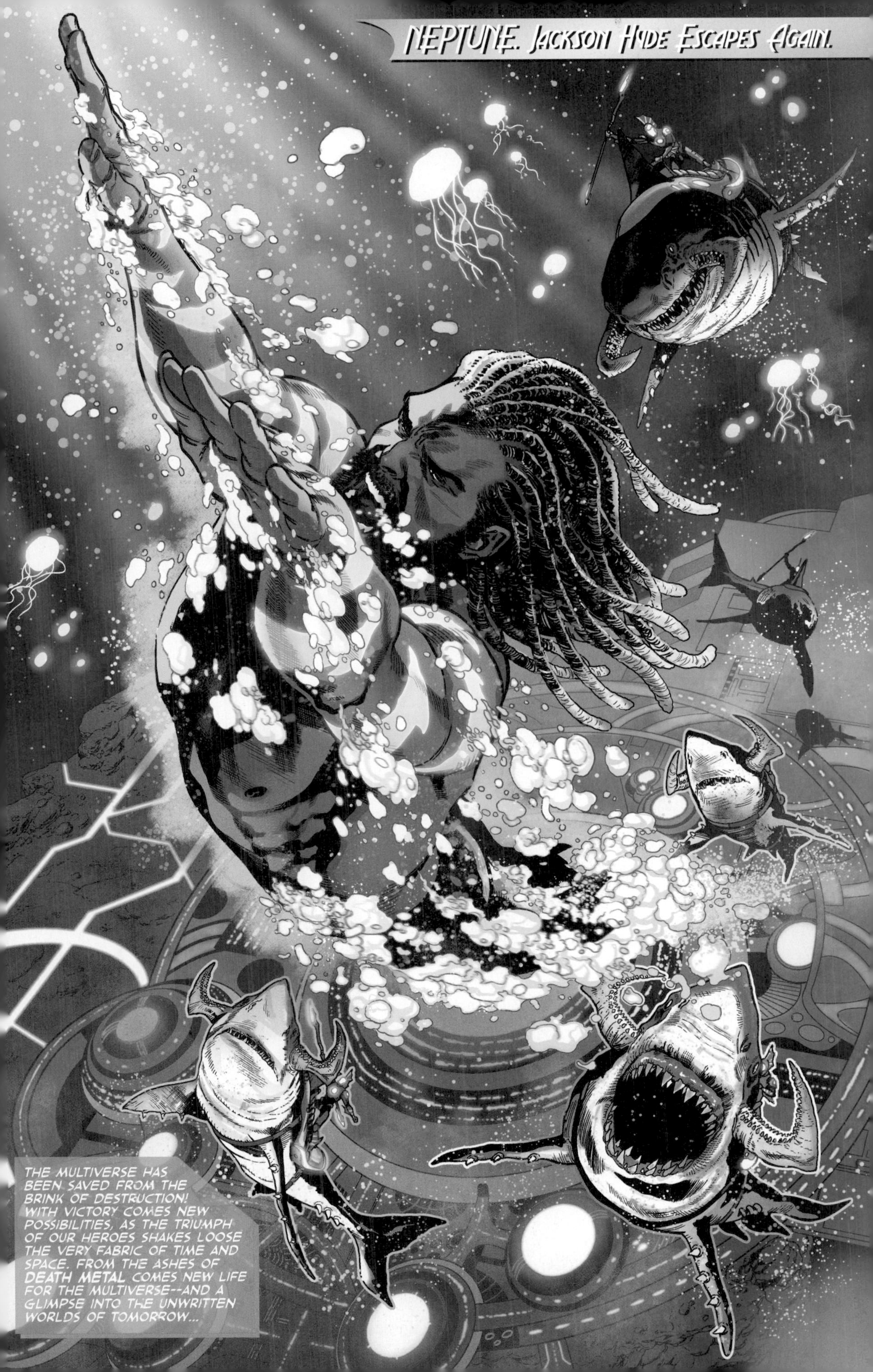
NEPTUNE. JACKSON HYDE ESCAPES AGAIN.
THE MULTIVERSE HAS BEEN SAVED FROM THE BRINK OF DESTRUCTION! WITH VICTORY COMES NEW POSSIBILITIES, AS THE TRIUMPH OF OUR HEROES SHAKES LOOSE THE VERY FABRIC OF TIME AND SPACE. FROM THE ASHES OF DEATH METAL COMES NEW LIFE FOR THE MULTIVERSE--AND A GLIMPSE INTO THE UNWRITTEN WORLDS OF TOMORROW...

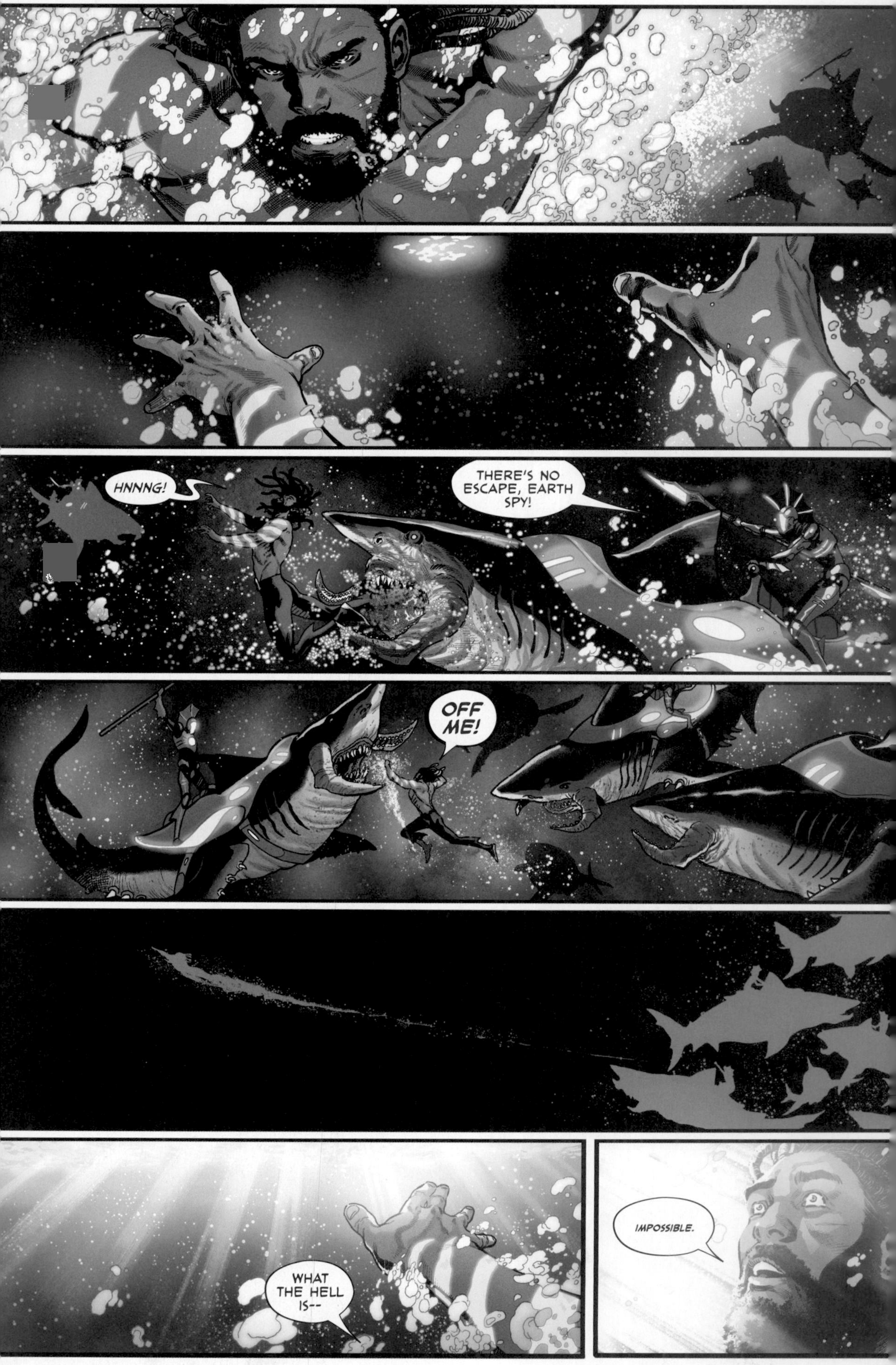
HNNNG!
THERE'S NO ESCAPE, EARTH SPY!
OFF ME!
WHAT THE HELL IS--
IMPOSSIBLE.

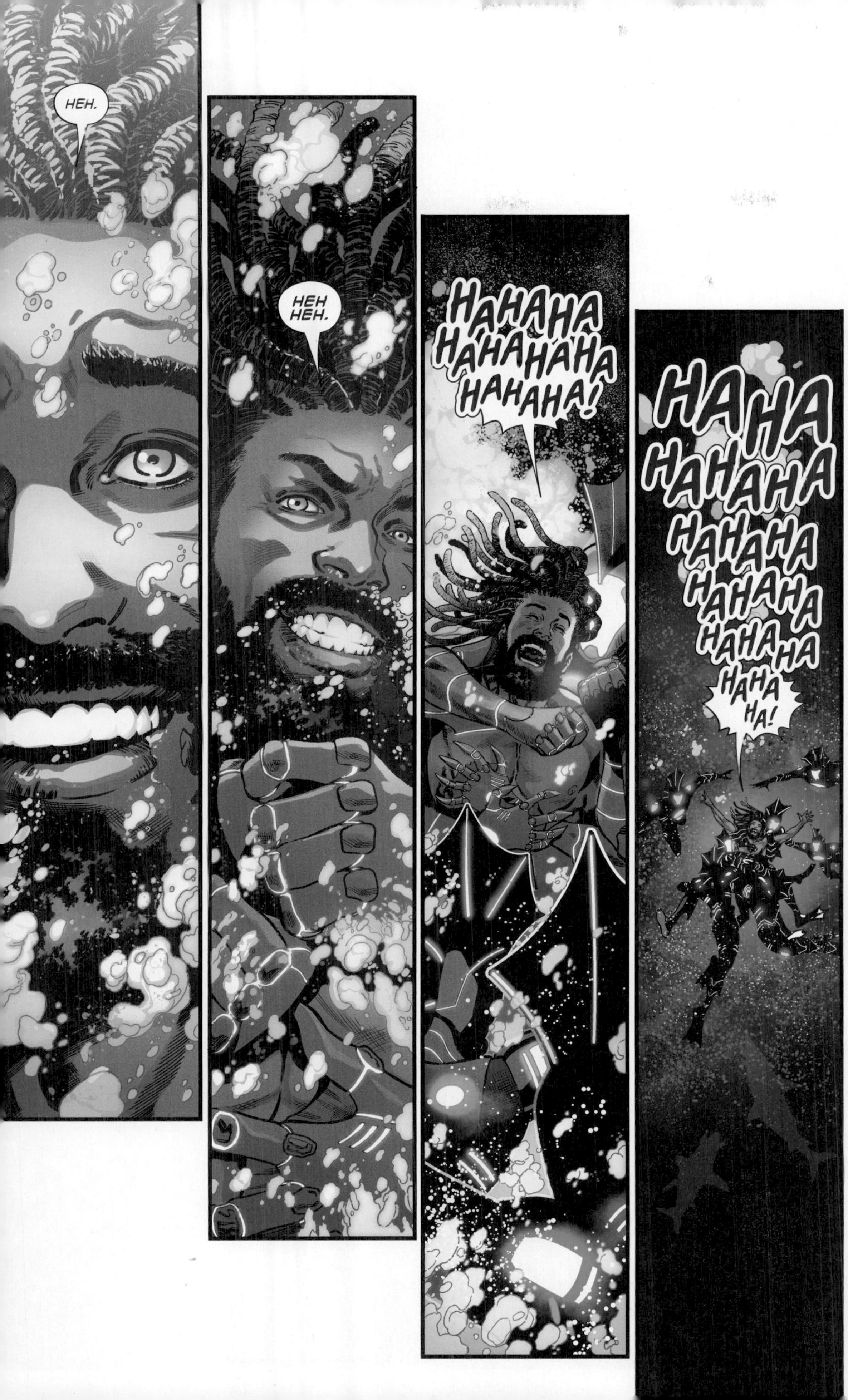
HEH.
HEH HEH.
HAHAHA HAHAHAHA HAHAHA!
HAHA HAHAHA HAHAHA HAHAHA HAHAHA HAHA HA!

FUTURE STATE: AQUAMAN

THE CONFLUENCE

PART ONE

BRANDON THOMAS WRITER DANIEL SAMPERE ARTIST
ADRIANO LUCAS COLORIST CLAYTON COWLES LETTERER
SAMPERE & LUCAS COVER ARTISTS
KHARY RANDOLPH & EMILIO LOPEZ VARIANT COVER ARTISTS
ANDREA SHEA EDITOR CHRIS CONROY SENIOR EDITOR
AQUAMAN CREATED BY PAUL NORRIS

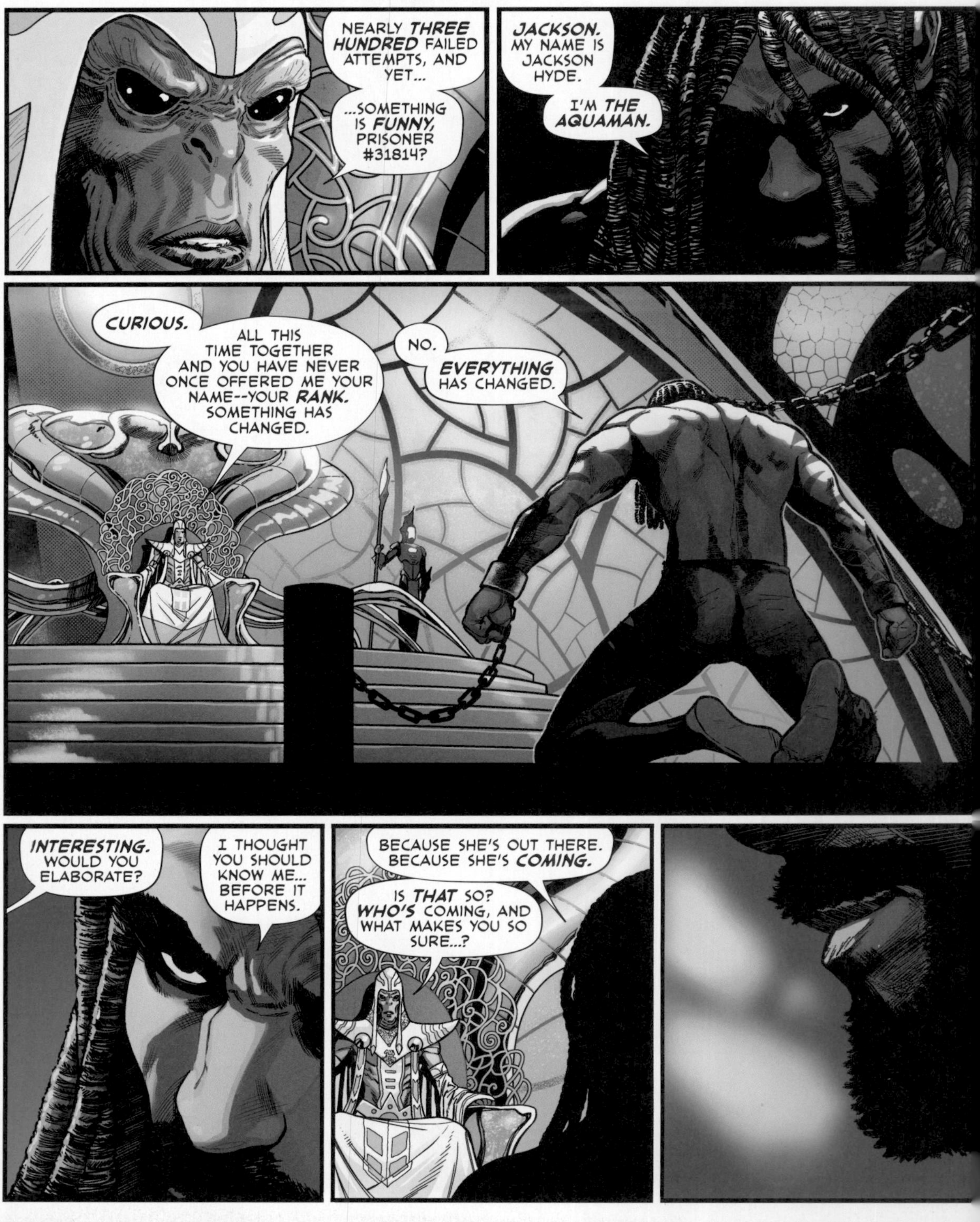
NEARLY THREE HUNDRED FAILED ATTEMPTS, AND YET...
...SOMETHING IS FUNNY, PRISONER #31814?
JACKSON. MY NAME IS JACKSON HYDE.
I'M THE AQUAMAN.
CURIOUS.
ALL THIS TIME TOGETHER AND YOU HAVE NEVER ONCE OFFERED ME YOUR NAME--YOUR RANK. SOMETHING HAS CHANGED.
NO.
EVERYTHING HAS CHANGED.
INTERESTING. WOULD YOU ELABORATE?
I THOUGHT YOU SHOULD KNOW ME... BEFORE IT HAPPENS.
BECAUSE SHE'S OUT THERE. BECAUSE SHE'S COMING.
IS THAT SO? WHO'S COMING, AND WHAT MAKES YOU SO SURE...?

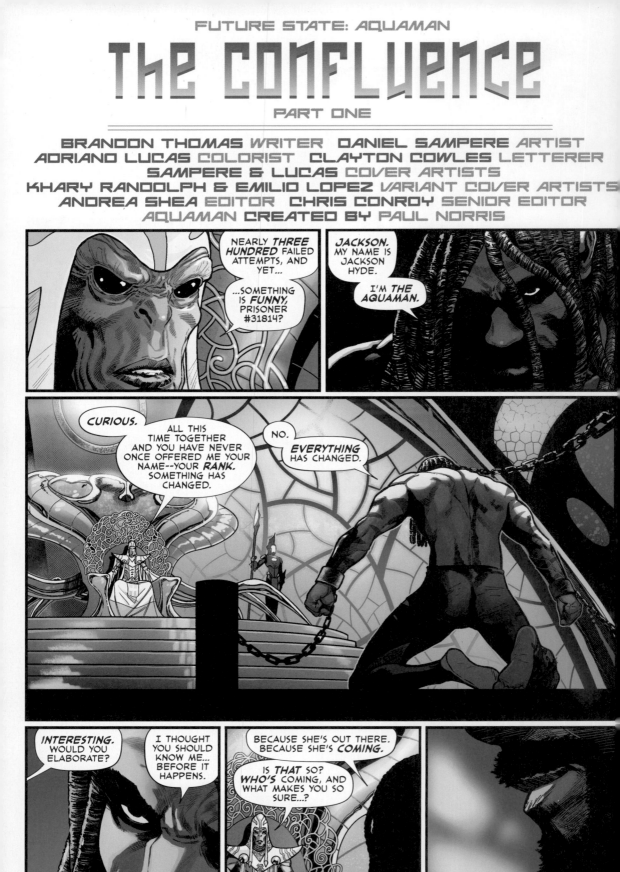

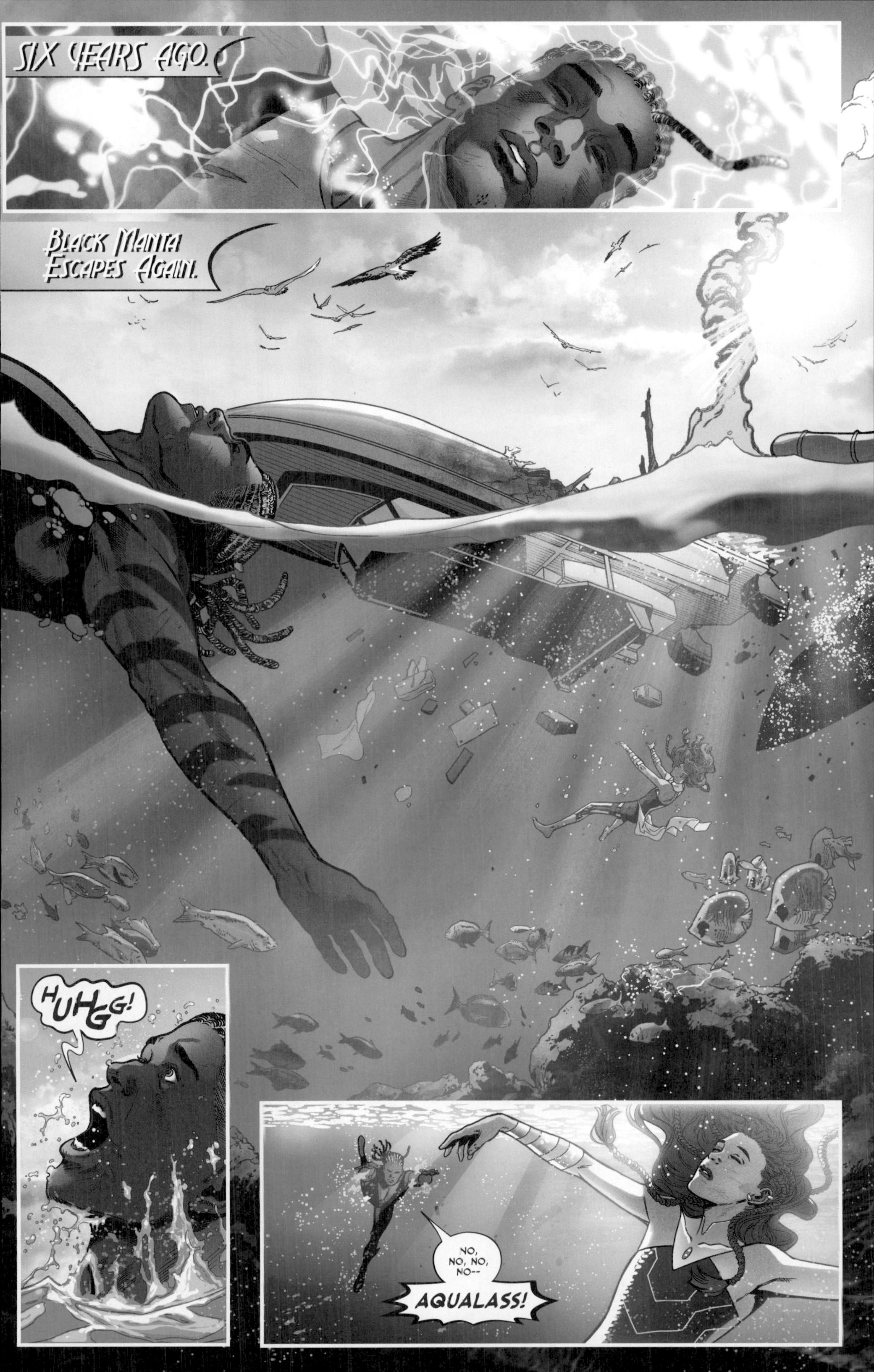
SIX YEARS AGO.
BLACK MANTA ESCAPES AGAIN.
HUHGG!
NO, NO, NO, NO--
AQUALASS!

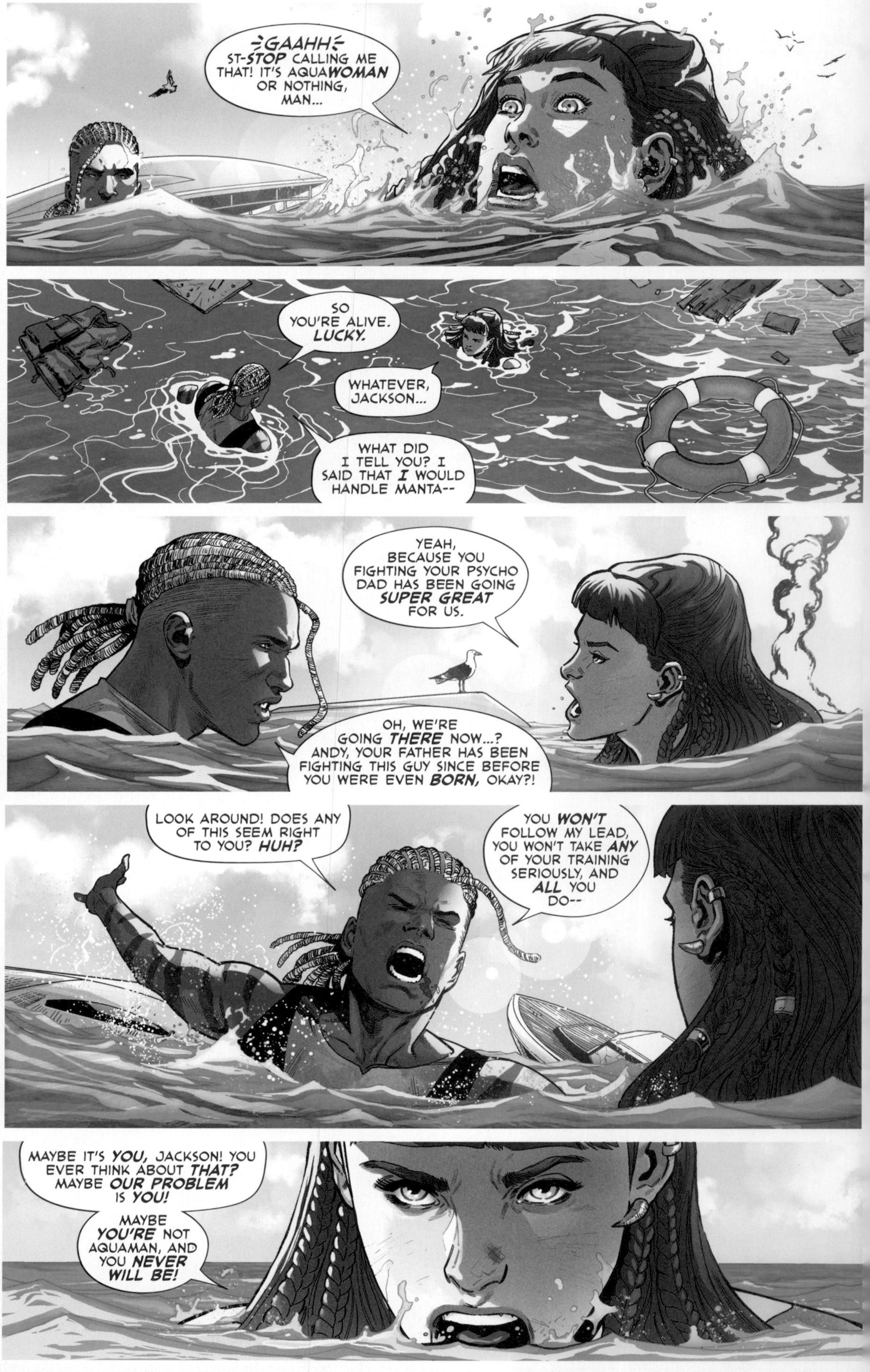
GAAHH
ST-STOP CALLING ME THAT! IT'S AQUAWOMAN OR NOTHING, MAN...
SO YOU'RE ALIVE. LUCKY.
WHATEVER, JACKSON...
WHAT DID I TELL YOU? I SAID THAT I WOULD HANDLE MANTA--
YEAH, BECAUSE YOU FIGHTING YOUR PSYCHO DAD HAS BEEN GOING SUPER GREAT FOR US.
OH, WE'RE GOING THERE NOW...? ANDY, YOUR FATHER HAS BEEN FIGHTING THIS GUY SINCE BEFORE YOU WERE EVEN BORN, OKAY?!
LOOK AROUND! DOES ANY OF THIS SEEM RIGHT TO YOU? HUH?
YOU WON'T FOLLOW MY LEAD, YOU WON'T TAKE ANY OF YOUR TRAINING SERIOUSLY, AND ALL YOU DO--
MAYBE IT'S YOU, JACKSON! YOU EVER THINK ABOUT THAT? MAYBE OUR PROBLEM IS YOU!
MAYBE YOU'RE NOT AQUAMAN, AND YOU NEVER WILL BE!

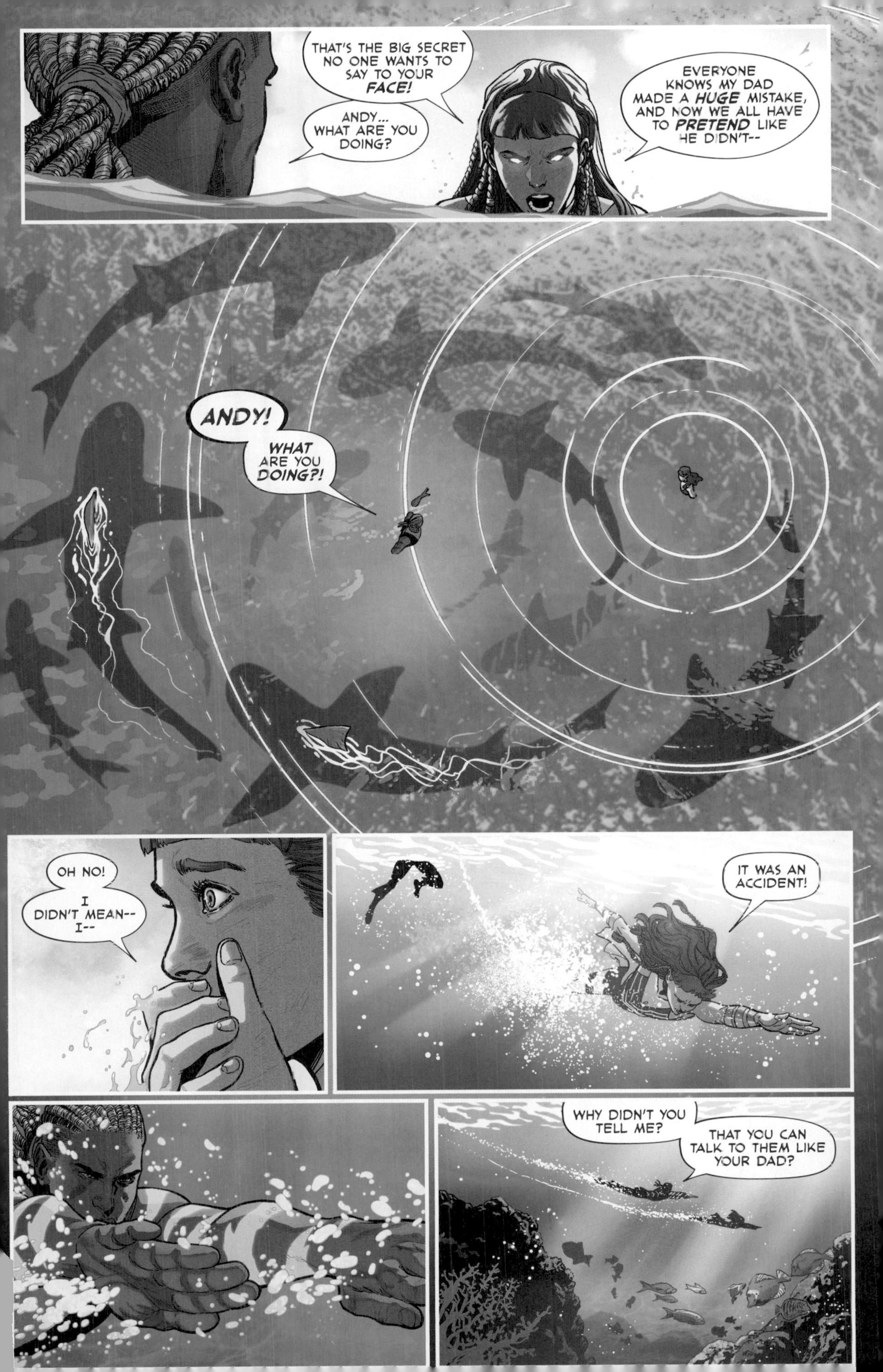
THAT'S THE BIG SECRET NO ONE WANTS TO SAY TO YOUR FACE!
ANDY... WHAT ARE YOU DOING?
EVERYONE KNOWS MY DAD MADE A HUGE MISTAKE, AND NOW WE ALL HAVE TO PRETEND LIKE HE DIDN'T--
ANDY!
WHAT ARE YOU DOING?!
OH NO!
I DIDN'T MEAN-- I--
IT WAS AN ACCIDENT!
WHY DIDN'T YOU TELL ME?
THAT YOU CAN TALK TO THEM LIKE YOUR DAD?

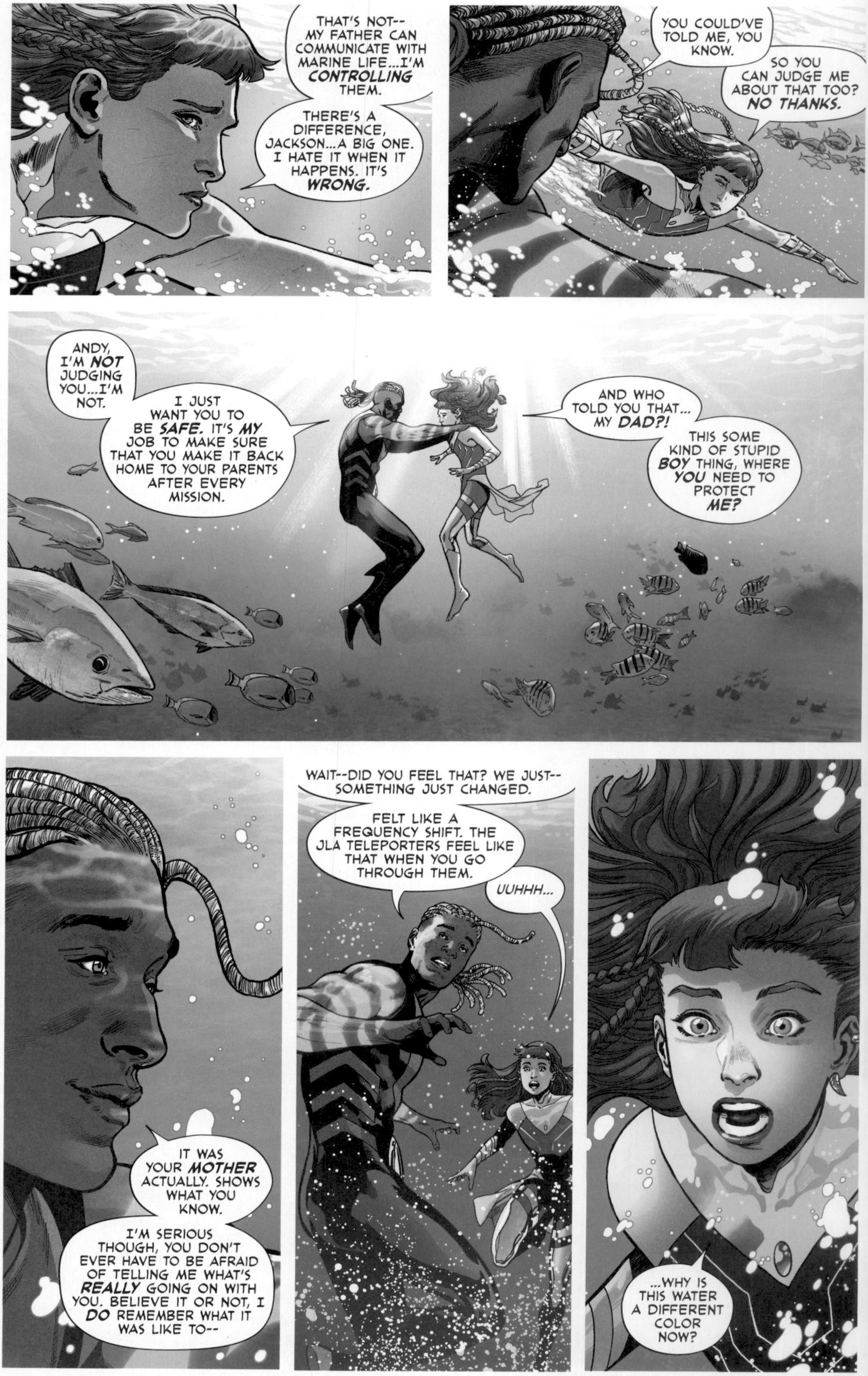
THAT'S NOT-- MY FATHER CAN COMMUNICATE WITH MARINE LIFE...I'M CONTROLLING THEM.
THERE'S A DIFFERENCE, JACKSON...A BIG ONE. I HATE IT WHEN IT HAPPENS. IT'S WRONG.
YOU COULD'VE TOLD ME, YOU KNOW.
SO YOU CAN JUDGE ME ABOUT THAT TOO? NO THANKS.
ANDY, I'M NOT JUDGING YOU...I'M NOT.
I JUST WANT YOU TO BE SAFE. IT'S MY JOB TO MAKE SURE THAT YOU MAKE IT BACK HOME TO YOUR PARENTS AFTER EVERY MISSION.
AND WHO TOLD YOU THAT... MY DAD?!
THIS SOME KIND OF STUPID BOY THING, WHERE YOU NEED TO PROTECT ME?
IT WAS YOUR MOTHER ACTUALLY. SHOWS WHAT YOU KNOW.
I'M SERIOUS THOUGH, YOU DON'T EVER HAVE TO BE AFRAID OF TELLING ME WHAT'S REALLY GOING ON WITH YOU. BELIEVE IT OR NOT, I DO REMEMBER WHAT IT WAS LIKE TO--
WAIT--DID YOU FEEL THAT? WE JUST-- SOMETHING JUST CHANGED.
FELT LIKE A FREQUENCY SHIFT. THE JLA TELEPORTERS FEEL LIKE THAT WHEN YOU GO THROUGH THEM.
UUHHH...
...WHY IS THIS WATER A DIFFERENT COLOR NOW?

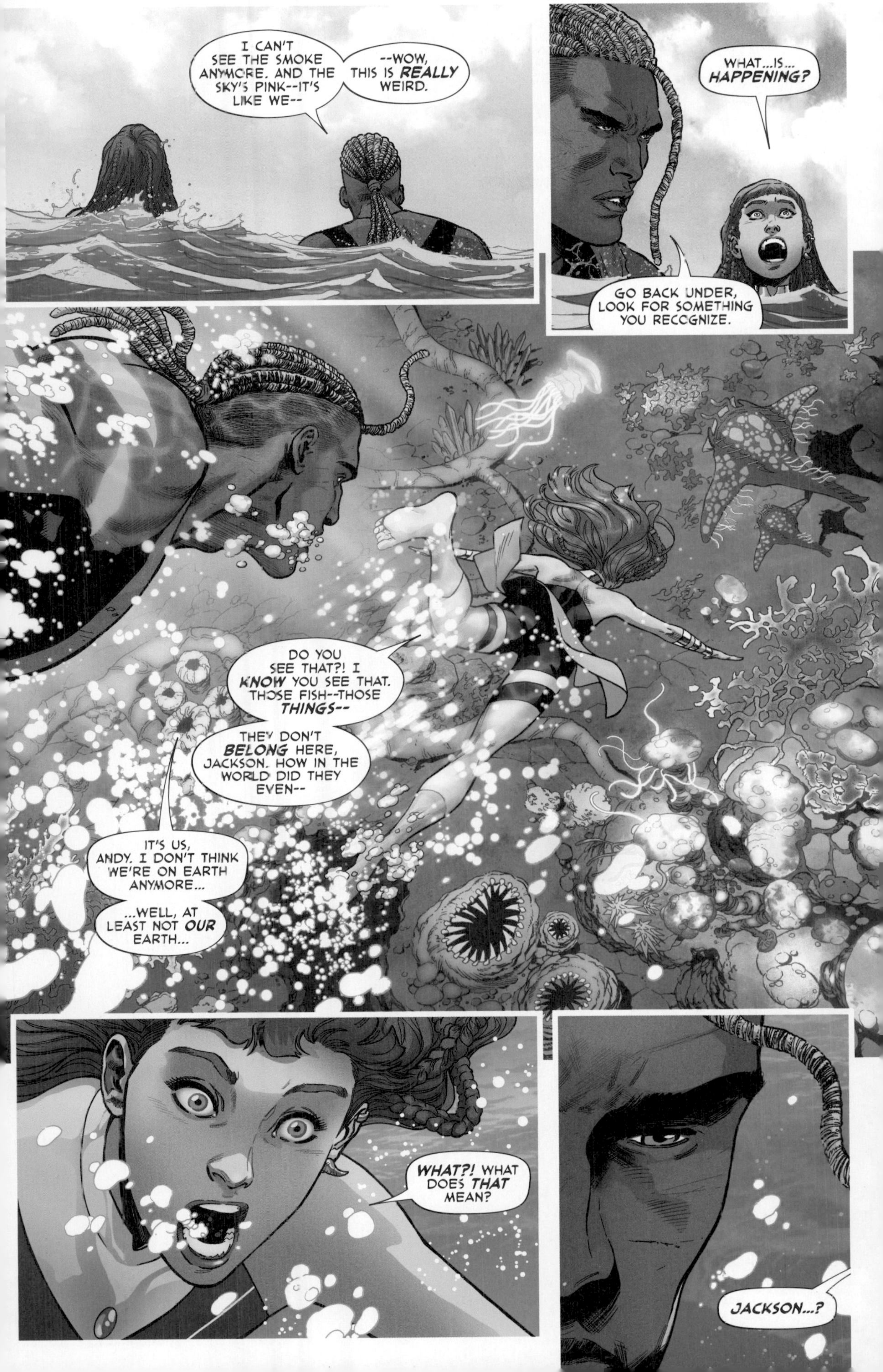
I CAN'T SEE THE SMOKE ANYMORE. AND THE SKY'S PINK--IT'S LIKE WE--
--WOW, THIS IS *REALLY* WEIRD.
WHAT...IS... *HAPPENING?*
GO BACK UNDER, LOOK FOR SOMETHING YOU RECOGNIZE.
DO YOU SEE THAT?! I *KNOW* YOU SEE THAT. THOSE FISH--THOSE *THINGS--*
THEY DON'T *BELONG* HERE, JACKSON. HOW IN THE WORLD DID THEY EVEN--
IT'S US, ANDY. I DON'T THINK WE'RE ON EARTH ANYMORE...
...WELL, AT LEAST NOT *OUR* EARTH...
WHAT?! WHAT DOES *THAT* MEAN?
JACKSON...?

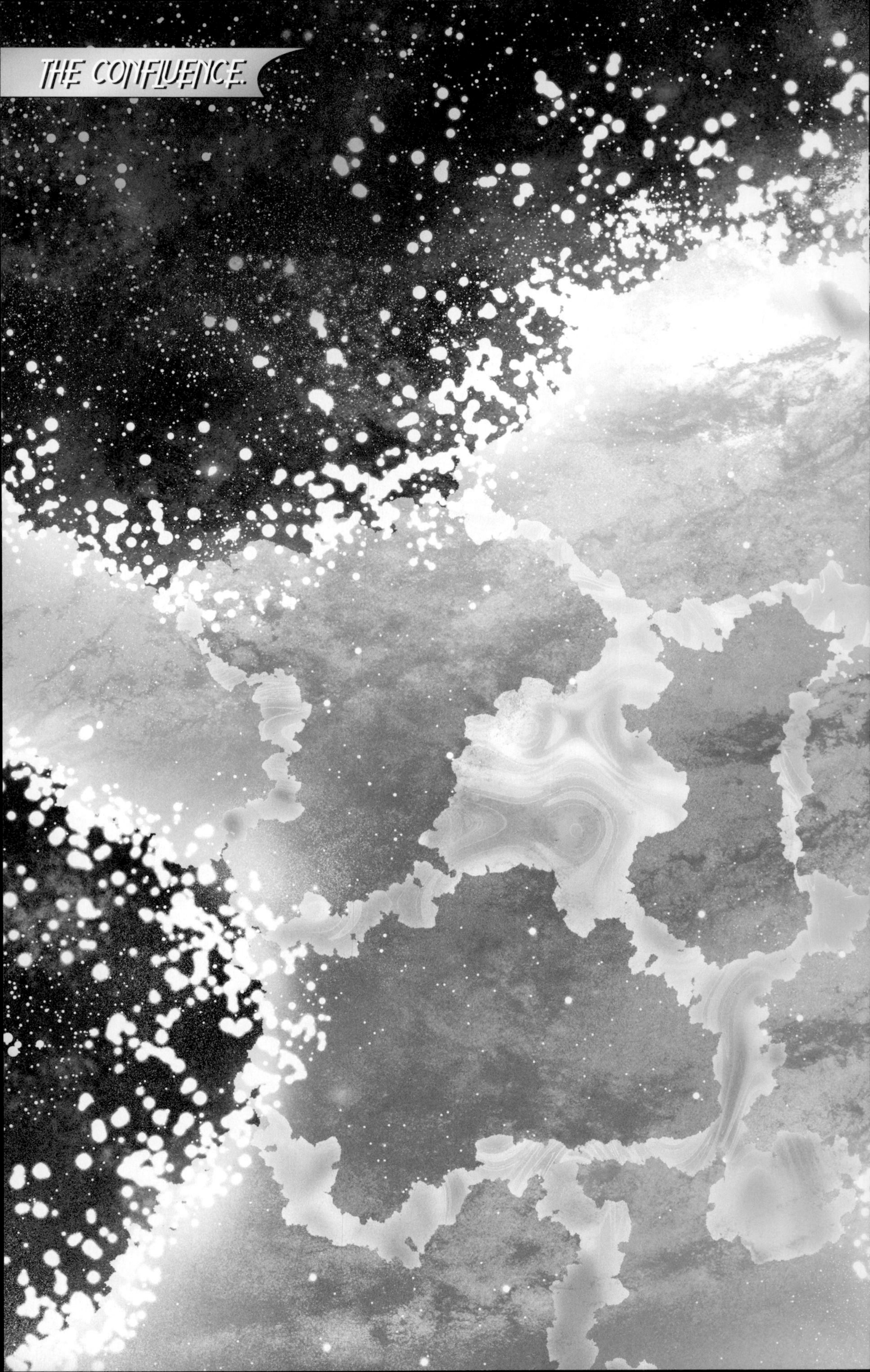
THE CONFLUENCE.

JACKSON, WHERE ARE WE...?

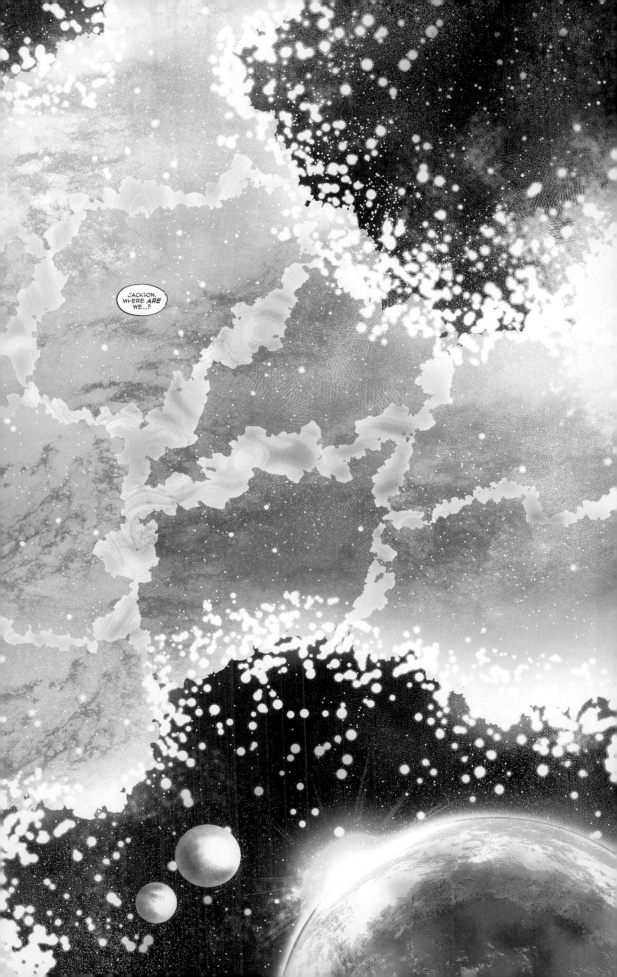

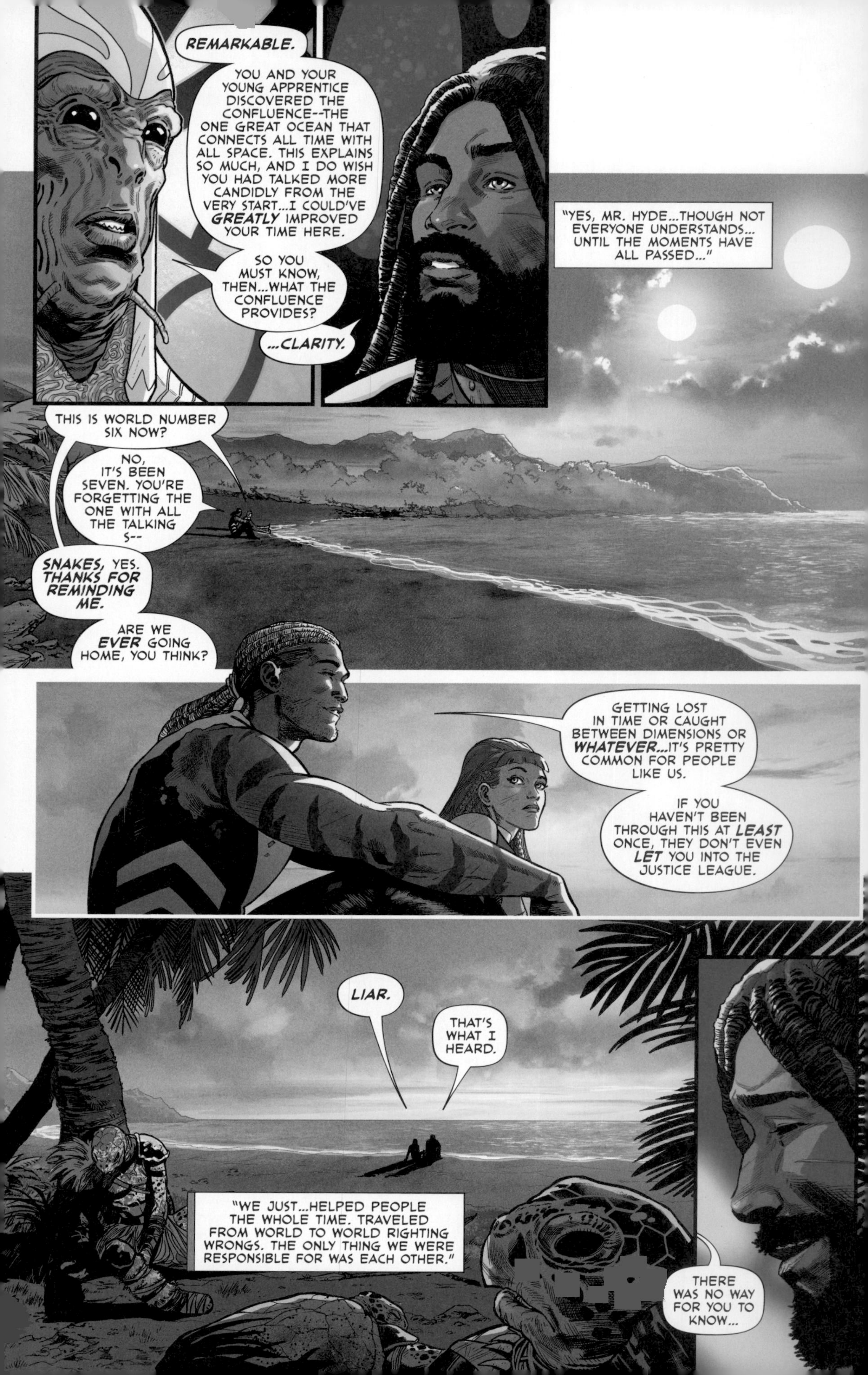
REMARKABLE.
YOU AND YOUR YOUNG APPRENTICE DISCOVERED THE CONFLUENCE--THE ONE GREAT OCEAN THAT CONNECTS ALL TIME WITH ALL SPACE. THIS EXPLAINS SO MUCH, AND I DO WISH YOU HAD TALKED MORE CANDIDLY FROM THE VERY START...I COULD'VE GREATLY IMPROVED YOUR TIME HERE.
SO YOU MUST KNOW, THEN...WHAT THE CONFLUENCE PROVIDES?
...CLARITY.
"YES, MR. HYDE...THOUGH NOT EVERYONE UNDERSTANDS... UNTIL THE MOMENTS HAVE ALL PASSED..."
THIS IS WORLD NUMBER SIX NOW?
NO, IT'S BEEN SEVEN. YOU'RE FORGETTING THE ONE WITH ALL THE TALKING S--
SNAKES, YES. THANKS FOR REMINDING ME.
ARE WE EVER GOING HOME, YOU THINK?
GETTING LOST IN TIME OR CAUGHT BETWEEN DIMENSIONS OR WHATEVER...IT'S PRETTY COMMON FOR PEOPLE LIKE US.
IF YOU HAVEN'T BEEN THROUGH THIS AT LEAST ONCE, THEY DON'T EVEN LET YOU INTO THE JUSTICE LEAGUE.
LIAR.
THAT'S WHAT I HEARD.
"WE JUST...HELPED PEOPLE THE WHOLE TIME. TRAVELED FROM WORLD TO WORLD RIGHTING WRONGS. THE ONLY THING WE WERE RESPONSIBLE FOR WAS EACH OTHER."
THERE WAS NO WAY FOR YOU TO KNOW...

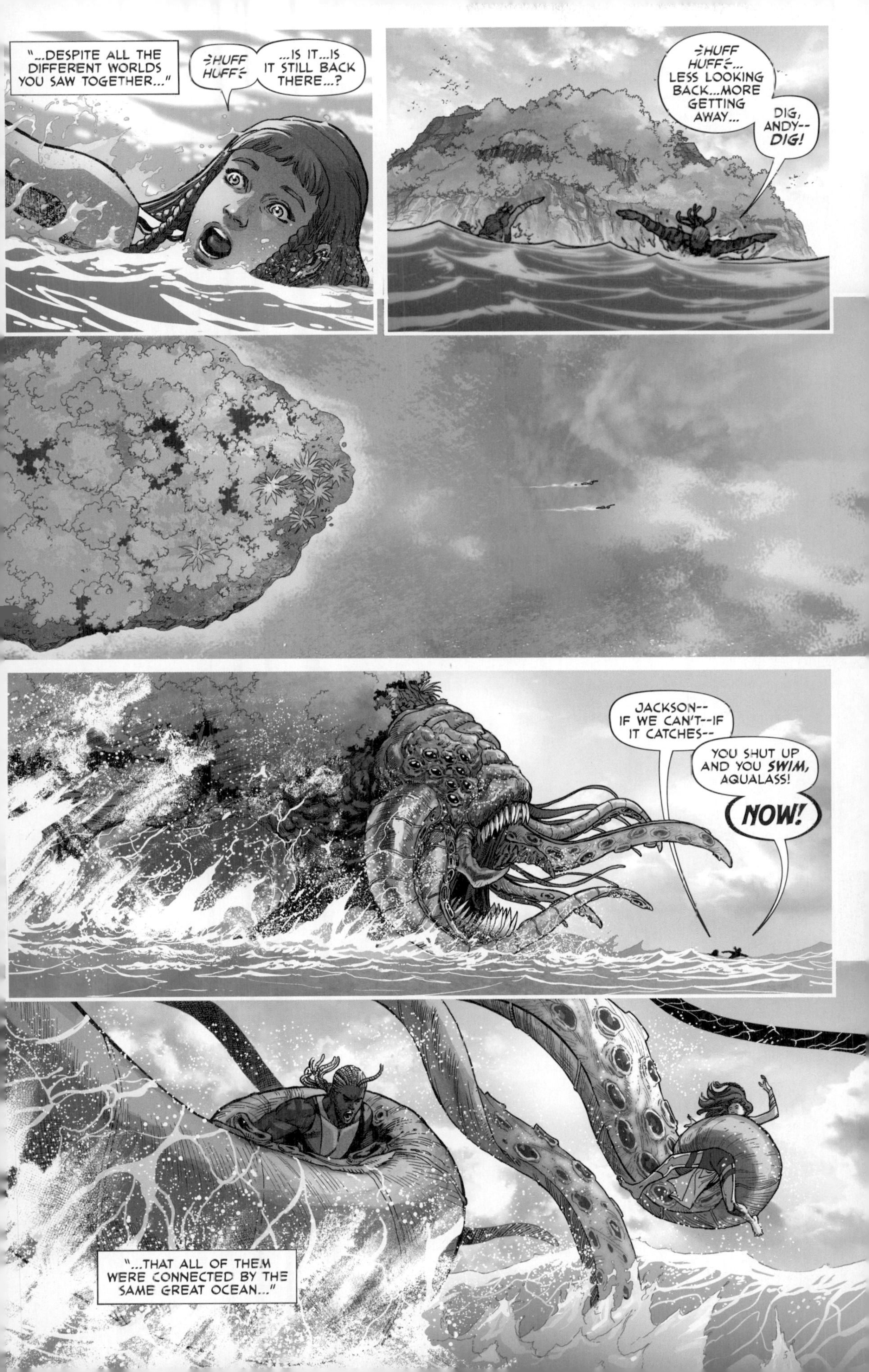
"...DESPITE ALL THE DIFFERENT WORLDS YOU SAW TOGETHER..."
HUFF HUFF
...IS IT...IS IT STILL BACK THERE...?
HUFF HUFF... LESS LOOKING BACK...MORE GETTING AWAY...
DIG, ANDY-- DIG!
JACKSON-- IF WE CAN'T--IF IT CATCHES--
YOU SHUT UP AND YOU SWIM, AQUALASS!
NOW!
"...THAT ALL OF THEM WERE CONNECTED BY THE SAME GREAT OCEAN..."

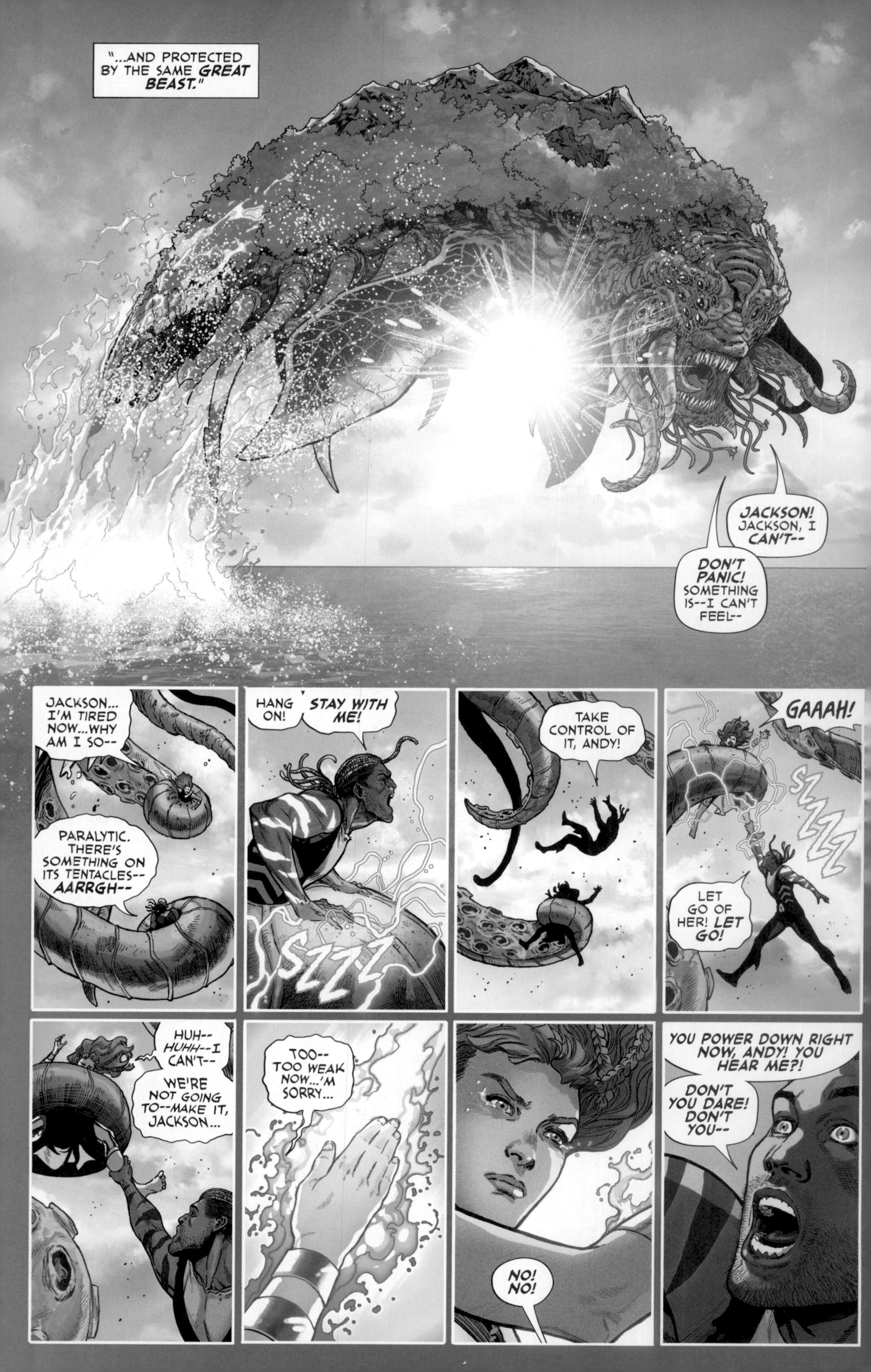
"...AND PROTECTED BY THE SAME GREAT BEAST."
JACKSON! JACKSON, I CAN'T--
DON'T PANIC! SOMETHING IS--I CAN'T FEEL--
JACKSON... I'M TIRED NOW...WHY AM I SO--
PARALYTIC. THERE'S SOMETHING ON ITS TENTACLES-- AARRGH--
HANG ON!
STAY WITH ME!
SZZZ
TAKE CONTROL OF IT, ANDY!
GAAAH!
SZZZ
LET GO OF HER! LET GO!
HUH-- HUHH--I CAN'T--
WE'RE NOT GOING TO--MAKE IT, JACKSON...
TOO-- TOO WEAK NOW...'M SORRY...
NO! NO!
YOU POWER DOWN RIGHT NOW, ANDY! YOU HEAR ME?!
DON'T YOU DARE! DON'T YOU--

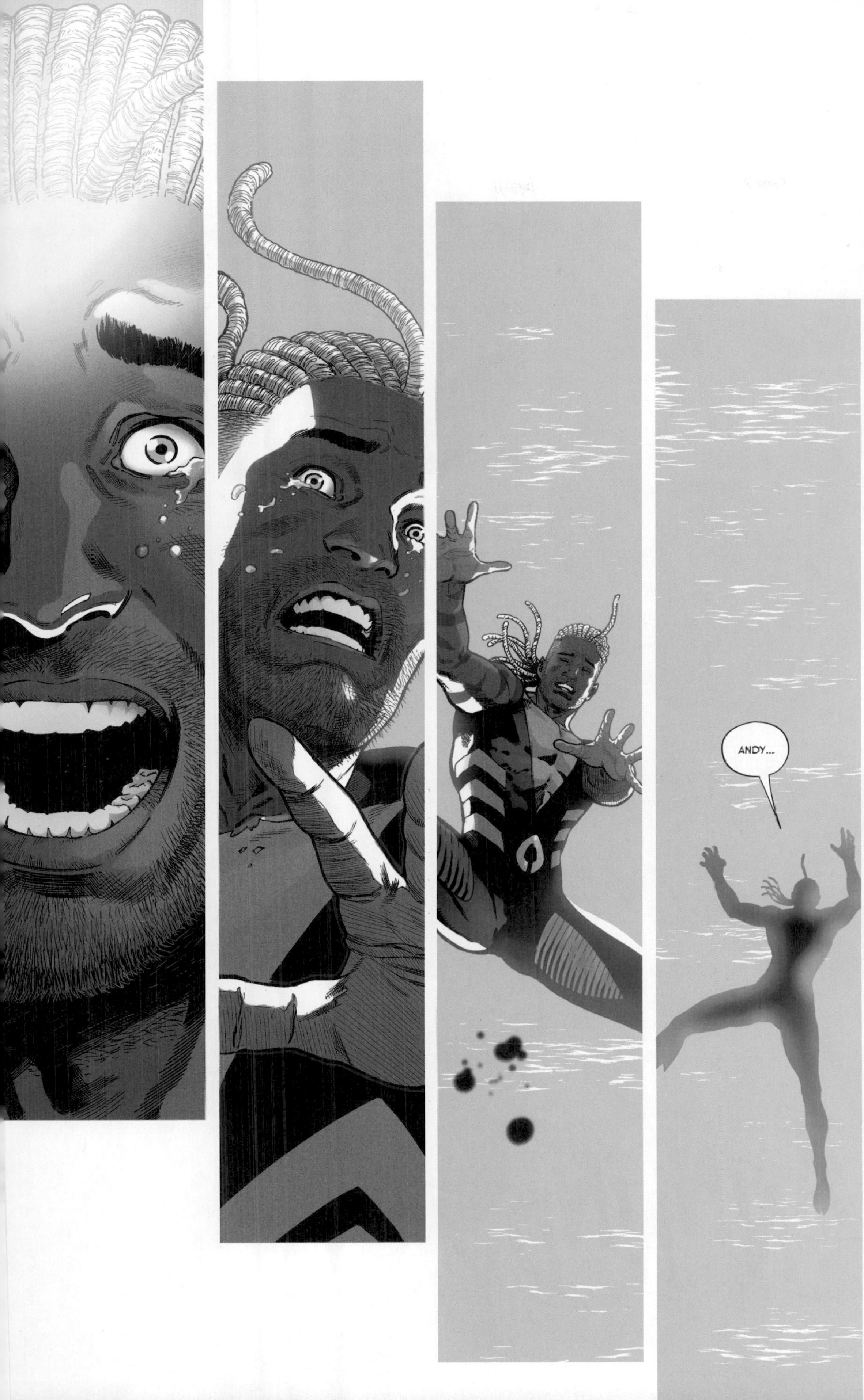
ANDY...

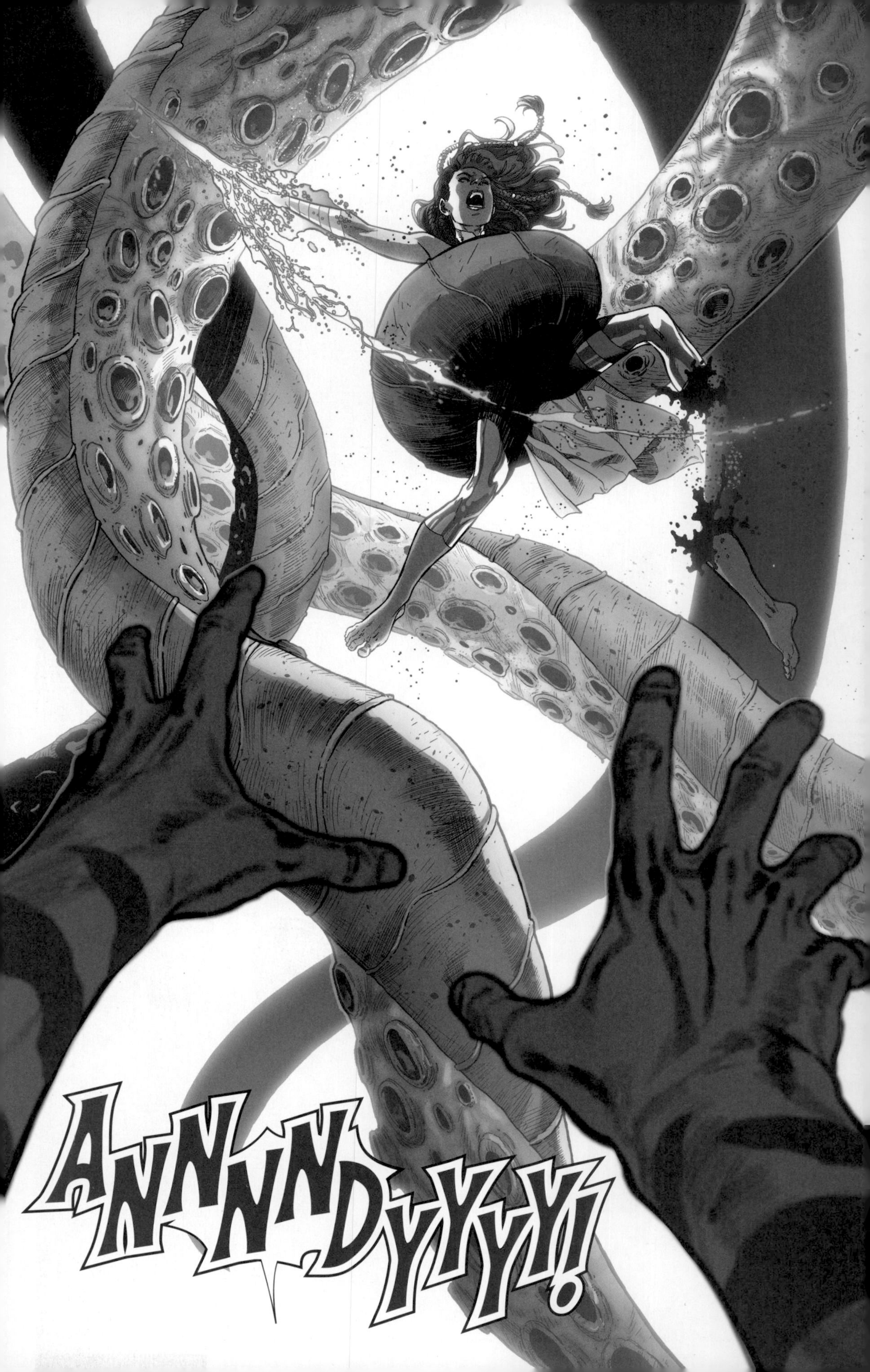
ANNNNDYYYY!

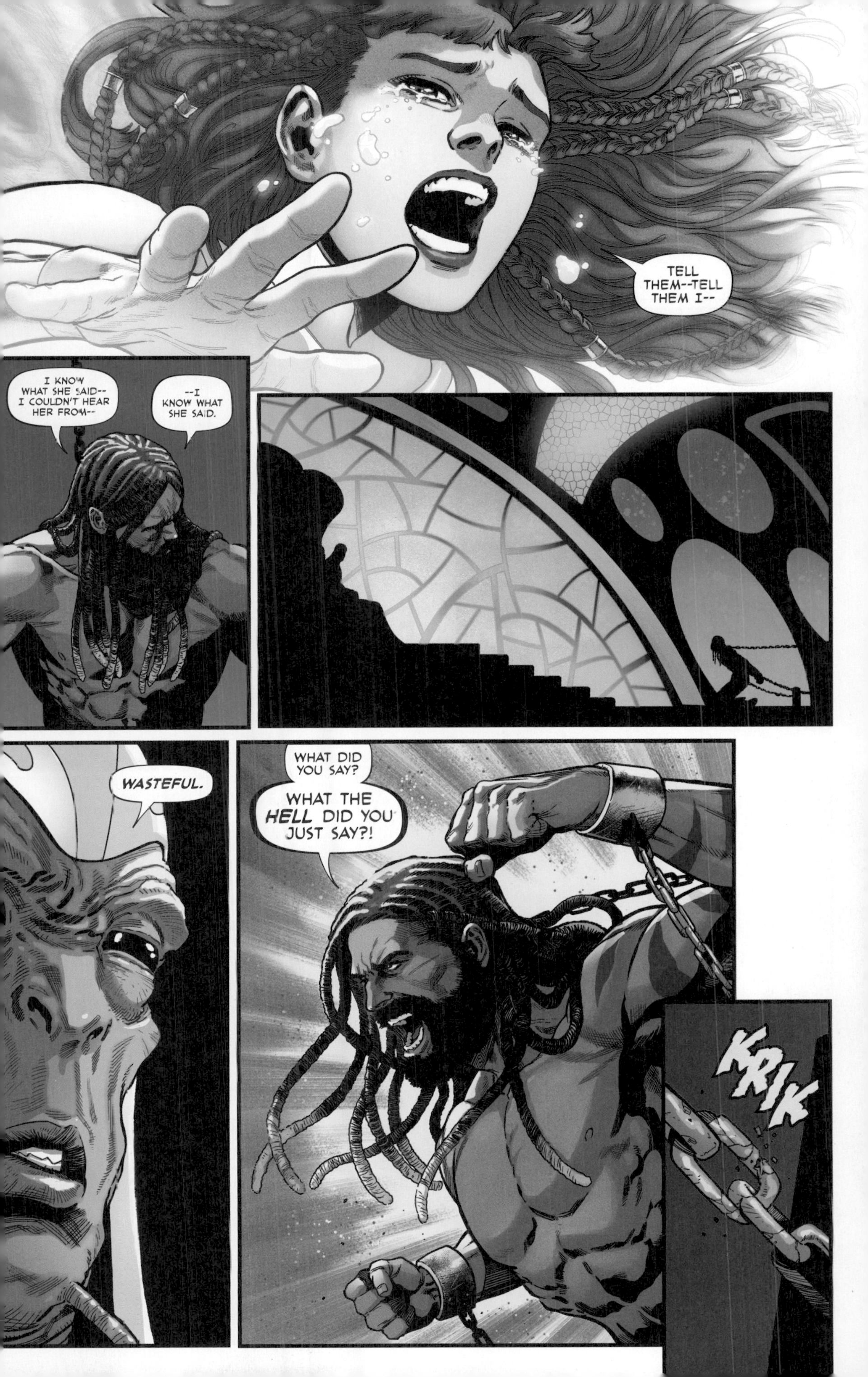
TELL THEM--TELL THEM I--
I KNOW WHAT SHE SAID-- I COULDN'T HEAR HER FROM--
--I KNOW WHAT SHE SAID.
WASTEFUL.
WHAT DID YOU SAY?
WHAT THE HELL DID YOU JUST SAY?!
KRIK

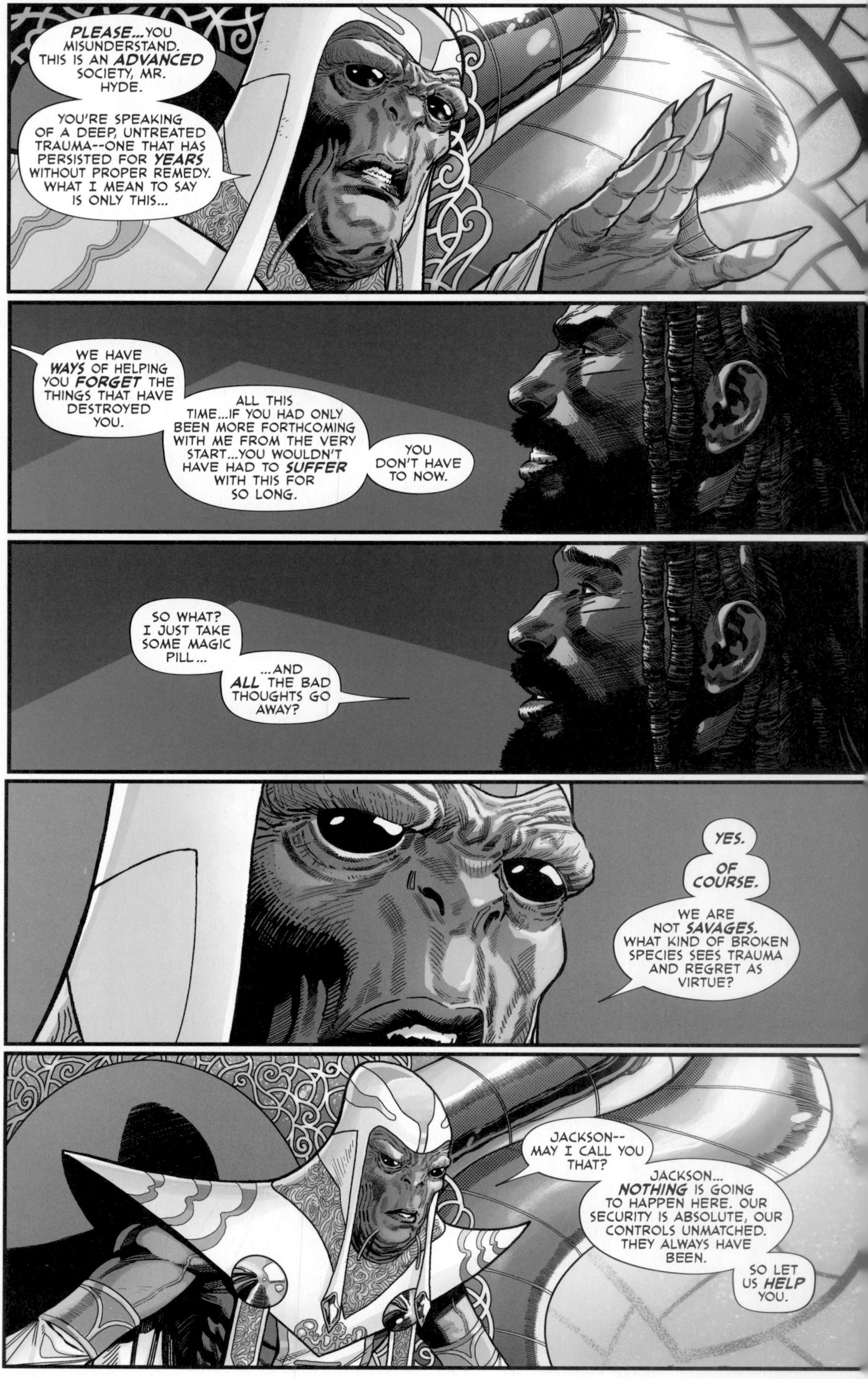
PLEASE...YOU MISUNDERSTAND. THIS IS AN ADVANCED SOCIETY, MR. HYDE.
YOU'RE SPEAKING OF A DEEP, UNTREATED TRAUMA--ONE THAT HAS PERSISTED FOR YEARS WITHOUT PROPER REMEDY. WHAT I MEAN TO SAY IS ONLY THIS...
WE HAVE WAYS OF HELPING YOU FORGET THE THINGS THAT HAVE DESTROYED YOU.
ALL THIS TIME...IF YOU HAD ONLY BEEN MORE FORTHCOMING WITH ME FROM THE VERY START...YOU WOULDN'T HAVE HAD TO SUFFER WITH THIS FOR SO LONG.
YOU DON'T HAVE TO NOW.
SO WHAT? I JUST TAKE SOME MAGIC PILL...
...AND ALL THE BAD THOUGHTS GO AWAY?
YES.
OF COURSE.
WE ARE NOT SAVAGES. WHAT KIND OF BROKEN SPECIES SEES TRAUMA AND REGRET AS VIRTUE?
JACKSON-- MAY I CALL YOU THAT?
JACKSON... NOTHING IS GOING TO HAPPEN HERE. OUR SECURITY IS ABSOLUTE, OUR CONTROLS UNMATCHED. THEY ALWAYS HAVE BEEN.
SO LET US HELP YOU.

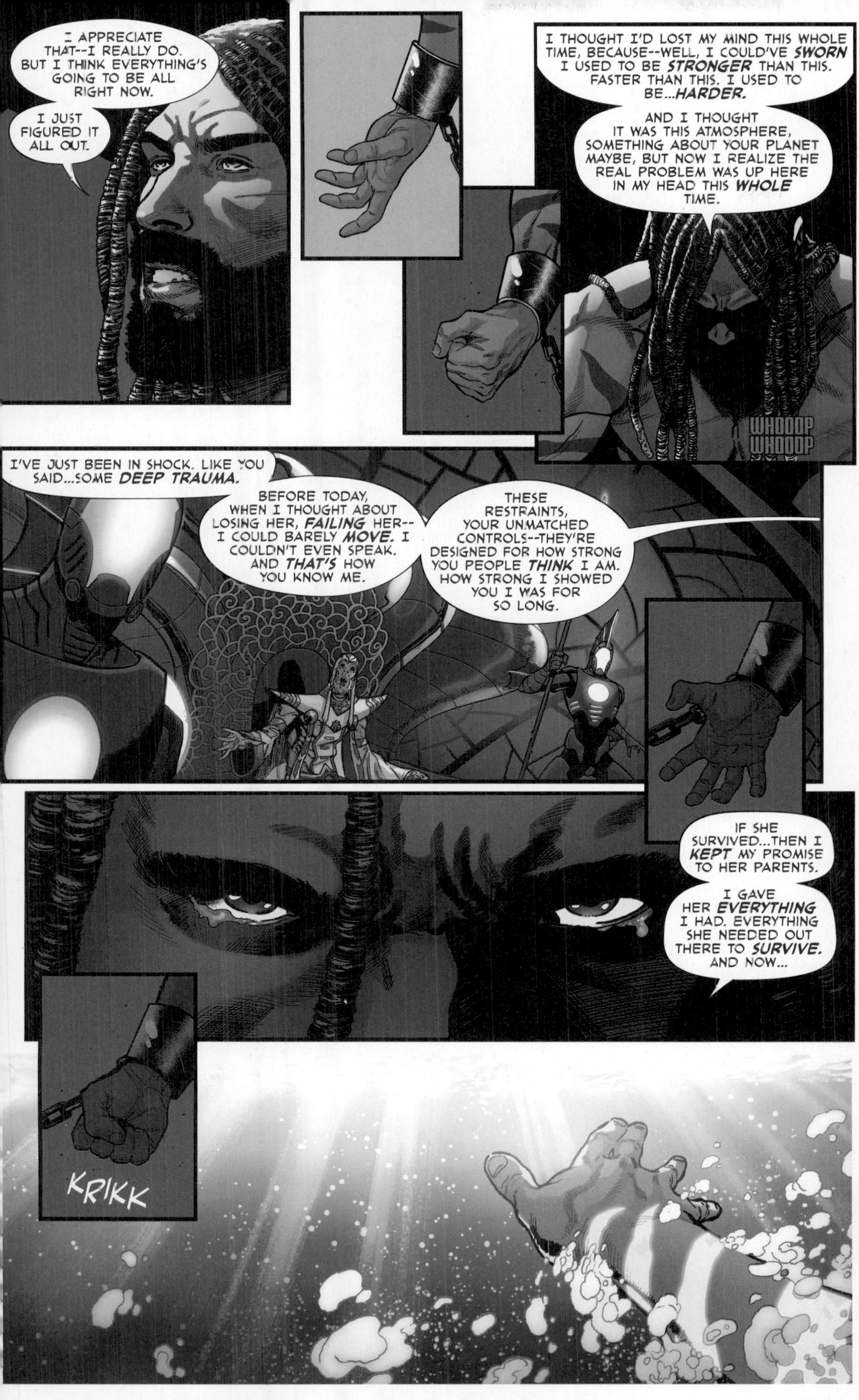

I APPRECIATE THAT--I REALLY DO. BUT I THINK EVERYTHING'S GOING TO BE ALL RIGHT NOW.
I JUST FIGURED IT ALL OUT.
I THOUGHT I'D LOST MY MIND THIS WHOLE TIME, BECAUSE--WELL, I COULD'VE SWORN I USED TO BE STRONGER THAN THIS. FASTER THAN THIS. I USED TO BE...HARDER.
AND I THOUGHT IT WAS THIS ATMOSPHERE, SOMETHING ABOUT YOUR PLANET MAYBE, BUT NOW I REALIZE THE REAL PROBLEM WAS UP HERE IN MY HEAD THIS WHOLE TIME.
WHOOOP WHOOOP
I'VE JUST BEEN IN SHOCK. LIKE YOU SAID...SOME DEEP TRAUMA.
BEFORE TODAY, WHEN I THOUGHT ABOUT LOSING HER, FAILING HER-- I COULD BARELY MOVE. I COULDN'T EVEN SPEAK. AND THAT'S HOW YOU KNOW ME.
THESE RESTRAINTS, YOUR UNMATCHED CONTROLS--THEY'RE DESIGNED FOR HOW STRONG YOU PEOPLE THINK I AM. HOW STRONG I SHOWED YOU I WAS FOR SO LONG.
IF SHE SURVIVED...THEN I KEPT MY PROMISE TO HER PARENTS.
I GAVE HER EVERYTHING I HAD. EVERYTHING SHE NEEDED OUT THERE TO SURVIVE. AND NOW...
KRIKK

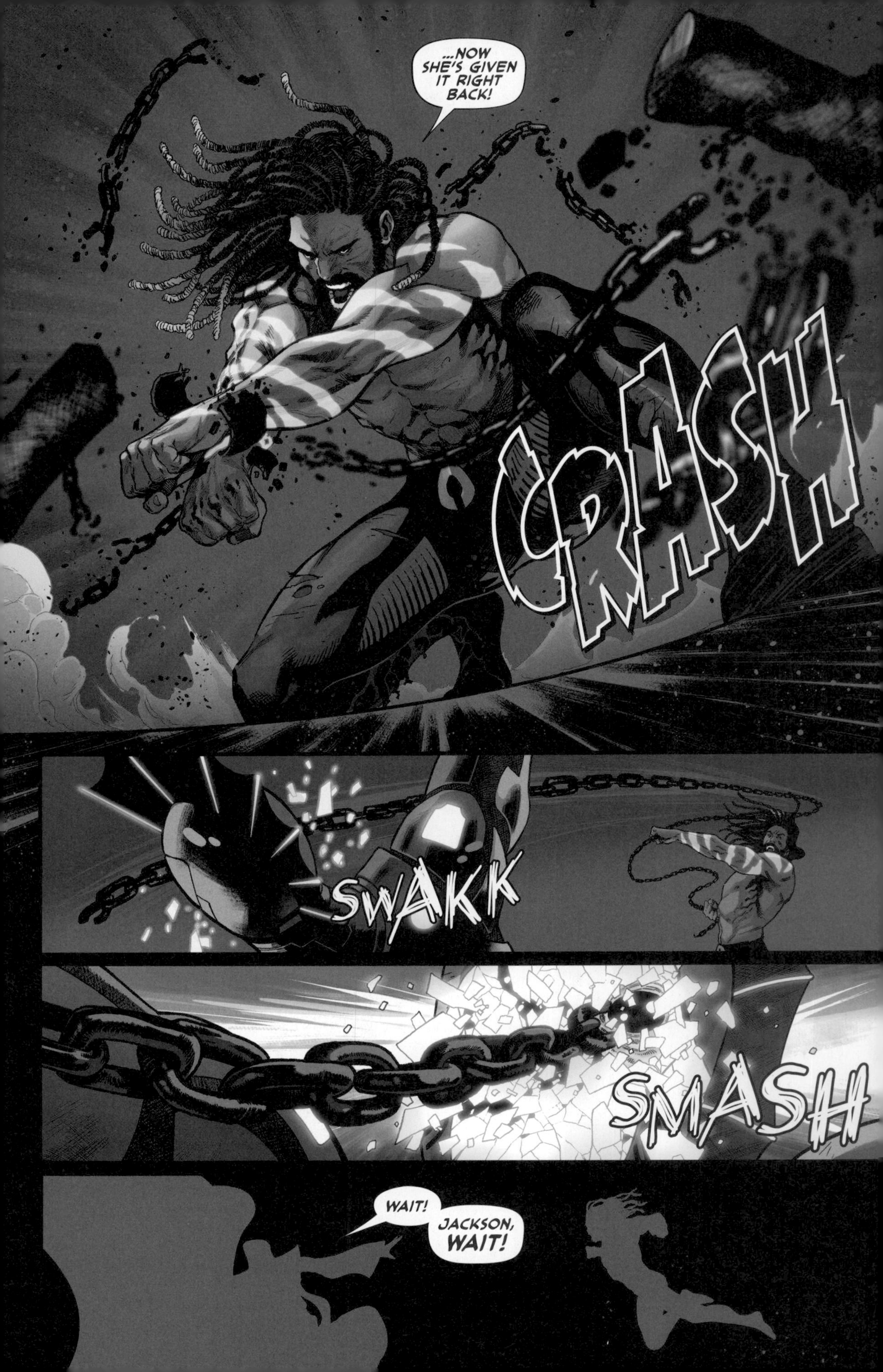
...NOW SHE'S GIVEN IT RIGHT BACK!
CRASH
SWAKK
SMASH
WAIT!
JACKSON, WAIT!

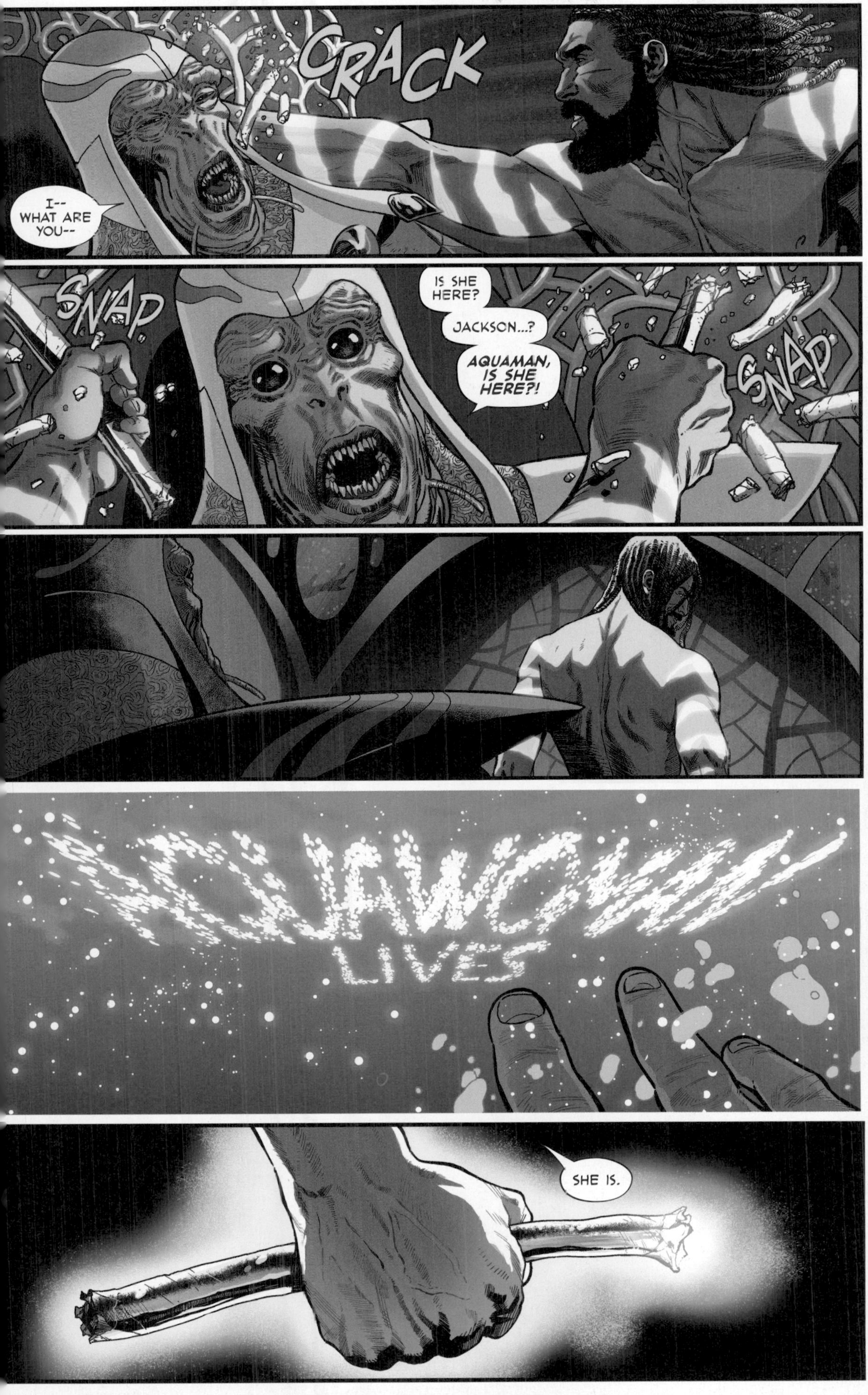
CRACK
I-- WHAT ARE YOU--
SNAP
IS SHE HERE?
JACKSON...?
AQUAMAN, IS SHE HERE?!
SNAP
AQUAMAN LIVES
SHE IS.

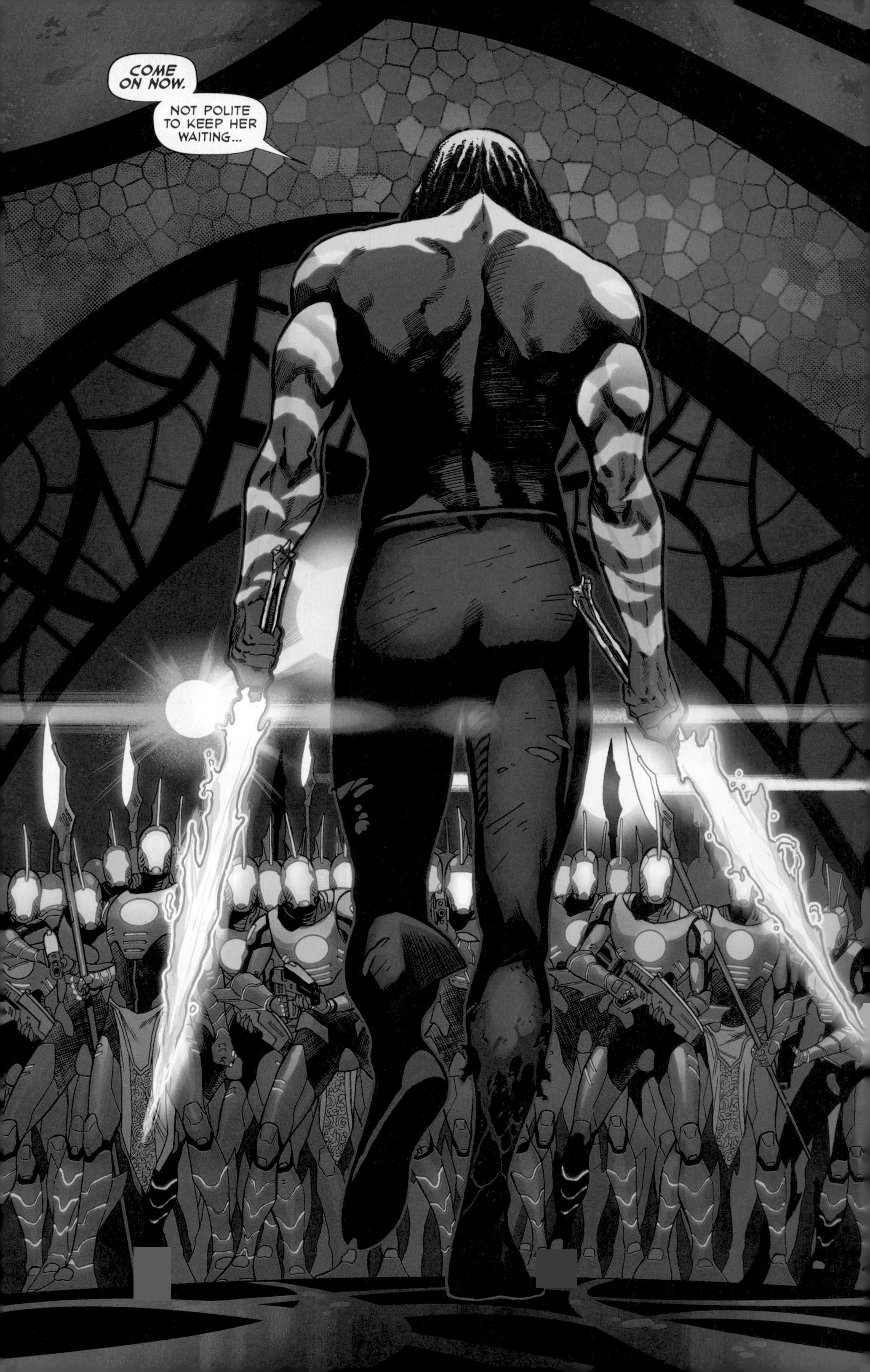
COME ON NOW.
NOT POLITE TO KEEP HER WAITING...

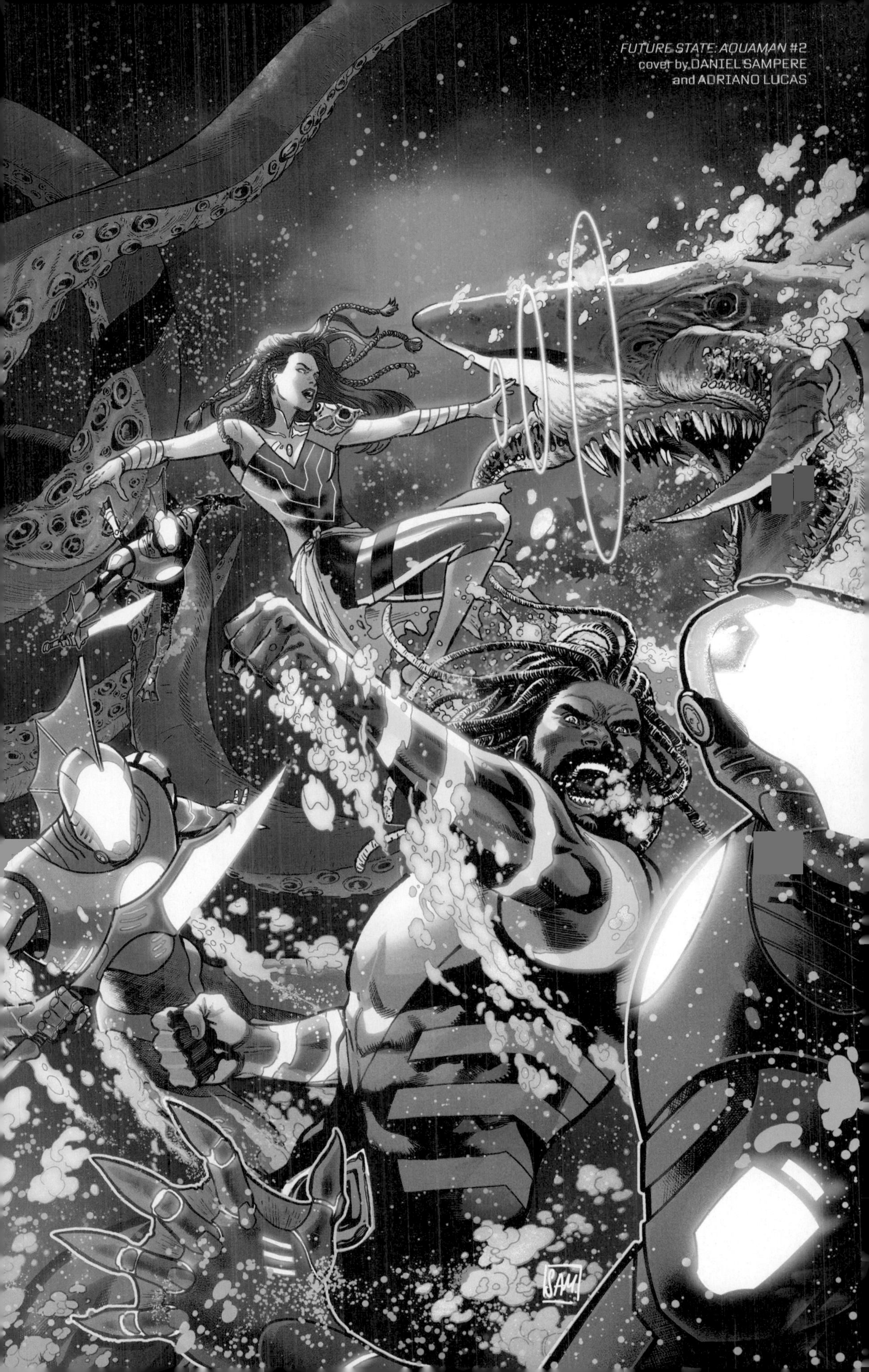
SAM

FUTURE STATE: AQUAMAN #2
cover by DANIEL SAMPERE
and ADRIANO LUCAS

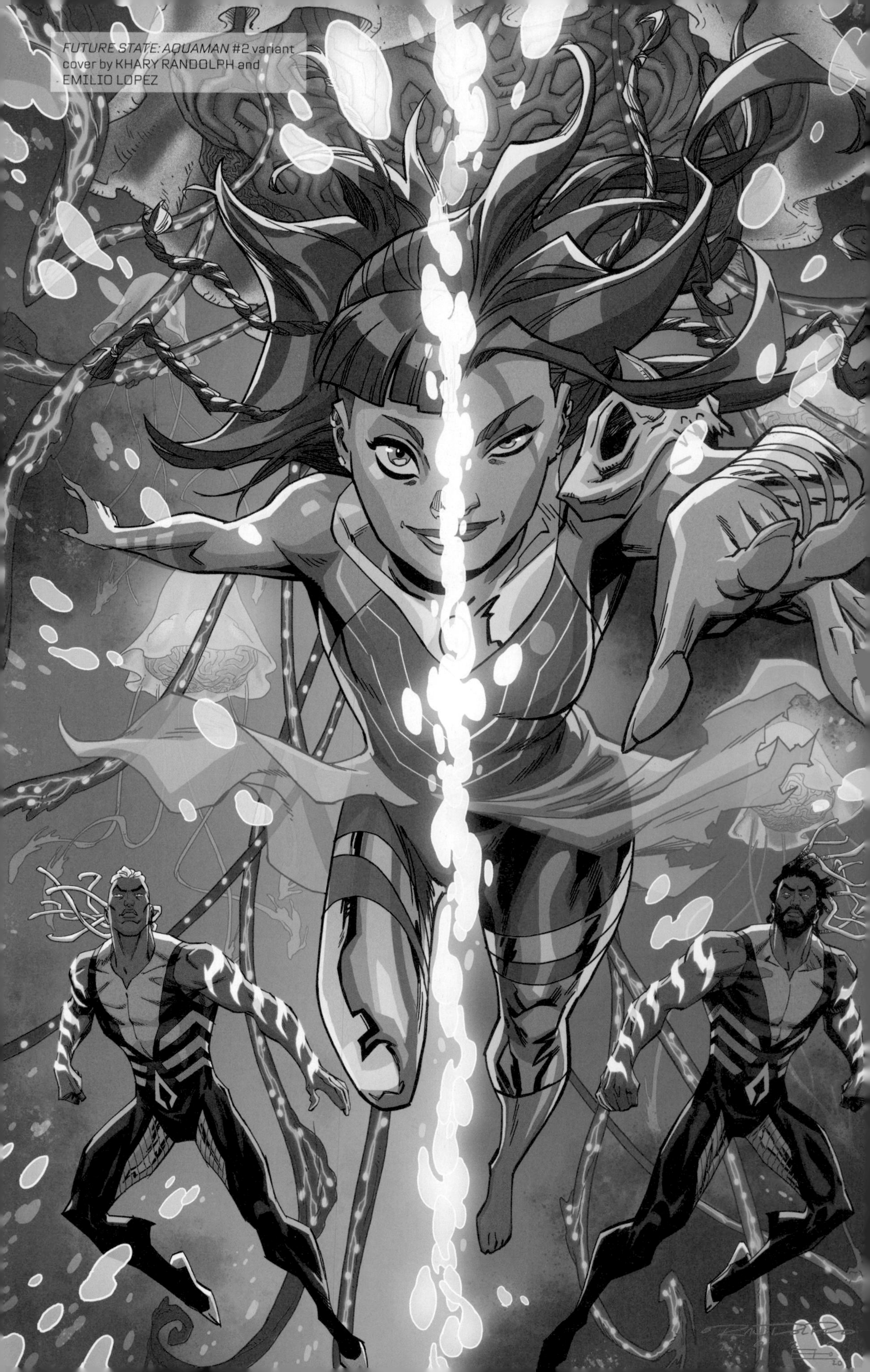

FUTURE STATE: AQUAMAN #2 variant cover by KHARY RANDOLPH and EMILIO LOPEZ

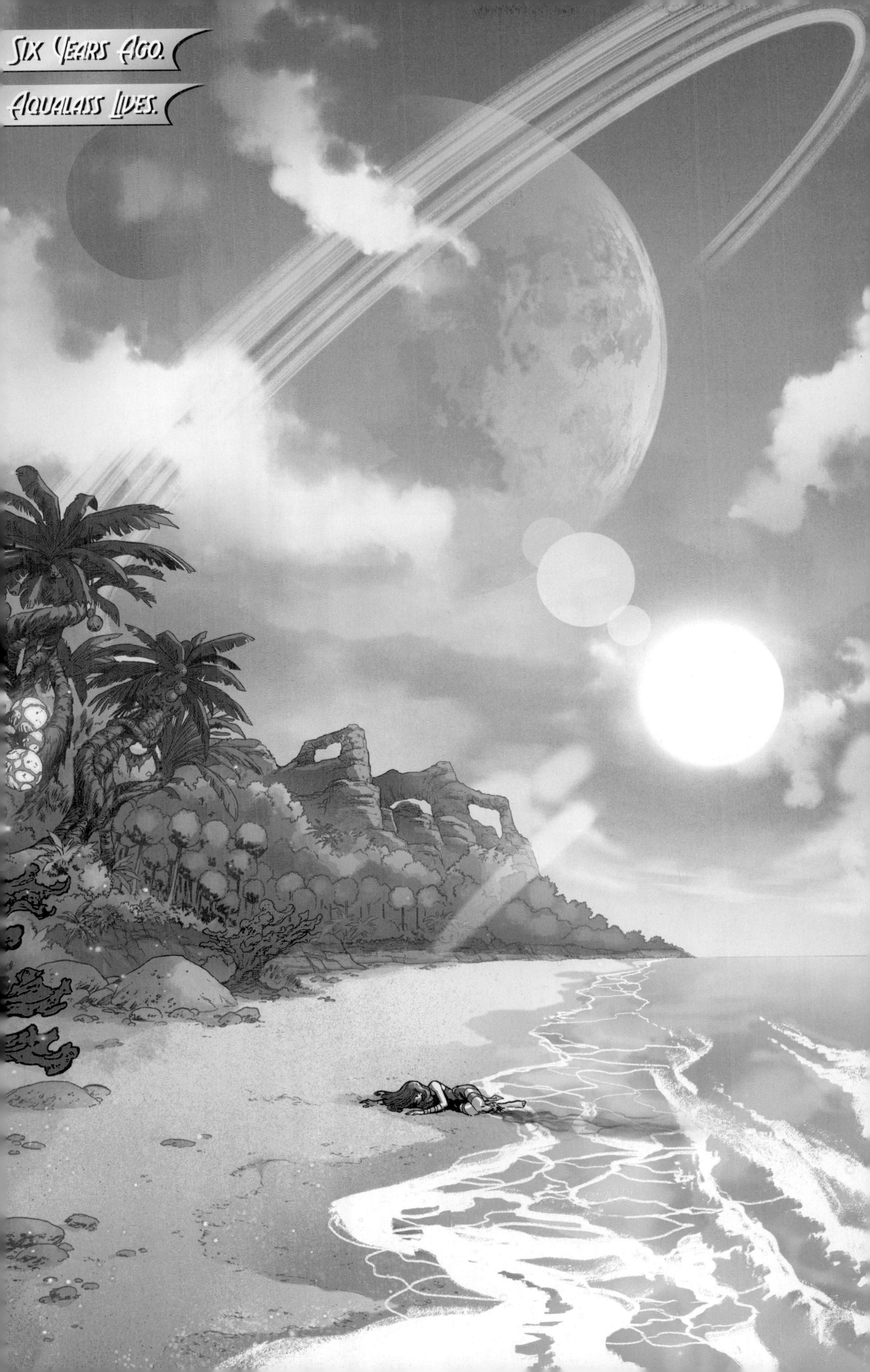
Six Years Ago.
Aqualass Lives.

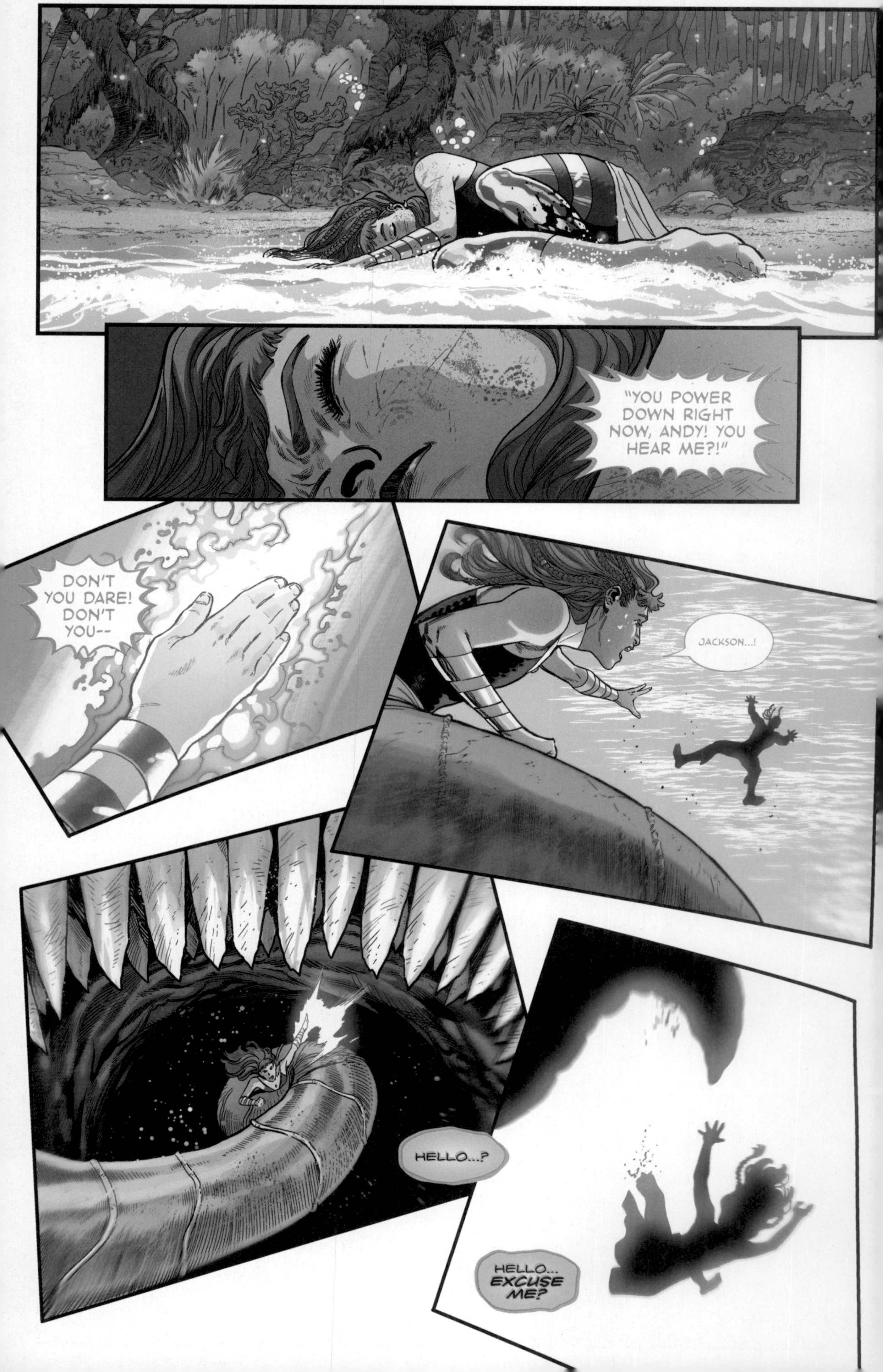
"YOU POWER DOWN RIGHT NOW, ANDY! YOU HEAR ME?!"
DON'T YOU DARE! DON'T YOU--
JACKSON...!
HELLO...?
HELLO... EXCUSE ME?

FUTURE STATE: AQUAMAN

THE CONFLUENCE

PART TWO

BRANDON THOMAS WRITER DANIEL SAMPERE ARTIST
ADRIANO LUCAS COLORIST CLAYTON COWLES LETTERER
SAMPERE & LUCAS COVER ARTISTS
KHARY RANDOLPH & EMILIO LOPEZ VARIANT COVER ARTISTS
ANDREA SHEA EDITOR CHRIS CONROY SENIOR EDITOR
AQUAMAN CREATED BY PAUL NORRIS

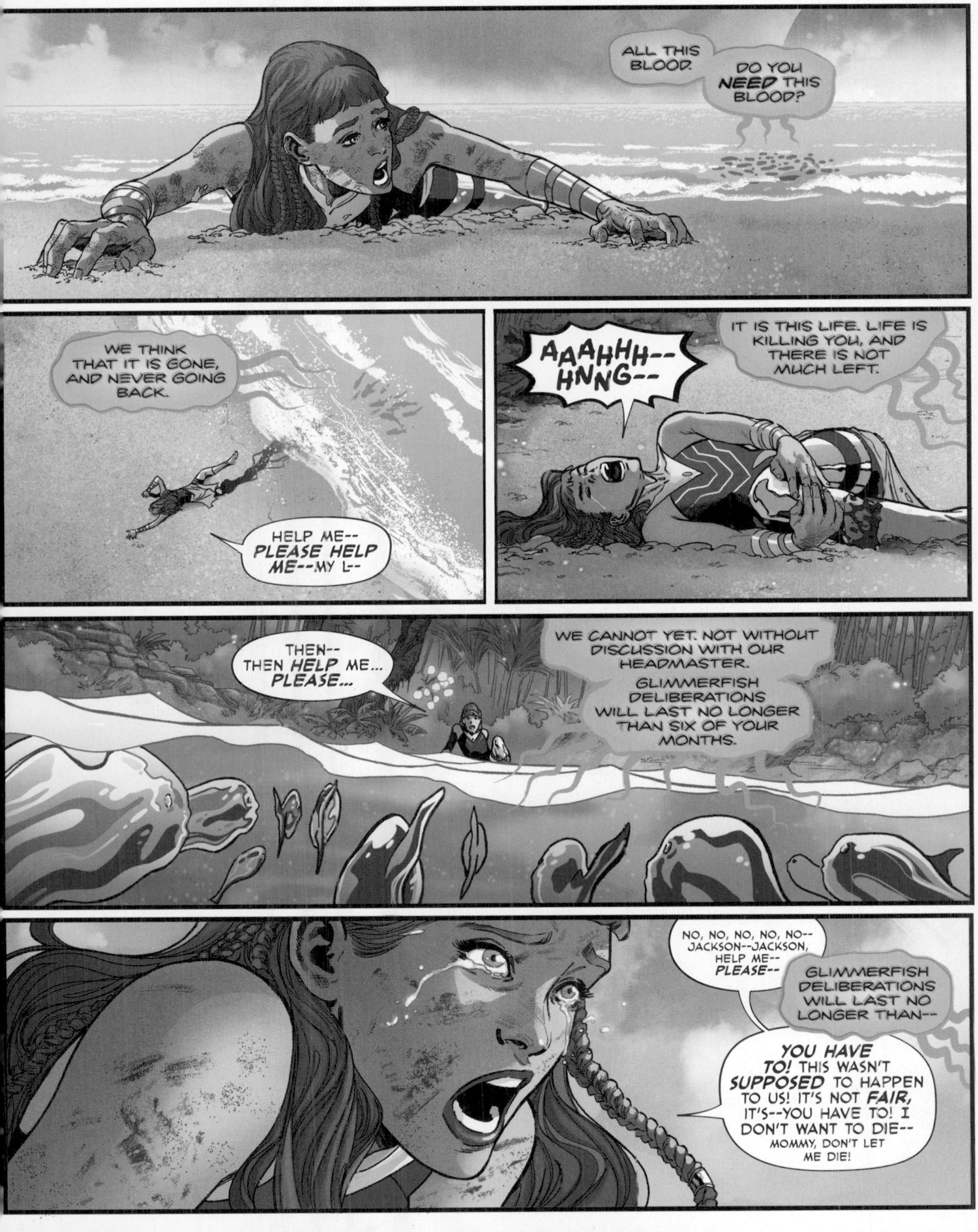
ALL THIS BLOOD.
DO YOU NEED THIS BLOOD?
WE THINK THAT IT IS GONE, AND NEVER GOING BACK.
HELP ME-- PLEASE HELP ME--MY L--
AAAHHH-- HNNG--
IT IS THIS LIFE. LIFE IS KILLING YOU, AND THERE IS NOT MUCH LEFT.
THEN-- THEN HELP ME... PLEASE...
WE CANNOT YET. NOT WITHOUT DISCUSSION WITH OUR HEADMASTER.
GLIMMERFISH DELIBERATIONS WILL LAST NO LONGER THAN SIX OF YOUR MONTHS.
NO, NO, NO, NO, NO-- JACKSON--JACKSON, HELP ME-- PLEASE--
GLIMMERFISH DELIBERATIONS WILL LAST NO LONGER THAN--
YOU HAVE TO! THIS WASN'T SUPPOSED TO HAPPEN TO US! IT'S NOT FAIR, IT'S--YOU HAVE TO! I DON'T WANT TO DIE-- MOMMY, DON'T LET ME DIE!

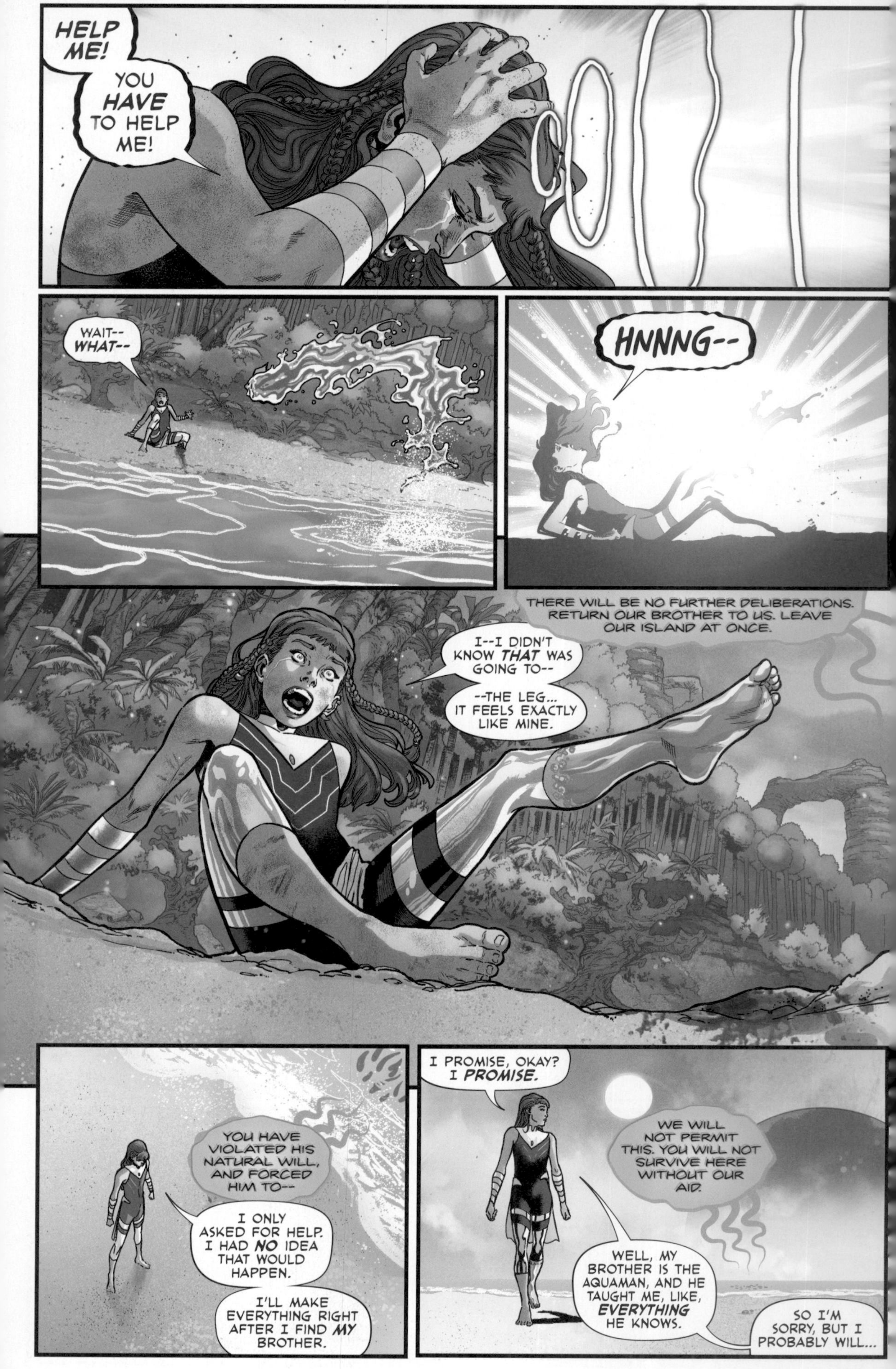
HELP ME!
YOU HAVE TO HELP ME!
WAIT-- WHAT--
HNNNG--
THERE WILL BE NO FURTHER DELIBERATIONS. RETURN OUR BROTHER TO US. LEAVE OUR ISLAND AT ONCE.
I--I DIDN'T KNOW THAT WAS GOING TO--
--THE LEG... IT FEELS EXACTLY LIKE MINE.
YOU HAVE VIOLATED HIS NATURAL WILL, AND FORCED HIM TO--
I ONLY ASKED FOR HELP. I HAD NO IDEA THAT WOULD HAPPEN.
I'LL MAKE EVERYTHING RIGHT AFTER I FIND MY BROTHER.
I PROMISE, OKAY? I PROMISE.
WE WILL NOT PERMIT THIS. YOU WILL NOT SURVIVE HERE WITHOUT OUR AID.
WELL, MY BROTHER IS THE AQUAMAN, AND HE TAUGHT ME, LIKE, EVERYTHING HE KNOWS.
SO I'M SORRY, BUT I PROBABLY WILL...

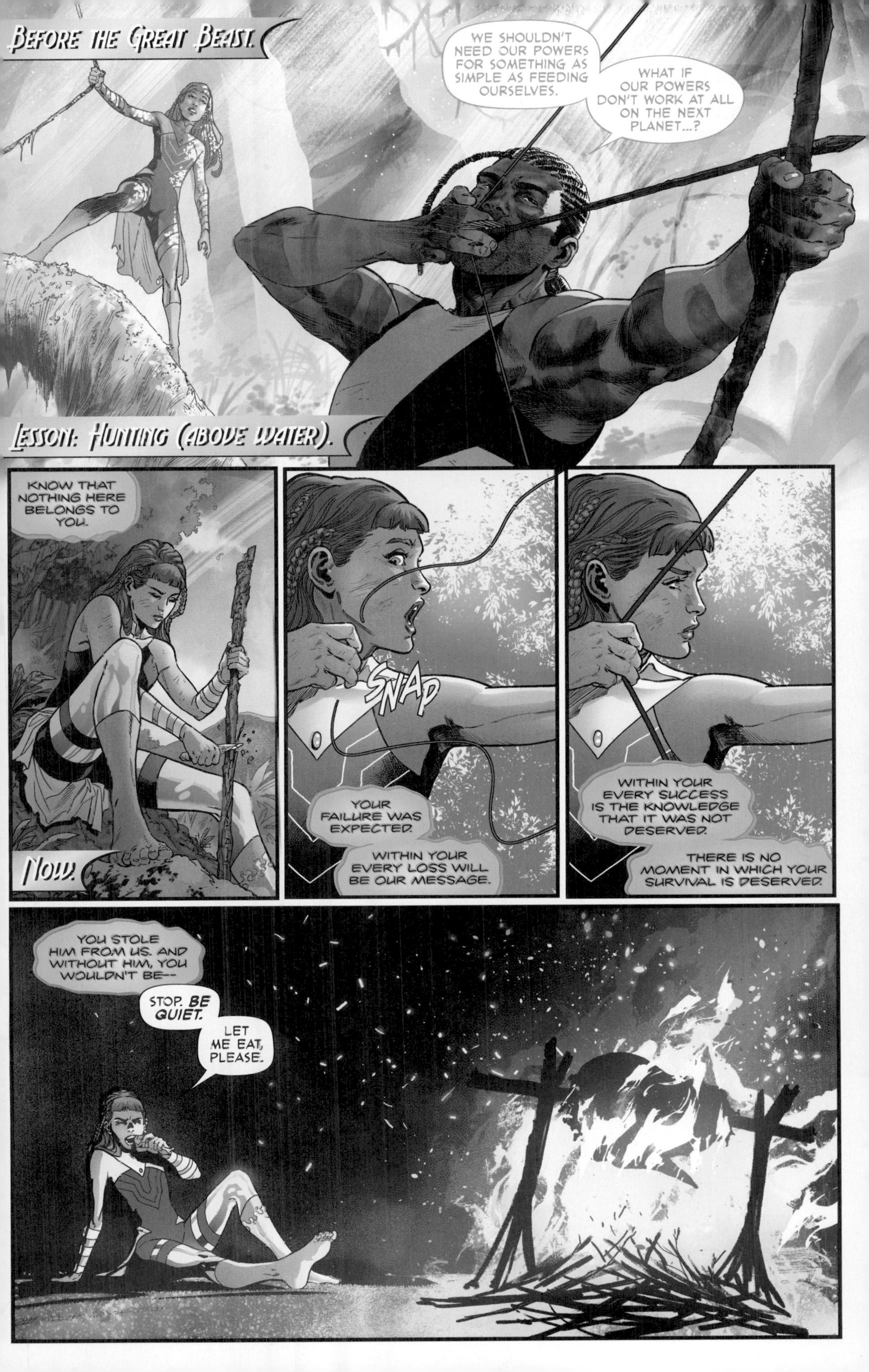
Before the Great Beast.
WE SHOULDN'T NEED OUR POWERS FOR SOMETHING AS SIMPLE AS FEEDING OURSELVES.
WHAT IF OUR POWERS DON'T WORK AT ALL ON THE NEXT PLANET...?
Lesson: Hunting (above water).
KNOW THAT NOTHING HERE BELONGS TO YOU.
Now.
SNAP
YOUR FAILURE WAS EXPECTED.
WITHIN YOUR EVERY LOSS WILL BE OUR MESSAGE.
WITHIN YOUR EVERY SUCCESS IS THE KNOWLEDGE THAT IT WAS NOT DESERVED.
THERE IS NO MOMENT IN WHICH YOUR SURVIVAL IS DESERVED.
YOU STOLE HIM FROM US. AND WITHOUT HIM, YOU WOULDN'T BE--
STOP. BE QUIET.
LET ME EAT, PLEASE.

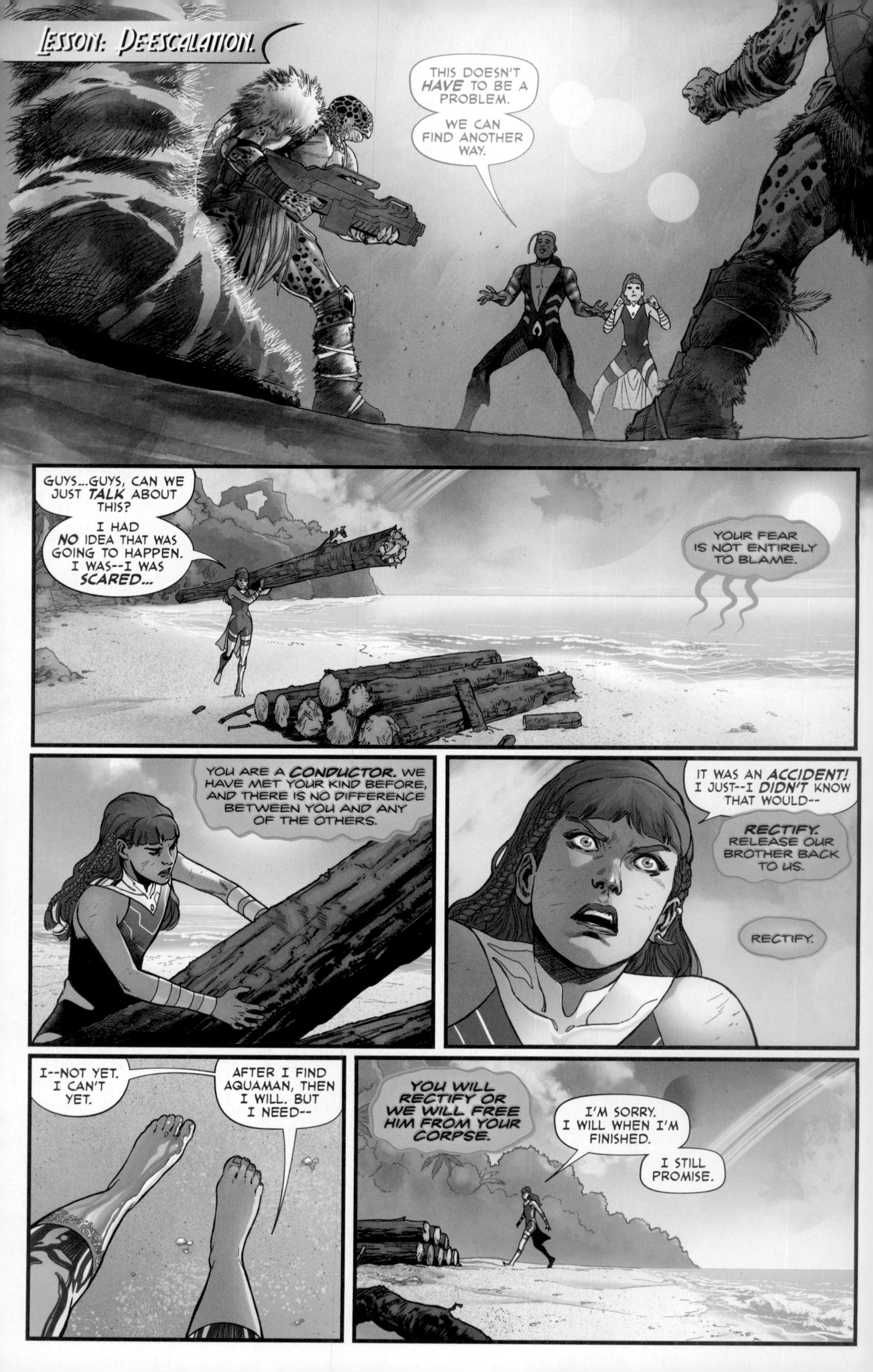
LESSON: DE-ESCALATION.
THIS DOESN'T HAVE TO BE A PROBLEM.
WE CAN FIND ANOTHER WAY.
GUYS...GUYS, CAN WE JUST TALK ABOUT THIS?
I HAD NO IDEA THAT WAS GOING TO HAPPEN. I WAS--I WAS SCARED...
YOUR FEAR IS NOT ENTIRELY TO BLAME.
YOU ARE A CONDUCTOR. WE HAVE MET YOUR KIND BEFORE, AND THERE IS NO DIFFERENCE BETWEEN YOU AND ANY OF THE OTHERS.
IT WAS AN ACCIDENT! I JUST--I DIDN'T KNOW THAT WOULD--
RECTIFY. RELEASE OUR BROTHER BACK TO US.
RECTIFY.
I--NOT YET. I CAN'T YET.
AFTER I FIND AQUAMAN, THEN I WILL. BUT I NEED--
YOU WILL RECTIFY OR WE WILL FREE HIM FROM YOUR CORPSE.
I'M SORRY. I WILL WHEN I'M FINISHED.
I STILL PROMISE.

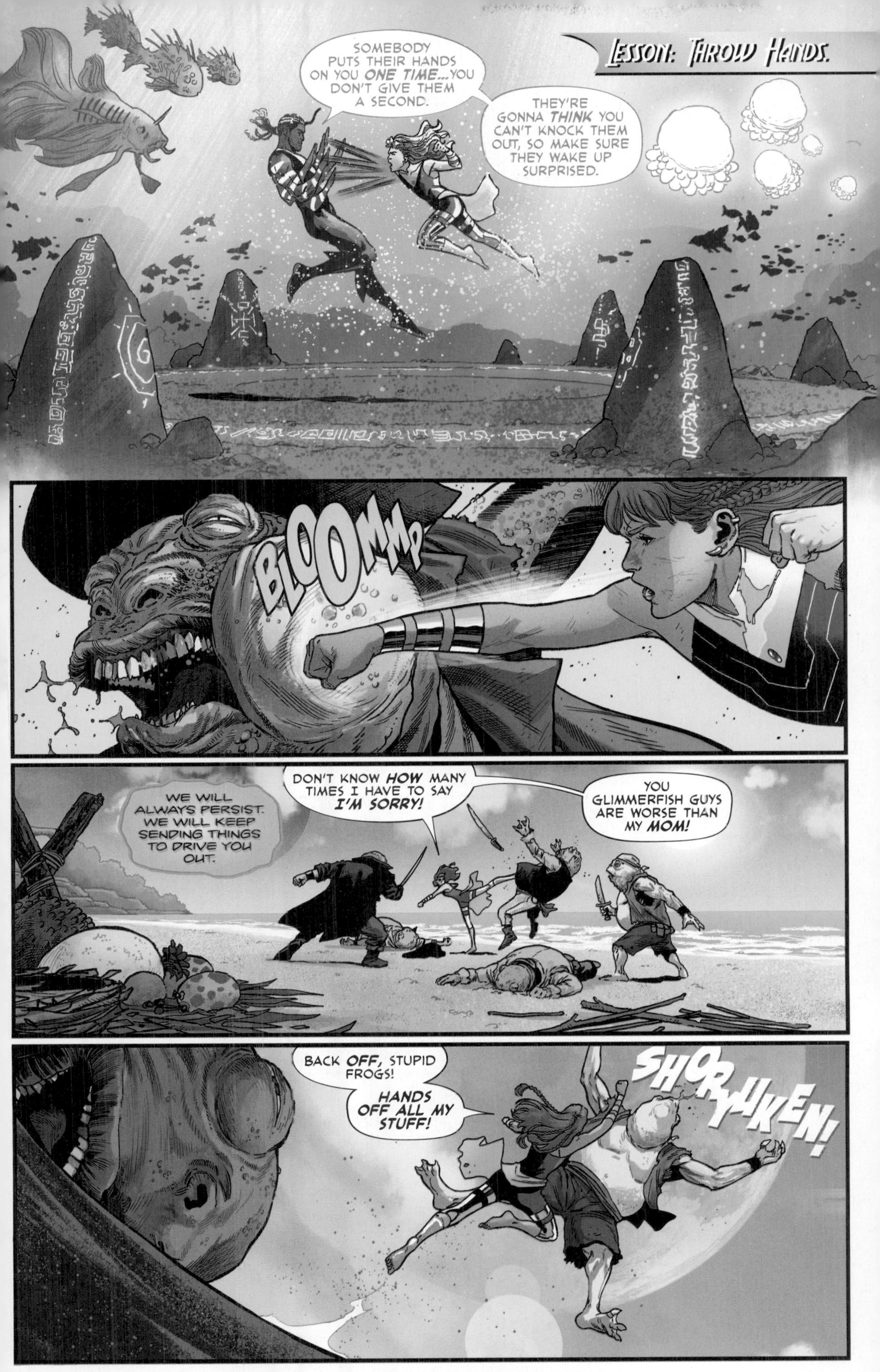

Lesson: Throw Hands.
SOMEBODY PUTS THEIR HANDS ON YOU ONE TIME... YOU DON'T GIVE THEM A SECOND.
THEY'RE GONNA THINK YOU CAN'T KNOCK THEM OUT, SO MAKE SURE THEY WAKE UP SURPRISED.
BLOOMMP
WE WILL ALWAYS PERSIST. WE WILL KEEP SENDING THINGS TO DRIVE YOU OUT.
DON'T KNOW HOW MANY TIMES I HAVE TO SAY I'M SORRY!
YOU GLIMMERFISH GUYS ARE WORSE THAN MY MOM!
BACK OFF, STUPID FROGS!
HANDS OFF ALL MY STUFF!
SHORYUKEN!

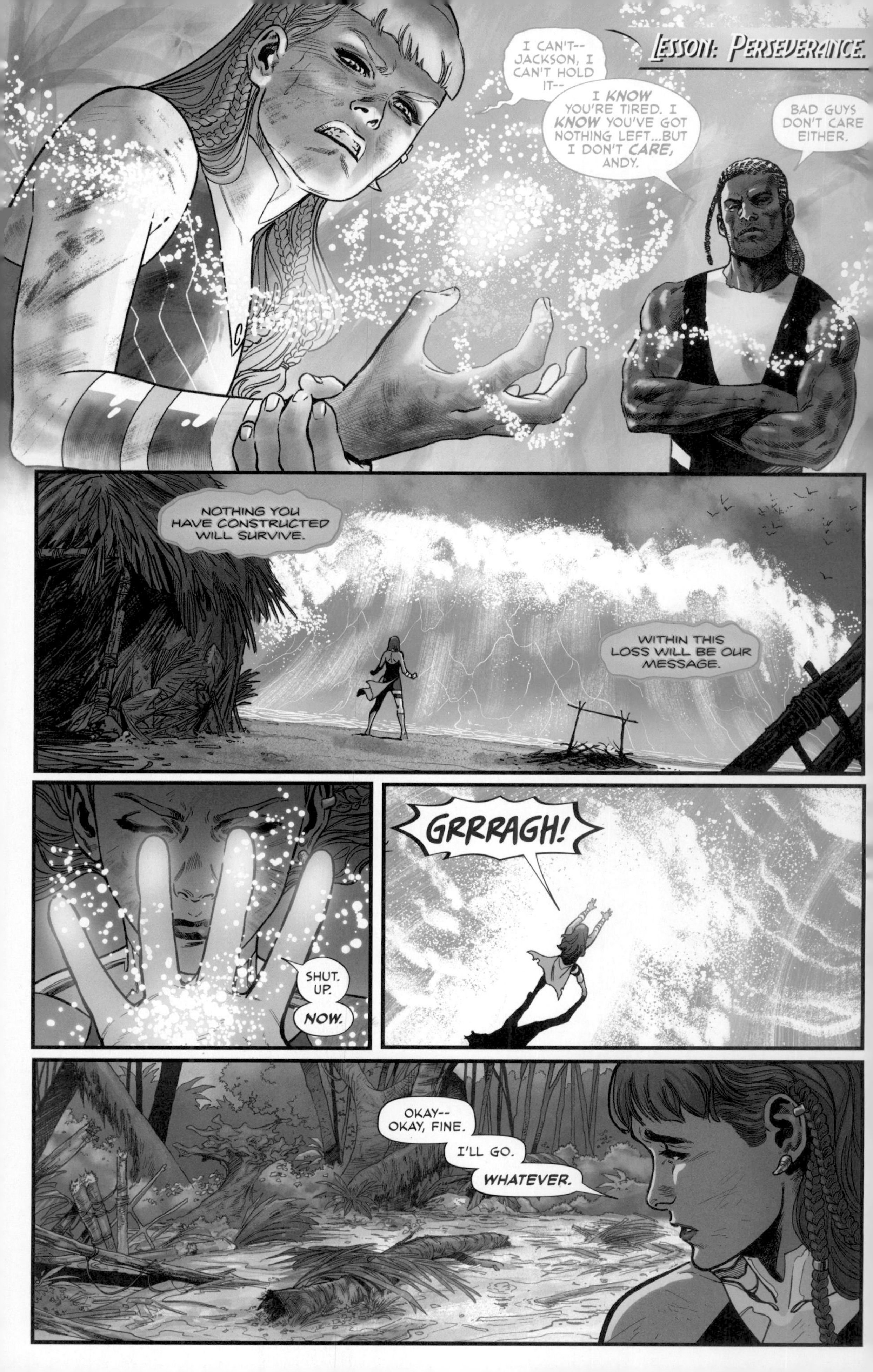
LESSON: PERSEVERANCE.
I CAN'T-- JACKSON, I CAN'T HOLD IT--
I KNOW YOU'RE TIRED. I KNOW YOU'VE GOT NOTHING LEFT...BUT I DON'T CARE, ANDY.
BAD GUYS DON'T CARE EITHER.
NOTHING YOU HAVE CONSTRUCTED WILL SURVIVE.
WITHIN THIS LOSS WILL BE OUR MESSAGE.
SHUT. UP.
NOW.
GRRRAGH!
OKAY-- OKAY, FINE.
I'LL GO.
WHATEVER.

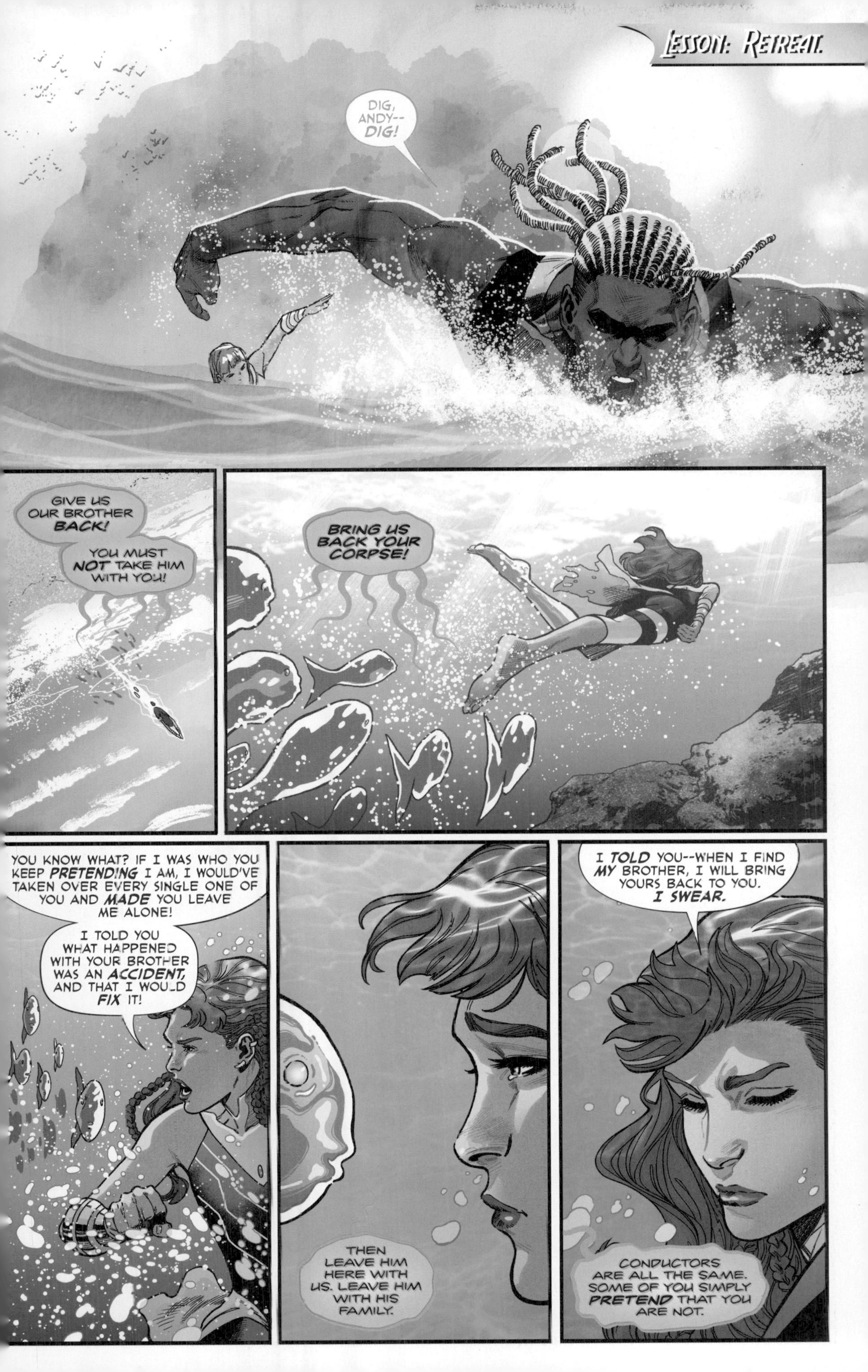

LESSON: RETREAT.
DIG, ANDY-- DIG!
GIVE US OUR BROTHER BACK!
YOU MUST NOT TAKE HIM WITH YOU!
BRING US BACK YOUR CORPSE!
YOU KNOW WHAT? IF I WAS WHO YOU KEEP PRETENDING I AM, I WOULD'VE TAKEN OVER EVERY SINGLE ONE OF YOU AND MADE YOU LEAVE ME ALONE!
I TOLD YOU WHAT HAPPENED WITH YOUR BROTHER WAS AN ACCIDENT, AND THAT I WOULD FIX IT!
THEN LEAVE HIM HERE WITH US. LEAVE HIM WITH HIS FAMILY.
I TOLD YOU--WHEN I FIND MY BROTHER, I WILL BRING YOURS BACK TO YOU. I SWEAR.
CONDUCTORS ARE ALL THE SAME. SOME OF YOU SIMPLY PRETEND THAT YOU ARE NOT.

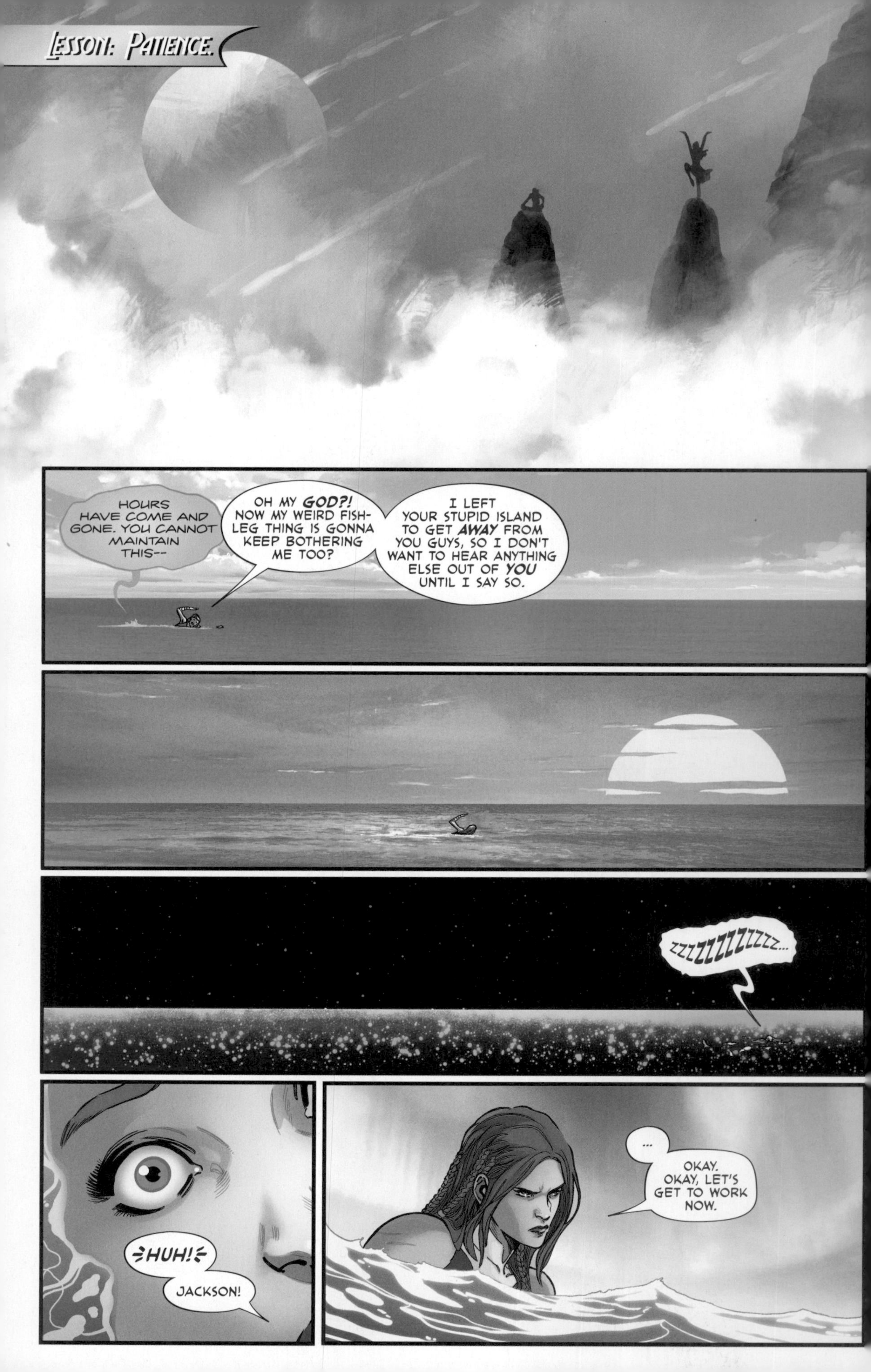
LESSON: PATIENCE.
HOURS HAVE COME AND GONE. YOU CANNOT MAINTAIN THIS--
OH MY GOD?! NOW MY WEIRD FISH-LEG THING IS GONNA KEEP BOTHERING ME TOO?
I LEFT YOUR STUPID ISLAND TO GET AWAY FROM YOU GUYS, SO I DON'T WANT TO HEAR ANYTHING ELSE OUT OF YOU UNTIL I SAY SO.
ZZZZZZZZZZZZ...
HUH!
JACKSON!
...
OKAY. OKAY, LET'S GET TO WORK NOW.

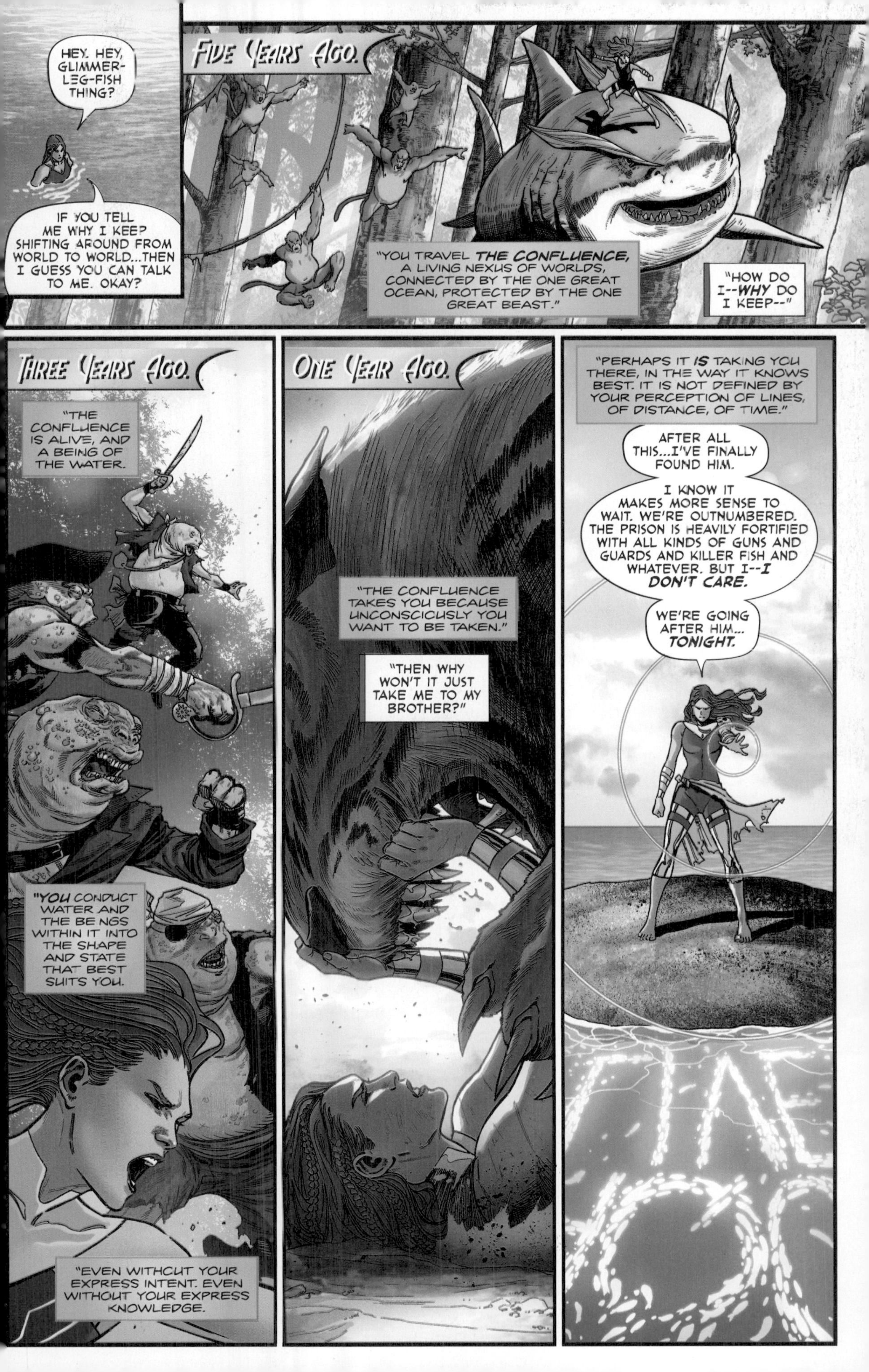

HEY, HEY, GLIMMER-LEG-FISH THING?
IF YOU TELL ME WHY I KEEP SHIFTING AROUND FROM WORLD TO WORLD...THEN I GUESS YOU CAN TALK TO ME. OKAY?
FIVE YEARS AGO.
"YOU TRAVEL THE CONFLUENCE, A LIVING NEXUS OF WORLDS, CONNECTED BY THE ONE GREAT OCEAN, PROTECTED BY THE ONE GREAT BEAST."
"HOW DO I--WHY DO I KEEP--"
THREE YEARS AGO.
"THE CONFLUENCE IS ALIVE, AND A BEING OF THE WATER.
"YOU CONDUCT WATER AND THE BE NGS WITHIN IT INTO THE SHAPE AND STATE THAT BEST SUITS YOU.
"EVEN WITHOUT YOUR EXPRESS INTENT. EVEN WITHOUT YOUR EXPRESS KNOWLEDGE.
ONE YEAR AGO.
"THE CONFLUENCE TAKES YOU BECAUSE UNCONSCIOUSLY YOU WANT TO BE TAKEN."
"THEN WHY WON'T IT JUST TAKE ME TO MY BROTHER?"
"PERHAPS IT IS TAKING YOU THERE, IN THE WAY IT KNOWS BEST. IT IS NOT DEFINED BY YOUR PERCEPTION OF LINES, OF DISTANCE, OF TIME."
AFTER ALL THIS...I'VE FINALLY FOUND HIM.
I KNOW IT MAKES MORE SENSE TO WAIT. WE'RE OUTNUMBERED. THE PRISON IS HEAVILY FORTIFIED WITH ALL KINDS OF GUNS AND GUARDS AND KILLER FISH AND WHATEVER. BUT I--I DON'T CARE.
WE'RE GOING AFTER HIM... TONIGHT.

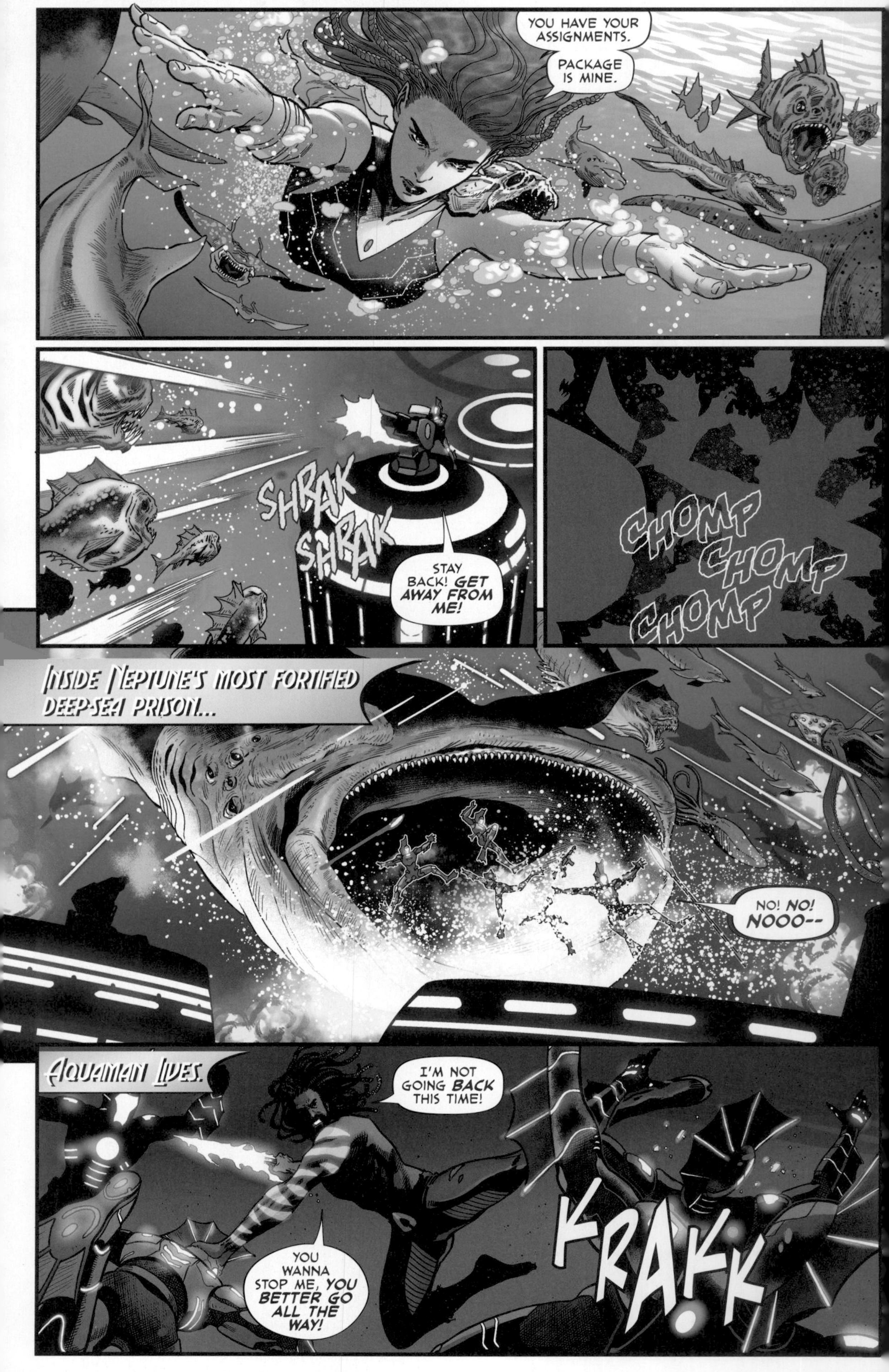

YOU HAVE YOUR ASSIGNMENTS.
PACKAGE IS MINE.
SHRAK SHRAK
STAY BACK! GET AWAY FROM ME!
CHOMP CHOMP CHOMP
INSIDE NEPTUNE'S MOST FORTIFIED DEEP-SEA PRISON...
NO! NO! NOOO--
AQUAMAN LIVES.
I'M NOT GOING BACK THIS TIME!
YOU WANNA STOP ME, YOU BETTER GO ALL THE WAY!
KRAKK

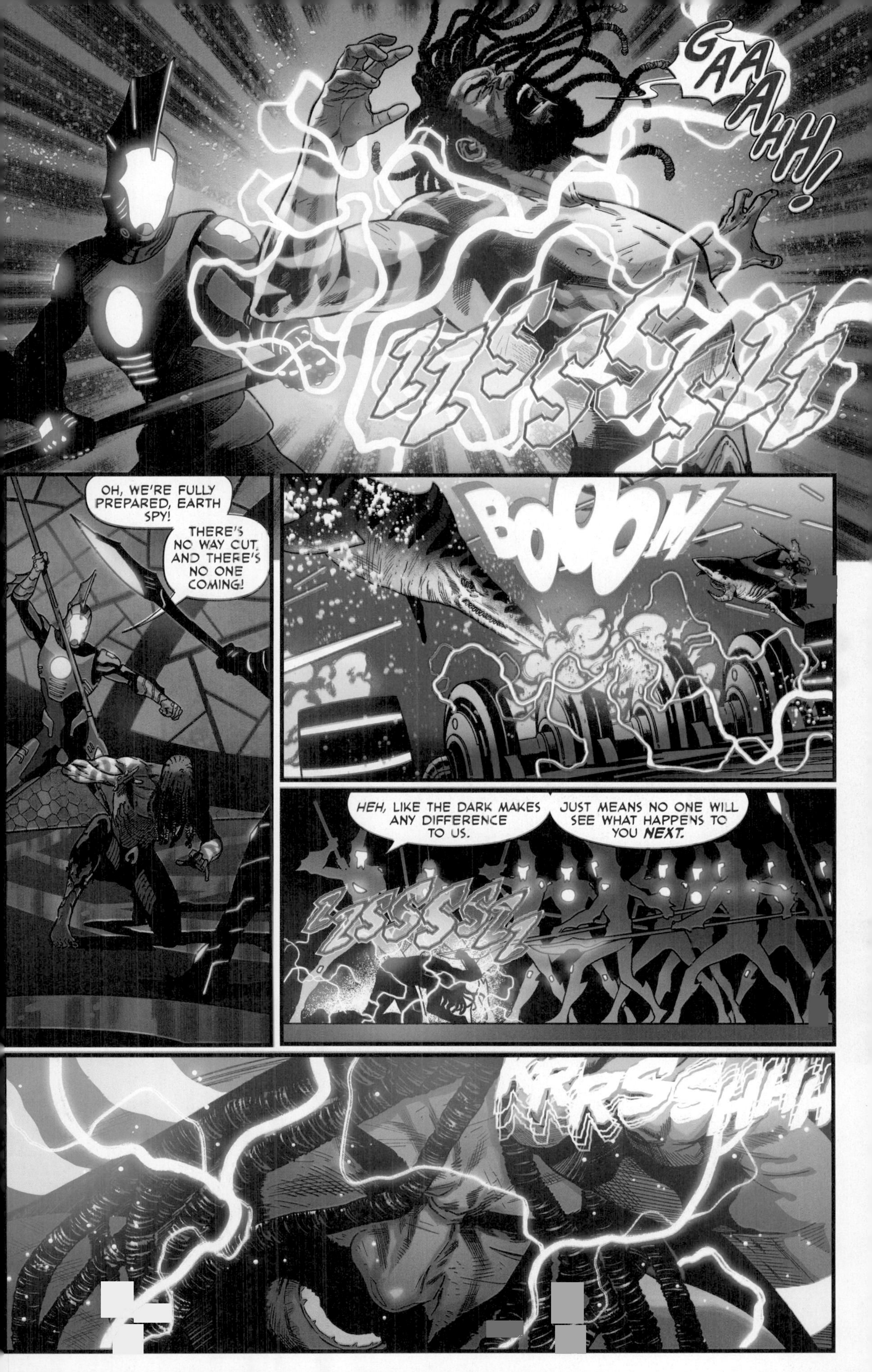
GAAAHH!
OH, WE'RE FULLY PREPARED, EARTH SPY!
THERE'S NO WAY OUT, AND THERE'S NO ONE COMING!
BOOOOM
HEH, LIKE THE DARK MAKES ANY DIFFERENCE TO US.
JUST MEANS NO ONE WILL SEE WHAT HAPPENS TO YOU NEXT.
KRRSSHHH

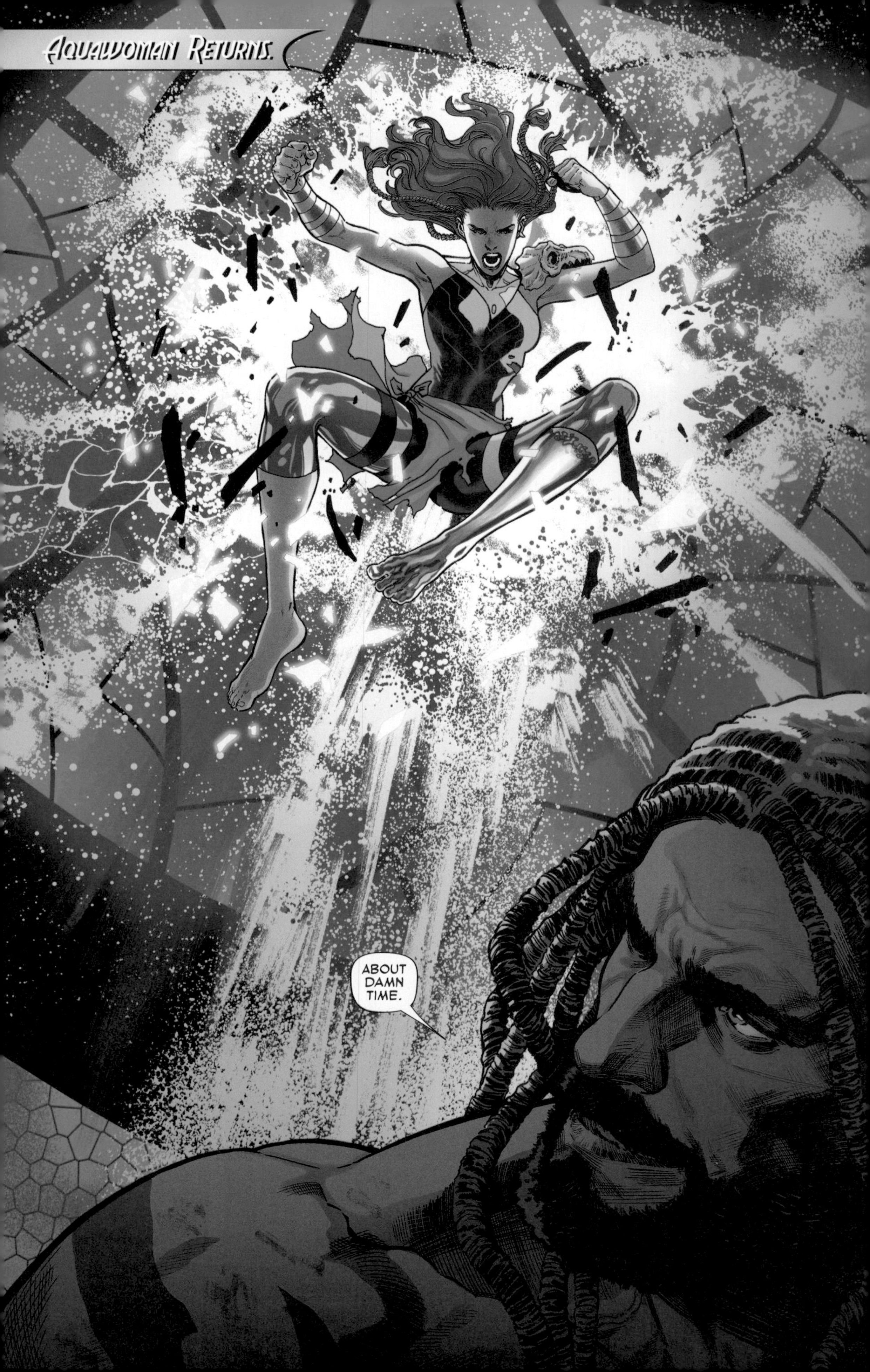
Aquawoman Returns.
ABOUT DAMN TIME.

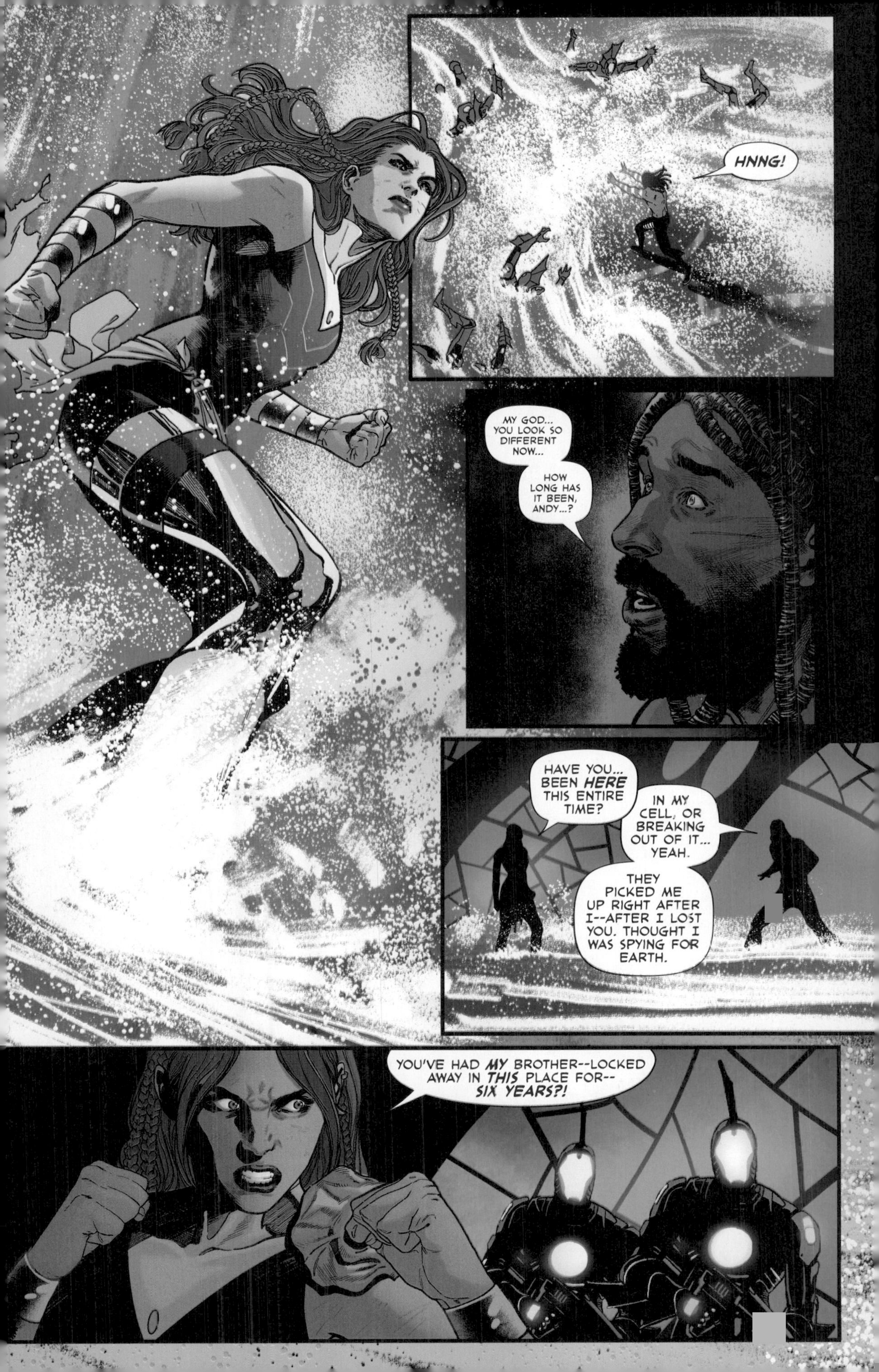
HNNG!
MY GOD... YOU LOOK SO DIFFERENT NOW...
HOW LONG HAS IT BEEN, ANDY...?
HAVE YOU... BEEN HERE THIS ENTIRE TIME?
IN MY CELL, OR BREAKING OUT OF IT... YEAH.
THEY PICKED ME UP RIGHT AFTER I--AFTER I LOST YOU. THOUGHT I WAS SPYING FOR EARTH.
YOU'VE HAD MY BROTHER--LOCKED AWAY IN THIS PLACE FOR-- SIX YEARS?!

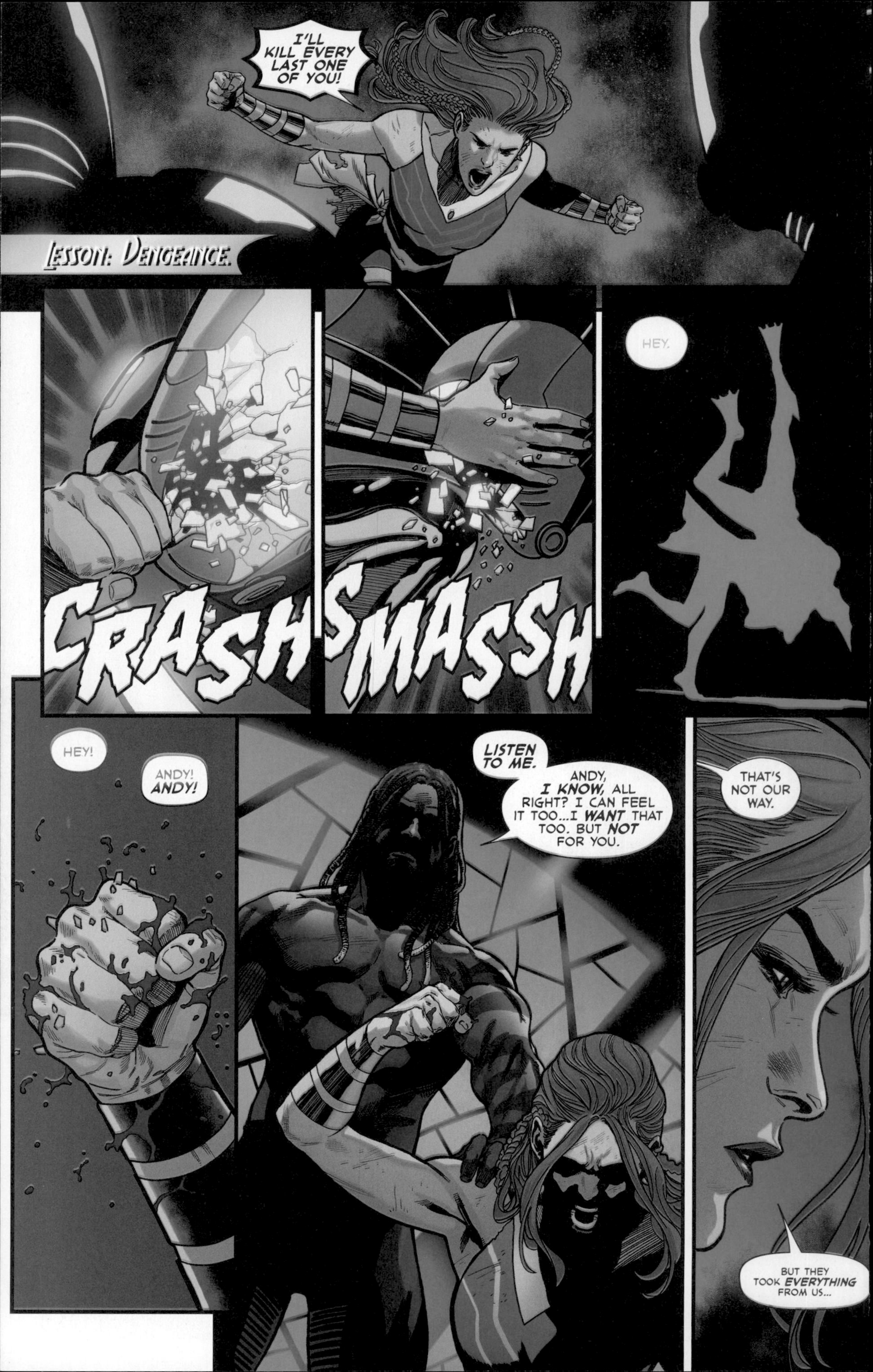
I'LL KILL EVERY LAST ONE OF YOU!
LESSON: VENGEANCE.
CRASH
SMASSH
HEY.
HEY!
ANDY! ANDY!
LISTEN TO ME.
ANDY, I KNOW, ALL RIGHT? I CAN FEEL IT TOO...I WANT THAT TOO. BUT NOT FOR YOU.
THAT'S NOT OUR WAY.
BUT THEY TOOK EVERYTHING FROM US...

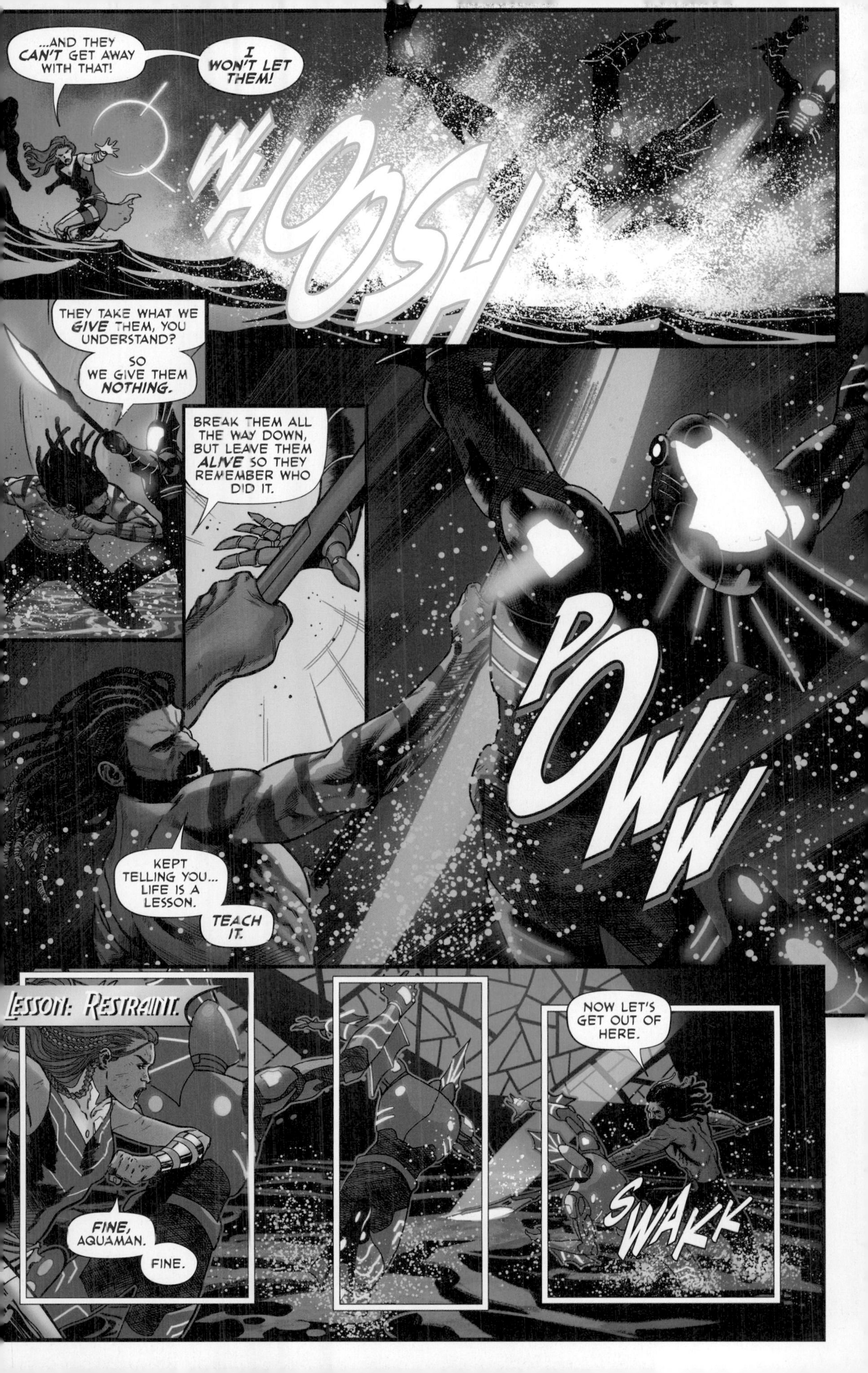

...AND THEY CAN'T GET AWAY WITH THAT!
I WON'T LET THEM!
WHOOSH
THEY TAKE WHAT WE GIVE THEM, YOU UNDERSTAND?
SO WE GIVE THEM NOTHING.
BREAK THEM ALL THE WAY DOWN, BUT LEAVE THEM ALIVE SO THEY REMEMBER WHO DID IT.
POWW
KEPT TELLING YOU... LIFE IS A LESSON.
TEACH IT.
LESSON: RESTRAINT.
FINE, AQUAMAN.
FINE.
NOW LET'S GET OUT OF HERE.
SWAKK

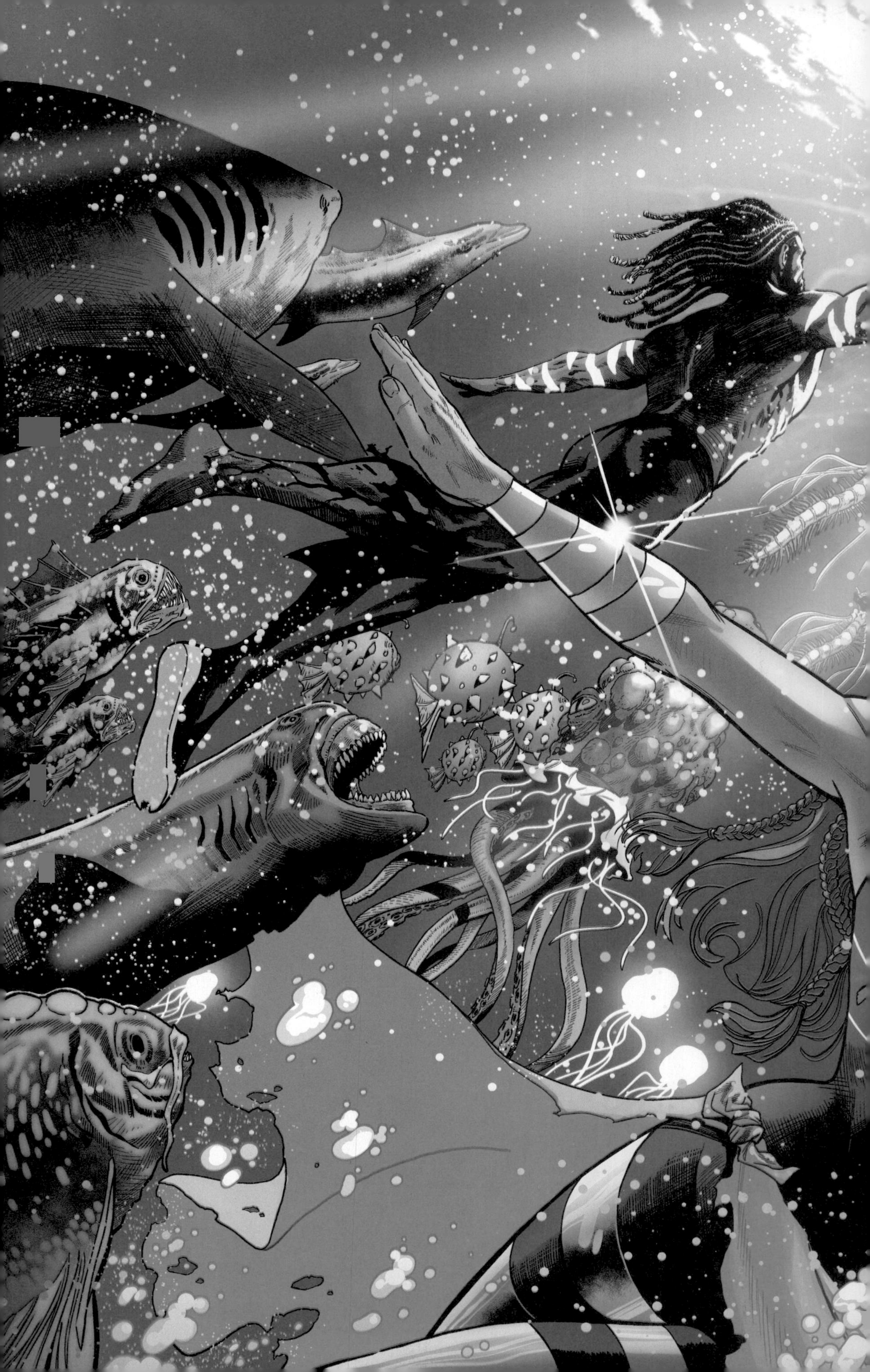

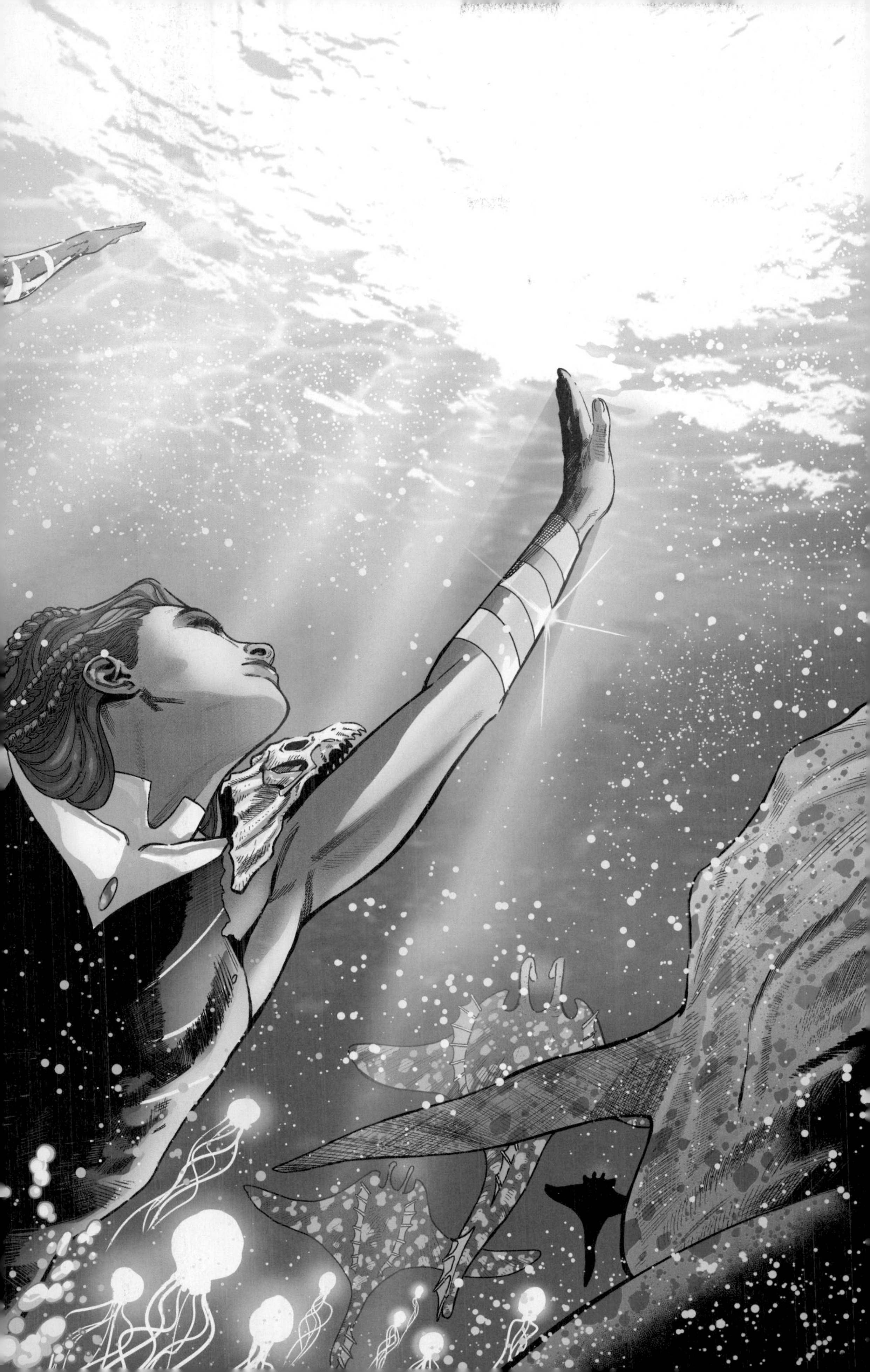

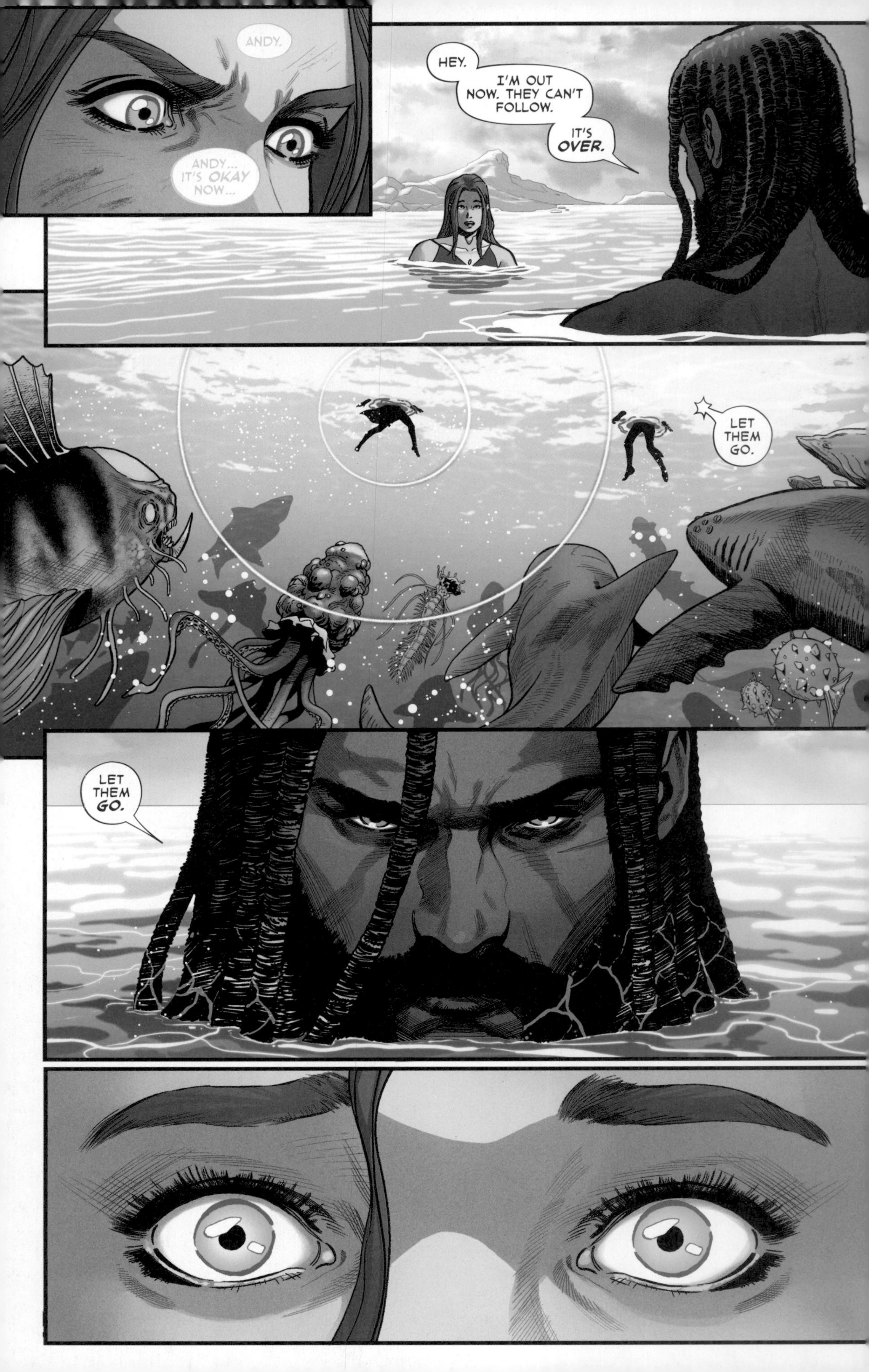
ANDY.
ANDY... IT'S OKAY NOW...
HEY.
I'M OUT NOW. THEY CAN'T FOLLOW.
IT'S OVER.
LET THEM GO.
LET THEM GO.

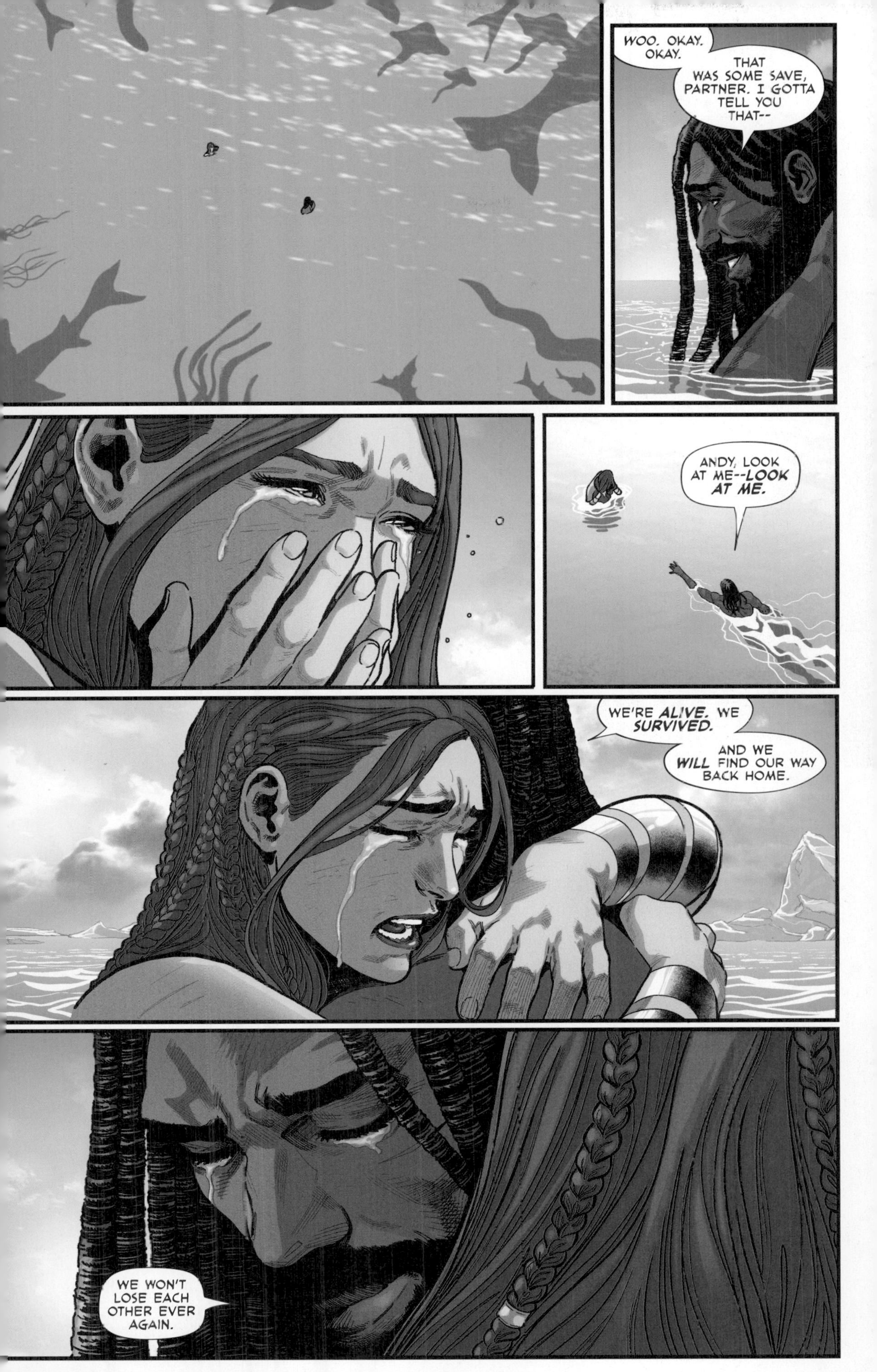
WOO. OKAY. OKAY.
THAT WAS SOME SAVE, PARTNER. I GOTTA TELL YOU THAT--
ANDY, LOOK AT ME--LOOK AT ME.
WE'RE ALIVE. WE SURVIVED.
AND WE WILL FIND OUR WAY BACK HOME.
WE WON'T LOSE EACH OTHER EVER AGAIN.

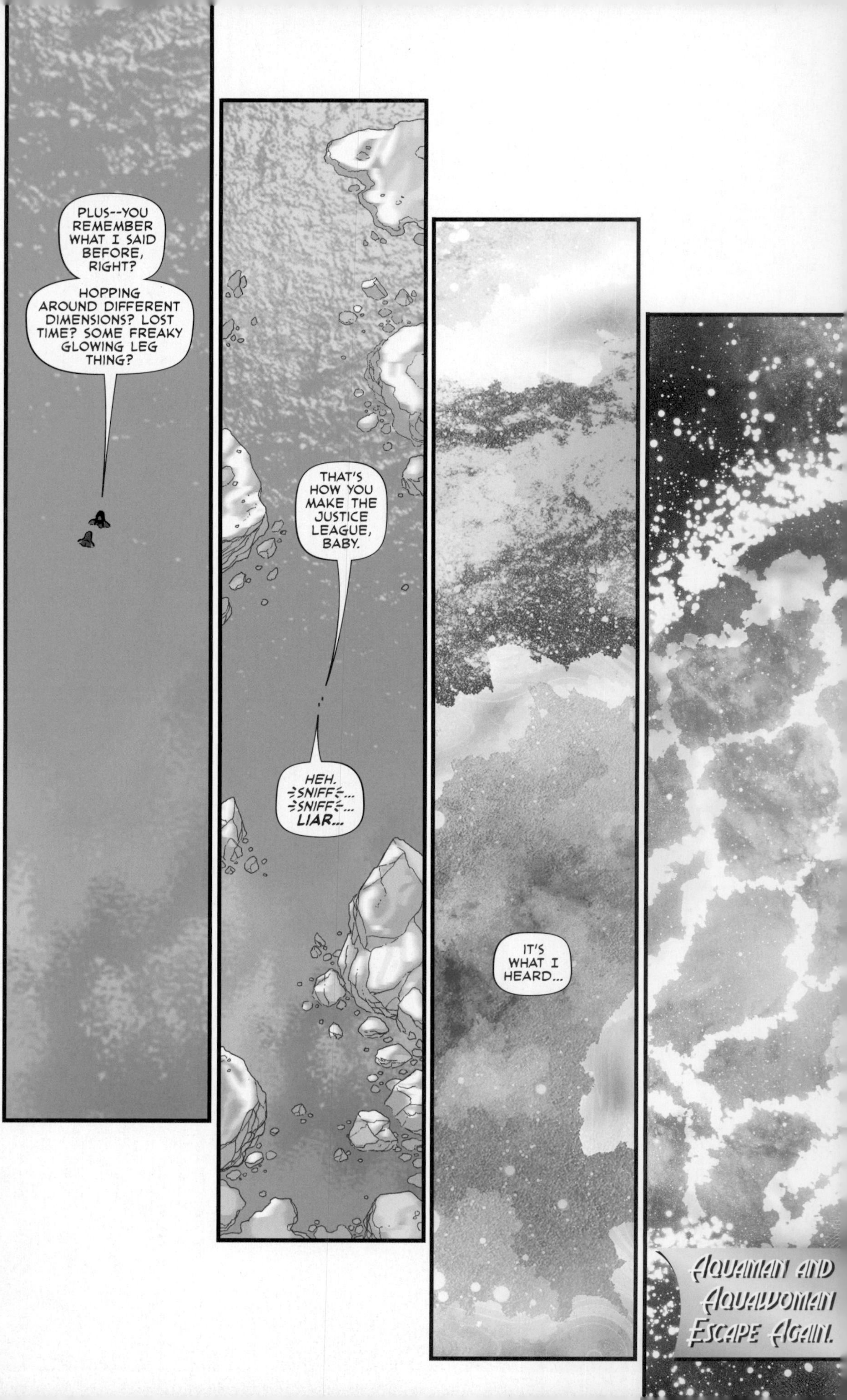
PLUS--YOU REMEMBER WHAT I SAID BEFORE, RIGHT?
HOPPING AROUND DIFFERENT DIMENSIONS? LOST TIME? SOME FREAKY GLOWING LEG THING?
THAT'S HOW YOU MAKE THE JUSTICE LEAGUE, BABY.
HEH. =SNIFF=... =SNIFF=... LIAR...
IT'S WHAT I HEARD...
Aquaman and Aquawoman Escape Again.

DEEP

The Art of *Aquaman: The Becoming* and *Future State: Aquaman*

DIVE

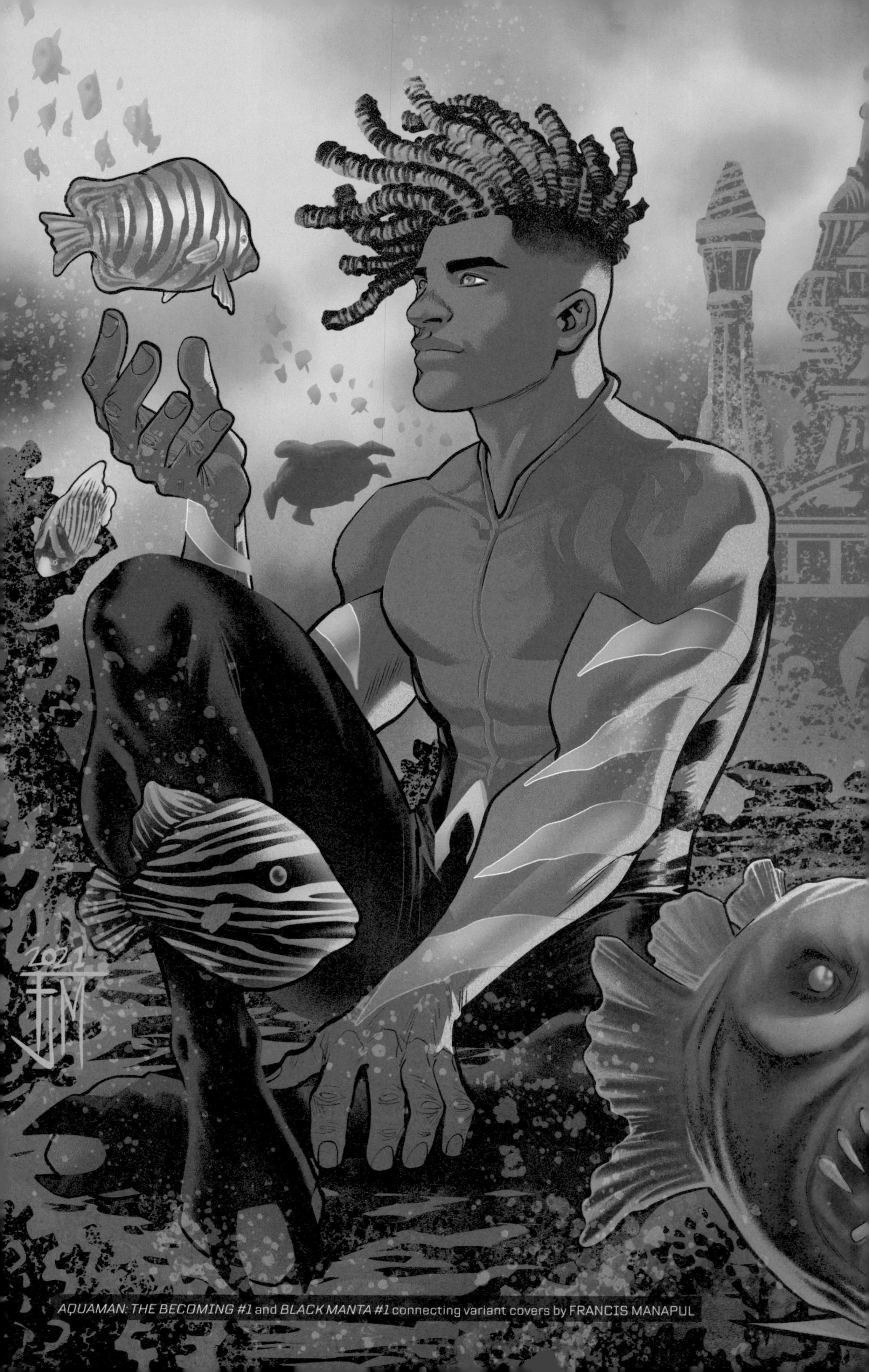
2021
FJM
AQUAMAN: THE BECOMING #1 and *BLACK MANTA #1* connecting variant covers by FRANCIS MANAPUL

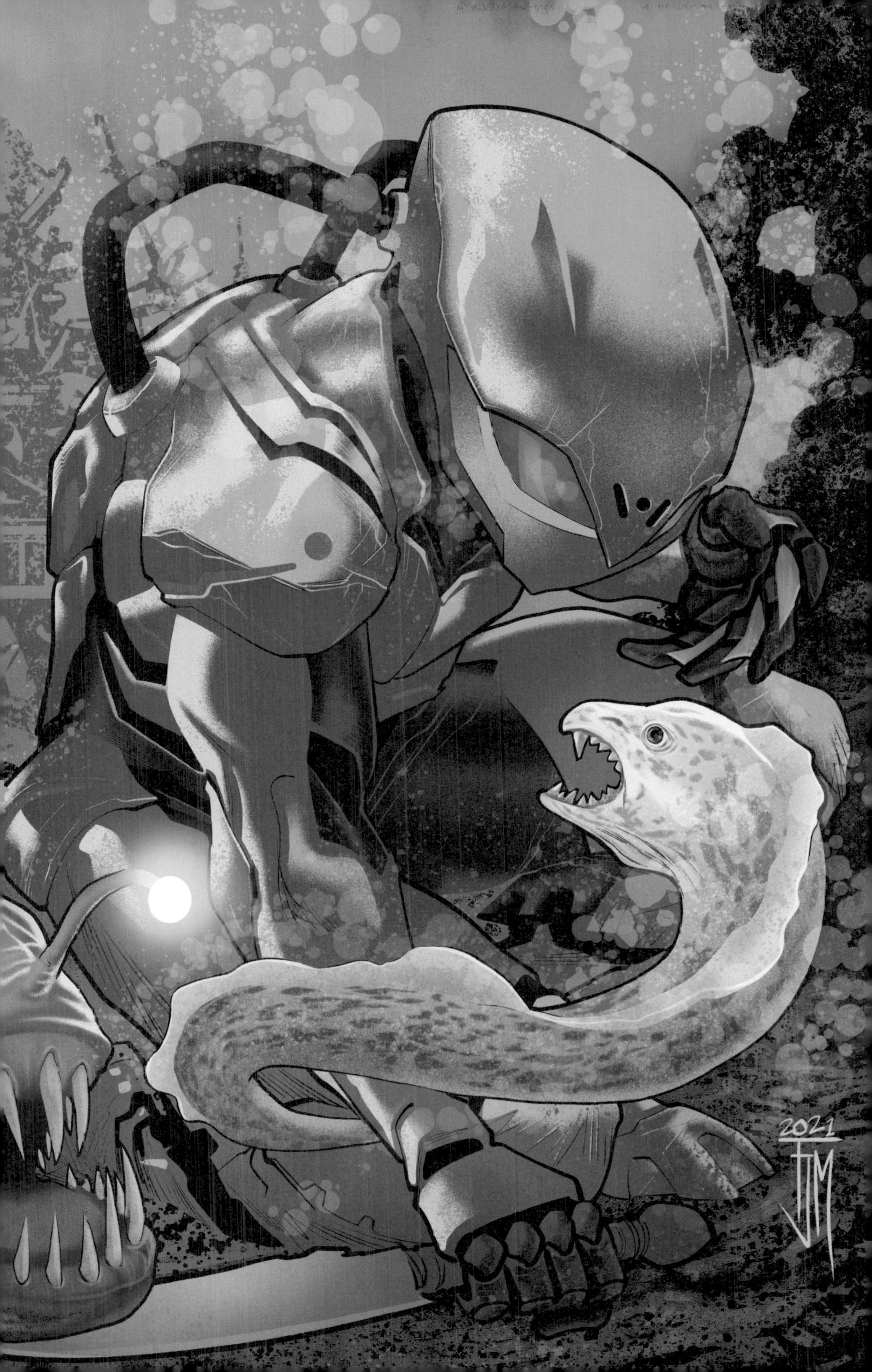
2021

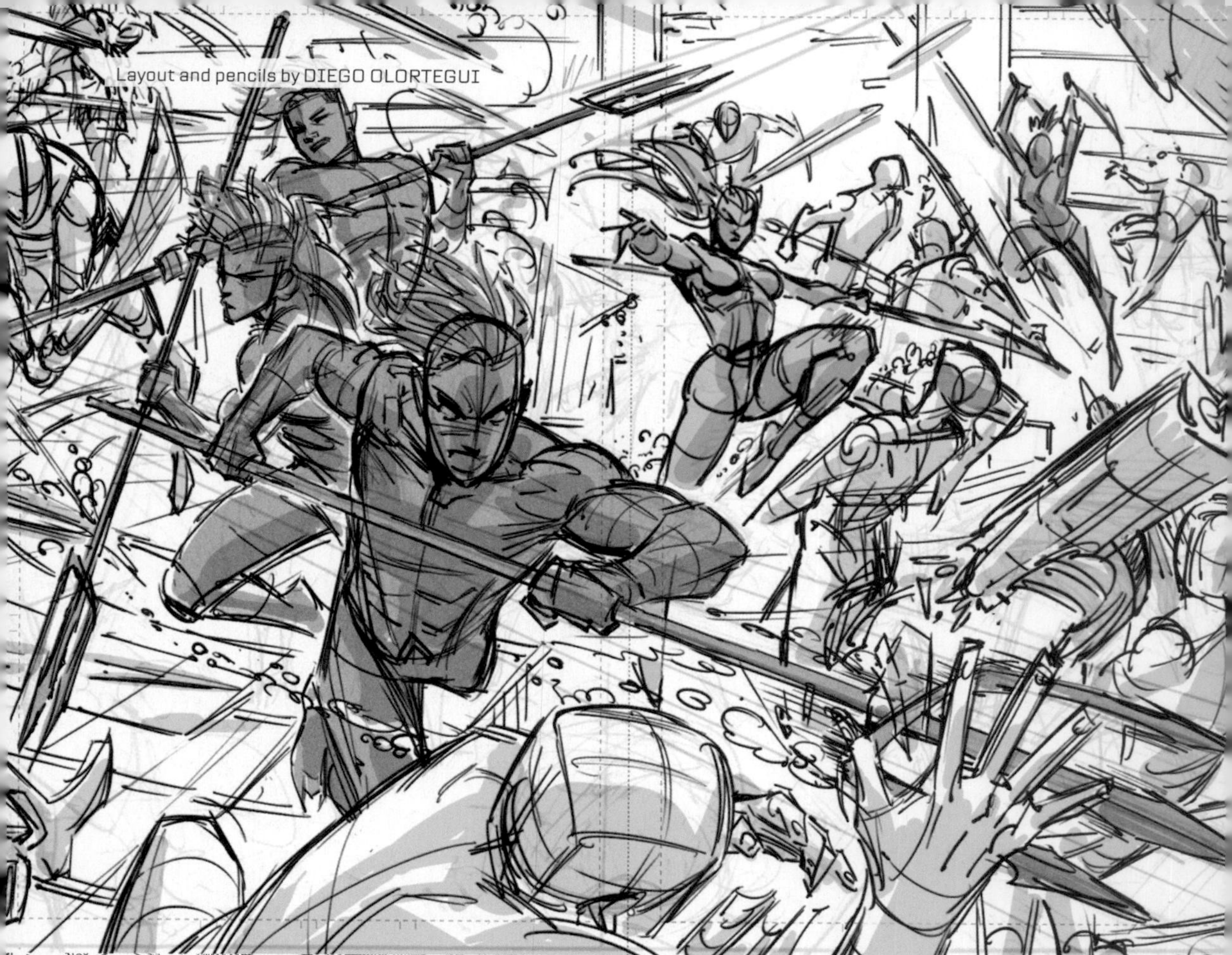

Layout and pencils by DIEGO OLORTEGUI

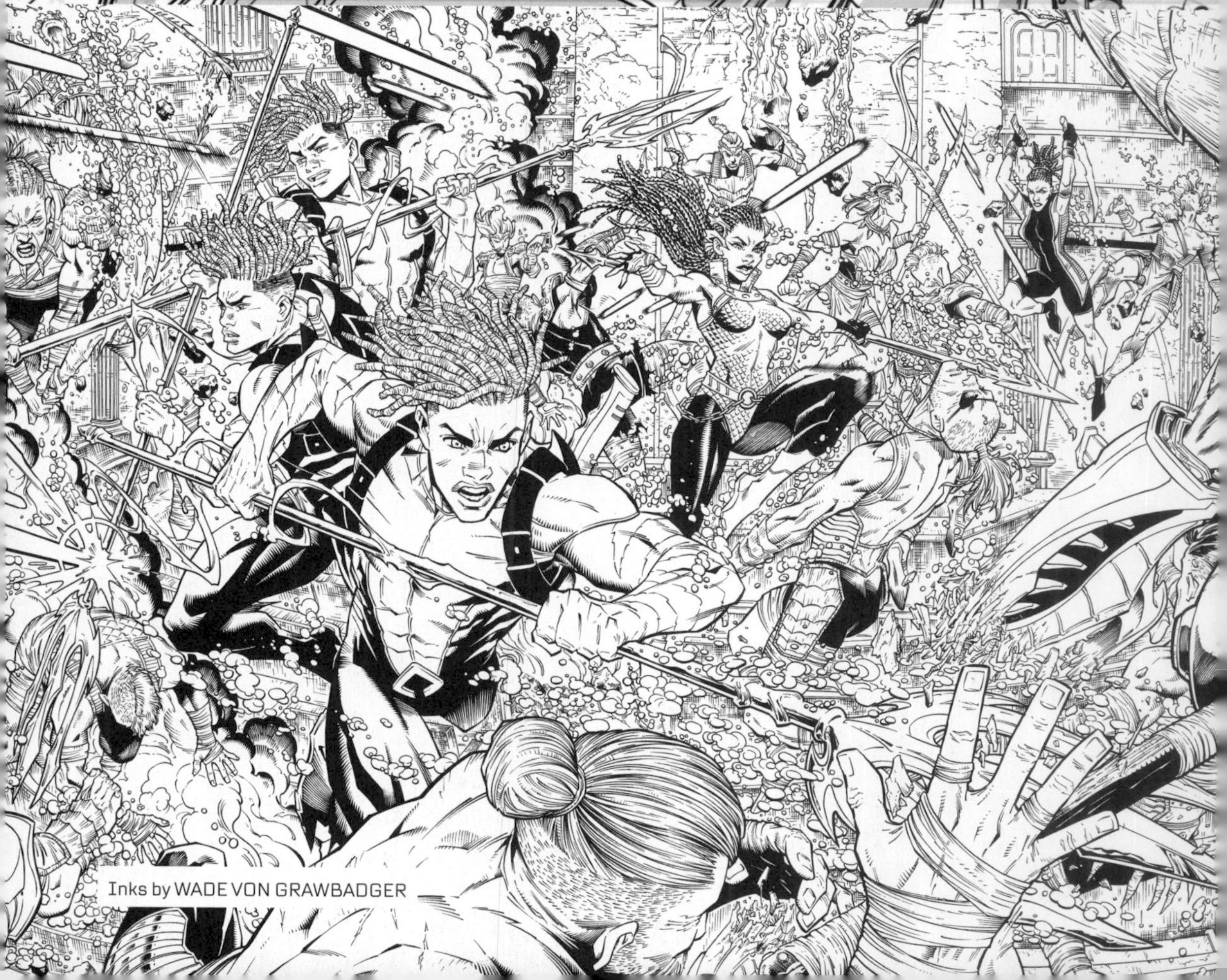

Inks by WADE VON GRAWBADGER

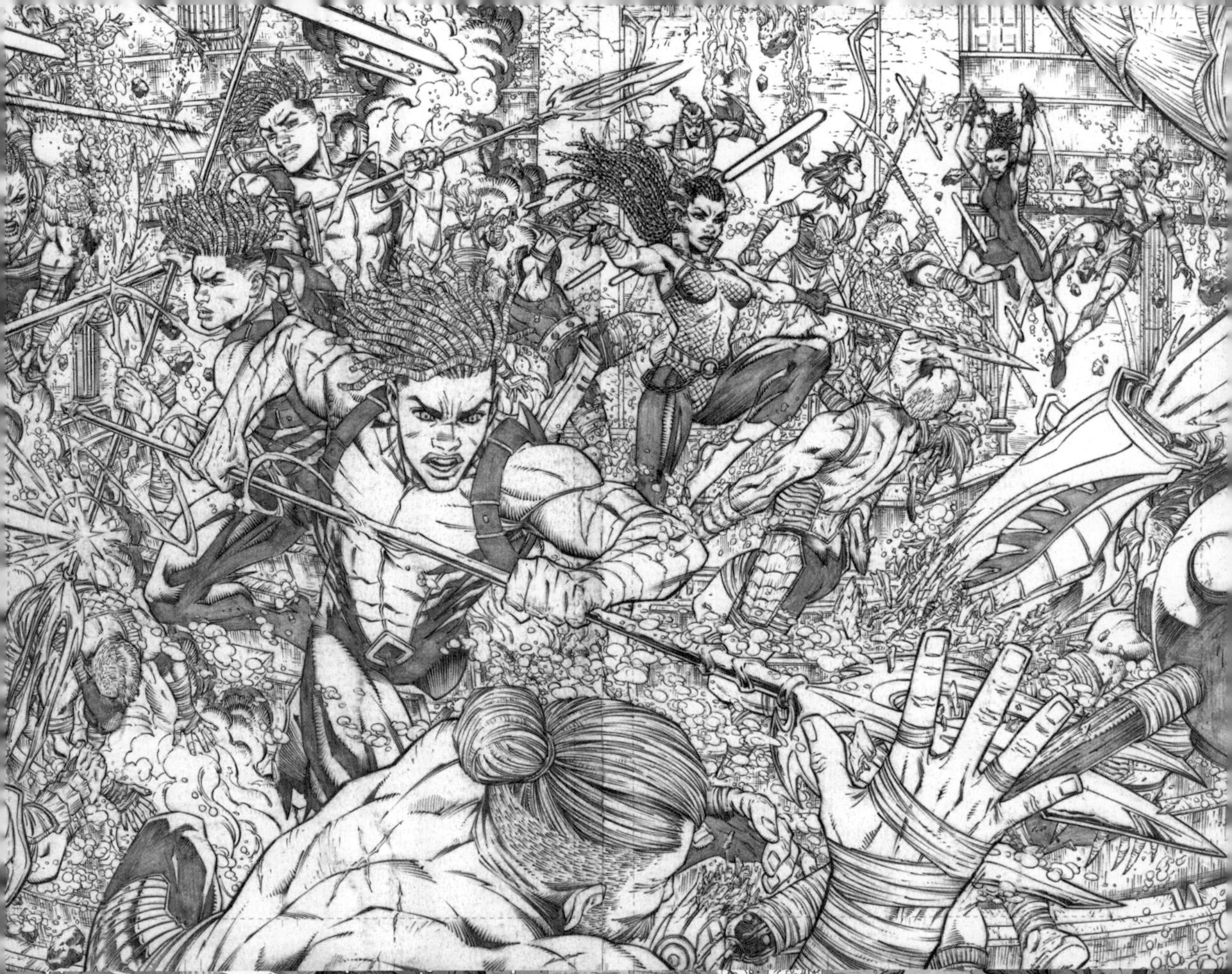

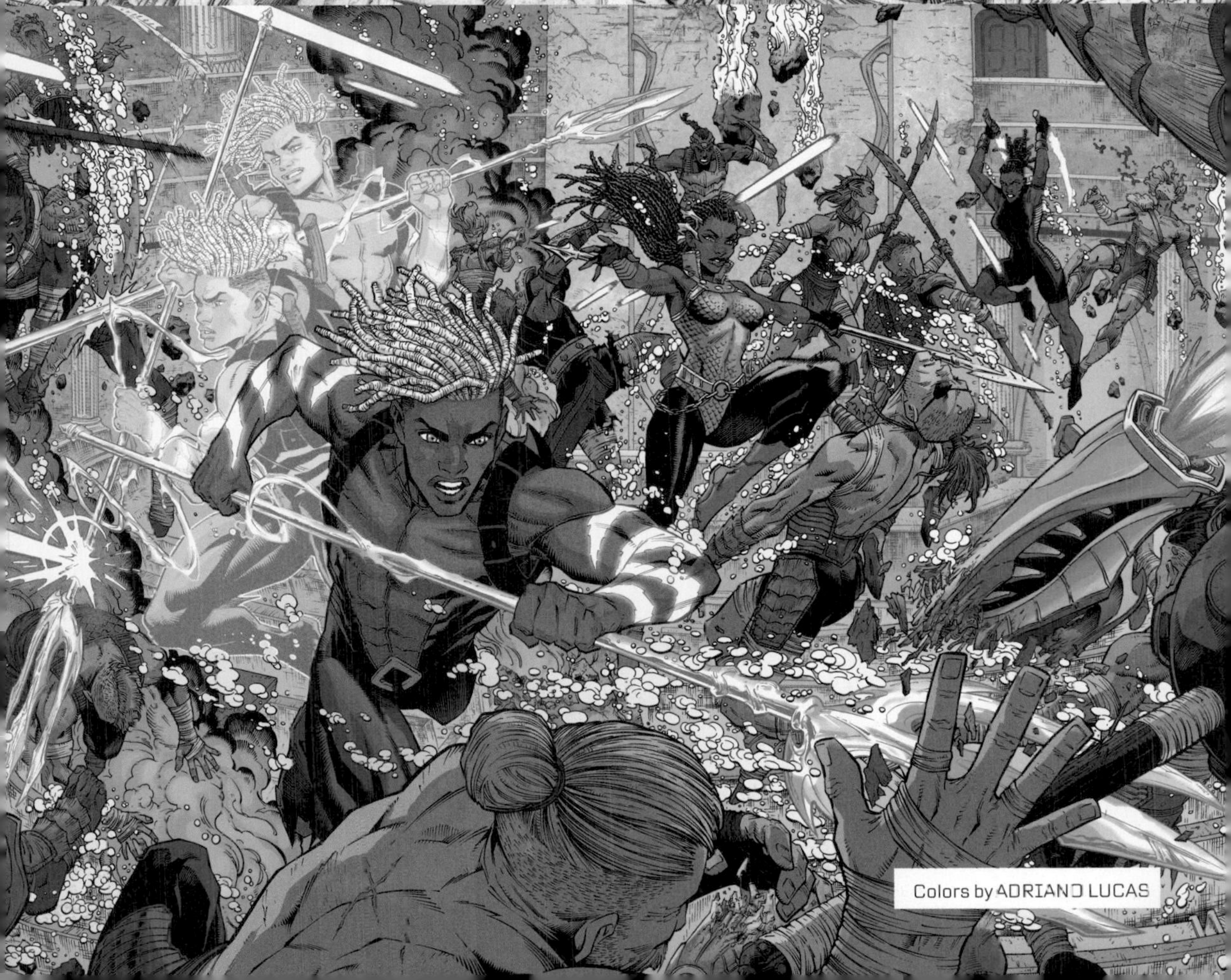
Colors by ADRIANO LUCAS

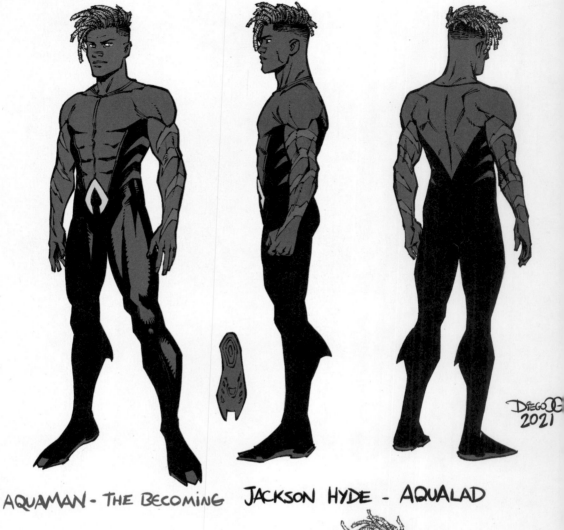

AQUAMAN - THE BECOMING   JACKSON HYDE - AQUALAD

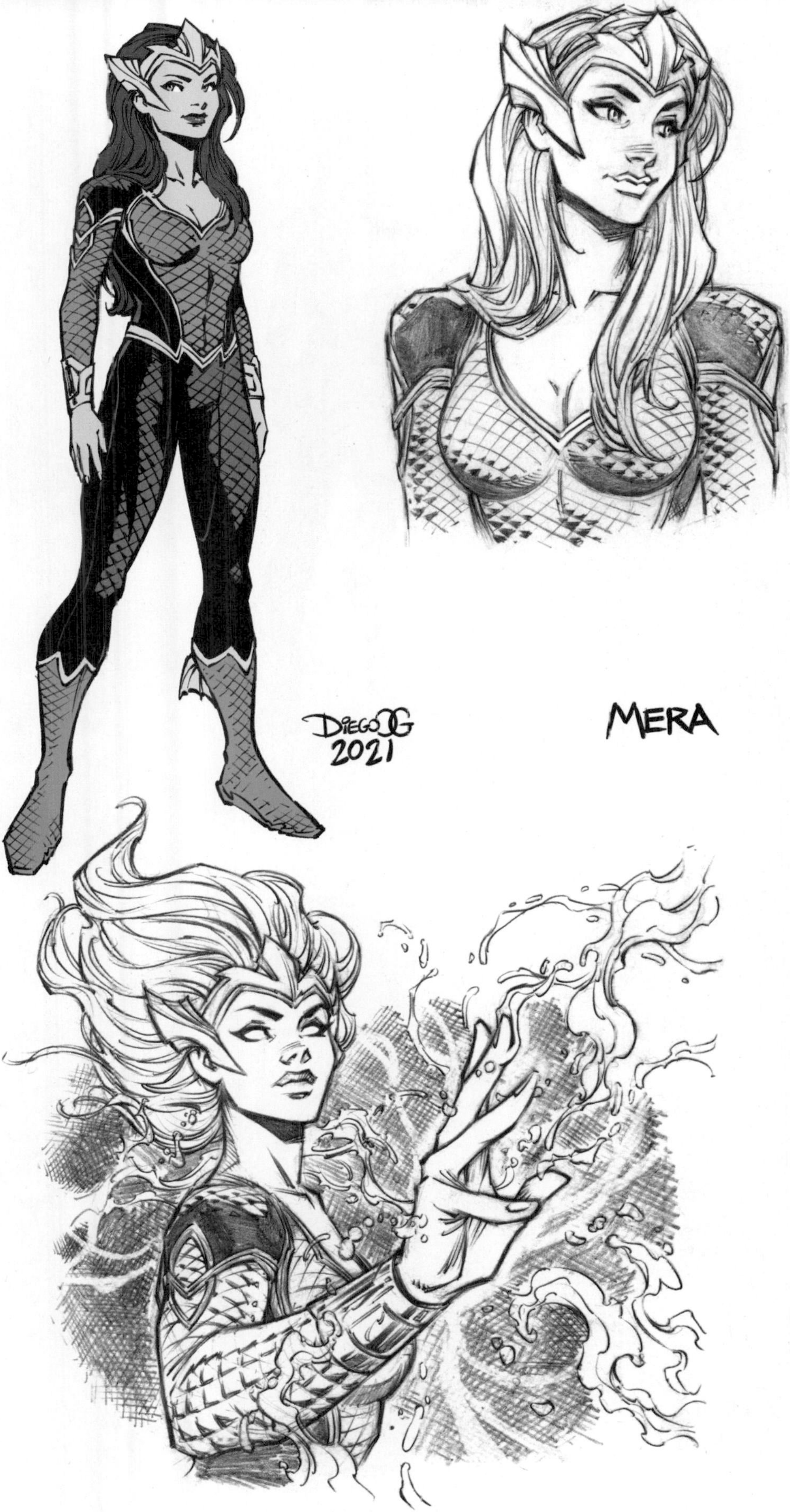
DiegoOG
2021
MERA

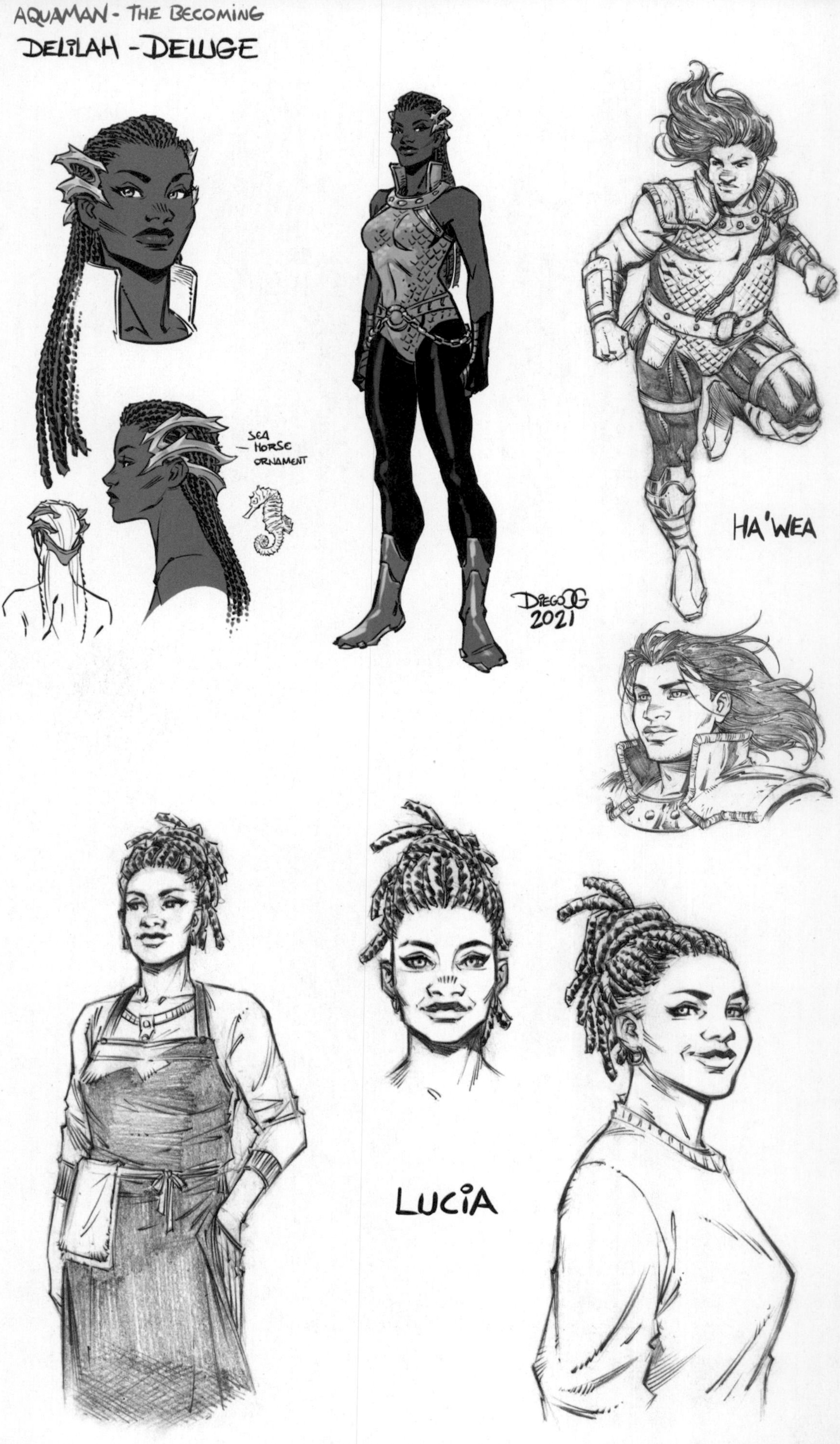
AQUAMAN - THE BECOMING
DELILAH - DELUGE
SEA HORSE ORNAMENT
DIEGO OG 2021
HA'WEA
LUCIA

JACKSON

FUTURE STATE: AQUAMAN
designs by DANIEL SAMPERE

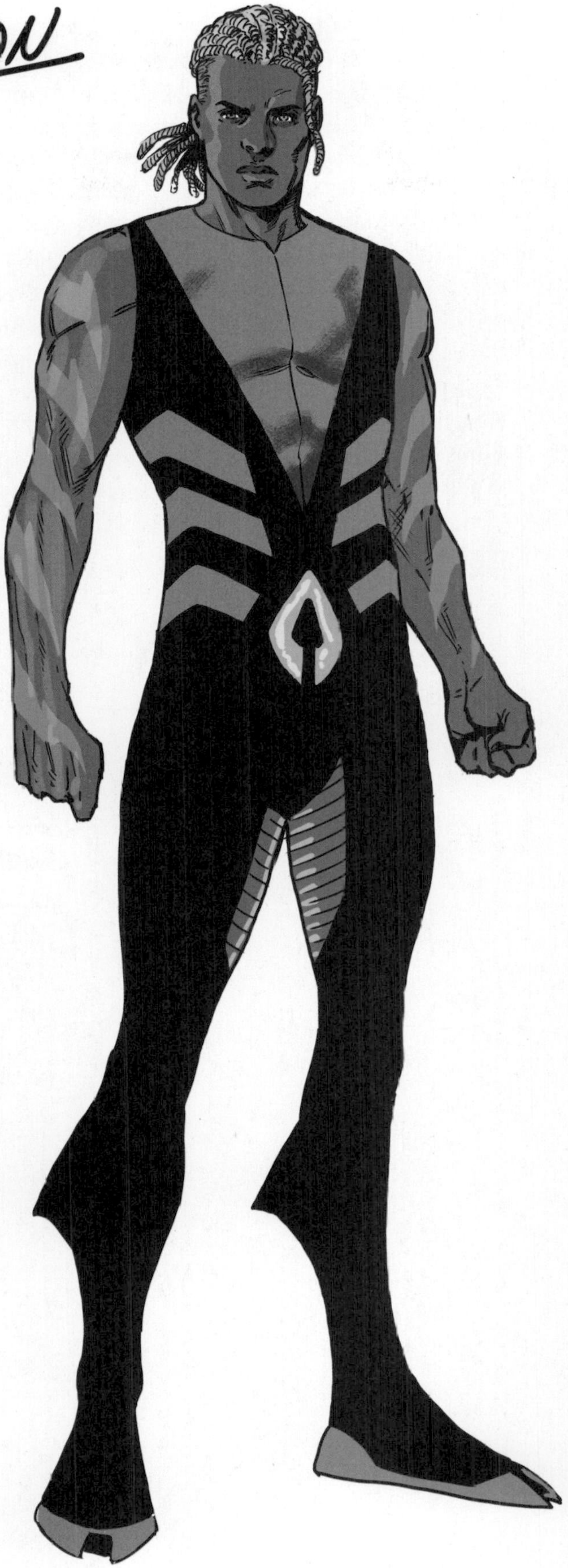

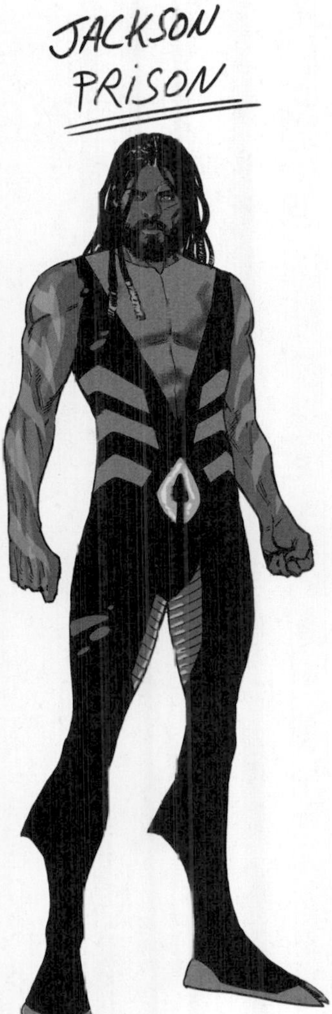
JACKSON
PRISON

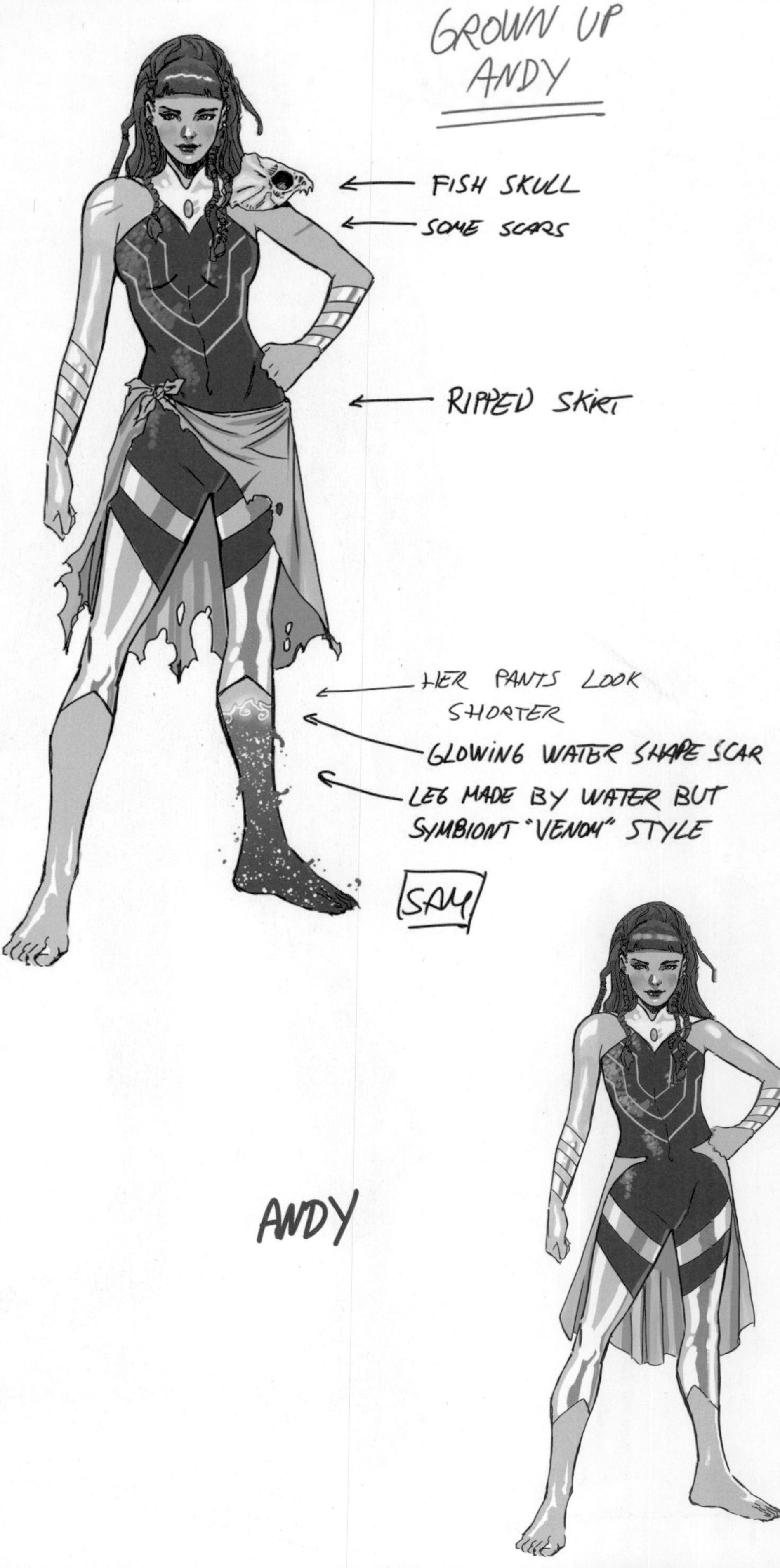
GROWN UP ANDY
FISH SKULL
SOME SCARS
RIPPED SKIRT
HER PANTS LOOK SHORTER
GLOWING WATER SHAPE SCAR
LEG MADE BY WATER BUT SYMBIONT "VENOM" STYLE
SAM
ANDY

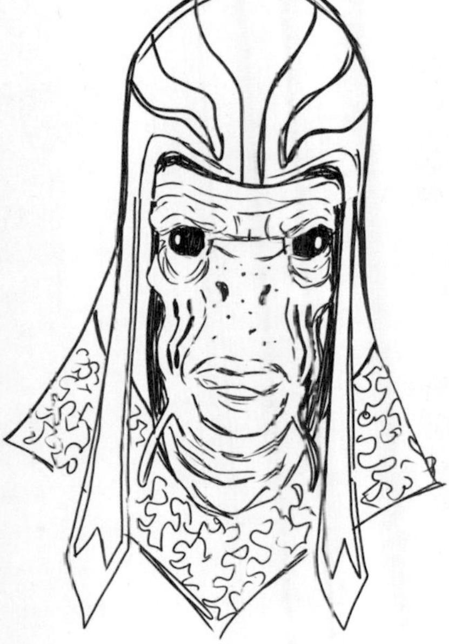

INTERROGATOR

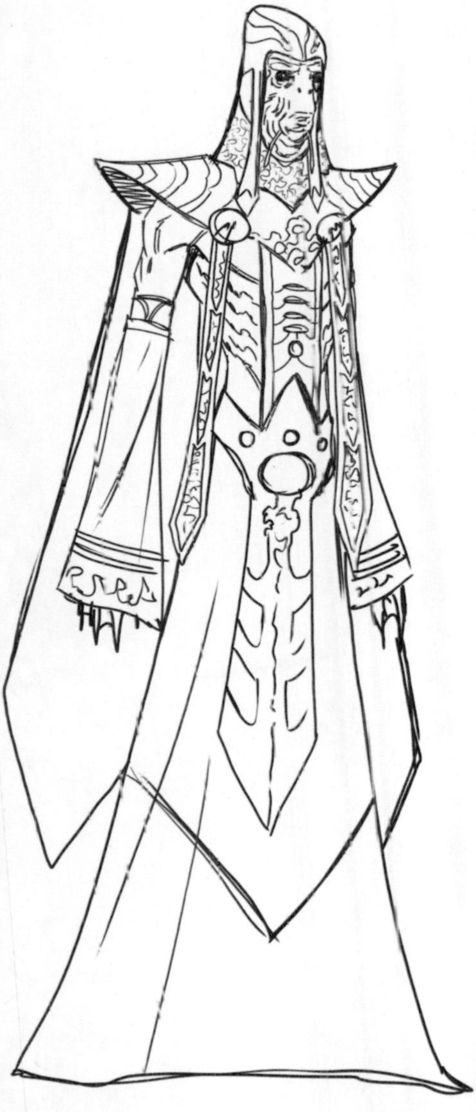

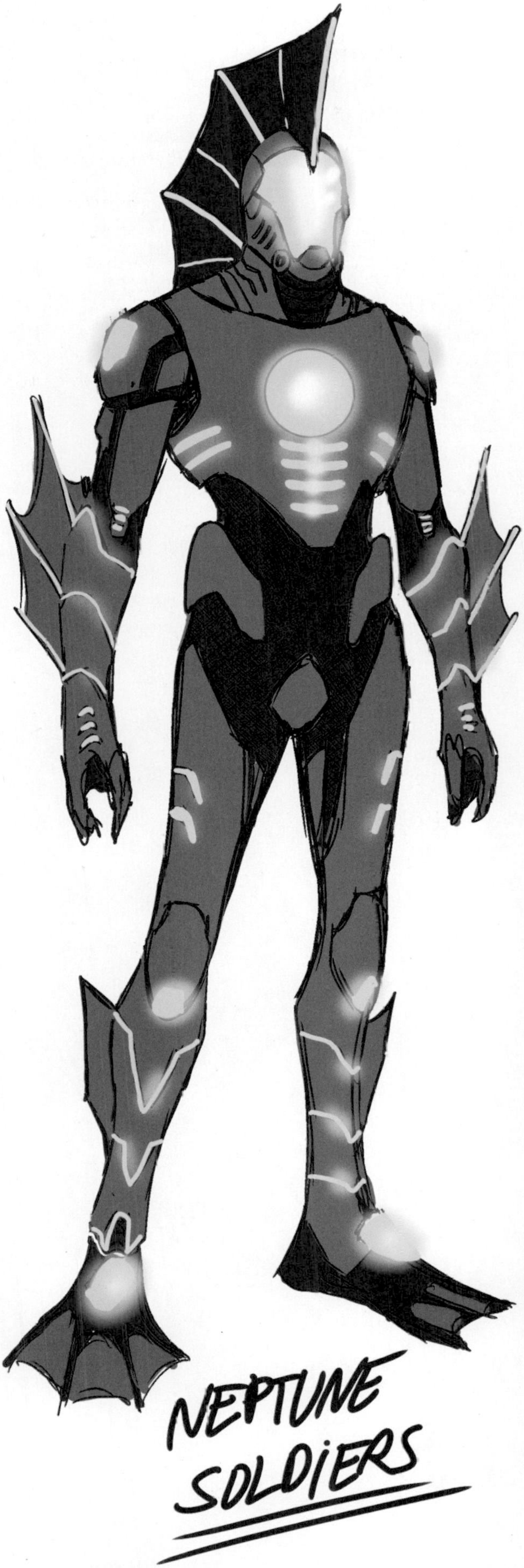

NEPTUNE SOLDIERS

The adventure continues in...

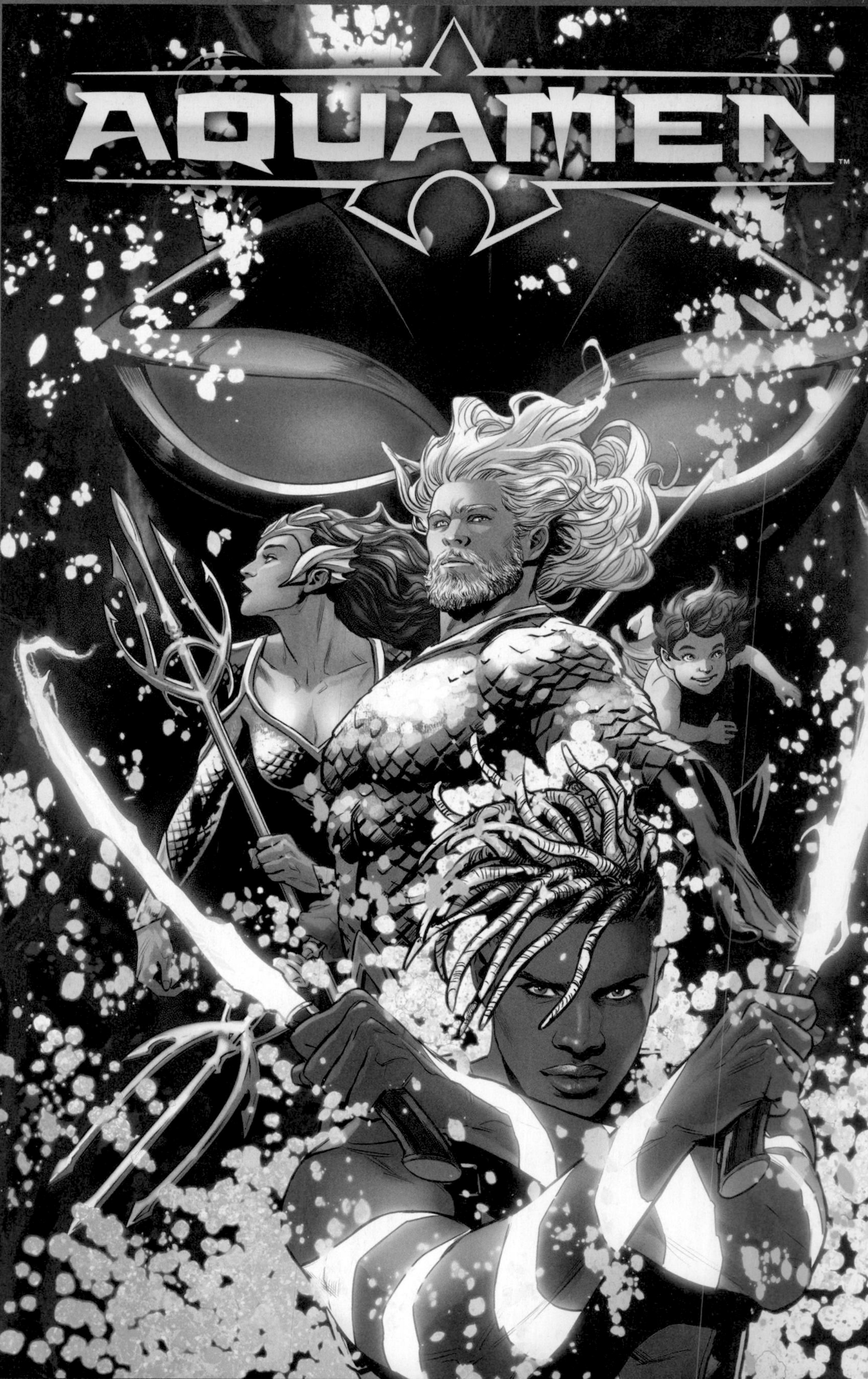
AQUAMEN